The Concept of Dance Education

Expanded Edition

The Concept
of Dance Education

Expanded Edition

Graham McFee

Pageantry
Press

The Concept of Dance Education
Expanded Edition

© Graham McFee 2019
Reprinted 2019 by Pageantry Press, UK
ISBN: 978-0-578-22144-1

. . . .

Earlier publication:

© Graham McFee 2004
Expanded Edition published 2004 by Pageantry Press, UK
ISBN-10: 0-9547147-0-9

© Graham McFee 1994
First published 1994 by Routledge, UK
ISBN-10: 0-41-508376-1

. . . .

Cover design — Myrene McFee
Cover graphic figure — Nikolay Kurkin/Alamy

Contents

vii

Introduction to the Expanded Edition

Preamble: The fate of the original edition

As the Preface to the original text of *The Concept of Dance Education* (here-after 'CDE') makes clear, that book grew from some powerful commitments of mine. Ten years on, I find little or nothing in the original design with which to disagree in principle. Yet the virtues of CDE never really made their way into the public domain, though it found a loyal (if limited) following. There are several reasons for this. First, the 1994 edition never appeared in the relatively inexpensive — and hence accessible — format for which I had hoped: rather, it appeared only in an expensive hardbound version. The projected paperback would have both emphasised its connection to its predecessor *Understanding Dance* (McFee, 1992a: hereafter 'UD'), and increased its availability to the teachers and students of dance (in education) who were its intended audience. Instead, the practical concerns of CDE were rarely noted. Even when it was discussed in the literature, for example by Frances Sparshott, that projected audience was not identified: instead, it was presented as assuming 'a national school system with a common examination system' (Sparshott, 1995: 151–2) when in fact the intention was simply to consider the place of dance in an education system that recognised *accountability*.

Second, CDE was especially couched in terms of examples drawn from the National Curriculum for England and Wales, as it was being drawn up at the time of composition. This was in part a marketing strategy: to show how the abstract ideas had concrete application. But it was also to exemplify (in a concrete way) the abstract ideas — the context of writing at that time made the emergent National Curriculum my preferred example. But the rapid meta-morphosis of that legislative structure meant that CDE *appeared* to date rapidly. Of course, this was an illusion. As the preface to the 1994 edition makes plain, the ideas central to CDE were partly a result of consideration of what, in England, dance education should be like (as formalised by the National Curriculum for England and Wales). But a more fundamental question — which is what that book really discusses — is how dance education should be understood in a way that permits it to be accountable. So it connects up theoretical ideas about dance with theoretical ideas from educational studies: the changes in detail were actually not important, except insofar as they better (or worse) exemplified these ideas. But, of course, some readers may have missed this feature. Curiously, here, where it is more explicitly a *worked-example* from the past, the reference to the National Curriculum may be more apposite.

Third, the audience for philosophical interventions in dance did not expand in ways some of us hoped it would. In part, this point is a reflection of the previous one — dance teachers (like other teachers) became overwhelmed by the form-filling the National Curriculum came to require; or so it seems to me. As a result, less time was available for detailed consideration of, say, *my* teaching this, as opposed to *your* teaching it, and of *our* teaching it, as opposed to its not being taught. But such consideration is fundamental to a flourishing curriculum. In this sense, then, the National Curriculum seemed to begin taking from teachers some areas of (autonomous?) decision in which variety had flourished. And this represented a loss of a key *context* for philosophical reflection on what is taught and why: those questions *seemed* to be answered 'from on high'. (That the answers offered were regularly bland, merely rhetorical or rooted in outdated theory exacerbated this problem.)

A fourth reason could also be mentioned here: those of us who saw the National Curriculum has having a *liberating* potential were disappointed — it tended to ossify existing conceptions of, say, the value of dance, or even to be reductive of choice. This need not have happened; but it did. And teachers with different conceptions did not flourish. Or so it seemed.

An additional consideration, of an autobiographical kind, is that changes such as these resulted in a lack of recruitment for a Masters degree in which I had been discussing these ideas with practicing teachers. With its demise, and the demise of similar programmes to which I had been contributing, I had no *ready* source of places for advocacy of the importance of the questions CDE addressed — and hence less opportunity to urge the relevance (or even the correctness) of my interventions or answers, as represented by CDE. This simply reinforced its neglect.

Publishing an expanded edition?

Although the discussion above suggests reasons why CDE might have been found difficult to read or might have been not read, it *still* found its way onto reading lists and the like. And once it was no longer in print, I was regularly asked if I had 'spare' copies of the text. Then I became aware that with 'publishing on demand' technology I could produce a small edition of CDE and offer it to those interested at (approximately) cost price — and all without expanding the sense in which my house was a repository for books!

But then, once the idea of producing the book seemed feasible, the opportunity to augment the original text, in ways discussed below, became irresistible. If the heart of the plan of CDE was to discuss the (necessary) *accountability* of any dance education worthy of the name — and to *distinguish* it from within education (especially arts education) more generally — perhaps this direction was not as transparent to readers as its author hoped, and might be newly clarified. Yet that was in the original version, and I was loath to produce a radically altered CDE, even granting the points recognised above.

So what you have before you is designed to meet two related requirements: the first is for *continuity* with the original edition, the second to suitably *augment* it. Thus the original pagination is (roughly) retained, and expansion achieved by the addition of material. [This model was suggested by the revised edition of Wollheim's *Art and Its Objects*, which faced similar problems. There the original pagination was preserved, and augmentation was achieved by the addition of Supplementary Essays (Wollheim, 1980a).] So the changes in the body are limited to the correction of minor errors, chiefly typographical. Also, I have occasionally added new notes, where there seemed something in CDE suitable for brief comment.

The original edition (CDE: 192) made plain both that certain issues had not been discussed, and that — as my plans then were — I had no intention of discussing them: indeed, my claim (CDE: 199) was that I might be writing no more on dance. But no sooner had these words been put down than a number of invitations prompted me to continue writing about dance, and to write on at least *some* of the topics I had originally put aside. Further, other discussions — about dance in general, rather than dance education — seemed to have a direct bearing on what was written in CDE. These suggested ways of both expanding and up-dating the original ideas but without changing the original text.

So, to generate this expanded edition, I have put together three Supplementary Essays. All share passages with previously published elements, as well as drawing on new(-ish) material from lectures on these topics: at their hearts, Supplementary Essays 1 and 2 more or less replicate papers published elsewhere (McFee, 1998; McFee, 1994b respectively), if with expansions. Essay 3 offers a new combination of previously published material (McFee, 2003a; McFee, 2003b). And, for each, I have written a new introduction and modified/expanded the text appropriately.

Three related discussions may clarify the direction here. The first returns us to the comments by Sparshott (1995), who goes on to suggest that, for me, an emphasis on the (educational) *value* of should be such as 'should suffice to satisfy Her Majesty's Inspectors' (Sparshott, 1995: 476). The implication, of course, is that there is a trivialising dependence on what is *now* thought valuable by *some* people. But this was never part of my plan. Instead, my claim was we should consider the value of dance in education by considering the distinctive value of *art* in the educational context; and the distinctiveness of dance from within the arts. Here, a central issue will turn on how (or when) we have a particular dance under consideration — this topic, sometimes called 'the identity of dances' — is sketched in Supplementary Essay 2.

The second comment raises a similar point, most easily presented via a review of UD — as CDE explicitly inherits its account of art. Trevor Whittock (1994: 70) urges that institutional accounts in general cannot give due weight to the roles of choreographers and dancers, giving weight to 'secondary figures instead of the actual makers and performers of dance'. This matter is complex: it is important to give *due* weight to choreographer, and to the dancer. But that requires not over-rated them — as, say, subjectivist accounts do — as well as not under-rating them. So Supplementary Essay 3 tries to sketch considerations here in respect of both the place of the audience of dance and of the role — within dance study — of the experience of dance.

The third comment has two dimensions: sometimes it involves a questioning of the firm contrast between the artistic and the aesthetic, on which CDE insists. This, too, is taken up in Supplementary Essay 3. But sometimes the view is put to me more forcefully (say, at conference). Then it is suggested that the principle thesis of CDE is refuted by changes in the nature of (the art of) dance or of the condition of society — both characterised under the general heading 'postmodernism'. Now, CDE (pp. 194-196) had explicitly recognised that there were a number of related issues here. My brief remarks there are now expanded into Supplementary Essay 1.

Yet there is still one substantial 'omission': namely, there is no discussion here of changes to the National Curriculum for England and Wales, neither to its detail nor its general framework. But the explanation is that given earlier — that these changes would be *philosophically* irrelevant, from the perspective of *this* project.

Afterword

When all that is said, there remain questions about the *revision* of CDE that this expanded edition represents. Here, an answer would point out both the (original) distinctness of CDE and what this edition adds. Let us consider each in turn.

The major differences between this and any other interventions into the field of dance education reside (I suspect) in two or three key dimensions. First, the argument draws the distinctiveness of dance education from the *artistic* distinctiveness of dance among other physical activities — thus (roughly) it differs from gymnastics in being *art*, and from music in being (essentially) *physical*: that is, (partially) *constituted* by or *comprised* of movements of human bodies, rather than simply caused by them. Second, the argument was conceived as a project in philosophy; and one with implications into, for instance, the nature of *research* into dance and dance education. For one cannot deal with dance educators for long without realising that — at least if one looks at the best of them — they are truly expert in a difficult field. So they *know* what to do. In the jargon of CDE (p. 65), they have the relevant craft-knowledge. It follows that, since that is genuinely knowledge (assuming it is), it cannot be gain-said. Then any interventions must reside in how that knowledge is *explained*. Of course, not everything such teachers *do* is beyond question; but, more importantly, what they *say* (in description of what they are doing) is no good guide. So this perspective grants something, but not everything, to the practitioner.

Neither the artistic focus of CDE nor its recognition of craft-knowledge is undermined in what is added now in the Supplementary Essays. But three broad areas of expansion are entertained here.

First, the claims of postmodernism are really of two kinds. As Supplementary Essay 1 urges (following CDE: 194-5), some discussions identify a kind of dance ('postmodern dance') which may be problematic (especially educationally) — perhaps because of its eclecticism. Equally, some discussions stress how a 'postmodern condition' might generate problems for (traditional) understandings of dance. In putting aside both such worries, Supplementary Essay 1 stresses how each builds on an insight which, taken too far, it cannot sustain. And then we see how eclecticism is little other than a style of its own, and how the (real) pressure on 'grand narratives' of history or society actually amounts to no more than a rejection of typical pretensions of philosophy. We are entitled to the *truth* (with a small 't') of claim about dances — or, when they are not true, it is because they are false — but this does not commit us automatically to claims of unreasonable generality (to *Truth* with a capital 't'). In this way, then, the insights of CDE are preserved against objections of this sort.

As our second emphasis, Supplementary Essay 2 moves onward to address — applied to dance — a question of great importance applied to dance education: namely, one concerning the limits of understanding. It poses the question by disputing whether or not two performances are of *the very same* dance. Without coming to any direct conclusion, it stresses both the *under-determination* (by its score) of performances of a particular dance and the conception of *numerical identity* for dances — that is, of this being *the very same dance*, rather than one of the same kind — which *its* use of the type/token contrast would entail. In this way, it stresses constraints following from the fact that performing arts are both *performing* and *arts*. When we come to these ideas from an educational perspective, they impinge both on the emphasis on *masterworks* (CDE: 78-81), since they explain the *specificity* of the claim made of the particular work by (say) Martha Graham, and on the *various* difference among cases of re-staging and re-choreography. In these ways, they expand both what was said in UD and what drives some judgements in CDE.

Third, the whole question of the (essentially) *physical* nature of dance is confronted (in Supplementary Essay 3) by incorporating into a discussion of the *audience* for dance consideration of a suggestion which, applied to dance, would expand the significance afforded to (say) dance on video. But this requires making clearer (than in was in CDE: 17-18; 107) exactly what the artistic/aesthetic distinction amounts to in this context. For the *problem* at the heart of over-rating (say) video is, effectively, that the video lacks crucial features of the *dance* — and that means crucial features of the *art* of dance, as opposed to aesthetic interest in dancing bodies. And this in turn has connections to the possibilities of a genuine *audience* for danceworks: that is, an audience that can see the bodily movements (etc.) as comprising *dances*.

Indeed, my version of the artistic/aesthetic contrast — which is a pervasive theme of the analysis offered in CDE, relating it directly to the institutional account of art (CDE: 47-49) — is further clarified in Supplementary Essay 3. And crucial here is the thought that, properly understood (which means: as *artworks*), dances have artistic properties. For it urges that, even when the same term (say, 'beauty') has an artistic and an aesthetic *use*, (correctly) applying it to an artwork amounts to something different than it would if — mistaking the artwork for a mere aesthetic object, say, some elegant road-sweeping (CDE: 106) — one still called it *beautiful*. And this idea is fundamental to the *transformative* character of art-status (CDE: 107–8), although probably not sufficiently emphasised there. For the fact of dance as art is, on this view, fundamental to its educational profile. And, of course, this is central to the contrast between dance and (for instance) gymnastics or diving.

Of course, the elaboration of all these ideas will depend partly on the arguments offered for them in the Supplementary Essays and partly on what (in addition) might be said in their defence, even if I have not said it. But one will only be drawn to that defence if there is something mildly compelling about the positions as derived here: I can only comment that *I* find them convincing to at least that degree.

There still remain many problems from CDE which this expanded edition does not address: but at least one of those problems remains fundamental to the project of the expanded edition — that dance is important enough for its educational role to be *worth* justifying. And this in turn would not (or, anyway, should not) be disputed by those who grant dance *some* educational role, because even entering into the debate would be conceding too much. Instead, opponents might think of dance as simply movement regarded aesthetically; but then it can have no distinctive educational role. But that cannot be my starting point. Rather, I have urged the centrally artistic nature of anything that counts as dance for these purposes. But I did not argue the detail: if readers prefer to consider the whole text as hypothetical against that possibility ... well, at least I have no compelling argument against them. Yet, for me, we begin from the *value* (educational and otherwise) of dance as a fact to be explained. Then the contours of my explanation might be adopted; and that might suggest some directions for future investigations into the concept of dance education.

Acknowledgements to the Expanded Edition

Of course, this work inherits the acknowlegements from CDE. But it has some obligations of its own. More specifically, to those who have permitted the reprinting of material:

- To Routledge, for 'permission' to make this expanded edition; and for permission to reprint passages from McFee, 1998 in Supplementary Essay 1;

- To Springer Verlag, for permission to include sections of McFee, 1996 in Supplementary Essay 1;

- To Dance Research, for permission to include material from McFee, 1994b in Supplementary Essay 2;

- To Meyer & Meyer, for permission to include sections from McFee, 1999 in Supplementary Essay 2;

- To the Nordic Society for Aesthetics, for permission to reprint sections of McFee, 2003b in Supplementary Essay 3;

- To Praeger/Greenwood, for permission to include sections from McFee, 2003a in Supplementary Essay 3.

I would also like to acknowledge the support of Dr. Bonnie Rowell, for many discussions of dance and postmodernism, going well beyond what was required for my supervision of her PhD; and for invitations to speak on these topics.

I was also stimulated by presenting some of these ideas — and discussing others — at a colloquium at the Dance department, University of California, Riverside, on 2nd November, 2000; and at the conference, *The Challenge of Dance*, Uppsala, Sweden, 10th February, 2001. My thanks to all participants.

I would also like to thank all those whose continued interest in CDE — in spite of some difficulties sketched above — led me to think an expanded edition worthwhile.

As usual, this work would not be what it is without the contribution of my wife, Myrene, to whom my thanks are due. In this case, though, the expanded edition would probably not exist at all, since it was both her mastery of the technology that made it possible and her understanding, encouragement and devotion to my project that brought it into being.

Finally, I would like to note more generally the contribution of three late friends: the death of John Wisdom, whose picture of rationality is central here, was announced as I was finishing CDE; the death of Gordon Baker, whose view of philosophy I have long accepted, was announced as I was planning this expanded edition; and, as I was working on it, came the announcement of the death of Richard Wollheim, who had supported me ever since supervising my doctorate. This book would undoubtedly be less good without their support — as, indeed, the world is now a emptier place.

Eastbourne, February, 2004

Preface to the 1994 Edition

Any book — and particularly a scholarly book — should aim at convincing its readership through rational argument. Its author's convictions have no place in the body of the book. Yet they bring *that* book (rather than some other) into being. So a preface articulating such commitments, and even doing so polemically, is not out of place. Knowing the author's motivations may help readers understand what is at issue in any of the succeeding arguments.

This book is guided by two commitments of mine: first, to the value of dance — indeed of the arts more generally — and in particular to their educational value. Second, to the *distinctiveness* of dance, and hence to the (potential) distinctiveness of its contribution, educational and otherwise. But these are not *mere* commitments, for I am here providing *arguments* in support of each: arguments which must be judged for their soundness, and not for my investment in them. That is to say, then, that this is a work of philosophy.

However, the commitments are important insofar as they explain *why* I am discussing these topics at this time. The arts are under threat, both from forces external to the art world, and from internal forces. In considering the first category, the external, we should remember, as others have noted (Best, 1992a), that totalitarian regimes have regularly seen the arts as a threat, either censoring artists (as in Soviet Russia in the 1950s) or defending the 'True Art' against its 'degenerate' (that is, challenging) counterpart (as in Hitler's Germany [Chipp, 1968: pp. 474–483]). If what I say is broadly correct, these regimes had a point: art *is* important and (potentially) challenging. So regimes which *reject* the very idea of challenge might be expected to respond in these ways. In contrast to the seriousness manifest in such examples, the government in the UK has recently treated the arts as something trivial, as mere amusement, or of no great significance. This indictment of the present situation in the UK is sharply put by the late Peter Fuller, who writes against general Thatcherite values as they apply to art, considering the specific example of Charles Saatchi, an art collector as well as Mrs. Thatcher's former media orchestrator. Fuller (1988a: pp.79–80) comments:

> I believe Saatchi has been a catastrophe for art in Britain… because, as far as art is concerned, Saatchi has no taste or discrimination — one reason why he prefers to buy works of art by the baker's dozen.

Fuller's point — which he takes Saatchi to exemplify — is that there is an attitude which sees '…no merit whatever in the old spiritual and aesthetic idea of art as a "disinterested" pursuit' (1988a: p.63;). Given such an attitude, one might predict, first: '…the transformation of fine art courses into courses orientated towards the new technologies, design and mechanical processes' (pp.63–64). A second prediction might be that holders of this attitude would have '…starved the museums and galleries of resources' (p.64). And this is *exactly* what Fuller (1989) found to have happened in the UK recently.

Within the art world, things are not much better. So that, looking to our second case, from art's defenders we find many misty claims masquerading as analysis. Thus David Best (1990a: p.5a) perceptively comments on the extent to which, instead of a vigorous argumentative defence of the value of art, we encounter '…vague and soothing soporifics from supporters'. Applied to education, these 'soporifics' typically take one of three forms. First, an 'argument' is advanced to the effect that, in schools, classes in the arts represent 'the other side of the coin', light relief in contrast to the serious intellectual business of mathematics or physics. Second, there is the blithe assumption of aesthetic value'— which means that one is not—*required* to say anything about the arts, their value being self-evident. The third version takes the form of a commitment to 'expressive objectives' for the arts in contrast to the more serious and important objectives of other curriculum activities. In any of these forms, this is simply a commitment to a reprehensible form of subjectivism (see Chapter One, section 3; and *UD*, Ch.1).

Clearly, the precise details of these situations differ from country to country. To make the discussion in this text more concrete, I have sometimes used, as an example, the situation in the UK, with a few remarks directed towards North America. Such a procedure means that UK readers have a discussion of their own situation, while North American readers at least have a discussion with actual examples of practice rather than mere idealisations. I have assumed that the current picture in the UK is either familiar or that the documents describing it are available: however, I have included a brief summary (as an appendix to Chapter 1) for those for whom this is not true.

The account of dance here is centrally that of my book *Understanding Dance* (McFee, 1992a), and many of the arguments used in that book recur in this one. However, I have endeavoured to present them in different ways, and have generally noted the places where topics introduced here are treated more extensively (*UD* in brackets with page numbers). Also, the different purposes of each book mean that there is a lot in *Understanding Dance* which I judge not to be strictly relevant to my project here. Those who require an expanded version of the concept of dance developed here are directed to that work.

Those who hope for a blow-by-blow account of what to teach — in particular, what to teach to children of such-and-such an age, on such-and-such a day — will be disappointed by what is here. My concern is with the *reasons* which might be given for the inclusion of dance in an *entitlement curriculum*, suitable for all. This concern means, first, that I am not *primarily* concerned with how that curriculum is delivered or with what is taught when; second, that (as argued in Chapter One) it cannot follow that dance *must* be taught, only that it has a substantial claim for curriculum time and resources, to be weighed against other substantial claims.

Although I have been thinking and writing about these issues for a number of years, the precise impetus for this book was provided by an invitation to discuss the concept of dance education at a conference organised in 1988 by the Dance section of the National Association of Teachers in Further and Higher Education. This book expands and explores the themes of that presentation: and, to acknowledge its origin, something of the *style* of the talk has been retained in writing this work. Such a style is appropriate to a text polemical in defence of (as I said initially) two major commitments of mine. Moreover, there are three further reasons why the 'lecture' style is suitable here. First, it lends itself to an informality of presentation appropriate for the conveying of complex ideas where 'gist' rather than detail is what is important. Second, the level of complexity is thereby kept to a minimum. Third, it allows me to refer to arguments articulated in *Understanding Dance* which, while not of primary relevance here, might nonetheless be of interest.

In this text I attempt to deal with complex issues briefly (and hence sometimes brusquely). It might be objected that my discussions in some places are unduly superficial. I have endeavoured to ensure an *appropriate* level of consideration in each place: I accept that on most topics a whole book could be (and often has been) written. But my focus is on the needs of a typical dance teacher: and where I have gone beyond that, it has been into the areas of my own particular expertise (especially in Chapters Four and Nine), where I not only have a special interest in saying something, but something particular to say.

A word about the examples: they are largely British because they derive primarily from my experiences of particular dances — augmented by films or videos — and I have relied largely on works for which a literature is available. Unfortunately, this may give the examples a dated feel, since waiting for such literature will involve *waiting*. Moreover, our commitment to *master-*

works (see Chapter Eight) will tend to focus on works which 'pass the test of time', and so are not in the forefront of *contemporary* work in dance. But the virtues of having a literature should compensate. First, points made are to some degree accessible even to those who are not there on a particular night, and hence could see a particular performance; and, second, the points are *general* points, not dependent on the particular examples. Indeed, the intention is that readers should supply their own examples into all discussions, with my examples simply indicating the issues under consideration.

Some readers might view this text as simply a presentation of certain views of David Best's: in particular, I explicitly build on his artistic/aesthetic contrast, (a version of) his account of art in terms of life-issues, and his Personal Enquiry conception of education. It would not break my heart if that were all this text achieved. Each of these ideas is important and, suitably understood, correct (or so I shall argue).

But I see this as *more* than an exposition of Davis Best's views in three ways. First, and least, there are places where the positions adopted here diverge from Best's. There are specific arguments with his views, as well as ideas he would not adopt. Second, there are ideas here which are *not* not drawn from Best's work, some of them my own and some from authors Best does not draw on. Third, and most important, many of the key ideas have their origin in authors Best and I share: in particular, John Wisdom and Wittgenstein. So that one might, with equal justice, highlight my dependence on — for example — Gordon Baker as an expositor of Wittgenstein, given my general debt to Wittgenstein's ideas.[1]

Acknowledgements
to the 1994 Edition

I have benefited from discussing these topics, and some of these ideas, with colleagues and numerous generations of students. My thanks to Sue Jones, Rachael Lightfoot and Fiona Smith (now a colleague) can stand proxy for all these debts.

My thinking has developed under the (friendly) criticisms of David Best and David Carr; although, as usual, I have regularly not taken their advice. The influences of Terry Diffey and Gordon Baker are powerful here, too. I would thank all of these friends for their support, and for specific discussions on various topics.

As with *Understanding Dance*, my biggest debt is to my wife, Myrene, who — in addition to preparing the typescripts — read the whole text in draft, saving me from unclarities, infelicities of style and down-right mistakes. Without her support, the project would never have been finished. Of course, she is not responsible for any of the more arcane of my views or for any mistakes which remain.

In addition, I would like to thank my editor, Julia Hall, for all her support in this project, and indeed all those at Routledge whose skills have contributed to the realisation of this text.

Finally, I would like to thank the Editor of the *Cambridge Journal of Education* for permission to rework sections from my paper 'Some reflections on action research' (published in Vol.23, No.2: pp 173–183) in Chapter Sixteen.

Chapter 1

Introduction

This book's over-riding purpose is to sketch a satisfactory rationale for the place of dance in education. As such, it is centrally a piece of abstract argument, drawing on considerations employed elsewhere, for other purposes. It assumes that the context of education is *broadly* as at present: running from about five years of age to about sixteen years for everyone, with the possibility of continuing until eighteen, or even twenty-one, and with the possibility of returning later in life. But none of these numbers is crucial. The schooling could, for example, begin at four or six years and finish at seventeen. What *is* crucial is the rationale provided for dance: it will have application *wherever or whenever* the conditions it requires are satisfied. If, for example, a child psychologist were to demonstrate that conceptual understanding (or conceptual understanding of a certain sort) were possible in children at two years of age, and if that conceptual understanding played a part in our justification of dance education, then *to that degree* the justification would apply from age two, and so on. The qualification 'to that degree' is important. For if we show what all children are *entitled to* in their schooling, and that this entitlement begins at two years, we have as yet shown nothing about when the dance education *should* begin, only when it could!

The problem: the distinctive nature of dance education

Imagine that you are faced with the task of justifying the place of dance in the school curriculum — either its place as *part of* physical education, or as a distinct area in its own right (this was a situation which the Education Reform Act [1988] in the UK forced on those in England and Wales who wished to argue for some place for dance). What is needed is the articulation of a characteristic *distinctive* of dance: if one's argument is based on features shared with, say, gymnastics or synchronised swimming, then one does not have an argument for *dance* at all. The 'powers that be' might do all you are asking — and yet do it without having dance in their curriculum.

1

Moreover, the characteristic identified must have an *educational* significance, for otherwise it will not define the different *educational* 'role' for dance. So what is needed is a defence of the *educational distinctiveness* of dance. This could, in principle, turn into either a defence of a special *dance education* programme, or a defence of the distinctive place of dance *within* a physical education programme.

For better or worse, in the UK, the argument for a discrete dance education programme in schools has been lost: dance will now occur as part of the physical education programme. The Education Reform Act [1988], as interpreted, determined *that* (see Appendix to Chapter 1). But deciding whether or not dance should be within the physical education area was not an issue for this text as such. *Wherever* dance is to be located, if it is to have a rationale, *its* rationale must be different from the rationale of other aspects of the school curriculum. In particular, it must be different from other aspects of the physical education curriculum.

Of course, any decisions in a particular school will depend on what it is realistic for *that* school to offer. There may be no time (in a particular school) to run *all* the courses that are deemed desirable. Some desirable elements may have to be dropped. One cannot therefore have arguments that compel the inclusion of dance in a school curriculum — only arguments that *would* compel the inclusion of dance, other things being equal. That is to say, these would be reasons for including dance, but not reasons which are *always* compelling. One might might agree that dance could not be dropped without loss, and yet that loss might have to be tolerated in certain specific cases. Still, the argument here will include major reasons for including a dance education programme, although the claims might be met in other ways — by considering, say, the combined 'effects' of gymnastics, music and synchronised swimming. This recognition allows us to formulate the project of this text more clearly. For one might urge that articulating the concept of dance education is itself a sufficiently precise task. But it is more exactly localised when one recognises that the *real* questions concern the *educational* distinctiveness of dance: and that both these elements are important. Advocates of dance must identify a distinctiveness and then argue the *educational importance* of that distinctiveness.

Against subjectivism

One major aspect of my position — an aspect already identified in the Preface and an area of agreement with David Best — is a rejection of any subjectivist trend in aesthetics. This is not the place to argue for the objectivity of artistic judgement (*UD*: Ch. 1), or the precise version of objectivity it builds-in. But it is worth being clear both *that* something is amiss with subjectivist views, and *what* is amiss with them.

A subjectivist view might be roughly characterised as holding that, say, beauty is in the eye of the beholder, or that appreciation in art is just a matter of personal taste, or that everyone is ultimately entitled to his or her own opinion about art. Such a view is problematic in many areas — for example, it builds-in a self-defeating relativism, as we will see — but it is especially problematic when one thinks about the arts in education. For if an area is subjective, in this sense, it follows that this area is not one where *learning* can take place — for one's view before and after the (supposed) learning experience are of equal value; it is not an area where *teaching* is possible — for the views of the 'student' before and after the (supposed) teaching are equally valuable; and it is not area where *knowledge* is possible — for the very idea of knowledge implies that (in principle) some have and some lack that knowledge. If all claims were of equal value, this would make no sense. So finding an area subjective in this sense is finding that concepts of teaching, learning, and knowledge have no application to that area. Clearly, anyone committed to a place for dance education must *hope* that dance is not subjective in this sense. In this vein, it is particularly galling to be confronted with some of the 'defences' of the role of the arts in education, by its supposed friends.

We can bring out in two ways what precisely is amiss with the subjectivist view of dance. First, such views tend to a self-defeating relativism; second, they denigrate dance. Let us consider in turn each of these objections to subjectivism.

The simplest version of relativism has two key elements: that two views are *in conflict* or *disagreement* on a certain point, and that *both* are correct (say, relative to a culture, viewpoint, or some such). Such a position is clearly self-defeating. For if we ask a relativist if relativism is *true*, he has an insuperable dilemma. He can answer 'yes', but now *this* fact at least is not a relativist one. So relativism *isn't* true, at least for this one claim. And if our relativist answers 'no', then he gives us no reason to believe in relativism — nor any reason to accept that he genuinely believes it himself. One might put this point to a *relativist* by urging 'relativism isn't true-for-me' (Putnam, 1983: 288). And our relativist cannot — by his own lights — have any reply. Of course, there is much more to be said about relativism (*UD:* Ch. 14). But suppose we accept its self-defeating character. We immediately see that a subjectivist view of art is refuted in exactly the same way. Consider the claim that an object X^1 is a work of art, or that object Y is a great work of art. If our subjectivist urges that it is *true* (or *false*) that X is a work of art or that Y is a great one, it follows that judgements of art-status and artistic value are not subjective after all: it is *not* in the eye of the beholder. For he has urged the truth (or falsity) of one of these positions. Yet if our subjectivist *denies* that it can ever be true that X is a work of art or that Y is a great work of art (because the categories are not suitable for truth etc.) he is urging subjectivism: but, on this option, *what ever* is implied by subjectivism, it cannot be applied to *art*. To be a subjectivist in *this* way is to claim that it is not *true* that a certain object is art: or, more briefly, that there is no art. We should conclude, therefore, that one cannot genuinely be a subjectivist about art. For if one can discuss art, one cannot really (that is, consistently[2]) be a subjectivist. And one can only be a subjectivist by ceasing to talk about *art* at all.

That rather abstract discussion might not 'bite' immediately on the practical concerns of dance educators. The other consideration should have more practical import. It is that — if correct — the subjectivist position denigrates art. For suppose the subjectivist is correct: what place could art have in a school curriculum? Since notions of teaching, learning and knowledge have not application (on this position) in respect of an art form such as dance, it follows that any curriculum time given over to dance cannot possibly be viewed as teaching, learning, or the acquisition of knowledge. By extension, it clearly cannot be thought of as the acquiring of any *understanding*. Again, the notion of understanding implies (at least in principle) that some people do and some do not understand — a view at odds with the subjectivism we are presently considering.

So how might a place for dance be justified? In the Preface I noted three potential ways forward: (1) that dance might be seen as *an alternative* to the educational, a kind of light relief; (2) that artistic experience *as such* was *obviously* educational; or (3) that its educational value would be developed in terms of expressive objectives. Clearly, all of these come to roughly the same thing. They represent different ways of either making the best of subjectivism, or trying to have one's cake and eat it (see Eisner, 1972: 156–8). For, first, relegating dance to 'the other side of the coin', in contrast to *genuinely* educational activities, is simply giving up. Equally, claiming that the experience of art is *obviously* beneficial is mistaken in two important ways. Surely, taken literally, it is simply false. We do not accept that *any* experience of art is automatically valuable. Rather, we believe that experience of art must be guided or directed — for example, through structured participation, through classes in appreciation, through training in techniques and the like. Second, and more importantly, if *any* experience of art were beneficial, this would simply remove any *educational* justification for the place of an art form such as dance in a school. Pupils need simply to be directed to the local gallery; or perhaps not even that, if we accept that novels, music and (some) cinema count as art in this sense. So taking this line is tantamount to acknowledging that no *educational* justification for the arts can be given. Such an answer must also suggest evasion to theorists of education.

The third possibility to consider is that there are some specifically artistic kinds of educational outcomes. This possibility should not be ruled out without consideration. But it is difficult to see how such outcomes can both have *no* connection with other educational outcomes and yet be *definitely* themselves educational. As I will urge in Chapters 3 and 13, a narrow view of the aims and outcome of education is to be avoided. However, this avoidance must surely weld arts education into a more general educational process, concerned with personal understanding: and making available the possibility of teaching and (most especially) *learning*. And that is just another way of saying that arts education must not be treated in a subjectivist fashion.

If subjectivism is, in these ways and for these reasons, to be rejected, it follows that — at least in principle — we are faced with discussing a rationale for dance in the curriculum which is *similar to* the rationale we might offer for other activities. That is the kind of position adopted here. As David Best (1983: 155–6) urged in another context, there are many differences between our judgements in respect of works of art and the judgements we make about other events, objects, and persons: but those differences are not in respect of their *objectivity*, at least necessarily.

That qualification, using the word 'necessarily', is an important one. For I am not claiming that every remark made about any art form is *automatically* an objective remark. There are various ways in which it could fail to be so, the two most obvious being through prejudice or bias. I return to these issues in Chapter 15, when we consider accountability. For now, though, it is important to recognise that the *possibility* of bias, or the *possibility* of prejudice, are themselves confirmation of our thesis against subjectivism. As with the notion of *colour-blindness*, which presupposes that most of us see coloured objects as they are, the thought that a certain judgement might be prejudiced contrasts it with a judgement made in respect of the same area which was not prejudiced. And similarly for the notion of bias. So, this text campaigns throughout for the *importance* of dance in education, and that campaign is predicated on the rejection of subjectivism.

Plan of the book

A commitment to the role and value of dance education poses major questions — what should be taught?, in what relation to (the rest of) physical education? — as well as more fundamental questions about what benefit, if any, accrues from the practice and study of dance. The provision of the National Curriculum in the UK makes discussion of these issues especially timely: but they are perennial issues of significance for those who think that dance *should* have a place in the education of the young (and more generally).

In this text, I will defend the view that dance in schools must be thought of (at least centrally) as an *artistic* activity, continuous with the activities of dancers and choreographers. As we will see, this view provides a rationale for dance in educational contexts, and thereby suggests the employment of some dance forms rather than others.

The argument begins in Chapter 2 with a brief account of the nature of dance. This account is expanded by emphasising the uniqueness of artistic interest and understanding, and introduces the idea that the chief educational contribution of dance is rooted in its nature as an art form. Such an account is then integrated with the conception of education (Chapter 3), and expanded through a discussion of the mechanism of the process (emotional education) and its focus (life-issues) in Chapter 4. Finally, Part I closes by laying-out the account of dance education adopted in the work, the *artistic account*.

Part II addresses four ways in which that account needs to be supplemented or expanded to make its practical 'bite' more apparent. So that we consider why, on this account, the actual practice of dance is required, how dance is related to (the rest of) physical education, the potential role of dance artists in education, and the centrality, within the education role of dance, of the study and practice of dance criticism.

In Part III, I consider three positions which run counter to the *artistic account*: namely, (1) the view that dance is simply movement in which we take an aesthetic interest (and hence continuous with other enjoyable movement); (2) that dance is simply a popular cultural form, with the idea of *art* being either irrelevant or pernicious; and (3) that a multi-cultural approach to dance in education is essential, especially when one is living in a multi-ethnic society (such as the UK or the USA). Adopting all or any of these positions would undermine the *artistic account*, either by rejecting its central idea of art, or by robbing it of practical value since it would no longer point to *kinds* of dance to be studied. Each of these positions is considered, and ultimately rejected.

Part IV addresses a variety of issues in education more generally. For planning a dance curriculum requires that one explore the complex relationship between aims, objectives and processes. It is argued that a *process* model must be central to any coherent account of dance education, and that such a model indeed elaborates the account of education as Personal Enquiry given in Part I. Second, the relationship between *understanding* dance and actually *doing* dance (broached in Part II) will be expanded through a brief consideration of the *teaching* of dance in educational contexts. The argument will be that a process account of education requires the adoption of teaching/learning strategies which are 'child-centred' — but that this need not deteriorate into an 'anything goes' movement-based dance education: indeed, that the *artistic account* expressly militates against such a trend. Further, general issues of accountability and assessment for dance education will be considered. The emphasis will be on the objectivity of the informed judgement of the knowledgeable. Finally, there will be a discussion of one way forward for dance-in-education: namely, the extension of teacher-based research, exploiting Donald Schön's idea of *reflective practice*. For it is important to see that some of the knowledge required by the teacher of dance in educational contexts is *craft-*

knowledge, and hence is best acquired from the good practice of established teachers of such dance.

The outcome of this text, elaborated in the Conclusion, will be a vindication of the *artistic account*, a better understanding of its implications, some pointers towards its implementation, and a sketch of some directions (and some principles) for future research into aspects of the concept education.

Appendix. The National Curriculum in the United Kingdom — an introduction

The National Curriculum in the United Kingdom[3] is presented here as posing, in a concrete form, a set of major questions for the curriculum in general and the role of dance education in particular: and as offering *one* response to those questions. As Kenneth Baker (then Secretary of State for Education) said in a speech in January 1987, by the expression 'National Curriculum' was meant 'a school curriculum governed by national criteria which are promulgated by the Secretary of State' (quoted Maw, 1988: 49). In fact, this idea was enshrined in the 1988 Education Reform Act (for England and Wales[4]): by then it amounted to a specification of (1) subjects; (2) organised as core + foundation subjects; (3) representing a certain percentage of the curriculum; and (4) involving an elaborate pattern of regular testing. As it is summarised (DES, 1989: §3.3):

> The National Curriculum comprises
> * *foundation* subjects — including three *core* subjects and seven *other* foundation subjects which must be included in the curricula of all pupils;
> * *attainment targets*, to be specified up to ten levels of attainment, covering the ages 5–16, setting objectives for learning;
> * *programmes of study* specifying essential teaching within each subject area;
> * *assessment arrangements* related to the ten levels of attainment.

The core subjects were English, mathematics and science; the other foundation subjects were technology (including design), history, geography, music, art, physical education, and (from 11–16) a modern foreign language. Moreover, it is acknowledged that 'the foundation subjects are certainly *not* a complete curriculum ... the *whole* curriculum for *all* pupils will certainly need to include at appropriate (and in some cases all) stages other cross-curricular themes'; also necessary are (at least) (DES, 1989: §3.8):

* careers education and guidance;
* health education;
* other aspects of personal and social education; and

- coverage across the curriculum of gender and multi-cultural issues.

It is no part of the argument of this text to dispute the educational credentials of the 'proposals' in this Act: by now, they represent the legal obligations of Local Authorities in England and Wales. One might think of the whole idea as 'a folly of unprecedented proportions' (Simons, 1988: 89) or agree with White's tart comment (White, 1988: 113): 'You pick ten foundation subjects to fill 80-90% of the school time table, highlight three as of particular importance and arrange tests at different ages. I could have worked out the National Curriculum years ago. Anyone could'. Nevertheless, that is not to the point: the interest here is as a concrete example of how *dance* might be located within a school curriculum. However, it is worth recording that dance does not *always* have a place in the school curriculum at present. I am reliably informed, for example, that the school-based dance-experience of one Californian consisted in a brief introduction to square-dancing for 11 year-olds (6th grade), where the intentions were less artistic or cultural than they were social — as it was put to me, 'to get the boys to touch the girls and vice versa'. The more serious point is that any argument around what *should* happen in education, especially of the young, must be alive to the practical realities of the present situation. In this respect, too, the National Curriculum in the UK is an appropriate starting point since it does acknowledge a place for dance.

Not that this investigation locates the ideas of the National Curriculum seamlessly with our own. What will become apparent — of course — is the discrepancy between the conception of education espoused in this text, the Personal Enquiry conception, and key aspects of the Education Reform Act [1988]. We will see (Chapter 13) that the conception of the curriculum adopted here — which might be called a 'process model' — is much *better* represented in the physical education proposals than in the National Curriculum more generally, which is broadly (a) a 'product' model of the curriculum, and (b) misconceived on the *nature* of assessment/accountability. One might speculate on *why* this might be, but the crucial feature to notice (in Chapter 13) would be the tension between the proposal as a whole and the physical education version (see Kelly, 1990: Ch. 3).

Notice, too, that the National Curriculum involves testing 'at the ages of 7, 11, 14 and 16 for most pupils' (DES, 1989: §6.4) — these ages representing the end-points of the so-called Key Stages 1 to 4. It should also be noticed that dance does not feature as a foundation subject. And given the subject basis on which the curriculum *is* presented, it follows that dance has no explicit place in 80–90% of the school experience of an average child. Or, more precisely, that only does so *within* physical education.

PART I

DANCE, ART AND EDUCATION

Chapter 2

What is Dance?

Introduction

In line with arguments elsewhere (*UD*: Ch. 1), I will not attempt to *define* dance in the sense of giving a list of conditions which are individually necessary and jointly sufficient[1] for an activity's being dance. Indeed, I begin from the assumption that we know what dance is. No doubt there may be disputes about borderline cases, but these are built on a firm understanding of other cases. So we understand that, for example, ballet, tap, disco, reggae are dance forms, and that gymnastic floor work, diving and acting are not. We know that the waltz and the tango are dances; and so are the foxtrot and the pogo. And if all of these are not familiar, some are. Moreover, any 'gaps' could be filled-in with other uncontentious examples. In this chapter I will take us beyond that account of these activities in three ways. First, I will comment on the relation between dances and other human activities. Second, I will begin to distinguish the kind of dance that, for the purpose of dance education, are of central concern, or so I shall argue: namely, art-type dances. This will involve my distinguishing artistic interest and judgement from (other) aesthetic interest and judgement, and offering some remarks on the nature of art. The third area of discussion involves distinguishing characteristics of this art-type *dance* from the characteristics of other art-forms. In particular, it will focus on the status of dance as a physical art-form and as a performing art; and ways in which our interest in dance differs from our interest in other art works (*UD*: Part II).

The upshot of this chapter will be an account of the *uniqueness of artistic interest in dance*. This point will be crucial to the argument of this book since, as the Introduction stated, it is a defence of an *artistic* concept of dance education. Of course, not much of the material in this chapter is about dance education specifically — but I return to the nature of dance education in Chapters 4 and 5.

Action

Any informed discussion of dance must begin from the status of dance as *human action*: that is to say, from its role as the sort of thing *people* do, rather than the sort of thing that just happens (see also Chapter 10). If this kind of agency is crucial, dance must be described in ways which, first, permit talk of human agency and, second, do not confuse such actions with other events. An example may make these points concrete. To my doctor, a traditional Western general-practitioner-type, I am (primarily at least) a rather complex physical system, and his job involves returning that system to smooth-running, where this is typically achieved by bringing about chemical changes in the physical system — by giving me pills, in other words. Now, this way of thinking of me leaves little or no room for the concept of *action* to be applied to me. No doubt I am thought of as able to take the pills. But, from the doctor's perspective, I make no (other) contribution. The cure is, we might say, something which happens to me. Well, is such a medically-based understanding a suitable one if your concern is with dance? No, for if we conceive of an event as a collection of physical systems, embodying 'scientific laws' (the kinds of laws in place in physics and chemistry), we have not described a *dance* at all. As I put it earlier, that way of describing does not permit talk of human agency.

Additionally, this medically-based way of considering an event would not distinguish dance from other activities — all would be collections of physical systems, embodying the working-out of those same laws. So this way of treating dance will be confusing if we are trying to plan, say, a curriculum for physical education: it may lead us to confuse dance with non-dance. What is *distinctive* about dance is not picked-out in this way of thinking about it. So one *cannot* think about dance in this way, for this way of thinking does not distinguish dance from other activities.

This point is of central importance because, as we will see in Chapter 10, failure to notice it is *one* of the confusions embodied in thinking of dance as 'aestheticised movement' or 'a special kind of movement' (*UD*: Ch. 2).

What does such a point it tell us about dance? Two features are important. First, any satisfactory account of dance must distinguish dance from other, similar, things that people *do*. And, second, doing so must pick-out what *actions* the people were performing[2], not simply the movement they did. A related example may explain and expand this point (*UD*: 52–3). An intelligent, English-speaking being from another planet arrives at a church on a Saturday afternoon, and sees a number of people gathered there. In particular, three are talking together. Although the alien understands the words, their import escapes him. He does not understand the *action* of marrying. He does not understand that nexus of rules and the like which constitute marriage. For the alien, the event on the Saturday would not significantly differ from a similar event on the preceding Thursday evening with the same people in the same place saying the same words. The alien could not recognise that from the Thursday event, the rehearsal, nothing followed, in ways that the Saturday event did have implications, commitments and so on. These were different *actions* even though they were comprised of the same *people* in the same *place* saying the same *words*.

To apply, what makes an activity dance rather than some other thing is — like any other action — a complex matter of rules and contexts: certainly not one where simply performing certain movements is by itself sufficient. So to characterise an activity as dance we must build-into our characterisation the sense that it is *human action*. This perspective already takes the dance theorist away from conceptions which treat dance as centrally continuous with other human activities, for it recognises that two actions, although comprised of similar bodily movements, may be quite different.

This contrast — between descriptions which treat an event as action and descriptions which treat it simply in terms of movements of the body or as a physical system with the working-out of certain scientific laws — is important when we consider the nature of dance notation. For, typically, notations are so constructed to be able to describe *any* movements of the body, not just those that take place in dance. But this very capacity means that they do not identify what is *central* to dance in so doing. Thus notation systems too do not represent *unique* descriptions of dances. And this is a great strength. If one wished to compare or contrast dance with other movement, having a notation system which applied equally to both the dance and the other movement would clearly be an advantage. If there were a notation system which applied uniquely to dance, so that one could only characterise dance using it, it would be worthless for purposes of comparison: and therefore worthless to, say, the anthropologist.

Of course, much that is notated is dance. We recognise, though, that what makes it *dance* is not precisely what is being notated. The notation identifies the movements right enough, but the context evades the notation. It is this that is provided by, for example, locations for performance, the understanding of an appropriate audience, and so on.

Another important aspect of the idea of *action* is relevant. For — as we have said — actions are centrally something you *do*, as opposed to something which just happens to you. A nervous tic or the leg movement the doctor initiates by tapping my knee are good examples of cases where my body moves, but there is no *action*. Thinking of action in this way means that one has only done something, has only performed an action, if it makes sense for you to have *tried* or *attempted* or *intended* to do that thing. This connection between the concepts *action* and *intention* comes out clearly through a simply problem case: say, belching. In general, belches are involuntary and we are not criticised — or not much criticised — for them: we couldn't help it. However, it is apocryphally told that in certain countries it is impolite to *fail to belch* after a meal. Hence, one is held responsible for one's belch (or lack of it). The point to notice is that it *makes sense* to hold people responsible for their belching *to the extent* that it is something they control, something they could try to do or refrain from doing. The conclusion to be drawn, of course, is a connection between the notion of action and notions such as *intention* and *trying* (Winch, 1973: 130–50; Winch, 1987: 177–8).

As we will see in Chapter 4 (section on 'The nature of art'), the idea of *intention* is an important one for the understanding of dance as art. For dance-making is possible only in societies or cultures which have the concept *dance*: only then can one attempt or intend to make dance — hence, only succeed in the *action* of dance-making under such conditions. But we are moving ahead too fast. We must return to the understanding or appreciation of dance.

Perception and aesthetic interest

It is important to recognise that understanding dances is a matter of seeing them, where this means *seeing them as dances*. Yet that is no easy matter. Two issues are of central importance. The first, considered in this section, concerns the distinction between taking a purposive interest in something and taking an aesthetic interest in that thing. The second issue, considered in the next section, involves distinguishing — from *within* aesthetic interest — the special interest we can have in works of art (artistic interest). On the first of these issues, we contrast the interest we typically take in dances (but also in other objects in which we take an aesthetic interest — sunsets, motorcars, gymnastic sequences) with the interest we take in those same objects when our concern with them is, say, the economic interest that we have in a dance because we are its 'backer', or the mechanical interest we have in our new car, and so on. That is to say, we can take a number of different kinds of interest in a car. We could, for example, concern ourselves with its brake horse power, with its design, with its speed, reliability and so forth. Thus, on one occasion we could take an aesthetic interest in the car — be struck by its line, grace, and the like; and an another occasion we might take a mechanical interest in the car and be impressed by its complicated engine. This same thought applied to dance, that we can take more than one kind of interest, is crucial here. In particular, two characteristics of the taking of these other (non-aesthetic) kinds of interest must be noted. Before we get to them, though, it is worth noting a general feature of considerable importance: that our perception of the dance work is *concept-mediated*.

The point is that what I see (or hear, or whatever) depends on the concepts that I have available to me. Thus, to use an example used elsewhere (*UD*:

39), looking out of the window I see simply trees whereas you, with your greater botanical knowledge, see oaks, ashes and elms. Here we have a difference in what we *see*, explained in terms of the different concepts we bring to bear. I am only able to bring to bear the concept 'tree', whereas you can employ the concepts 'oak', 'elm', 'ash' etc. This is a perfectly general point. Applied to our situation, it is that thinking about the different kinds of interest one can have in dance is another way of recognising the contours of the concepts under which we perceive the dances: that is to say, when I take an economic interest in a dance I am perceiving that dance under economic concepts.

So what two key features distinguish *aesthetic interest* from the other interests that we might take in, say, a dance? We can summarise both by saying that taking an aesthetic interest in something (a dance, or a car, or a firework display) is not viewing that 'something' as a means to an otherwise specifiable end. David Best (1978a: 103–10) presents the root distinction in a clear and helpful way applied to the case of sport. He urges that sports may be divided into two kinds: aesthetic sports and purposive sports. Purposive sports are defined in terms of the achievement of a specifiable end: say, the scoring of tries and drop goals for rugby. Then success in that sport is explained in terms of acquiring points in those ways and any method of achieving those points, within the rules of the game, is permitted. Thus, the elegant running of the Australian rugby player David Campese may score a try, but equally fumbling, staggering and mauling by some forwards might achieve a try: the first one, let us say, achieved with elegance, grace and so forth, the other with brute force and luck. But both count equally as a try. Here we see one feature of a purposive sport. Not merely are purposive sports defined in terms of a particular end — say the scoring of points in rugby — but it is recognised that there is more than one route to that end: the elegant and graceful route counts no more towards the final score than the lucky or ungainly. Moreover, as a consequence, a second feature can be identified. There are many characteristics of the route to that end, the *way* that the points are achieved, which are irrelevant to the overall result. So that, again, the number of passes, for example, which take place prior to the scoring of the try are simply irrelevant. More passes or fewer do not affect whether or not the try is acceptable. But the irrelevance here has no further consequences — it is not, for example, that the number of passes *stands in need* of some justification, which is missing. Rather, it does not *need* to be justified at all.

Consider, by contrast, David Best's *aesthetic* sports, such as gymnastic vaulting. Here the two characteristics we have identified for rugby disappear. First, the aim is not simply to get over the box, but to get over it in such-and-such a manner: one cannot specify the *end* independently of the means of achieving that end, for end and means combine. One must get over the box *in such-and-such a fashion.* So speaking means/ends language here is going to be confusing. We cannot really differentiate means from ends, the manner of achieving the result from the result itself. Thus there cannot be 'many means'. Moreover, the second characteristic too is missing. If the gymnastic vault includes irrelevant material, irrelevant twirls, say, then that will run counter to high scoring because it will mean (for example) that the vault was not performed as cleanly as it could be. Thus we have here two characteristics which, Best urges, distinguish aesthetic sports from purposive ones.

Whatever one thinks of the distinction as a way of dividing up sports, at the least it directs us to an important contrast between purposive interest and aesthetic interest. That contrast has two related elements. In aesthetic interest, we do not have a means to an otherwise specifiable end: the end *involves* or *includes* the means of achieving it. This would not be so for purposive interest. Moreover, and second, all features are aesthetically relevant — at least in principle. So that finding a feature which did not contribute to the aesthetic significance would be — from the perspective of *aesthetic* interest — finding a flaw. Again, this is not a characteristic shared by purposive interest (Beardsmore, 1971: 8–9).

I have suggested thus far that we recognise aesthetic interest as rooted in perception of objects using aesthetic concepts, and that aesthetic concepts should be contrasted with purposive concepts.

Two aspects of our achievement so far should be noticed. First, it determines the *large* concept of the aesthetic (*UD*: 39–42) by separating aesthetic judgement from purposive judgement. But, thus far, this tells us nothing about the case of art, although we would expect artistic concepts and artistic interest to be non-purposive in the way which we have presently identified. This point will be important later on. For David Best (1984) urges that the term 'aesthetic education' is confusing just because it runs together our concern with fountains, firework displays and landscapes on the one hand, and our concern with art on the other (appendix to Chapter 4; also *UD*: Ch. 13). The *reason* such a confusion might take place is that our aesthetic concern with the fountains, firework displays and landscapes is also non-purposive, as is our concern with art. But, from that, nothing follows about other similarities.

The second aspect is that taking a *purposive* interest in art (as in any aesthetic object) is failing to see it as *art*. So the producer whose concern with a dance is simply a concern with its economic success, because he is taking an economic interest in it, is not really concerned with *dance* at all. To put the point figuratively, he would not care what the actual dancers did at all, as long as they attracted a sufficiently large paying audience. His concern is not with the features of the work, but with something extraneous to those features.

The nature of artistic interest

We now turn to the second key characteristic of our concern with dance, as identified in the previous section: the distinction, within the general category of *aesthetic* interest, between the interest we take in works of art, and the interest in other things where we take an aesthetic interest, such as waterfalls, sunsets, fountains and firework displays. From within that large concept of the aesthetic, following David Best (1978a: 113–16), we therefore distinguish the interest that we take in works of art — *artistic interest* — from the interest that we take in other aesthetic objects (fountains, firework displays and natural beauty and so on). We can call this second '*merely aesthetic interest*': it represents a *small* conception of the aesthetic. Both artistic interest and merely aesthetic interest will be centrally non-purposive (although as the earlier discussion of aesthetic sports may make plain, there may be some residual purposiveness in some instances of merely aesthetic interest). This distinction between the artistic and the aesthetic amounts to the claim that the interest in *art* is importantly unlike the interest in other things in which we take an aesthetic interest. Of course, this is not straightforwardly a *verbal* distinction, nor is it one regularly respected by writers on aesthetics[3]. Still, neither of these points undermines the importance of this contrast. For what is at issue is not what *words* we should (or do) use, but what contrasts we respect.

Now let us turn to the distinction between *artistic* interest, judgement and appreciation, our judgement etc. of works of art, and aesthetic interest, judgement and appreciation of natural beauty, fountains and firework displays — perhaps better called *merely* aesthetic judgement. The clearest way to introduce this distinction is to consider the case where a spectator confronts a work of art but does not confront it *as* a work of art; and this means that the spectator is not able to bring to bear on that 'object' the concepts appropriate to the appreciation of art — concepts such as form, style, meaning etc. For example, I typically hear a particular piece of music, say, as in a certain *category* of art (Walton, 1978), as having a certain form. For Webern's *Symphonie Opus 21*, the category would be *serial music*. To fail to hear this work as serial music would be to misperceive it. Now consider a listener who knows nothing of serial music, and attends to a particular piece, Webern's *Symphonie Opus 21,* as though it were a pleasing succession of natural sounds (for example, birdsong). This might be a highly enjoyable experience, but it is not an experience of art — it does not involve artistic appreciation or the making of an artistic judgement. This listener lacks the kind of understanding required to avoid misperceiving the work. So this listener is not really confronting a work of art at all, for he is not confronting this work *as* a work of art. He could not, for example, discern its structure. So his appreciation is *merely* aesthetic. Again, a parallel case: a person who, knowing no French, is entranced by the reading of a particular poem in French. She cannot be said to understand *the poem*; rather, she confronts the poem as though it were merely a succession of pleasing sounds; she has missed its meaning, its form, and so on. And again, this is not to say the she might not find listening to the 'poem' enjoyable.

But how is this contrast between artistic judgement and aesthetic judgement to be articulated? Best uses two ideas to hold the contrast in place. The first — key here — is most easily seen through one of Best's own examples. Attending a performance of the classical Indian dance Ram Gopal, Best (1978a: 115) is 'enthralled by the exhilarating quality of his [Gopal's] movements'. But, as Best acknowledges, his appreciation was merely aesthetic, not artistic, because he (Best) did not understand Indian dance. Similar movements might also have been exhilarating and so, for Best, 'equivalent': but different movements would not have amounted to the same thing for those in the audience taking an *artistic* interest. What is emphasised here is the importance of detail in relation to meaning/understanding. David Best does not understand Indian dance (of that style?), and hence is not appreciating it artistically, even though, first, he is enjoying/appreciating it and, second, it is indeed art.

We can usefully expand this point. First, this example takes for granted that the dance *is* art: that, roughly, it was the product of the intention to make art — or, to put that another way, that it was constructed under the concept 'art'. Second, this example suits our purposes in that there is something *specific* that Best did not understand: namely, the precise meanings of the hand gestures. Since the hand gestures *have* these precise meanings, we can recognise what, as it were, Best was missing. But the point is a wholly general one. For a similar failure to understand, say, the formal significance of repetitions — or, for poems, the significance of rhyme — would lead to misunderstanding (and hence misperception) in just the same way. One's grasp *did not allow* artistic appreciation, or the taking of an artistic interest. This picks out the sense in which a different kind of understanding is operative in the case of artistic interest from that which operated vis-à-vis aesthetic interest.

The second idea which holds in place the artistic/aesthetic contrast for Best is one of considerable importance for us: it concerns the way in which artworks have the possibility of expressing a conception of what Best (1985a: 159) calls 'life issues' or 'life situations' (Best, 1978a: 115). For Best, this most truly marks the artistic from the aesthetic. But for our purposes here it is sufficient if the *distinction* is accepted, and accepted as a difference in kind of *understanding* — given the concept-mediated character of experience, as a difference in kinds of experience. We will return in detail to the notion of life-issues (Chapter 4).

The upshot of viewing dance as action

Thus far I have argued that dance must be seen as action, and that doing so requires that we differentiate between apparently similar kinds of human action. Two actions comprising similar movements may still be very different. Further, I have suggested one important characteristic of at least some dance: that it is an art form, and therefore an appropriate object for artistic interest. This offers a powerful way of justifying the place of dance in education more generally and in the school curriculum in particular. Faced with the question, 'Why include dance?', and seeing dance as competing, say for curriculum time, with other activities (gymnastics, games, music, etc.), it will be important to have a specific reason for including dance; and the possibility of taking an artistic interest in it will at least distinguish it from gymnastics and from team games, since these are not appropriate objects for *artistic* interest.

So we have a justification for dance in the school curriculum if we can first justify the role of the arts and, secondly, justify the role of dance from within the arts. That first task will be undertaken in Chapter 4, but it is important to say something here about the status of dance from *within* the arts. For if the educational justification consisted simply in providing pupils with the opportunity to make, to develop *artistic interest*, this could clearly be served by any one of music, literature, drama, painting, etc.

Dance as a performing art

Asked what marks off dance education from (other) physical education, our reply has been its artistic dimension or possibility. For, in explaining the concept of dance education, we will be localising dance education; and this means comparing and contrasting it with physical education (or with the rest of physical education). In this context, though, it is worth stressing also what distinguishes it from the other arts. Two features are of particular importance. The first is its *physical character*: I shall think of dance as the only essentially physical art form, although drama and (especially) mime should not be excluded[4]. Not that music and visual art do not *require* human action for their creation and/or existence, but the art objects are not physical (that is, not human action) in quite the same sense. Participating in them is not, of itself, physical training (although it may require physical training). So dance is a physical art form: that already distinguishes it from music, literature and visual art. Moreover, dance is a performing art. This idea has many complexities, only some of which we can look at here (see *UD*: Ch. 4).

It is important, for any performing art, to recognise that we have (as it were) two objects for discussion. To take a particular example, we must consider both *Swan Lake* itself and Tuesday night's performance of *Swan Lake*.

That is to say, there is the dance and particular performances of it. This has a number of interesting implications for the nature of dance education. So it is worth making some remarks in respect of it. First, the dance itself is an abstract object — one never meets *it*, although of course seeing the performances is, in another way, seeing *it*. Second, the dance can be seen in two places at the same time — by groups seeing different performances. So that the dance could be going on simultaneously in London and in New York, and both would be *Swan Lake*. The third thing to notice is that the London *Swan Lake* and New York *Swan Lake* will typically be different, if only because they have a different cast, are performed on stages differing in size, and so forth. In fact, the differences will typically be more profound than that. When the dance is staged in London, the stager may emphasis different of its characteristics, perhaps to suit the dancers in his cast. And, for similar reasons, different aspects may be stressed by the person staging the dance in New York.

It is useful to have a way to talk about this phenomenon, and my preferred way is a type/token distinction[5]. I will introduce this idea by considering the case of flags (*UD*: Ch. 4). For, like dances, flags have this dual aspect. Suppose I give a flag each to ten people. Asked how many flags there are, there is a clear answer to the question: there are ten flags, because each person has a stick with a piece of cloth on it. But all of the flags are the Union Jack. So there is an equally clear answer that there is only one flag here: there is only the Union Jack and not, for example, the Stars and Stripes, the Tricolour, and so forth. We call the sense in which there are ten flags the *token sense*, and the sense in which there is one flag the *type sense*. Thus our Union Jack is the type, and our sticks with cloth on them are tokens of that type. Notice too that the type is an abstract object. One never confronts the type directly. For what one sees is always some token. Further, notice that all tokens are equally tokens of that type. All the flags given out are equally the Union Jack.

This idea is important in considering art forms since some theorists have wished to give priority to, say, the handwritten manuscript of a novel, or the version of a dance staged by its choreographer. But the nature of the type/token relation means that one cannot privilege one token above others. All are equally tokens; equally but no more. So seeking this kind of prioritisation is giving up a type/token conception of the relation between the dance and its performances[6].

Our type/token language helps us to be clear on the three points noticed earlier. Since we are claiming that *Swan Lake* is a type, then our language informs us that it is an abstract object (the first point). As an abstract object, we would expect it to be encountered only through encountering tokens, and hence for it to be possible for there to be more than one token around at one particular time (the second point). In my flag example, there were ten flags. All the flags were equally the Union Jack, even though, for example, some were big, some were small, and so on. In the same way, all the various performances are equally *Swan Lake*, despite their differences (the third point).

In the case of dances a further feature should be noted. For the type/token distinction does not, of itself, decide what is to count as a token of what. There is a difficult borderline between re-staging a dance and re-choreographing it to produce a different dance. In some of Nureyev's productions, for example, it is difficult to say with certainty whether he has restaged or re-choreographed. But that simply recognises a difficulty in *deciding* whether a particular performance is or is not a token of a particular type. That is to say, recognising re-choreography as the production of a different work of art is a way of saying that its tokens are tokens of a different *type*.

This way of presenting the matter poses a major question for the nature of dance by asking us to see particular performances as tokens of an abstract type. But how does a type *constrain* its tokens? What makes them tokens of *that* type? This is a complex question, stretching in many directions. Here I will simply assert two aspects of an answer (*UD:* Chs 3 and 4).

The first aspect of the answer is the Thesis of Notationality, which states that a work is a token of a particular type if it satisfies a notation agreed by the knowledgeable in that field to be an adequate notation for that dance. So that if we have a notated score for a particular dance, say Christopher Bruce's *Black Angels* (1976), and we come across a performance which satisfies that score, then we are at least some way towards recognising that the movements we have seen comprise *Black Angels*. This account puts weight on the notation system in question. For a different notation system would have taken as *crucial* different features of the dance, so that movements which satisfy a Benesh score might not satisfy a Labanotation score, and *vice versa*. All we can do is to urge that only reputable notation systems count here: that the knowledgeable about that art form decide what is and what is not reputable. Moreover, a related issue is raised by the discussion in the section on perception and aesthetic interest in this chapter (see p. 14). For notation *alone* does not guarantee that the activity is dance. Hence it will be important to be able to identify a sequence of movements *as a dance*: that is, to pick it out as the right kind of action. But once this is done, the Thesis of Notationality provides us with a necessary condition[7] for the identity of a particular work.

The second aspect is implicit in the first one. For talking about 'the knowledgeable in respect of a particular art form' is a way of recording that — in the end — it is a dance-critical matter as to whether something is or is not a token of a particular type. In the example as we had it before, that Nureyev has made certain changes may mean that his work no longer satisfies a particular notation for — *Swan Lake* — but one alternative here would be to doubt the appropriateness of the notation. So, I am suggesting, it will be an art-critical matter (more precisely, a dance-critical matter) as to whether a work is a token of a particular type.

Of course, other performing arts, such as music, will be equally be given a type/token treatment on this analysis. So the mere fact that dance is a performing art, and hence analysed in a type/token way, does not of itself give it any additional claim to a place in an education system. Noting its differences from music — for example, that it is a physical art — may give us grounds for wishing to include, in our justification of dance, not *merely* its artistic status or *merely* its performing status; but certainly to include those.

The heresy of paraphrase and the importance of individual works

But is there a justification for the inclusion of a variety of art forms into the educational experience of the young or whether one is enough? The argument here is sometimes confusingly referred to as 'the heresy of paraphrase', the confusion arising because some writers treat it as heresy that one *can* produce paraphrases of art works, others that it is a heresy that you *can not*. To be clear, though, my position is that a paraphrase of an art work — either into words or into some other art form — is impossible. If this is accepted, along with the potential importance of art works in education (see Chapter 4), we have a justification which separates not merely one art form from another but also one art work from another. In an ideal world, then, the inclusion of *every* art work would be permitted by the success of this argument.

Why should this idea be accepted? The 'heresy of paraphrase' point may be put somewhat grandly by speaking of 'the inseparability of form and content' (Best, 1990a: 4b). Although difficult to establish conclusively, some examples clarify both the thesis and its direction. Suppose that art works were interchangeable in the way I am presently denying. In such a case, faced with the unavailability of a particular novel (Beardsmore, 1971: 17–18) or a particular dance, I might say, 'Well, go and read such-and-such or go and see such-and-such instead — they come to much the same thing'. But what weight that can be laid on the idea of 'much the same thing'? It may well be that, for some purposes, the differences between one dance and another, or one play and another, or one novel and another, is of no great significance. If I wish you to understand a certain kind of Nordic *angst*, perhaps any of Ibsen's plays will do. But clearly this attitude denigrates the plays by failing to pay attention to the importance differences between them. To return to a point made in an earlier section, the precise details of *this* play as opposed to *that* one are becoming lost: I am treating the two plays as equivalent in spite of these differences. The point is well put by Betty Redfern (1979: 18) in a favourite quotation of mine:

'There would be no need to see, for example, Martha Graham's *Night Journey*, since we could get the same experience by listening to Stravinsky's *Oedipus Rex*; and neither of them need really have bothered since Sophocles already "said it all" in *Oedipus Tyrannus* centuries before'. This example brings out clearly the way such an attitude denigrates the art works by ignoring their differences, and also — as Redfern intends — the absurdity of so doing.

An amusing and instructive discussion of the 'heresy of paraphrase' idea occurs in the work of Stanley Cavell. Considering the possibility of an art work being transposed into words, Cavell (1969: 79) urges that this is unproblematic, so long as one's 'translation' is allowed to include enough *et ceteras* and dots of continuation. But this is precisely *not* what the advocates of paraphrase had in mind. Their thought was that a particular art work — say, a dance — might be *equivalent* to either (a) another art work or (b) some string of words. If Cavell's point is accepted, he has effectively proved that paraphrase in this sense is impossible. But what is Cavell's argument? It proceeds in broadly the way that we have, by considering the adequacy of rendition into some other form, as though the form the work originally had was somehow inadequate or inappropriate. Referring to some poetry, Cavell (1969, 81) says, 'Paraphrasing the lines or explaining their meaning, or telling it, or putting the thought another way — all these are out of the question'. This is the key sense here: that we cannot explain fully what a work of art amounts to — either in words or via some other art work. But this does not mean that we cannot explain it at all nor that art works might not profitably have artistic reflection upon them. One thinks here of, for example, the Picasso *Man with a Blue Guitar*, which serves as a starting point for a long poem by Wallace Stevens which in turn is the subject of illustrations by David Hockney. Notice, though, that each of these represents a separate art work, although one related to an earlier work. We see this kind of relationship most clearly is we consider a fairly crude characterisation of the topics of certain works. So that, for example, Richard Austin's account of Christopher Bruce's *Black Angels* can make it sound quite a lot like a section from Milton's *Paradise Lost*: 'There is...no sense of the once bright angels of god; these are debased beneath the human, so that they can only crawl on their bellies like maimed animals though the atrocious fire' (Austin, 1976: 97).

The point, though, is that making this criticism more precise would involve showing how it follows from the movements performed by those dancers in that context in the case of Bruce's dance and by those words in the case of Milton's poem. So if we are to explain precisely what is going on in either case, we shall have to highlight both the similarities — say, that the passage quoted from Austin might be applied to either — but also the differences, and in particular the differences in the reasons we might have for claiming this set of words to be true of them. For example, finding the truth in Austin's claim involves looking at the dance, while finding the truth in a claim about *Paradise Lost* would be looking elsewhere (at the poem!).

Of course the difficulty here lies in seeing precisely what could make paraphrasing possible. The *reasons* one offers in respect of the dance seem to have very little in common with any reasons one could offer in respect of the poem: in particular, the first would relate *centrally* to movements, the second to words. The point to be got from the heresy of paraphrase argument comes out fairly clearly if we consider, say, a poem with a very obvious theme and message, like Wilfred Owen's *Dulce et decorum est*. For what does this poem 'say' or mean? That war is nasty business? That we should not trick the young with war films and the like into thinking it is a glorious one? Put like that, the point sounds trite. One is left asking why Owen bothered so much to say so little, why he fiddled with small details of the verse, why he opted for just that formal structure. Of course, our reply should be that Owen says far more than that trite summary. But what more? As we go on to fill-in more and more, we see why it would be absurd to urge, 'Well, read another of Owen's poems if you can't get this one, it's saying the same thing" — for it would not be saying *exactly* the same thing. Crucial to what it is saying is *how it is saying it*. To put that point in a way I used earlier (see pp. 15-16), it is not a means to an otherwise specifiable end. It follows therefore that the only way to get to *that* end is with *that* work. And that is simply to repeat the importance of individual works.

Conclusion

Where have we arrived?

- I have urged that it is crucial that dance be seen as action, and that means (amongst other things) bearing in mind the concepts under which it is intended and the context in which it is performed.
- I have urged that artistic interest should be distinguished both from mere aesthetic interest and from purposive interest such as economic interest.
- Further, that one distinctiveness of dance is its appropriateness as an object of artistic interest.
- I have elaborated the distinctiveness of dance from within the arts as both a physical art and a performing art, and the importance of individual works of art via the heresy of paraphrase argument.

This amounts, I suggest, to the beginnings of a powerful answer to the question set in the introduction: what justification can one find for dance education? For if dance education focuses on the artistic aspects of dance (as I have urged), recognising dance as an art form, a physical art form, and one not open to paraphrase, its distinctiveness is established.

But is that distinctiveness of educational importance? In Chapter 3 I shall sketch a view of education, which I think independently appealing, and then in Chapter 4 discuss the nature of art so as to bring out the sense in which the distinctiveness of dance is very clearly of educational significance.

Chapter 3

Education and Personal Enquiry

Introduction

This chapter sketches the account of education to be employed throughout this work. It is not an *argument* for that account: much of it draws on the writings of previous theorists and, to the extent their conclusions are accepted, it too appears plausible. At its centre, this is a picture of education which stresses kinds of personal development which cohere around our notion of *the educated person*. This will mean giving due weight to the development of the *rational* capacities of the person, in contrast — perhaps — to the acquisition of factual information. We are introducing a view of education which is neither the currently fashionable one, nor one for which full argument can be given here. Nevertheless, what follows should give at least *some* reason for adopting this view, as well as spelling it out more fully. For the nature of education is notoriously complex.

Education

In the formal education system, manifested through schools, it is obvious that the job of the teacher is not *one* job at all. As Lawrence Stenhouse (1975: 80) remarked: 'Education as we know it in school comprises and necessarily comprises at least four different processes'. Stenhouse called these *training, instruction, initiation* and *induction*. He saw training as 'concerned with the acquisition of skills, and successful training results in capacity in performance' (Stenhouse, 1975: 80). Instruction he saw as 'concerned with the learning of information and successful instruction results in retention' (p. 80). Initiation was 'familiarisation with social values and norms', while induction 'stands for introduction into the thought systems — the knowledge — of the culture' (p. 80). Such a categorisation requires a more elaborated discussion than is appropriate here. My point is simply to show a major educational theorist recognising the diversity within educational roles: there is not just one thing going on. Nonetheless, some issues seem of more central concern than others. As I said in the Introduction, I shall be sketching a Personal Enquiry account of education, highlighting this as the *crucial* aspect if education is to take place. But how are we to proceed?

One place to begin is with the term 'education': what do we mean by it? Two sorts of views may be distinguished[1], each of which will be briefly considered. The first view interprets education in terms of a *bringing forth* or *bringing up*. On this popular view, education is preparation for life, the sum of life's experiences. In consequence, one never stops being educated — education extends from birth to death. And a useful slogan, to address the extent to which this is a 'socialisation' view of education, would be 'Life is the best educator'.

Such views are commonly held. But how plausible are they? Two criticisms in particular are pertinent. First, there is an inevitability about education on this view. Since (on such a view) education is *everything* that happens, everyone becomes educated. Yet this is surely an improbable conclusion. Surely education involves the selection of some things rather than others, and that this selection be made for *reasons*, on the basis of *values*. The account under discussion does no justice to this relevant feature of education. Second, and relatedly, the need for specialist educators disappears. Since there is, on this view, no *selection* from within experience to be made, nor any need to *structure* experience for children, no one needs to be trained as *selector* or *structurer*. Again, this is highly implausible.

A major reason for mentioning that account of education — apart from its having a certain misguided prominence — is that the other view builds on its weaknesses. This second view interprets education in terms of a *leading out*. Here the thought is of someone, the teacher, doing the leading. So this conception of education brings with it the idea of a *sense of direction* for the educational process. Roughly, those with knowledge or skill — or at least an understanding of these things — teach them to those who lack them. So this view implies decision-making in relation to a *value system*: and hence makers of those decisions.

Put in that way, two questions are prompted. First, what value system? Second, who are the right people? Answers to these questions may be developed in what follows. But something introductory can be said which bears on them.

As a beginning, notice that the idea of *leading out* in this context suggests encouraging those things which are distinctively or characteristically *human*. After all, it seems a waste of time teaching people to do what could be done by machines or animals. [As a precaution against this point being misunderstood, let me note that, for example, the possibility of calculators doing arithmetic does not, on this view, lead to the conclusion that humans shouldn't be taught mathematics. First, one has to have some understanding to know which buttons to press. But second, and more important, *mathematical theory* — the progress of mathematics — is not within the province of machines (Carr, 1984; Searle, 1984: Chs 2 and 3).] But what is characteristically human? Our answer will be that reason and rationality are the province of humans (Seneca, 41st Letter, 1969: 88–9). It is humans who make rational choices, perform independent or autonomous actions, applying (or mis-applying) rules and standards to appropriate experiences. Humans, one might say, *understand* and *control* actions, rather than respond to stimuli.

One way of seeing this point is to study the myriad relations between teaching on the one hand and changes of behaviour on the other. Teaching is regularly and characteristically contrasted with a whole set of other activities — training, instruction, drilling, perhaps coaching, indoctrinating — largely because in those other activities there is little or no room for autonomous action from the pupil. This point holds good even though it may be difficult to precisely characterise, for example, indoctrination. So, when compared to teaching, those other activities are not equally defensible in educational terms. For example, if one could train pigeons to 'play' table tennis, the concern would be with repeating certain performances. So there would be nothing here about tactics, subtleties of skill, nor could there be, since these imply what is also necessarily absent: namely, considerations of rationality (Carr, 1984). Similarly, if one *trained* rats to run mazes, one could not begin with problem solving other than by trial and error. By contrast, *education* would require making decisions, being selective. Yet there is a complication here; one could only show or recognise the sort of understanding characteristic of learning to grasp an activity through one's performance of that activity — perhaps supplemented by discussion of it. So an emphasis on education does not lead us away from performances into some ephemeral mental realm. Rather, it makes us aware that, in general, performance must *display* understanding if it is to be relevant.

A summary to date should be useful. Implicit in the contrast in conceptions of education between *bringing forth* and *leading out* was the contrast between inevitable learning (that is, the acquisition of behavioural changes) and deliberately promoted learning — learning in someone's (society's or the individual's) *best interest*. (As an aside, we recognise the difference between what is *in one's interest* and *what interests one*. An interested party — say, at the reading of a will — could still be very bored!)

Three key terms for our discussion are emerging:

a. *Freedom*. The idea that we have developed is that pupils must make their own choices. But this idea is easily misunderstood. For example, it may become (as in some discussions of dance) the view that children can do whatever they want to, at their own pace. Instead, we have emphasised the need to learn to discriminate and make choices.

b. *Interest* (in both senses of the word). To misunderstand the role of interest here is to look, within education, for 'spontaneous, instant and constant entertainment'. This is impossibly idealistic. One wants to engage the *interest* of pupils, but in a way that is *in their best interest*. And this leads us back to the role of the *values* of educators.

c. *Enjoyment*. As with 'interest', one can misunderstand the importance of enjoyment, and treat it as indicating a need for 'spontaneous fun'. But of course one can't *teach* enjoyment as such. No doubt in teaching one should aim to make the desirable desired: that is to say, to make pupils want what is in fact in their interest. Yet this refers simply to the methodology of teaching, to how one teaches. An undue emphasis on enjoyment — as, for example, when physical education sessions are viewed as the — 'other side of the coin' from academic lessons — will encourage physical recreation without doubt, but there is nothing necessarily educational in that.

As we have seen, Freedom, Interest and Enjoyment are good *motivators* for learning, not a substitute for it. The conclusion of this discussion might be captured in the so-called *paradox of freedom*: that to have too much freedom is in fact to have too little. For one is only really choosing freely when one's choices are informed, considered, deliberate, and based on a sense of the alternatives. If one is allowed to select from *any* course of action, without guidelines suggesting a particular range of alternatives, one is not in fact *more free*: for one's choices are then arbitrary, random. One does not really choose option A freely unless one recognises option B, C, etc. and goes on to select A. David Best (1985a: 64) brings out this point with a quotation from Kant: 'The light dove, cleaving the air in her free flight, and feeling its resistance, might imagine that her flight would be still easier in empty space'. The point here, of course, is that only when there is a restriction of options, which means that one chooses *between* A,B,C etc., is one's choice an intelligible one; one for which reasons might be given. For those reasons might make reference, not only to what one *did* choose (A), but to what one *might have* chosen (B, C, etc.).

We have seen how the idea of education implies consideration about choices, reasons, deliberate action; and these considerations bring with them the paradox of freedom.

To conclude this sketch, some general points on what can be educational are suggested, both in terms of the methodology and of the subject matter. Applied to methodology, the points above all come from the concept of education as *leading out*; for they mean that one cannot *just* start with the child. One's aim must include a *direction* for education, bearing in mind that stagnation will result if one does not go beyond previous practice. So, first, one must look for *progress* in educational thinking. Second, choice is clearly of importance, but what is needed here is *structured choice, structured freedom*, in line with the paradox of freedom. This means that choices are to be from the *possible within the lesson*. Third, pupils must learn (and teachers must know) the *appropriateness* of certain choices. It means that one can be wrong in what one does. One has to *learn* to structure experience, to make something of it. Fourth, teachers should explain the interrelations and interconnections, for example, between certain practices and the activities they relate to, not least as a part of trying to sustain the interest of pupils. Fifth, there is a need to test understanding. This will involve encouraging demon-strations and discussions which should both illustrate and develop the pupils' ability to *apply* knowledge. Finally, the teacher's aim is to make the pupil *independent* of him or her. Pupils should *care* about the work, and also be able to make choices of their own. All of the above are general points, which should apply (with appropriate modifications) for all curriculum areas.

Let us now see what can be said about subject matter. Material must be susceptible to the sort of treatment described above: and that means it must allow for individual interpretation, for an exercise of the imagination; there must must be scope for working-out of difficulties, for problem-solving; there must be the possibility of development and the material must be capable of sustaining challenge; there must be principles to understand, standards to aspire towards. If the aim is indeed to contribute to education, the central notion will be *respect for persons*; so the idea will be a sharing of one's understanding with the pupils. For then one might reasonably expect to lead the pupils towards making their own, independent, decisions.

Personal enquiry

If these general remarks are to be implemented — in particular if they are to be the rationale for formal curriculum proposals — it is important to say more about the nature of education by picking out, if possible, some kind of *centre* to the concept of education. This will clearly be highly contentious, and here necessarily both sketchy and abbreviated. No doubt very many things are peripherally educational, but what is the focal point (Best, 1985b; Carr, 1984)? The issue is to ask what education *must* do, principally (Best's primary qualities of education) and also what it could/should do additionally (Best's secondary qualities)[2]. At the heart of the first of these categories, Best rightly locates the education of values — for it is here that we are dealing with what is distinctly human: namely, rationality. And this is a point we have already introduced. As Best (1985b: 76) notes, although 'it is not immediately obvious that rationality depends on values and attitudes', it is indeed true that values are integral to what is rational. For the thought that X is (intrinsically) *valuable* is not a thought that we can distinguish from the reasons for the value of X. Indeed (as Anscombe, 1957: 71–5 and Best, 1985b: 76 recognise), what renders unintelligible the idea of valuing, for its own sake, a saucer of mud is the impossibility of giving reasons for such a judgement. If someone asserted it, we would doubt his sanity; or, at the least, his rationality. And central to the idea of an educated person is the need to be understood as a rational human being (*inter alia*) so that one's actions are intelligible as *human* rational activities. And the intelligibility of action is, of course, central to the understanding of dance (as we saw in Chapter 2). So when speaking of the education of 'values' here, as the centre of education, the intention is not the teaching of a *specific* value system — that would be preposterous in a multi-cultural, multi-ethnic society (if not anywhere). No, what is intended is the provision of the sorts of intellectual 'tools' needed for questioning perceptively and thinking independently. As Best (1985b: 81) puts it, this Personal Enquiry conception of education is 'concerned to develop qualities such as curiosity, originality, initiative, cooperation, perseverance, open-mindedness, self-criticism, responsibility, self-confidence and independence'. It takes these sorts of things as the *primary, principal,* or *crucial* target for educational practice. Its aim is to develop the 'greatest possible *variety* of individual potential and initiative' (Best, 1985b: 82). And this justifies its title, for its aims cluster around Personal Enquiry — its possibilities, scope and limits.

On such a view the secondary qualitites of education, all those things that it could/should do in *addition* to stimulating Personal Enquiry revolve around factual knowledge and 'useful' skills. At the centre of this discussion is a difficulty concerning the nature of so-called 'propositional' knowledge: that is, the sorts of knowledge which can be stated in a sentence which is then either true or false. For it was once asserted (Hirst, 1974: 84–100) that propositional knowledge was the major and most crucial part of the target of education. This is problematic since very many of the things which are characteristically human are not amenable to this sort of treatment. An example may illustrate. A 1988 survey conducted for the *National Geographic* Magazine in the USA considered the ability of different nationalities to answer simply questions concerning geography: questions such as where their own country was, where other major countries in Europe were, and so on. One response — clearly the intended one — to finding that the young and old in one's country were unable to fulfil these tasks would be to throw up one's hands in horror, bemoaning the state of contemporary education. No doubt there is an element of appropriateness in such a response. But another kind of reply might be to question the general relevance of this kind of information. Much better, one might think, to have people who know that such information is readily available in an atlas, without necessarily being able to reproduce it themselves. And this kind of response must be particularly appealing to those of us whose knowledge of African geography, once rendered elaborate by mind-numbing exercises in rote-learning for examination purposes, has with the passage of time become simply out of date. Most of the countries whose names and capitals I so laboriously learned at school simply no longer exist! What is illustrated here is a general problem about the relative importance of propositional knowledge (Best, 1991). But, to be clear, the Personal Enquiry conception of education does not say that such matters are not the business of education: rather, it says that they are not its *primary* or *principal* business.

Moreover, the Personal Enquiry conception of education is true to another insight articulated already — the importance, for human understanding, of the notion of *action*: for one capacity characteristic of humans is the capacity for *action* (in this sense). So education is partly developing a capacity to understand, and hence to initiate, *appropriate* and *rational* actions.

Consider the case of how we are to correctly describe a particular human action when that action itself is up for moral consideration[3]. In an extreme case, calling an action *manslaughter* rather than *murder* is clearly not just a matter of *describing it differently*. As Stanley Cavell (1979a: 265) memorably remarked: 'Actions, unlike envelopes and goldfinches, do not come named for assessment, nor, like apples, ripe for grading'. So there is a genuine issues here concerning the nature of human action. In any discussion of that issue, what the agent (the person who did it) *says* about the description of the action clearly has a central place. Not, of course, an authoritative place; the agent can be *wrong*. But the account given by the agent is important because it is of a piece with other things he would say of himself: his commitments, intentions, relations with others and the like. But if this is correct (or to the degree which it is correct), it follows that we have a basis for a rough and ready idea of *respect for another person*: it involves 'taking seriously his own conception of himself, his actions and his relations with others' (Winch, 1987: 177). That is to say, the agent's *conceptions* of all these things are important.

Now this possibility — the possibility of respecting another — is a distinctly human one. If we succeed in mastering it, we will have taken an important step towards becoming a moral agent: we will have begun learning to be a *human being*.

Further, this case highlights two other key characteristics: the first is that a kind of *fairness* or *justice* underlies this commitment to others, the second is that the justice is '*self-legislated*' (Winch, 1987: 177). Treating anothers' claims about his or her actions with due weight, respecting those claims (even when one finds them false), is treating that person *justly*. I am not doing that if I merely rehearse conclusions learned by rote. No doubt the outcome might be just treatment: but *I* could not be said truly to be treating that person justly. At best, I am going along with a treatment derived from whatever authority I am parroting. Again, this may be inevitable in parts of our lives: it may even be essential or desirable — do we really want *every* action to be *always* up for grabs in this way[4]? As Wittgenstein (1969: §§310–316)) noted, if we question *everything* a history teacher says, we will never learn enough history to begin asking historically-rooted questions. But a central aim of any education system must be to *allow for* the *possibility* of the kind of self-legislation described here, at least from time to time. And that, to reiterate, is (one aspect of) what the Personal Enquiry conception of education urges.

Values, practices and learning outcomes

One major difficulty for a conception of education such as the Personal Enquiry conception is that it does not seem to generate *specific learning outcomes*: for what is it to have taught such things? How could one be sure that one had succeeded?

The work of Stenhouse, which — as noted earlier — underlies much of the thought here, offers an answer. For Stenhouse argued that a satisfactory account of education did not depend on prespecification of learning outcomes. Two of his ideas are of special significance here. First, Stenhouse emphasised the importance, for the understanding of educational achievements of pupils, of *the capacity to be surprised*. This means, of course, that one cannot *begin* from an account of some specific behavioural requirements. And this is just what the Personal Enquiry conception of education 'predicts'. Stenhouse (1975: 82) summarised his position as follows, considering a history essay: 'an essay should be individual and creative and not an attempt to meet a pre-specification'. Stenhouse made the point vivid, as well as explaining it, by reference to an experience familiar to all who have been engaged in assessing work of such a discursive nature: 'From the pile of essays a few leap out at the marker as original, surprising, showing evidence of individual thinking. These, the unpredictable, are the successes' (1975: 82).

The second characteristic idea of Stenhouse involves seeing the point of education as *intrinsic* to the activities of teaching and learning, rather than external to such activities. Consider why the works of Shakespeare should be included in a curriculum. In the case in point, we do not — Stenhouse urges — study great writing in order to improve our mastery of the language. As he puts it (Stenhouse, 1975: 83), '*Hamlet* must not be justified as a training ground for literary skills'. To see it in this way is to make the educational value of *Hamlet* something which is external to it, something equally applicable to other works of literature, and indeed to non-literary texts. For Stenhouse, the situation should be precisely the reverse: 'Literary skills are to be justified as helping us to read *Hamlet*'.

These two ideas from Stenhouse come together when we recognise that they imply that the *value* of education, as practiced through schooling, should be seen as an *intrinsic* value. This point is made sharply by Elliott (1991: 50) with reference to the way in which education is the *value* which constitutes the 'end' of the practice of teaching:

> What makes teaching a vocational practice is not simply the quality of its educational outcomes, but the manifestation within the practice itself of certain qualities which constitute it as an *educational* process capable of fostering *educational* outcomes in terms of student learning.

Thus, if Elliott's view is accepted, we should not simply expect education to be manifest in the *outcome* of such teaching, but also in the intrinsic quality of the *practices* of teaching. Certainly we cannot expect to be able to *specify* the outcomes independently of the practices.

Adopting these ideas puts practical flesh on the bones of the Personal Enquiry conception: but it also highlights a further crucial feature — that the 'aims' of educational practice are *essentially* value aims, which is another way of saying that the aims are *internal* to the practice itself. There are three complex and related ideas here: first is the idea of a *practice*; second, the idea of an *internal relation*; and third, the idea that values can, in serving as the *aim* of practices, have an *internal relation* to those practices. The next section will begin to articulate those three ideas and to apply them in the case of the practices of teaching and learning.

The importance of internal connections

The discussion of purposive interests in Chapter 2 introduced to us some crucial characteristics of means/end thinking: that such thinking involves a *separation* of means from end — we can characterise each *independently* of the other, so that the means to a particular end are always just one means among many, at least in principle. But, as we saw in Chapter 2, artistic interest is not of this means/ends kind. Nor, I shall argue, should we think of the outcomes of education in a means/end fashion. A clear way to bring this point out might be through a comparison with Bertrand Russell's theory of desire. Russell (1921: Ch. 3) urged that the *object* of desire, or more generally 'what one wanted', was *whatever* would, when you got it, make the desire go away. Thus he *separated* the object of desire from the desire itself. For him, the *end* (that the desire go away) was separate from the *means* — whatever you did to make the desire go away. As a result, if a punch in the stomach removes my desire for a pint of beer, it follows (on Russell's theory) that the punch was what I wanted all along. This is clearly nonsense: and it comes about because Russell ignored the internal connection between the *desire* itself and what is desired. What makes it a desire for, say, a pint of beer is, of course, partly that a pint of beer would satisfy it. The essential feature here is that the *desire* is only correctly characterised when its object is included in that characterisation (Baker & Hacker, 1984b: 107–8). To use a form of words we will introduce more fully in Chapter 4, the idea of *desire* is *intentional*[5] in just this sense.

Russell's mistake, then, was to imagine that one could understand *desire* independently of what would satisfy that desire. In a similar way, a theorist might assume that the *end* of education could be understood entirely independently of the practice, teaching, which led to that end. In contrast, I am suggesting that to characterise an activity as teaching (in this context) is to build-in a value-outcome: namely, education. Thus the practice of teaching is *essentially* and not just accidentally or instrumentally educational: the values which hold it in place are educational values.

To argue for this conception of an internal relation between the outcome (education) and the process by which that outcome is arrived at, we may usefully draw on two ideas which might well be shared with our opponents. The first is that education is a matter of *values*. This might be thought to mean that what is and what is not educational is somehow not a *factual* matter: what we see, in contrast to that view, is that *what* is educational cannot be separated from the *how* of education — that is to say, teaching. Once we see that the value in question should not be conceived of separately from the activity, we lose the temptation to think of it as an *abstract* value: rather, it is concrete in what we do.

The second idea is of education as a *practice*. To introduce that idea we should notice immediately that teaching (and educational research) are *social activities*: they involve a collaboration with colleagues etc. and with students. To better understand this idea we might turn to Pettit (1980: 5–6) for an account of a practice as 'a species of regularity' of behaviour[6].

> A regularity of behaviour is a practice in a given society only if: (1) nearly everyone conforms to it; (2) nearly everyone expects nearly everyone to conform; (3) this expectation gives nearly everyone some reason for wanting deviance discouraged.

Thus practices, in this sense, are normative regularities in societies, and that means that they are not *mere* regularities. For what is specified is not just what people *do* as a matter of fact do, but also what they *should* do or refrain from doing[7]. As Pettit (1980: 6) notes, 'general conformity to such regularities ... would appear to be a precondition of society'. It follows that people are generally reliable, truthful, honest and so on. For if they were not, such regularities could neither be established nor maintained. So practices are a *species* of social behaviour, but a rather important one. In this sense, recognising teaching as a *practice* is recognising that it has value-connections built-in: it is a *normative* activity. But what is the *end* or *aim* of such a practice? As our previous remarks might lead one to conclude, such a question cannot be answered as it stands.

The values which constitute that aim cannot be defined independently of, and prior to, the practice — for (as our quotation from Pettit makes plain) they are what makes it the practice that it is. That education, and more specifically teaching, is a *practice* in this technical sense is an important conclusion, especially when we consider the role of *objectives* in the characterisation of education (in Chapter 13). For now, though, it is sufficient for us to recognise that this conception of the educational locates the values of educational activity *within* (or internally connected to) the activity of education itself.

An objection might be raised at this point, one which will make clearer for us the nature of our thesis here. The objection is that, contrary to the position just urged, the aim of education is fairly clear: namely, the acquisition of knowledge. Further, that knowledge itself should be treated as a series of *propositions*, stating *facts* (Hirst, 1974: 85). A weak reply to this objection, already briefly indicated earlier in this chapter, would be to acknowledge that *an* aim of education is the acquisition of knowledge, but to insist that this was not education's *primary* aim. Such a response, however, does not take us very far. In particular, it does not get us to the root misunderstanding which gives rise to the objection. To reach that point we must bring in two further theses. The first thesis concerns the importance of understanding: that understanding should be thought of as the outcome of education — understanding, that is, rather than knowledge. However important it may be *that* the Battle of Hastings was in 1066, it is clearly far more important that one *understand* the significance, or otherwise, of the Battle of Hastings. Indeed, the date of the battle might — other things being equal — be something one always had to look up from a textbook; but if one understood the legacy of the Norman invasion of England, and also its impact on the previous Anglo-Saxon culture, one would have a good grasp on the significance of the battle: one would be educated in respect of it. Thus the importance here resides not so much in what one *knows*, but in what one can *do* — which, in context, broadly means what one understands (Best, 1991). This reiterates points made earlier about the relevance of propositional knowledge.

The second thesis, however, involves a more vigorous attack on the notion of a *fact*. For it is central to the objection we have imagined that the notion of a *fact* be clear and unambiguous — moreover, that facts be always and every-where *valuable* to us. Neither of these conditions is satisfied. To take them in reverse order, there are large numbers of facts which have absolutely no relevance for humans, and which even the objector would wish to *exclude* from an educational package for that reason. Other things being equal, what I had for breakfast today is simply not something the young of this country need to concern themselves with. Nonetheless, a sentence which related what I had for breakfast would indeed be stating a *fact* — just one of no educational significance. But, more importantly, many supposed facts are far from obvious and far from determinate. The most straightforward case, mentioned earlier, concerns the *facts* propounded by science. We should notice two characteristics here. First, what is taught to children is typically not the mature views currently holding sway amongst major scientists. To put the example crudely, we teach the young sorts of mechanics which give them an *understanding* of mechanical concepts, rather than what is at the boundaries of contemporary mechanical thinking. Similarly, the intention in school history classes is not that *all* that we know about, say, the impact of the Norman conquest in England is conveyed to children, but rather that certain salient characteristics are got across. In this sense, all the 'facts' presented to children are likely to be mere approximations to what is going on in the higher reaches of the relevant disciplines. And second, still typified by science, it is of the nature of such 'facts' to be revisable in the light of later findings, or later theory. All in all, such facts are not definite and determinate. Rather, they are revisable. This does not mean, of course, that they are tentative, nor that we should cease using them in our teaching. The point to make, though, is that *this* conception of a fact does nothing to license the objection posed initially.

Conclusion

In this chapter I have attempted to articulate, to explain, and partly to justify a conception of education which — following David Best — I have spoken of as a Personal Enquiry conception of education. This conception has emphasised 'process values' (Kelly, 1990: 62–3) for education, with educational value internally connected to educational *practices*. At the heart of this conception is the view that to be *educated* depends on the realisation of characteristically *human* potentialities: putting that less grandly, that the Personal Enquiry conception emphasises the sort of spirit of enquiry which one would hope for in all educated people — and which might be contrasted with narrow-mindedness or a blinkered approach to one's thinking. Of course, a great deal more could, and should, be said about this conception of education. Some of it will be explored in later chapters. And, as my references to Lawrence Stenhouse indicate, his writings offer another rich source of insight on this matter. However, it should be recognised that — in arguing for the educational potential of dance — I am arguing that dance is a suitable medium for satisfying aspects of a Personal Enquiry conception of education. So questions about the kinds of *propositional* knowledge which dance does or does not impart, or even questions about its achievements as socialiser or in engendering physical fitness, are simply beside the point. The value of dance would, on this conception, be an *intrinsic value*. And, of course, this is just what a *defender* of the distinctive educational place of dance would have hoped all along!

Chapter 4

Emotional Education and Life Issues

Introduction

The aim of this chapter is to consider three major but related concerns. The first is the nature of the contribution of the arts to human life in general and to education in particular. This involves paying attention both to the mechanism through which the arts contribute to human life — namely emotional education — and the area of understanding in which that contribution takes place; that is to say, 'life issues' (Best, 1985a: 159) or 'life-situations' (Best, 1978a: 115). Considering the matters of life issues and emotional education will highlight some of the differences between the position espoused here and David Best's position. Having broadly ascertained, then, the nature of the contribution of the arts, it behoves us (second) to say something specific about the contribution of dance. The third matter, which can be treated only briefly here (*UD*: Ch. 3) concerns the nature of art. For, as promised in Chapter 2, it is important to see what it is that distinguishes the arts from other areas of human concern.

The outcome, though, is a picture of dance which focuses on its *artistic* character, and develops its importance in those terms.

Concepts and conceptual change

As we saw in Chapter 2, perception is concept-mediated. We did not, however, fully explore what this might mean. In this section I will discuss the nature of changes to understanding which might be brought about by conceptual change. To do so is in part to reflect the kinds of changes in *experience* which might result from comparable conceptual changes. The key thought here has two related aspects. First, for most of the areas of concern of the arts, critical response to the arts typically involves a reference to the feelings: more specifically, to the emotions. Now, ascribing emotions is always a matter of mentioning what the emotion is directed *at* (Kenny, 1963: 187–202). In the jargon, emotions take *objects* (Beardsmore, 1973): so that one is afraid *of*, in love *with*, angry *at*, and so on. And if we are to understand what the precise anger is, or the precise nature of the love, or the exact characteristics of the fear, we shall have to make reference to those objects. So that, subjectively, there may be no difference between my fear of axe murderers and my fear of escaped leopards. But if we wish to recognise, correctly, that these are *two kinds* of fear, we will do so by noticing that they have two different objects. This is central to our experience of dance, once we recognise that the understanding of a particular dance depends in just that way on the concepts that we bring to bear on it; and the dance itself serves as an object for the emotion (or more generally the feeling) that we have in respect of it (*UD*: 171–3).

This means that identifying *what one experiences* when one confronts a particular dance is a matter of (a) articulating the concepts under which one perceives the dance — given that all perception is concept-mediated, and (b) recognising the dance thus perceived as the *object* of one's feelings or emotions. So reference to *the dance itself* is crucial if one is to characterise an appropriate experience of that dance (see Chapter 2 on the heresy of paraphrase). Further, the concepts must not just be *available* to one, but that they must be *mobilisable* in one's experience (Wollheim, 1986: 46). That is to say, it is not simply a matter of 'knowing about' a certain issue, but rather a matter of being able to make something of that knowledge *in* one's perception of the dance in question.

I want at this stage to put aside three misconceptions that might arise. The first concerns the scope of my claims here. I am not claiming that there is some *correct* batch of concepts under which a particular work *should* be understood. But I am claiming that the work itself provides constraints on this understanding. (That is an issue addressed directly in Chapter 9.) Secondly, it is important that the *scale* of my remarks be clear. For I am not claiming, in using the expression 'conceptual change', anything very grand. An image catching the right thought here is that of two spider's webs, differing in the placement of one strand: these are different webs, but not *that much* different. Hence conceptual changes might be clear without involving *necessarily* any very radical reorganisation of the material under review.

Finally, it is important to consider the sense in which these really are *conceptual* changes: for a critic might urge that they are better characterised in some other fashion. I have no knock-down argument on this topic. But, since experience is concept-mediated, changes in *experiences* are best thought of as changes in the concepts under which those experiences take place. This is an improvement if only because it is very hard to characterise the experience except in terms of our two related notions: the concepts under which it takes place and its object. So that if I wish to understand what my joy in viewing a particular dance has to do with other kinds of joy, that is at least partly explained by the commonality implicit in the my use of the same concept. But if we wish to ask about the differences, then a fundamental notion here will be that they have different objects. For different *dances* serve as the objects for such emotions.

Emotional education

The idea of *emotional education* is extremely complex, for two related reasons. First, although I call it 'emotional education', its scope ranges more widely that *just* the emotions. I am not placing any particular weight on my use of the word 'emotion' here. Second, this might *sound* like the articulation of an *aim* for art, external to its more general concerns, as we describe them when thinking about the nature of artistic education. For is it not true that, in thinking about the arts as achieving emotional education, I am finding an *external purpose* for it? Of course, my answer here will be that this is not so. I am simply urging another way of articulating the general point made in Chapter 2 about the *intrinsic* nature of artistic value: but that is something that further discussion must demonstrate, rather than simply something I can assert.

How should we think of this emotional education as taking place? David Best (1978b) offers the beginnings of an answer here. If asked what the arts have to offer, and in particular what they have to offer in education, we reply with a key thesis: that arts provide us with a kind of 'emotional education', and do so because they allow conceptual change in respect of the concepts through which the works of art are experienced. So this thesis has two dimensions, identifying (respectively) the *outcome* of interaction with the arts, as emotional educatio; and the *mechanism* of that interaction, as conceptual change. A conceptual change — a change in the concepts available to a person — might change the range of desires open to her or him, and hence the range of experiences open to that person. The experience of the arts allows us to experience finer shades of feeling, and may do so *because* it may allow the refining of those concepts under which those feelings are experienced, and under which those experiences are characterised. Best (1978b: 76) puts the point in this way: 'a pre-condition for experiencing the subtle and finely discriminated feelings which are the province of art is that one should have acquired the imaginative ability to handle the appropriate concepts' But what is at issue here is not just the *mechanism* of emotional education (which, recall, we are urging is conceptual change), but also the *impact* of that mechanism. On this point, Best (1974: 159) notes: 'in exploring and learning new forms of expression, we are ... gaining and refining the capacity for experiencing new feelings'. This is emotional education.

Best's thesis has a number of difficulties of interpretation. The most important concerns his use of the expression 'imaginative ability' in the first quotation, which I shall not discuss here (*UD*: 218). However, the general conception — that the value of the arts is elucidated in terms of a refining of one's discrimination, and hence of one's capacity to experience finely discriminated feelings — is what we wish to get out of this section of his writing. So that the expression 'emotional education' describes the outcome of a crucial mechanism — namely the mechanism of conceptual change — through which (I am claiming) the arts enhance our understanding: and hence, since experience is concept-mediated, our experience of art and of life more generally.

Such a picture may mislead in two ways which will tend to obscure the later argument. So, without discussing them in detail (see *UD*: Ch. 8), let us record them, in order to put them aside. Both concern the scope of what I have called 'conceptual change'. The first asks whether all the changes brought about by the arts should genuinely be thought of as *conceptual* changes; the second urges that some of the changes in understanding brought about through the arts are of too small a scale to warrant the title 'conceptual change'. The reply to both consists in underlining how small a thing conceptual change (on my version) can be, as we noted before. If we think of a particular concept — say, love — having a wealth of connections with other concepts, then a breaking of just one strand of that web will (on this model) result in a new conception of love, by making what follows from the application of that concept just slightly *different*. And once we accept that all experience is concept-mediated, we see how such changes have this conceptual character. It is in this small-scale sense that I speak of art as bringing about *conceptual change*, and of such changes as resulting in a change of what can be experienced.

In this section I have argued that the method by which art achieves its 'aims' is *conceptual change*; but what is the outcome? To answer that question is to address the matter of 'life-issues'.

Life-issues

The key thesis here again derives from David Best, although (as we have noted) he puts it differently in different places in his works. In articulating a fundamental characteristic (as he sees it) of artistic interest, Best (1978a: 115) says: 'It is distinctive of any art form that its conventions allow for the possibility of the expression of a conception of life situations. Thus the arts are characteristically concerned with contemporary moral, social, political and emotional issues'. And Best uses similar forms of words in other places. For example, he says 'It is intrinsic to an art form that there should be the possibility of expression of a conception of life issues' (Best, 1985a: 159). Best articulates this as a *necessary* condition for art-hood or art status. In the next section I shall contest this claim. Nonetheless, I agree with Best that the life-issues connection, however made out, is crucial to an articulation of the nature of the arts. Moreover, such a view has a direct educational significance. For if the arts really do make some kind of 'impact' on our conceptions of life-issues, their educational relevance seems guaranteed.

It is important to correctly identify the object of my discussion here. Stanley Cavell (1984: 99) speaks of what what makes art 'wantable': that is to say, of how we articulate a connection between art and value. Best's conception of a life-issues connection represents *one* way to do just that. It seems to me that it is the correct way, as I will argue in the rest of this section. Even more importantly, these are issues to which *some* answer must be given. It will not do simply to imagine that the value of the arts is obvious, or to reduce that value to some merely aesthetic value.

Much can usefully be said in discussion of this notion of 'life-issues' (see *UD*: Ch. 8). But here I wish to go along with a common-sense understanding of what the expression might mean, supplemented by my own comments and by the reading of David Best's texts, to which I have referred. The term 'life-issues' may not be the best term to have chosen: however, it has a currency in the literature and makes a direct connection with other writings with which someone concerned with dance education might well be familiar. So I prefer to remain with it than to launch off into the use of some other expression.

I have been taken to task (Hirst, 1989) for urging that art is good *in proportion* to its comment on life-issues. But this is not my position. I accept that one could make bad art (or non-art) about whatever is *the* important life-issue (God, immortality or whatever). Indeed, I know quite a number of student dance which attempt to explore such issues and are bad — perhaps even bad for that reason. My point here is merely to say that all art should/ would make the life-issues connection: and that an object could not be art unless it did.

There seems one obvious counter-example. For one cannot insist that *all art* has this connection with life-issues. At best, one should urge that there is always something to *explain* here. Now consider an artist who *decided* to make a work which had *no* such connection with life-issues. Is this possible? Of course, that possibility must be conceded. Still, this is the work of *an artist* — that is, someone whose other works have the life-issues connection (or so I claim) — and there is an *explanation* of his work: an explanation which makes explicit reference to life-issues (by denying that it picks them up!). To say this is to reiterate a point that Stanley Cavell (1969: 253) made in respect of the notion of intention, as it applies to art (*UD*: 181): that whenever a work did not imply some artistic intention, it operated in contrast to intention, and at the same level as intention. This is a central idea here. It amounts to urging that a work which *lacks* the life-issues connection must still be *explained* in terms of that connection.

It has also been urged (Hirst, 1989) in this context that a concern with life-issues implies a kind of high seriousness in art: LIFE-ISSUES. This is not what is intended. One of Best's examples, 'contemporary ... emotional issues', illustrates clearly that there is no need for absolute seriousness: the issues need only be of importance. For example, the nature of love is an important business, but not (always) a serious matter, in the sense of making one glum-faced. And we might well expect that, through watching a dance, our under-standing of love might become altered. Indeed, perhaps the most famous of ballets, *Swan Lake*, might have exactly this outcome. But so might Jiri Kilian's *Silent Cries* (1989), a work with a comic thread despite its intensity, or Christopher Bruce's *Swan Song* (1987) with its tap-dancing torturers.

Further, it might be thought that the case of *abstract art* provides a clear-cut counter-example: that here no life-issues connection is possible. But this cannot be correct. Just because a work makes no connection with such narra-tive themes cannot mean that our understanding of it precludes a relation to human thought, feeling and the like. Indeed, one might wonder what *reason* one could have for acknowledging *as art* an object with no connection with human ideas, thoughts, or feelings — in short, with life-issues. So a challenge of this sort should meet that kind of objection. In these ways, then, the impor-tance of a 'life-issues connection' may be urged. For it is a way of explaining the *value* (in particular the educational value) of the arts by showing how they have, in the last instance, a 'bite' on human thoughts, feelings and the like.

Works or forms?

Thus far I have articulated a conception of the importance of art, drawing on its connection with life-issues, which derives (at least immediately) from the writings of David Best. It is important to notice, however, that the view espoused here (and elsewhere: *UD*: 179–82) is not precisely Best's view. To recognise exactly how, we must turn to Best's characterisation of the life-issues connection for art:

> It is distinctive of any art form that its conventions allow for the possibility of expression of a conception of life situations. Thus the arts are characteristically concerned with contemporary moral, social, political and emotional issues. (Best, 1978a: 115)

Notice that Best's claim has two important qualifications. First, it refers to art forms, rather than art works. So if a particular work is in a *form* which allows the possibility of expression of a conception of life-issues, this work satisfies Best's condition. Second, all that is required is the *possibility* of the expression of a conception of life-issues. So a form would satisfy Best's condition if, even though no conception of life-issues was ever *actually* expressed, the *possibility* of its doing so existed.

The rationale for both of these qualifications should, I hope, be clear. Best wishes to state a necessary condition for something's being a work of art. In doing so, he wishes to rule-out elementary problem cases. In particular, he wishes to defuse the objection raised by, for example, dances where the choreographer designs them so as to *not* express a conception of life-issues. On Best's account of such a dance, first, it is in a *form* which allows the possibility of expression of a conception of life-issues; second, all that is at issue is the *possibility* — and this form may have the *possibility* even though that possibility has not been realised or actualised.

Although the motivation for Best's position is clear enough, the position must still seem evasive. As a way of seeing this point, consider the art form *poetry*. Once we accept that, say, Wilfred Owen's *Dulce et decorum est* expresses a conception of life-issues — and given its connections with the nature of war, that can scarcely be denied — we have established rather a lot. For one work in which a conception of life-issues is expressed guarantees that, for such works, the *possibility* of that expression exists. If a certain thing happens, that thing is possible! On Best's account, establishing the possibility here, for this one poem, establishes it for poetry — at least if 'poetry' refers to the relevant art-form. So one poem which *actually* expresses a conception of life-issues means that *all* poems satisfy Best's necessary condition for art-hood.

One difficulty with a necessary condition with this degree of generality is that it hardly seems to rule-out *anything*. For surely we can imagine, for any art form, one rather obscure case in which some comment on, say, man's in-humanity to man was presented. By Best's condition, this establishes the possibility of art-hood for *all* works in that form. Its very power illustrates the problem here. For if this necessary condition for art status is so easily fulfilled, it is hard to give it much weight.

I wish to offer an alternative account of the life-issues connection to that Best has developed (*UD*: 179–82). Although superficially more complex, we will see that my account is more straightforward. It urges simply that art–*works* express a conception of life-issues; but that this condition operates *defeasibly* (Baker, 1977). By this is meant three things. First, that there is an almost universal generalisation to the effect that if something is a work is art then it expresses a conception of life-issues. Second, if, in some particular case, someone wishes to deny that a particular work expresses a conception of life-issues, the onus of proof is on that objector. Third, that when we find, for a particular work, that it does *not* express a conception of life-issues, this is always something we can *explain* — and explain, as it were, at the same level as talk of life-issues (*UD*: 61–5).

Two reflections on these points are pertinent. First, this notion of *defeas-ibility* is a familiar one in English law: the notion *contract* is defeasible in just this sense. Given that certain conditions C are fulfilled, there is a contract between us. But any contract builds-in the 'heads of exception' that the contract must be 'true, full and free' (Baker, 1977: 33). This condition only applies when some objector wishes to deny that, conditions C having been satisfied, there is a contract between us. The objector must show that the contract was not true, or not full, or not free: that is to say, he must show that one of these 'heads of exception' is satisfied. The onus of proof lies with the objector. So the notion of defeasibility is actually not an obscure one. Secondly, this account of the life-issues connection may be re-formulated into a challenge, after the fashion of the 18th century philosopher David Hume[1]. The challenge comes to this: would we be willing to accept as art an object which *did not* bear some connection with human thought or feeling? The short answer to such a question must be 'No'. In this sense, our position states a *necessary condition* for art-hood. Nonetheless, there may be some cases in which we would be willing to countenance an artwork which lacked a connection with human thought and feeling, although that fact about it would be explicable, and explicable at the same level as discussion of human thought and feeling.

At this stage, an objection might be that non-literal dances (Turner, 1971: 23–6) — such as (a contemporary example) those of Siobhan Davies (Burnside, 1990) — do not satisfy this condition: that they are *about* nothing, have no connection with human thought and feeling. But such an objection misses two key considerations. First, seeing an activity *as* dance at all, and understanding it as dance, connects it with other activities we see as dance. Hence the connections those *other* activities had with human thought or feelings feed-in to the reasons we have for taking this new activity to be dance. Second, and relatedly, we can ask why such non-literal dance should be taken seriously if it really has no connection with what humans value. This is a version of a kind of philosophical challenge David Hume employed (in a different context): what could make us accept that a movement sequence was dance if it lacked this connection with the human? The implied answer is 'nothing' (*UD*: 253–4). These two considerations lead us to conclude that the case of non-literal dance — or of abstract painting — is not a knock-down refutation of my claim about the life-issues connection (Ziff, 1981: 107).

Two points are important at this stage. First, this conception is more powerful than David Best's. It would allow us to rule-out certain objects as artworks, even though they were in forms where a conception of life-issues was expressible. But the point is a complex one. For there are a large number of ways of satisfying the connection I postulate. First, imagine a dance whose art status is under discussion. Now suppose it were *impossible* to trace that dance's claims to art status to either a conception of life-issues or to some other explanation, standing in a similar role to remarks about life-issues, that connected the dance — perhaps negatively — to human thought and feeling. That would appear to be a counter-case to my thesis about the centtrality of the life-issues connection. Nevertheless, if some choreographer *sets out* to compose a dance running counter to my thesis, that fact alone could serve as explanation for why this dance *is* art, even though it does not express a conception of life-issues: it is art because, roughly, its author *conceived of it* in relation to matters of life-issues, but negatively. The second point is that the variety within the notion of life-issues must be recognised, so that, for example, the possibility of abstract art should not be taken as an immediate counter-example. Indeed, in most cases, it is relatively straightforward to see abstract art works as celebrating some humanly-important characteristic — although this may turn out to be colour, landscape, or the like, rather than love, war, or something more *obviously* human.

There are two specific things we *can* say here, and an explanation of what we are *not* saying (and probably cannot say) about this idea of *life-issues*. First, if there is to be *any* connection between art and emotions — and few theorists would deny it — then it must, roughly, involve some life-issues connection. If the emotional experiences associated with art were to have no connection with other experiences, we would with justice wonder why they counted as emotions (or thoughts or feelings) at all. For if they were *so* totally unrelated to out *other* emotional (etc.) experiences, we would have no grounds for recognising them as of joy, or whatever. So life-issues are no more than issues that humans value: but, then, that is quite enough. Second, the notion of life-issues acknowledges that these are not just mine or yours but, at least in principle, have some more general 'bite': they are not *subjective* (*UD*: 175–6). Indeed, we would surely not accept *as art* an object whose appeal was *in principle* restricted to one person or to a small group (as opposed to just being so restricted by requirements of our knowledge and experience). And where a person treats an art work in such a purely personal manner (as, for example, when he uses it as pornography: see *UD*: 175–7), we recognise that his interest is no longer artistic, for such a way of treating a work *undermines* (by ignoring) the life-issues connection.

Why can we not be more specific about the life-issues connection for, say, a particular dance? Why are we not more explicit on this point? In part, the answer is that the particular life-issues connection, its peculiar workings, are unique to that specific dance (or art work more generally): there is nothing to be said which is both *general* and *accurate*. But, further, we run up against the 'fact' about humans that they are typically capable of finding dances meaningful or expressive or pleasurable in these ways. This possibility is realised in any society which has the concepts *dance*, *art*. But that is not true of all societies or cultures (see Kaeppler, 1985: 92; *UD*: 284-92); and, when it is, the conception does not always apply in *exactly* the same way. In all cases, of course, we might summarise life-issues (as did Best, 1978a: 115) as 'contemporary moral, social, political and emotional issues'. Yet what these are, and how they are realised in art works, will be specific in ways which elude our general (abstract) discussions in a work such as this. In short, they are art-critical matters.

Summary to date

The argument thus far in this chapter has been primarily directed towards establishing (and expanding) two points:
- That the mechanism of emotional education is conceptual change.
- That the focus of emotional education is life-issues.

If I have established both of those points then I have developed a distinctive educationally relevant conception of the arts and of dance within those arts. If, further, the 'heresy of paraphrase' remarks from Chapter 2 are accepted, it follows that I have established an educationally distinctive value for *individual* dances.

The nature of art

A text such as this, which emphasises the educational distinctiveness of dance *as an art form*, must have something to say about the nature of art. This is a vexed question. I will advance three related theses here, although a defense of them would require much more space than this chapter can include. The theses are (1) that the arts have a distinctive value; (2) that 'art' is an *institutional* concept; and (3) that art has an historical character.

The first thesis is the distinctive value of the arts: I wish to defend the idea of artistic value. In a sense, the defence of that thesis is already achieved. For if the arts offer emotional education in respect of life-issues, it will be hard to see them as other than valuable.

The second thesis concerns the way in which *I* would characterise one aspect of the nature of art: that art is an *institutional* concept, in a sense articulated in philosophy. This point is confusing for at least two reasons. First, the word 'institutional' has two different but related uses in philosophy, so that, for example, Elizabeth Anscombe (1981b: 24) claims that morality is an institutional matter, and hence that 'moral' is an institutional concept, without meaning precisely what I mean. Second, the elaboration of institutional accounts of art has typically fallen to those with whom I differ on many points (*UD*: Ch. 3).

For now, I wish to identify three characteristics of institutional theories[2]. The first and most general is that, in an institutional theory of art, some object is art if *the right people* say it is. The second characteristic of an institutional account, which applies in virtue of our viewing art as an institutional concept, is that institutional concepts depend on an *authoritative body* (Baker &

Hacker, 1984a: 272–3). By this is meant that whether or not something *is* art is a matter for some, but not for all, to say. In fact, this is a way of elaborating the first condition — for my 'authoritative body' just is those 'right people'. In the case of the arts in general, they will include artists, gallery managers, producers, and art critics, art historians, aestheticians, and performers. Not all will have an equal role in any particular case. So perhaps it is better to regard it as a set of particular authoritative bodies in respect of particular areas of the arts, rather than as *one* authoritative body. Third, that process can be made more precise by dividing it into two parts. The first phase, *self-election*, has an artist putting forward an object *as art*. For example, I might send my work to a poetry magazine, or offer my services as a choreographer to a dance company. In this sense, I am claiming the status of artist for myself, and the status of artwork for my creations. The other aspect, *other-acclamation*, involves the institution accepting, or adopting, or acknowledging one's work *as art*. So that, for example, the poetry magazine might accept my work; the theatre management might accept my choreography as part of an arts festival, or some such. Both stages are crucial. Accepting that art-status requires self-election incorporates the idea that one must *mean* to make an art-work, or make it under the concept 'art', if the end product is to be art. This picks up a connection between *action* and *intention* noted earlier (Chapter 2). For insofar as we think of art-making as an action — which, for the case of dance, is *very far* — it only makes sense if it could, in principle, be intended. That is to say, it only makes sense in a society or culture which has the concepts 'art', 'dance'[3]. Any object not viewed *as* dance will not *be* dance — that is one aspect emphasised by the self-acclamation condition. Thus objects might be *mistaken* for art because, although otherwise satisfying conditions for art-hood, they fail to satisfy this condition. So the idea of *self-election* may help to rule out *putative* art-works. Moreover, the other-acclamation condition means that works are not just art because I say so: it is not just a matter of my whim.

These three conditions begin to articulate my account of the nature of art. It is worth noticing that this model is not entirely fanciful. Acceptance of *bizarre* works as art has typically been predicated on both the recognition that their makers were *artists* (self-election) and the acceptance of those works by members of the relevant authoritative body (other acclamation). But if what one's work is not adopted in this way? That is to say, suppose one puts one's work forward *as* art, but the institution, the Republic of Dance (Diffey, 1969), does not other-acclaim one's work? In fact, there are three alternative outcomes in such a case. First, one might simply concede that one's work was not, after all, dance; one might adopt the judgement of the institution. Second, one might resist the judgement of the institution, continue asserting that one's work was art, and wait for the judgement of posterity. A moment's thought shows this to be a doubtful procedure. For while it is undeniable that some artworks have been found which, having been rejected by the institution at the time of their composition, are now highly regarded. But these are surely the exception rather than the rule. In the case of dance, it seems deeply improbable that there would be anything *left* of one's work if one took this line. After all, one's work would never have been seen, would have had no influence, and so on. The third alternative is to conduct a kind of public relations exercise on behalf of one's work — either doing this oneself or 'hiring' a suitable critic. Thus (at least arguably) T.S. Eliot established the kind of taste by which his own poetry was then judged; while the writings of Clive Bell and Roger Fry did much to bring about acknowledgement in the institution of the work of Cèzanne. In a parallel way, the writing of XXX (Chapman, 1984) might be seen as establishing the artistic credentials of certain dance works of his time.

Of course, my claim that art-status is an institutional matter is a large and complex one. But the point to be made here is simply that *whether or not* a dance is indeed art is not a matter of opinion, but rather a matter which, in principle, could be settled — in my case, by appeal to the Republic of Dance: if one rejects this account of art one must build-in some *alternative* manner of arriving at comparable definiteness.

The third aspect of the nature of art, on my account, has already briefly surfaced. It is what I call the *historical character of art* (McFee, 1992c). It is simply the thesis that the meaning of a work of art at a particular time may be different than its meaning at some later time. In practice, this might even amount to a work which *was* art at one time ceasing to be art at some later time, or vice versa. Of course, one could adopt an institutional account of art without accepting that art had an historical character. Nonetheless, the two views seem to fit naturally together. Consider a particular dance: question 1 — is that dance art? Well, we know that, although the artist puts it forward as art (self-election), it is not acknowledged by the Republic of Dance. Thus, on our institutional account, that work is not dance, not art. Suppose though, at some later date, the claims of this dance are yet again pressed. In the interim, we can imagine that ideas in the Republic of Dance have been re-shaped — perhaps by changes in critical theory, perhaps by changes in other theoretical areas (such as psychology), and perhaps simply by the passage of time. For whatever reason, let us imagine that the work is *now* given other-acclamation by the Republic of Dance. Thus at the later time our answer to the question will be that the work *is* dance, *is* art.

How should these two judgements be accommodated? Or, to put that another way — question 2: when, at the later time, we acknowledge that the dance *is* art, will we say that it *is* but *was not*? It seems to me that, as a critical matter, this is *not* what we would say. We would say that the work *was now* art, and had always been. But that is because we are adopting the per-spective of the critic. Just like the scientist committed to the views of Einstein who, looking back on the views of Newton, concludes that they always were mistaken, this is a judgement that can only be made with hindsight.The view of the philosopher, a more detached view, would urge that, at the time of the dominance of Newton's theory, it was (institutionally) *correct*, but ceased to be so at some later date.

This brings us to the second dimension of our historical character of art: its dependence on reasons. For what changes between one time and another are the *reasons* which can be given in respect of a certain judgement of a particular dance. So that, once one comes to understand better the workings of a certain psychological theory, one sees the psychological insight in, say, Christopher Bruce's *Ghost Dances* (1981) rather differently. This may affect one's judgement of the work. In part, it may increase or decrease one's valuation of the work; in part, it may allow one to acknowledge the work as art when one previously had not (or *vice versa*).

So I am urging that art status is valuable, that 'art' is an institutional concept, and a concept with a historical character. All three considerations bring out the importance of the *reasons* which might be offered in defence of artistic value or art-status. For these reasons may change as theoretical accounts change; and that one locates such reasons — at least typically — by considering the work of art critics. If we are to pursue that idea further, we must say more about the nature of criticism. And that is the topic for Chapter 9.

Conclusion

This chapter has laid out our picture of dance as an art by identifying the impact of art such as dance in terms of *emotional education* via *conceptual change* in respect of *life-issues*. Further, it has articulated an account of art which will be employed through this work. It has explicitly drawn the morals for dance, although much of that is implicit and the rest of the text should make some more explicit. But these ideas are fundamental to this work, for they constitute — with the artistic/aesthetic distinction — our artistic account of dance education.

Appendix: two issues

Two issues in this area have generated heat but little light. These are the use of the expression 'aesthetic education' and the idea of a *generic* relation between the arts. On both these topics David Best has trenchantly (and correctly) criticised the developing orthodoxy. However, his criticisms are liable to misunderstanding — at the least, they have been misunderstood. So here I shall attempt to adjudicate among the warring parties. The outcome — as might be expected given my general position — will be a vindication of Best's central points.

However, these points are tangential to my main concerns; hence they are merely an appendix. Anyone who has followed my arguments should never be making these mistakes.

When one considers the expression 'aesthetic education', Best (1984) wishes to urge two key points. First, and crucially, the activity concerns itself with artistic appreciation (in our terminology: see Chapter 2) and hence is best called 'artistic education' or 'education in and through the arts'. So the first point is that there is something misleading about persisting with the expression 'aesthetic education'. Second, using that expression can lead one towards subjectivism, by directing attention away from the distinctiveness of the arts — by treating them as just another area of aesthetic concern. There is at least some plausibility in the view that my appreciation of, say, a sunset is *mine* in the strong sense in which 'aesthetic beauty is in the eye of the beholder'. Whatever the truth of that thesis applied to (mere) aesthetic judgement, it is clearly entirely *false* in respect of art. For a characteristic of the arts simply is their amenability to reasons. And my judgements of the sunset are precisely *not* amenable to rationality in this way.

However, this argument does not seem to me especially compelling (*UD*: Ch. 13). I accept both of David Best's points, but they amount to no more than the suggestion that one reorganise one's language: for my claim throughout has been that the *distinctions* to which Best refers must be respected. But I do not defend one form of words over another. I do not mind, that is to say, if people continue to *call* the activity 'aesthetic education' as long as they do not fall into either of these errors. Then any dispute is simply about which procedure is most *likely* to achieve that: the Graham McFee procedure of noting the distinctions, or the David Best procedure of offering alternative words. I have no particular philosophical reason for preferring one strategy over the other: this not seem to me to be a philosophically central matter. Best and I are in agreement on the key points: nothing I have asserted could be used *against* any position of his by any serious thinker.

If the issue of aesthetic education is thus dealt with, the issue of a *generic* conception of the arts is more problematic. As David Best (1990a) has urged, at the root of some theorists' use of the term 'generic' in this context is an assumption of some underlying *essence* for the arts, shared by all arts, and in virtue of which they are arts. And this is what *must* be meant if justice is to be done to the term 'generic'. The kind of definition which specifies *sufficient* conditions (as well as necessary ones) is rightly called 'definition *per genus et differentiam*': that is to say, in terms of a *genus* and the differentiating characteristics. Clear examples of such definitions occur in biology. For example, we may study a particular insect, but our concern is with its structural characteristics — body divided into three parts, six legs, wings and so on — which are the characteristics of the *genus*, as well as with the what marks out this insect from others. Notice too (since it will be important later) that here one can study insects by studying *one* insect. So defenders of the 'generic' notion for the arts must be asserting that the concept 'art' functions *somehow* like the concept 'insect' here. Best's arguments seem to me to dispose of this, anyway rather implausible, suggestion. Can we really say that there is something shared by the arts and distinctive of them? Surely, given the diversity between painting, literature, dance and music, this implies an untenable position.

It is worth reviewing in more detail the considerations which led Best (1992a) to disparage as a *myth* the idea of the arts being *generically* related. In essence, his arguments have five prongs. *First,* this conception is widespread, and hence important to evaluate seriously. In support of this claim Best cites, among other documents, the influential *The Arts in Schools Project*: 'the different arts disciplines have common characteristics and should be planned for together as a generic part of the school curriculum' (1992a: 2). Indeed, Best (1992b: 18) explicitly claims *The Arts in Schools Project* as 'the principle source of the misguided generic arts notion'. Either way, the Project report does seem to be an influential document embodying this view. *Second,* Best urges that no coherent *rationale* for this assumption of the generic nature of the arts has been provided: and this means both that *typically* none has been offered, as though it were just obvious (Best, 1992a: 31), and that, if offered, such rationales have been inadequate, or poorly argued, or both. So that, for example, 'There must be something in common among all the arts, something which justifies the same word 'art' being used of all of them' (compare Bell, 1914: 7). But, as has been recognised in aesthetics, this is mistaken as a philosophical thesis: one can use the same word without there being some *one* underlying commonality (Baker & Hacker, 1980: 331–43). Yet, more important, we see here that this claim is insufficient. For Best is arguing against some characteristic '*common to all the arts ... and distinct from all other areas of the curriculum*' (Best, 1992a: 33). In this way, we see clearly Best's *target.*

If these first two elements of Best's argument are accepted, it follows that this is an *important* topic, and one still awaiting informed discussion. The third element of his argument is that it is dangerous to urge a generic relationship between the arts. In support of this claim, he recounts an anecdote in which a higher education institution seriously considered closing its visual art department since students could acquire artistic (aesthetic) education from cognate or generic areas: music, dance etc. I *hope* the absurdity of this suggestion is apparent. But, notice, it is *correct* by the lights of those who believe in the 'generic relation' idea — that, as with the insects, one can study *art* by studying *one* art. Each art *does* become expendable, given that some others are maintained. In fact, *one* ought to be enough!

Of course, we may *hope* that the arts lack this generic relation. But hope alone is not sufficient. Now Best reverts to the kinds of consideration raised earlier to suggest — as his fourth point — that it is *false*. How plausible is it to see the kinds of commonality at issue within such varied art forms such as painting, poetry and dance? This is not to say that there are no commonalities — but that what painting shares with poetry it might not share with dance, and so on. Indeed, this point would be obvious were it not that *other* notions — and especially the idea of a creative process — are inserted at this juncture. Yet these too will not do the job. For creativity in *dance* is centrally related to the actions of dancers; creativity in painting to the properties of paint; and so on (*UD*: Ch. 13; Best, 1985a: 64–89): there is no *one* process common to all the arts.

Best's attack continues (its fifth point) by showing how *confusing* adherence to this doctrine might be. For if, by his earlier points, we *need* to understand the relationship between the various art forms, a big danger would be in thinking (mistakenly) that we already do. That would stifle future investigations. For these reasons, Best correctly urges that it is *dangerous* and *confusing* to saddle oneself with the false belief that the arts stand in some generic relation, sharing a characteristic common to all of them, and not shared by other activities, events or objects.

But, an objector might urge, did I not claim (see p. 17) and reiterate (pp. 43–7) just such a central characteristic? Did I not urge that all art works must express a conception of life-issues or life situations? Well, I have urged that there is a *necessary condition* for art-hood here. But it is important to see what its status as a *necessary condition* brings with it. Consider my claim that the connection with life-issues was *essential* for any art form, focusing on the word 'essential'. This is a *negative* condition, used to rule-out candidates for art-hood (for example, sport: see Best, 1978a: Ch. 7). *My claim* is not that *only* art works have this connection with life-issues. Indeed, in other places I have explicitly recognised the way in which a variety of experiences might well bring one to an awareness of life-issues in a way not dissimilar from the arts (*UD*: 188–9). One of my favourite examples here is a remark by Alvarez (1971: 236) in respect of his attempted suicide: 'It seems ludicrous now to have learned something so obvious in such a hard way'. Alvarez's experiences did offer him insight into life-issues; but it would be a mistake to think that suicide therefore was an art form.

In contrast, the objector reads the word 'essential' as meaning that this is a *sufficient* condition for art-hood, or what makes the object in question art. He is seeking characteristics unique to art-forms, in virtue of which they *are* art-forms. It is this that is being denied. As noted above, Best correctly urges that such a claim is not justified as an assumption, nor supported by the evidence.

A reader who correctly understands Best's position — in particular, one who understands the distinction between necessary and sufficient conditions — will not make this mistake. As a result, Best's insistence on it (in the work cited) seems overdrawn. But that is because he is so obviously right as to make the issue not worthy of sustained discussion. Such discussion is only included here for two reasons. First, the view has some currency, as Best has illustrated. Second, it could be especially pernicious applied to dance education, for it may undermine the distinctiveness of *each* art form by appearing to give weight to the idea of a unique 'area of experience' (HMI, 1977): as Best (1990b: 12) quotes it from the Gulbenkian Report, *The Arts in Society* (1982), 'A distinct area of human experience'. And that point could be crucial here, since arguing for *dance education* is arguing for its distinctiveness within artistic education as much as for the place of artistic education within the curriculum more generally.

Chapter 5

Summary: The 'Artistic Account'

As a conclusion to Part I of this book, I will attempt to state bluntly, and without qualifications, the theses I have been urging in the preceding chapters. It is worth saying, however, that I have not done much more that *urge* them there: that many have *not* been argued for, or not fully argued for. I have been interested to lay out the position and give some reasons for its attractiveness. In what follows I shall give more reasons for that attractiveness by expanding the position and by meeting potential lines of criticism, as well as by exploring its practical ramifications.

In effect, my argument has some major theses which have a direct reference to the chapters in this section. I have urged the need to establish a *distinctive* character for dance education, and suggested that this can only be done on the basis of a *distinctive* character for dance. I have located that distinctiveness within the artistic *possibility* of dance: that is to say, within those kinds of dance which are art forms. Then, in Chapter 4, I have urged that the arts have a particular relationship to education since the arts allow the possibility of emotional education which consists in conceptual change in respect of concepts appropriate to our understanding of life-issues. Earlier, in Chapter 3, I sketched some aspects of a conception of education which permits us to think of the arts as suitably educational: this is the Personal Enquiry conception of education.

One might ask where the Personal Enquiry conception of education leads one in respect of dance education. The answer here emphasises the education of taste or judgement: that is to say, the education of the feelings. This shows the congruence between this Personal Enquiry conception of education and the *possibilities* which dance has in virtue of its *artistic* character, namely the possibility of bringing about conceptual change in respect of life-issues. And to actualise that possibility of *artistic* interest was to employ the artistic/aesthetic distinction. So that our concern with dance was centrally an *artistic* (as opposed to merely aesthetic) concern. Thus the whole argument turns on the artistic/aesthetic contrast.

Adopting these theses establishes, at least arguably, two facts of great importance. First, that the educational distinctiveness of dance is related to its art status; second, that the art status applies to only *some* dance. One project for later must be to defend both of these claims. But accepting them indicates at least *some* of what should be included in a programme of dance for education. It emphasises the importance of the *art form* of dance, and therefore implies that the dance curriculum should have this artistic possibility at its centre. Indeed, to deny this, supposing our earlier reflections are correct, will be to fail to find a place for *dance* at all. It seems to me that if any of the points that I have urged thus far is denied, then the possibility of a *distinctive* dance education disappears.

To see this point, consider what happens if some of the key theses are rejected: the outcome, as we will see, is the disappearance of our argument for the educational distinctiveness of dance. Denying the artistic/aesthetic contrast means that the value of dance in education becomes *equivalent* to the value of other physical, aesthetic activities — such as gymnastics and synchronised swimming. Denying the importance of the concept *art* has a similar effect. If, for example, the concept *art* is no more than some bourgeois notion, not reflecting a real feature of the world or people's experience, it follows that there can be nothing distinctly educational about art. Again, if we deny the Personal Enquiry conception of education, it may be very difficult to explain how the idea of a non-propositional knowledge or understanding can be sustained. And any account of dance must recognise a non-propositional dimension.

Therefore, these claims should be adopted by anyone who wishes to urge the distinctiveness of dance in education. They might be disputed, of course, by someone who urged that dance has a *different* distinctiveness than the one I have here articulated. I shall consider three such possibilities in Chapters 10, 11 and 12. It is important to notice, however, that the *artistic account*, as I am calling it, has at least *some* practical implications for the emphasis of the dance curriculum: it emphasises the artistic possibilities of dance. Programmes of study for such a curriculum might be expected to differ radically from programmes of study which took some different basis. In this sense, the artistic account has a direct practical relevance[1].

Taking the artistic account further (2004)

The arguments here are still of direct relevance to the state of play. The requirement for a distinctive (of dance as *dance*) account which here led to the artistic is still not widely recognised. Some theorists are content to explore related issues: for instance locating the value of dance in its contribution to health and/or fitness. Other theorists simply assume that the arts have a distinctive value (and hence that dance does) without saying where that distinctiveness lies. This simply leaves the field open to the assumption of alternative claims for the character of the values (especially the educational value) of dance — claims like those discussed in Part Three of CDE.

PART II

CONTEXTS FOR
DANCE EDUCATION

Chapter 6

Dance Performance and Understanding

Understanding and participation

Thus far I have begun to articulate the *artistic* account of the place of dance in education: and have reached the conclusion that this gives us at least a centre for the drawing-up of programmes of study for dance, and of a dance curriculum more generally. That centre is the *artistic* possibilities of dance. At this stage, I imagine a fundamental objection being raised, discussion of which takes us further into this important topic.

The objection is this. Where is the *practice* of dance? Where is the crucial *practical* dimension? Notice that this objection is important since I have urged, as a crucial characteristic of dance, that it is a *physical* art form. But have I concluded that the programmes of study for dance in schools must include *practical participation* in dance, or have I simply gone along with the thought that classes in dance appreciation might be sufficient? This objection is an important one, for it concerns the nature of my conception of dance education. Moreover, it allows for three kinds of clarification of that conception of dance education.

There is a distinction here between the different roles that dance theorists might see themselves playing. In my role as *philosopher*, my concern is with what is essential to education and to dance in education particularly. The precise way in which what is essential is achieved is not strictly my business (although whether or not it could be achieved in principle might have some important bearing). So one way of my responding to the objection just posed would be simply to wave my hands airily, remarking that whether or not the practice of dance is included in programmes is an empirical matter. This would be a way of dismissing the objection as somebody else's business: in particular, relating it to considerations of pedagogy for dance. Clearly there is something right about this response to the objection. One should not claim to know in advance what are the best *methods* of bringing about an unfamiliar outcome. However, in the case of artistic education through dance, the outcome is not so very unfamiliar. And appropriate methods for delivering at least some of it are established in the profession.

It follows from my acceptance that this issue has a bearing on my concerns, and my commitment to dance as a *physical* art form, that I must say something about the relationship between one's understanding of dance and one's practice of it. It is well established that one's appreciation of technique, etc., in all art forms (including dance) is typically sharpened by the sorts of insights that practical involvement offers. Thus practical involvement in dance might well be justified on such a conception; however, if it is, it is justified in terms of its contributions to the understanding of dance (and hence, indirectly, of life), as one possible method (amongst many). No doubt, in practice, it will be a major method. So emphasising the physical character of dance and the corresponding need to understand technical resources already gives us already some justification for including a practical dimension to our programmes of study in dance. However (the second point), none of my arguments, of them-selves, require the active participation in dance of pupils in dance education (although of course they do not exclude it). Consider for a moment the *out-come* of dance education. I have presented that outcome (in Chapter 3) in terms of *understanding*: in terms of changes, refinements and developments of understanding (see Chapter 4). Therefore, practical participation in dance will be justified to the extent that it supports this aim. As I have urged, this might prove to be quite a large extent. If I am interested in educating to appreciate the artistic qualities of dance — its expressive qualities, for example (*UD*: Ch. 12) — the best way to do this may well be to give pupils practical experience of dance. That reiterates the conclusion just reached. If, additionally, we couch the goals of education in terms of the development of educated persons, then — by extension — we might look to dance education for the dance-educated person. That might imply some role for practical work, if to be dance-educated requires, minimally, to have had some practical involvement in dance. But, again, the point would be to see the understanding *through* the movements performed: the justification for practical involvement would still lie in the understanding achieved. That is to say, the justification would be an *educational* justification, in terms of the aims of education (in particular, understanding).

The third point is simply a warning of the kinds of mis-justifications which might be offered here, focusing on one example. As I have urged elsewhere (*UD*: 264–73), it is very plausible to deny the *existence* of any genuine kinaesthetic sense. But crucial here is the recognition that neither the kinaesthetic sense, nor its siblings — kinaesthetic awareness, kinaesthetic empathy etc. (Best, 1974: 142–4) — can play any part in the understanding of dance. *If* such a sensory modality existed, it would (roughly) only give me 'knowledge' of the position etc. of *my* limbs and (some) other body parts. Yet the understanding of dance is, centrally, the understanding manifested by a spectator: at least, forced to choose between participant and spectator viewpoints, we would be obliged to choose that of the spectator. But to the spectator, the state or location of *my* body parts is simply an irrelevance. (This point might be put by saying that the 'kinaesthetic' cannot be a *projective* sensory modality; see *UD*: 266–7.) And if I am supposed to be empathising — well, with whom? With one of the dancers I am watching? Or with all of them? (This sounds roughly like the need to be able to play all the instruments in an orchestra, and simultaneously, in order to understand orchestral music (Best, 1974: 142). Again, such a view is untenable. So far we have seen that to imagine a *kinaesthetic justification* for the place of participation in dance education must be misguided.

Further, the role of the senses in understanding in general is widely misunderstood (Hacker, 1987: 48–78). For, although the functioning of the eyes obviously provides a minimal *condition* for perceptual understanding, it would be a mistake to attribute any larger role to it than this. Perception is concept-mediated (as we urged earlier). Hence any role attributed to the *mechanisms* of perception — to rods, cones and the like — will automatically be leaving out a great deal. In particular, leaving out the *real* perception — what is seen by the person. For the person just *sees* using these mechanisms. The central idea is that of a *perceptual act* — the capacity to learn or understand by looking, rather than mere sensory experience. Our interest is in the seeing — and in the understanding it may engender — not in the mechanisms as such. This is a point R.G. Collingwood (1938: 135–41) groped towards when he claimed that the work of art proper is not seen or heard: he meant that our understanding of the work is the key to our experience of it as art, and this is not purely reducible to sensory interaction (Wollheim, 1973: 250–60). Moreover, vision is — perhaps with hearing — the *key* sensory modality for the understanding of dance. Both of these are *projective* modalities. So if no significant role in relation to understanding exists for other sensory modalities, it becomes highly improbable that a role might be discovered for kinaesthesis.

Once such points are acknowledged, we have a picture of dance education which focuses on its relation to understanding, and to the distinctive kind of understanding it offers. Practical participation in dance is only justified if — and to the extent to which — it is in service of such understanding.

Understanding and composition

As we have accepted, to recognise an activity as dance (of the art-type) is to recognise it as *intended* under the concept 'dance'. It follows that an appreciation of how that intention works may be of considerable significance. But if our pupils are to understand this mechanism, we may require to teach those children to become (at least temporarily) *creators* of dances —

speakers in the language of dance, as it were (*UD*: Ch. 5). With this in mind, it seems obvious that excessive concentration on verbal reports of dances, or even notations of those dances, is unlikely to be adequate. These are not appropriate as the sole tools for the choreographer. Hence, they are not what our pupils should employ. Here there are three fundamental points.

First, even for the most basic understanding, it is the *dance* that is to be understood, and the dance is only confronted when one confronts (minimally) an assemblage of moving bodies. So that by itself the notation, for example, will not do. Of course, it may be that I can get a group of dancers to perform my choreography without myself being able to move at all. My choreography, after all, is predicated on the technique of just such dancers. (That is, technique in dancers is a pre-condition of style in choreographers: see *UD*: Ch. 9.) To expand this point, notice that there are two ways in which the *dancers* might be led to produce the art work that is my dance: I create the type-work (see pp. 20–1) that is my dance *either* by creating a token (moving the bodies of dances) *or* by writing a score, which is then performed by dancers. In either case, the successful performance of that dance is a token of the relevant type. (I argue in Chapter 4 of *Understanding Dance* that we have reasons for preferring the notated score as a mechanism here: but that is not to our immediate point.) Faced with with of these alternatives, it becomes apparent that, for all *I* need to be able to do, practical participation in dance is not essential.

This takes us to the *second* point, for the dancers who perform my choreography must be *taught* the technique that underlies it: learning such a technique is essentially a matter of bodily training. A technique in this sense might roughly be characterised, after all, as a set of fairly specific bodily skills. But the dancers are not not *thereby* taught to 'speak' the *language of dance*. Rather, they are trained to be the *medium* of the 'speech' of the choreographer. So, if our aim were to produce choreography, at however minimal a level, active participation in dance would not yet be required. One can be a choreographer without being a dancer (our first point), and now we have seen that one can be a dancer without being a choreographer (our second point).

However, as with language, one develops one's fluency in such 'speech' with practice. Thus the *third* point will be that trainee choreographers will need bodies on which to practice. We can see how being able to begin with one's own body would give one two major advantages: first, an easy method of explaining to the others what one wants — the 'do this' method — and, second, a very basic supply of a limited (to one) number of such bodies always at one's disposal. But such considerations are conceptually irrelevant. What is learnt from the art of dance — as opposed to, say, what exercise one gets or what friends one meets — is essentially a function of *observers* of that dance. A training in the bodily skill might make one a better observer, perhaps teaching one the sorts of thing to look for; yet surely that could be taught in other ways. Again, a performer may be in a rather worse position to actually see what is going on than a well-situated audience, since the dance is after all staged to provide a view to that audience, at least in typical cases.

Of course, the situation for education is rather more complex: most of the works produced by pupils are *not* art works: so these points apply to them only tangentially. And we return later to the big questions about the relation of pupil's achievements to the art products (see also Chapter 14).

Understanding and Personal Enquiry

However, it is important to bring to bear on this issue another area of our discussion thus far. For, if the intention is to employ a Personal Enquiry conception of education, one might ask whether or not, in respect of dance, active participation in dance is required. The difficulty, of course, is that traditional educational justifications for dance tend to deal with matters which, from the Personal Enquiry perspective, appear as merely peripheral or, at best, secondary characteristics of dance — for example, its ability to provide exercise, and hence cardiovascular fitness; or its contribution to socialisation. However, if we ask ourselves about the degree to which participation in dance might be expected 'to develop qualities such as curiosity, originality, initiative, co-operation, perseverance, open-mindedness, self-criticism, responsibility, self-confidence and independence' (Best, 1985b: 81), it seems clear that — for many of these characteristics — practical participation in dance as an art form will have little relevance. At least in so far as one is operating as a dancer, the initiative, independence, etc. lies in the hands of the choreographer. Indeed, to display independence here would be to interfere with the structure of the dance. In some cases this might be to the good, but it would involve a change of role. (In a parallel way, one might make innovations to the sentence structure of something one were reading. That might even improve the passage, but would not constitute reading.)

Nonetheless, there does seem to be some important connection between the practice of dance and the kinds of Personal Enquiry values advocated here. We bring out the connection by reminding ourselves that the knowledge and understanding to be gained from confrontation with art works is not, typically, *propositional* knowledge: that is to say, one cannot state simply and briefly *what* one learned, at least if one attempts to do this comprehensively. But how are teachers to know that one has understood? It is here, paradoxically, that the ability to *demonstrate* one's understanding may be of significance. This brings together points made in the previous two sections. For, if I am to be able to *demonstrate* my understanding, I may well need the kinds of *technical resources* (here in a specific dance technique) which only practical involvement with dance could provide for me. In this way, there is a connection, although a rather oblique one, between performance and understanding, at least in the sphere of dance education (this is a point to be considered in more detail in Chapter 14).

Understanding and 'transferable skills'

Responding to the ideas in the previous section, and my defence of the educational possibilities of dance (see p. 60), I imagine a critic asking me to specify exactly what the educational benefits of dance are. This is indeed an important task, and a difficult one. One part of the difficulty is especially worthy of note, since it leads us into our reply. For if we do *not* adopt a narrowly propositional conception of knowledge, on which whatever is known can be stated in (true) propositions (see Chapter 3), we will implicitly be conceding that there are things we *know* but cannot say ... or anyway cannot say without sounding vague or truistic. And the same goes for things we have *learned*. Now, this difficulty is a familiar one (see Alvarez, 1971: 236, quoted above); and, while it is by no means confined to the arts, it is widely recognised there. For at the centre of what I have learned is, roughly, a new way of looking at some aspect of life or the world (*UD*: Ch. 8). As I have urged in Chapter 4, this learning takes the form of conceptual change in respect of the concepts under which we perceive or consider the objects or events — what we have learned is a greater sensitivity, and one in respect of 'life-issues': those matters which bear on human thought and feeling.

It might be thought that to have an understanding of dance is *not* to have certain skills at all. But this idea is to be rejected. At its simplest, we can see this point by contrasting my (limited) understanding with that of a major critic of dance, such as Marcia Siegel. She can *do* certain things, make certain fine discriminations, which I cannot. And this sort of point will be central in our arguments to reject *subjectivist* accounts of the understanding of dance. Indeed, more generally, just this sense of 'being able to *do* certain things' — that is, to make informed judgements — is crucial in respect of the possibility of teaching (or learning) dance. It is connected with the possibility of what, formerly, we might call 'assessment' (see Chapter 15): the ability to tell good dance from bad, to put it briefly. The difficulty here is that *what* we know is not the sort of thing we can *say* or write down.

Increasingly (Brecher & Hickey, 1990), study of the humanities is seen as offering 'second-order' skills: in identification of the core of a problem and the means of solving it, in the integration and synthesis of disparate elements, and in the identification and clarification of values. In the relation between art and life-issues and the mechanism of that relation (the idea of emotional education), we see how similar thoughts might be developed for artistic education. Still, the skills for the humanities seem much more *closely* propositional, more readily described *independently* of content. Can we find some way of elucidating the relevant skills for dance education?

As we will see in Chapter 16, a fruitful discussion might employ the notion of *craft knowledge* or *community knowledge* (Deforges & McNamara, 1979; McNamara & Deforges, 1978). This is the practical knowledge that derives from practical experience and which underpins the activity in question. Such knowledge is typically not the sort of thing which one could write or say; in the jargon, it is not *propositional* knowledge. Though at present applied to professional (craft) knowledge of teachers, this idea has an obvious application both to dance teachers and those who 'professionally' understand dance: that is, to dance critics, formal and informal (*UD*: 159–63). There is a well-established line of research that makes craft knowledge explicit, *without* turning it into (mere) propositional knowledge. One fascinating possibility begins to emerge here. For to adopt a Personal Enquiry conception of the *essential* role of education, and to see the benefits of education in *craft knowledge terms* is to develop a strongly unified approach to the education — one which does *not* emphasise propositional knowledge. So that, for example, David Carr (1987: 350) remarks: 'it is obviously a matter of crucial importance for teachers and performers of dance to understand the nature of knowledge and learning in dance, to understand how dance *skills* are mastered or acquired'. Just so. But, as Carr recognises, this understanding is not describable in detail[1]. All that can be said is that it involves insight into an art form, and art forms are internally connected with life-issues. (Lest I be misunderstood, I could point out that this is not intended to pick out *all* that can be said: but all that can be said (a) above mere truism and (b) of the *central* achievement.)

It must be recognised that, although this *appears* to be a weak answer, it is actually a strong one. For the complex of powers and capabilities, of sensitivities and abilities which it describes constitutes a major achievement for human beings. In particular, it is one which might be contrasted (favourably) with the acquisition of the sorts of technical knowledge currently fashionable. But the worry was that the skill *itself* was not valuable: that is, it might be conceded that there is craft 'knowledge' to be acquired — but then the question asked — 'what is so good about it?'. In particular, does it warrant a place on the school curriculum — alongside (and hence competing for time with) such knowledge-generating, and wealth-creating, activities as the study of technology, or science, or mathematics? Or even, since the world is full of foreigners, the study of language?

A full reply would involved (at least) three aspects. Here I shall do little more than mention them, although some will be elaborated in what follows. So, *first*, the reply would point out what other objects of study — apart from dance — would be lost if such utilitarian thinking were to prevail: history and English literature, for example. And it would urge the impoverishment that this represents. We have already seen at least some of these considerations raised by Stenhouse (see Chapter 3). *Second*, the reply would contest the *obviousness* of the place of technology and science. What, *precisely*, do they offer? What *justification* can there be for their place in the curriculum? In particular, given the speed at which knowledge in these areas becomes outdated, these (if any) seem like areas which could be updated by the trained, inquiring mind, with a general background in them. So their claim to have a *permanent* place in the curriculum actually looks rather less certain. (Both of the 'moves' above should be seen as part of a general 'softening-up' of the opposition.) And, of course, one might attempt to undermine the conception of *the factual* sometimes invoked to hold science in place (*UD*: 30–2). That too we have seen, to some degree. It will be further elaborated in Chapters 13 and 16.

The third aspect of the reply involves retrieving some of the arguments used in respect of the *Personal Enquiry* conception of education (in Chapter 3). That is to say, it involves reminding ourselves that it is the possibility of man as a *moral agent* which is at stake here. For to act rationally — and, even more so, to act morally — is not something we can simply some to. Nor can we simply be told what rationality consists in: for then we are just 'parroting back' what others have decided for us. No, the values in question must be *our own*. Yet this does not mean that there are unique to us — indeed, they could not in principle be (McFee, 1984: 111–12) — but rather that we had *made* them our own: as some theorists put it, that we have *internalised* them (Bennett, 1976: 129–30). And what is lost if *this* is lost is not merely man's 'mastery' over the natural world, but any sense of direction to that mastery, and to human affairs more generally — at least, any direction distinctly human. No doubt that puts the matter unduly grandly. (Although, there is a long history of philosophical thinking, at least back as far as Seneca (1969), which puts the matter is broadly this way.) No doubt the powers and capacities at issue typically operate in smaller ways. Indeed, one danger lies in thinking of them too grandly: of only seeing them of importance in the 'big' things of life — the 'meaning of life' etc. For the smaller understandings that art works give us are also characteristically human. But there *are* big issues. And it can do us no harm to realise that, once in a while. Further, the sort of (moral) insight central to education, and delivered by the arts, cannot be just a matter of learning moral rules. For that would reinstate the 'parrot' conception of (moral) education. Rather, the only viable method for arriving at correct moral conclusions in new cases would involve seeing each case *as* new; and hence require us to develop the sort of sensitivity in such matters which will enable us to see the case in question — which means in the light of what one values and of past cases, but without being hidebound by them. To say all that is to reiterate, first, the need for sensitive and reformed understanding of life-issues and, second, the possible role of the arts in teaching us both the sensitivity and the understanding. It is also to reiterate our commitment to a Personal Enquiry conception of education. In these ways, then, the artistic account of dance education brings together both the *possibilities* of dance and the practical impact that it might have.

The place of practical achievement

One key question which remains concerns the *role* of pupils' practical achievements: since these are (typically) not art — at least for Jane and Joe Normal — how are they to be explained within the artistic account? My point will be that it is easy to *misrepresent* to oneself what is going on in the dance classes, and hence to misunderstand the (potential or actual) achievements of pupils. And in the next section I will consider the precise role of such achievements.

A parallel makes the point here. In schools, (visual) art class can *appear* to have the creation of, say, paintings, drawing, sculptures as their direction. Moreover, the major career opportunity might *seem* also to be in this *making* aspect, as artist or designer or the like. However, this is not as it seems. The achievements of the typical school art class are clearly not artworks: indeed, the production of large numbers of artworks is surely, by definition, not going to be achieved by Jane or Joe Normal. Contrary to appearance, the class is designed to enhance their sensibilities — and the teacher considers that this is better achieved through practical engagement than, for example, by showing them slides. There is a key *pedagogic* decision here — that the aim (of getting pupils to understand art) is best achieved through getting them to understand the properties of materials such as gouache, oil paint, clay and so on. But the aim of the visual art class is directly related to initiation into understanding.

Three lessons are suggested for dance education. First, like visual art, dance classes may *appear* to have the creation of dances as an outcome. In fact, this is just a method of achieving the understanding of dance. And, it seems to me, much of the nonsense talked about the role of dance in schools could be avoided if this point were better understood. Second, this concern with understanding is a reputable concern in education. It is one shared, for example, with history. Third, there is no real equivalent for dance of such day-to-day activities as counting and writing (for, say, mathematics and English respectively). But this is not a major difficulty. For these day-to-day activities are not fundamental to either of the disciplines themselves – they are not what is *educational* here.

Competence, understanding and education

Much is currently being written concerning the place (or otherwise) of *competence-based* education. In this section, I urge that there is one *important* way in which dance education is *not* concerned with competence. To bring that point out, however, it is essential to recognise that the word 'competence' could amount to many different things in this context: competence in analysis, competence in teaching, competence in demonstrating a historical under-standing or in reconstruction, for example. Here I am simply concerned with competence *in the activity*, that is, in 'doing' the dance. We might think of this as *technical* competence, although that too may be a confusing way of making the point. The question to be asked, then, is what importance is to be placed on competence in this sense. For example, should such competence be integral to the assessment of dance in education? In particular, is it a basis on which pupils might pass or fail?

Throughout this chapter I have been urging that the activity of dance was performed as a route to understanding: the *experience* of the activity was crucial only insofar as it was a mode of coming to understand that activity. Hence the assessment should reflect levels of *understanding* rather than levels of competence (in the sense previously picked out). Further, this idea of an emphasis on *understanding* is clearly more compatible with assigning a place for dance within the school curriculum, particularly when such a curriculum is led by academic concerns.

Against this position, it might be urged that the teacher required the confidence that competence would (or could?) give, and also the credibility that was attendant on the ability to demonstrate clearly. So, it might be argued, a teacher would need to be a master of dance *activity*: hence to have com-petence in that activity.

Of course, a concern with the training of dance educators is not our direct concern here. Nonetheless, this matter gives us insight into the case applied to the school curriculum. For the view just articulated does not locate the difficulty correctly. I accept, of course, the need for teachers to have this confidence and this ability to demonstrate (with one reservation I will come to). But that is part of the repertoire of the *teacher* and should be assessed insofar as we consider these people as *teachers*. It is as a teacher that this person is not succeeding, rather than as a performer in a relevant activity. The reservation that I have concerning demonstration is that we can very often learn (a) from demonstrating activity broken-down, which need not require the same facility in the whole activity, (b) from a demonstration whose faults are clearly identified, or whose identification is part of the pupil's task — perhaps supplemented by video, and (c) from demonstration by other pupils, if well-observed and analysed. So I am not completely convinced that the teacher-students whose competence levels are not high should be failing even in respect of their dance pedagogy. However that is resolved, dance teachers in training should not be assessed on their competence as such. For our concern is whether they *understand*, and that should be the focus of our assessment of them, just as it is in schools.

This leads to two major considerations. The first concerns the nature and place of assessment. For, as we will see later (Chapter 15), teaching should be *accountable* in the sense of being able to decide, in principle, whether or not one's teaching was successful. Thus it is essential to have some method of determining, at least in principle, whether pupils have learned what was intended for them, however broadly conceived (see Chapter 13). In this vein, one might *think* of giving marks for pupil *competence*, perhaps on the grounds that this was to some degree assessable.

That leads directly to the second point. For, clearly, we need to be giving the marks for *something*, but it needs to be the appropriate thing. Suppose we urge, as is integral to the argument throughout this chapter, that the pupils *understanding* may be recognised *through* their performance. If so, credit (say in the form of marks) given to pupils might *appear as* or *be mistaken for* marks given for competence. But they would not be. In this way, the mere fact that children *could* perform certain actions would not prove to us that they had understood what those actions amounted to in dances, nor that they had any grasp of how those actions might be used in the making of dances. There is clearly a major practical difficulty here: how are we to recognise *understanding thorough performance*? The claim here is that, however we manage it, we are required to do so. As the parallel with the training of dance teachers illustrated, an undue emphasis on competence as such will be beside the educational point.

There is, additionally, a complication. For it is sometimes difficult, especially when considering the understanding of choreography, to see the choreography clearly unless it is performed by dancers with technical competence. To illustrate the point anecdotally, I once attended a choreographic competition in which the works performed emanated sometimes from choreographers working in higher education institutions, sometimes from choreographers working in professional dance theatre. Typically, all the choreographers used, to perform their choreography, the people they had to hand. So those in higher education used their students, those in the professional world used members of the companies they were associated with. The short list, however, consisted solely of those with the professional company backgrounds. I do not believe for a moment that this truly reflects the range of choreographic ability. It was clear that the task of identifying sharply (and on one viewing) the characteristics of the choreo-graphy was made much simpler when the choreography was performed at a high level of competence. If this point is accepted, of course, it suggests that there is — at least for the case of choreography — a peculiar relation between the level of performance-competence and the level of understanding. Not, of course, that the choreographic understanding *as such* requires the per-formance competence, but that it might be lost to its audience without that competence.

Conclusion

The argument of this chapter has been somewhat diffuse. It has focused on the key educational role of *understanding* dance, bearing in mind that such understanding may reflect *craft knowledge* and may be recognised through *performance* of dances. It has argued that the requirement, within dance education in schools, for practical participation in dance classes derives from *pedagogic* concerns: that this may be the best way to initiate pupils into the understanding of dance. Further, it has argued that the considerations above do not preclude dance education having a role in the learning of 'transferable skills', once these skills are conceived of appropriately. And the whole picture — with its focus on *human* powers and capacities — fits neatly into our Personal Enquiry conception of the educational.

Chapter 7

Dance Within Physical Education

Introduction

As the philosopher Whitehead is reputed to have said (Kivy, 1989: 17), the universe is not divided into departments. But, of course, schools and higher education institutions are: and this is the level of organisation we must address. The topic of whether or not dance education should be the province of physical education departments was a 'hot' one in the UK few years ago, especially when education departments in Polytechnics and colleges were 'diversifying' into non-teaching qualifications. It no longer is. Indeed, one could be forgiven for thinking that, once the content of the dance education programme is clear, the precise details of such departmental locations are not important: that one can teach anything from anywhere. No doubt there is some truth here. The point, though, derives from my espousal of two key ideas, which together mean that its artistic possibility is central to dance education: namely, the point of dance residing in the *emotional education* in respect of *life-issues* which follow from its art-status (see Chapters 2 and 4). If the issue were simply the likelihood of exploiting the artistic possibilities within physical education programmes in schools, universities, polytechnics etc., no theoretical objection could be forthcoming to locating dance education in any department (even physics!) — although I envisage some concern that dance educators' natural colleagues (that is, those who are also concerned with the artistic) are in drama, art and English. Still, to repeat, that is not a theoretical objection to locating dance education in any department rather than any other.

Another matter has a slightly less direct connection. It might be put in the form of a question: why is there so little interest on the part of, for example, male physical education teachers, in the teaching of dance? (That this is so is borne out both by my personal experience and by discussions with colleagues and students.) Certainly, these physical education teachers do not see dance as centrally *their business*: they perceive its distinctiveness, and simply do not wish to accommodate it. No doubt many factors influence this kind of attitude — their own school experience, the way they were taught to teach dance while in training, the ethos of the school, a more generalised role for physical education teachers, and so on. My point here would be that *if*, as the National Curriculum in the UK now directs, the educational *home* for dance is in the physical education programme, to continue to locate dance *outside* physical education will simply reinforce that kind of attitude. An anecdote may explain. A graduate student of mine, interested in dance, wished to teach it in the school in which he was employed as a physical education teacher. Even more surprising to the 'powers that be' in the school was that he wished to teach dance for the male pupils! The school's reaction was, of course, to allow him to teach dance — but to locate this element of his work within the expressive arts department. And in the hierarchy of the school, expressive arts appeared even lower than physical education. As a result, the technique of removing dance from physical education served to further lower the status of dance education.

These points tell us that dance education has a *distinctive* identity, but that — at least pragmatically — establishing that identity *within* physical education many be at least as profitable as doing the opposite. But why should dance education not simply collapse into physical education? What — apart from my vested interest in dance — makes me defend the idea of a distinctive education? The answer lies in the unique character of the educational possibilities of dance, which is not to denigrate the contribution of other physical activities; but it is to make dance not just another way of getting exercise, social and moral development etc: that is, *not* just one activity amongst many. The unique character of the educational possibilities of dance rests, of course, in the emotional education which the arts have to offer. To repeat, to say this is not to under-rate the value, complexity or importance of (other) traditional activities traditionally used in physical education. It is simply to record (again) key differences between dance and such activities, and to note that this is an *educational* difference. So that while dance might — and no doubt does — also serve main of the other aims regularly (if mistakenly[1]) imputed for physical education, it also serves one unique to it amongst physical activities (unless perhaps drama and mime are also included).

Justifications for the place of dance

It is important, when assessing the possibilities of dance education, to see clearly the kinds of arguments which might be put for its inclusion in a school's curriculum. To do this I shall use, as a case study, some of the arguments which are actually given for dance in the National Curriculum in the UK. It should be remembered, of course, that this case is really there to exemplify the sort of justifications regularly offered.

Dance appears explicitly as part of the physical education programme, but also *implicitly* in cross-curricular initiatives — for example, in health education. However, for our purposes, I shall concentrate on the explicit remarks[2] about dance, as they appear in *Physical Education for Ages 5–16* (DES, August 1991 in Appendix B, §§23–28 of that report: 63–64)[3].

In effect, three justifications are offered for the place of dance. The first is that 'physical education offers an effective context for developing aesthetic appreciation' (Appendix B, §23). That is to say, there is a justification offered for dance as *aesthetic* education. The second justification is for dance as *artistic* education: 'of all the activities in physical education, only dance, as an art form in its own right, is characterised by the intention and ability to make symbolic statements to create meaning' (Appendix B, §28). So an account like that given here is employed for dance. It is accepted throughout the document that 'dance is also concerned with acquiring control, co-ordination and versatility in use of the body, and helps to maintain flexibility and develop strength' (Appendix D, §4). At this point, however, a further justification for dance is introduced. For the importance of dance in 'its broad cultural context' is recognised (Appendix D, §6). There dances are categorised as popular culture/art, traditional/folk and historical. Although the point is not made explicit in this section, it is apparent that an appeal is being made here to dance as a vehicle of *cultural* education. As this document recognises, the first of these justifications is a weak one. For aesthetic education — even in respect of physical activities — could be satisfied by 'gymnastics, skating, diving' (Appendix B, §24, §27). The question of the role of dance in cultural education will be discussed in Chapters 11 and 12, but — for now — it is sufficient to notice that this is not an area especially emphasised by the document (I had to extract this conception from it), and also it is one which is invoked only for dance — there is no suggestion of needing to contextual games or swimming, for example. So a distinctive characteristic for dance is invoked, but without being explained.

A second point to notice, central to the concerns of this chapter, is that none of these justifications requires dance to be part of physical education; that is, all are perfectly general justifications for the place of dance in a school curriculum, which might be invoked if dance were a separate area of study rather than (as in the National Curriculum) a part of physical education.

A third central consideration is that only one of these three justifications really makes the difference that we are requiring. That is, only one really justifies dance, in the sense of requiring *dance* and not something else. We can imagine aesthetic education satisfied (as the document acknowledges) *without* the inclusion of dance. And the cultural contribution of dance might be provided by a cultural study of games, say: one might venture to include, for example, the Indian game Kabaddi in one's games programme, and then to provide a broad cultural context for it. Thus, if one is looking for a *distinctive* rationale for dance, neither the aesthetic nor the cultural justifications seem promising.

I am suggesting, of course, that the rationale for dance is strong *only* if we argue for the difference between dance and other activities which go on under the general heading of physical education. Almost by definition, if we have a justification which *includes* dance as just one activity among others, we can satisfy the point of that justification *without* including dance. So, I am urging, consideration of the *place* of dance is yet another way of reinforcing our own artistic account of the justification of that place. Dance has a role while we think of it as an art form, and not to the degree to which we do not.

Here, then, we not only have a justification for the inclusion of dance within the school curriculum, but also a direction for *what* dance is to be included: it is to be that kind of dance that is art. So, our intention must be to offer pupils the possibility of artistic understanding, of making informed *artistic* judgements, in respect of dance. Precisely how we do that may be an importantly vexed question. It is not obvious that this will be achieved by unremitting concentration on the art form, nor by *beginning* with master works of dance-art (see Chapters 8 and 14). But precisely how it is taught is one thing; the rationale for teaching it quite another. And it is with that rationale that we have been concerned here.

Dance, physical education and the National Curriculum: a response

I will now consider a response to the National Curriculum that appeared in the newspapers while I was working on this chapter. That response focused on one aspect on which I have not so far commented: that, as it stands, dance would not be *compulsory* for all pupils in Key Stage 3 (that is, from 12 to 14 years of age), but — as we will see — its impact is more wide-ranging.

There is an important parallel between the situation in respect of dance in the National Curriculum and the situation in respect of music. As the *The Times Education Supplement* (TES, Feb.7, 1992: 1) noted, a lobby from musicians and those concerned with music had managed'to reverse the draft orders on music in the curriculum', which orders would have made music not *compulsory* in Key Stage 3. Nevertheless, the nature of the argument is not precisely clear. This article speaks of 'a campaign to persuade the Education Secretary to keep dance in the curriculum'. But, of course, there is no suggestion that dance *should* not be taught in Key Stage 3, and indeed Stage 4 (that is to say, for pupils aged 12–16). All the National Curriculum documentation requires is that dance not be *compulsory* at this stage. Nonetheless, given the pressures of time that the National Curriculum will create, what is not seen as *essential* may soon be marginalised: it is easy to be sympathetic to the fear, also expressed in this journalistic piece, that, if it is not compulsory, dance 'may now be dropped by schools'. This fear seems justified, in the current financial climate for education in the UK.

This response is interesting to us for three related reasons. First, there is an obvious way forward within the National Curriculum proposals as they presently stand: one simply makes dance so desirable that pupil choice (and associated 'parent-power') *requires* schools to offer it. That is to say, if dance were to become immensely popular in schools it would be unthinkable that it should suffer the decline feared. In that sense, concerted action by the dance education profession might be thought to be the way forward. Notice, though, other subjects are not forced to court popularity in this way: nobody requires that English, for example, be included because it is *wanted* — its educational status is not, in this way, under discussion. So we must be sympathetic to the suggestion that, if dance is relegated to the optional in Key Stage 3 in the National Curriculum, its educational potential — and in particular the educational *distinctiveness* argued here — is being denigrated. Second, the article in *The Times Education Supplement* also reports on 'the National Curriculum Council had taken on board comments that boys don't like dancing. That is a great insult to the many who do' (TES, Feb.7, 1992: 1). The point, of course, is that a strategy which required dance to be generally *popular* would be a strategy for doubtful success, and for two reasons. First, as noted above, the requirement for popularity amongst pupils is not equivalent to the requirement for educational desirability. Second, it cannot be denied that dance has been *perceived* as the province of girls rather than boys. An anecdote to illustrate that point: my book *Understanding Dance* was to have had a distinctly *female* form on its cover — the cover designers thought that that was an obvious thing to do! But such a move would simply have reinforced the stereotype that dancing is for girls. (The cover, in the end, shows a form that might be thought *arguably* female, but at least not one that is *obviously* so.) I am trying to emphasise of course, that 'dancing is for girls' is merely a *stereotype*, but (as illustrated by a story of the reaction of the 'powers that be' in a school to my graduate student's suggestion that he wished to teach dance) it is a stereotype with power, in particular amongst male teachers of physical education. That brings us to the nub of *this* point. For locating dance with physical education is placing the teaching of dance under the control, to some degree or other, of just those teachers.

This response to the National Curriculum proposals, a response wishing to make dance compulsory in Key Stage 3, is not justified insofar as it depends on the educational distinctiveness of dance, but would be justified if the delivery of dance were thereby hampered by being in the hands of those who accept the 'dance is for girls' stereotype. A third reason for including the discussion here is to bring out yet another misconception about the nature of dance. The article in *The Times Education Supplement*, cited above, also quotes the view of Robert Atkins, the UK Minister for Sport, saying 'I think there is a possibility of dance as a cop-out — a sixth-form disco as a substitute for physical activity. I don't think I agree with that' (TES, Feb.7, 1992: 1). This point is misleading in at least two ways. First, anyone who has sweated and strained in a technique class will find it had to believe that any well-taught dance might function as 'a substitute for physical activity', and this would surely be true *whatever* dance-form were being taught. Thus, well-taught disco will certainly count as physical activity for these purposes. Now we might have reservations, given our commitment to the *artistic* account of the value of education. But certainly the activity should be doing everything the Minister for Sport requires. The second point, though, concerns the recognition that pupils might, indeed, succeed in 'copping-out' of such dance classes — although, given the activities of the young in discotheques, this does not strike me as highly likely. Nevertheless, the possibility of pupils not concentrating, not trying, not participating, or generally becoming uninvolved, is surely a perfectly general problem for the delivery of all topics. Thus, these remarks might apply to the maths lesson as much as to the dance class.

The upshot of our consideration of this response, then, is to reinforce our original position. As the presentation in the physical education proposal suggested, the rationale for the distinctiveness of dance education is provided by the artistic account. But this account says nothing about *how* dance education is to find its way into the life of the pupil, nothing about which department it 'sits' in, nothing about how it is reported. These last three are all practical matters: as long as a clear *rationale* for the place of dance has been provided (and assuming that rationale is acknowledged in practice), there is nothing for us to add.

Conclusion

This chapter has shown that any arguments around the *location* of dance education are not strictly our concern. It has, in passing, identified some constraints on a satisfactory delivery of dance — constraints whose *practical* importance might lead one to prefer this or that 'home' for dance, given that dance education is to be justified via the artistic account. All-in-all, it has served to undermine any claims that, given its 'artistic account' justification, dance should *obviously* be the province of one department or another. This outline will be expanded when we turn, in Chapter 13, to an examination of the nature of our understanding of the school curriculum.

Chapter 8

Dance Artists in Education

Introduction

This chapter introduces a contrast crucial for our understanding of the concept of dance education: the difference between teachers of dance and dance artists in education. The thesis offered here is that both have an important role, and might usefully combine in an ideal situation. Nevertheless, this is not equivalent to saying that there is only one role. My strong impression is that the first forays onto the field of dance artists in education have the dance artists simply *being teachers*: as it were, trying to do exactly what the teachers had done, in terms of the same aims and objectives. Now, increasingly, their input involves the use of elements from the company's repertoire, which is the strength of the dance artists, their uniqueness; and breaking down the choreographic and technical structure of the art work of the company might be expected to foster insights into both these particular pieces of dance and dance as such. Here, they would not be functioning as teachers, for they would have neither the virtues nor vices of the teacher, but rather functioning as those who, through intimate knowledge, have a detailed understanding of the workings of particular art works. Perhaps (as my colleague Ann Cole would argue[1]), this process is not yet fully thought through. Perhaps the exact nature of the role of the dance artist is not yet clear. And perhaps its true benefits are not yet apparent. Yet the direction — the *artistic direction* — of their achievements is obvious enough. This exemplifies the artistic thrust of dance education: what is being done is the presentation, discussion etc. of works of art — together with their making.

What rationale might be offered for the practice of bringing dancers — as dance artists — into schools? What can they do that the school's own teacher cannot? If the school lacked a *specialist* dance teacher, one might think that the dance artist offers technical skills otherwise unavailable to the schools. This answer is inadequate, not least because the preparation of the pupils for the dance artist's visit or residency requires the sorts of understanding of dance which qualify one as a dance specialist. So, if that were the answer, the dance artist's visit would be a guaranteed failure. But even this answer is revealing. For the skills the dance artist has to offer are indeed those which support *dance as art*; and hence the taking of an artistic interest in dance.

The dance artist has, of course, two capacities on offer. The first, which I have been discussing, is the insight into particular dance works which the dance artist might be expected to have. The second is the detailed understanding of technique — also referred to above. Notice that the emphasis on *technique* — for example, Graham technique etc. (roughly, bodily training for the dance, including certain fairly specific sets of bodily skills) — cannot really explain the place of the dance artist in the school, for it does not give due weight to what those skills, that technique, is *for*; namely, the creation of meaning (or expression) in dance. And if what the dance artist brings is (elements of) repertory work of the company, we see the *artistic* connection very directly.

Masterworks and understanding

One important consideration which applies prior to any proper understanding of the place of the dance artist in education concerns the role of works which are *known*, or *recognised*, or *performed* in the current repertoire at any time. I shall call these, without intending any praise, *masterworks*. So that, for our purposes, a masterwork will be a work which has a current place in the repertoire of, let us say, major dance companies of the time. Therefore, *Swan Lake* will count as a masterwork, despite its long history, while we might have reservations about the degree to which, for example, Christopher Bruce's *Ghost Dances* (1981) counts as a masterwork, given that it is no longer in performance. That may not seem quite right, but these are minor difficulties. We can recognise that certain works have an established existence, that they have passed the test of time, and — as far as we can expect — they will be available to the students and theorists of the future. They can serve as masterworks for our contemporary understanding.

It is important to notice that masterworks in this sense are a key element in the teaching of music. For music teaching typically consists not only in, say, mastering fingering on the piano to give one technical virtuosity, but also the study of established works by major composers for (in this example) the piano. That is another way of saying that we study piano *masterworks*. As with the dance case, the exact contours of these masterworks may be problematic. Whose work is to be included? But, within such disputes, there is a high degree of agreement. In the case of music, a programme of masterworks which did not include, say, Beethoven, Bach and Mozart would be extremely bizarre. In a similar way, dance masterworks might be expected to include Graham and

Cunningham (among others). The point I am making here is that it is *possible* to envisage a teaching of dance which focuses on masterworks. The parallel with music teaching makes this especially plausible. Nor should we assume that such a focus on masterworks is equivalent to simply *observing* the dance works in question. We might easily study a section of a particular work by, say, Graham through performing some of its movements, discussing them and considering lines of their further development. In these ways, investigation of masterworks might — in practical circumstances — concentrate on bodily movements. So it makes sense to include the study of such masterworks within dance education, as the parallels with music education make plain.

But are there any advantages, for dance education, of the consideration of masterworks? I am not, of course, seeking to make a judgement about dance pedagogy as such, although colleagues in my own institution use a masterworks-method in a way which strikes me as deeply successful. My point, instead, is a purely conceptual one. Are there reasons for thinking that a concentration on masterworks, in the senses articulated earlier, could be educationally advantageous? Certainly, at least two related advantages are obvious. The first is in terms of the understanding of extant works. If I visit a theatre to watch dance, and the dance works include those I have studied, I am clearly advantaged. Second, there is a clear advantage if I am considering the ways in which the notion of 'development' applies to such dances. For, if I am to understand how a particular dance develops, I need to understand the *materials* of dance construction from which that dance originates. Again, the parallel with music is revealing. We would not expect to teach music by simply giving students the opportunity to make music for themselves. We expect their experience of masterworks of music to give them insight both into works that might still be in the repertoire (point 1), and also into principles of construction still current (point 2). Indeed, it would be surprising if dance composition could go far without blocks of 'material' to be explored and examined. As the parallel with music suggests, the natural place to start is with blocks from extant dances: what we have here described as *masterworks*. So if we are to provide students with *concrete* material for the construction of their own dances, it makes sense to give them material which can be broken down into comparable blocks. and a good way to do this would be via masterworks.

I am not, of course, arguing exclusively for a pedagogy for dance education based on the use of masterworks. The development of creativity (*UD*: Ch. 13) is clearly of central importance: if my job involves the cons- truction of dances for my pupils, it will not do if all I have at my disposal is the reiteration of dances of the past. But this point is not equivalent to the suggestion that I leave my pupils with *no* material on which to base their dance construction. Indeed, there is something very strange about the sug- gestion that one might teach dance *ideas* in isolation from teaching the material of dance: that is, from considering actual dances. Of course, there is no need to draw those dances from the contemporary repertoire. Yet, as urged above, there are independent reasons for doing so. For those reasons at least, it makes sense to *begin* from masterworks, wherever one concludes.

A third consideration is of some relevance here. It is perhaps best brought out by an example. A critical response to the public reaction to, say, the Cubist works of Picasso is to urge that the 'general public' has not absorbed sufficient of this century's progress in visual art to understand 'what Picasso is all about'. Whatever one makes of this point, in this specific example, it describes an issue for the development of the arts: the history of the *understanding* of any art form seems to involve a distinct lag between its general understanding and its understanding by those centrally involved in the form. How is such a transition in understanding to be achieved? A sense of the development of particular art forms must be built into education in that art form: to apply, we should build-in understanding of transitions in dance for those involved in dance education.

But how are such transitions to be negotiated? Let us take a particular example and consider Mats Ek's *Swan Lake* (1987). Here we have a work which has obvious connections with the past — with Petipa's choreography from 1895 — and connections with contemporary choreography. Indeed, it is precisely this combination which means that Ek's ballet is still appropriately entitled *Swan Lake*, despite its comprising different movements from Petipa's, different costumes, and a different theme. Someone ignorant of the Petipa version would miss much of the humour in Ek's ballet; but, more important, what makes it a *suitable Swan Lake* for today (*UD*: 67–71). For without seeing the connection to a Romantic past, it is doubtful if the quest for an understanding of the 'realities' of sexuality in Ek's *Swan Lake*, (where, even with swans, everything is not black or white) will be intelligible. That is partly a matter of recognising the expressive potentials of the technical resources at Ek's disposal. If a student is to understand how to use today's resources for choreography, it seems desirable that such a student should have an understanding both of the past — as represented through historically-rooted masterworks — and of the present, as represented by masterworks by contemporary choreographers, as well the interrelation between these two. And that inter-relation might be best explored through works, such as Ek's, which explore such a boundary area.

The conclusion, of course, is that there is the possibility of an important role, within dance education, for *masterworks*. But who are the best presenters of such masterworks? At one level, a well-prepared teacher with a good stock of video, a good grasp of the relevant notations and wide access to scores looks like a suitable candidate. But one must doubt the wide availability of such *superpersons*! Indeed, one might doubt whether these requirements could realistically be met by a teacher. More important, though, is the point articulated earlier: that the dance artist may offer an insight into the particular repertoire of a particular company which it would be unrealistic to expect of any teachers. Indeed, the dance artist might well have been integral in the *construction* of that repertory work.

I am suggesting, of course, that the general benefit from masterworks should be seen in terms of insight into the choreography — and hence the artistic opportunities — of the works in question. Such an understanding may well be predicated on a developed grasp of the *technique* within which that work is constructed. But one's interest in the technique extends as far as is required for understanding the works, and no further. Or, to be exact, one's understanding is so circumscribed by one's consideration of them as master-works. It may well be that one wishes to go further into the technique for one's own choreographic achievements. But it is no part of my purpose here to argue that point, one way or the other.

A brief introduction to the dance artist movement

Rather than survey the history of the use of dance artists in education, we achieve a helpful focus by concentrating simply on one moment in that history, a moment where the contours of the movement were sharply delineated. With that in mind, I shall discuss the 1980 report of the dance artists in education pilot projects produced by Valerie Briginshaw (Briginshaw, Brook and Sander-son, 1980), acknowledging of course that a concern with dance artists in edu-cation has moved on since that time. But the gain in clarity which lucid docu-mentation and hindsight provides more than justifies this look into the past.

The report sketched three pilot projects in which dance artists were in educational environments, under the aegis of the Arts Council of Great Britain (ACGB). As Briginshaw *et al.* (1980: 15) report, the press release 'invisaged that the scheme will benefit both the children and the dance artists taking part and facilitate a constructive exchange of ideas'. Although the projects lacked more clearly state aims, the projects proceeded on the assumption of some shared agreement as to 'the fundamental purposes of the joint venture' (Brigin-shaw *et al.*, 1980: 15). In the eventuality, this was not unproblematic: for example, even when a shared concern was clearly located — say, in improving 'body awareness" — all did not go swimmingly. As Briginshaw *et al.* (1980: 15) identify the matter:

> the educationalists' child-centred approach to achieving this sometimes caused them to query the artists' emphasis on training and technique. Similarly, a number of educationalists were disappointed that in some instanced pupils were not encouraged to contribute more to the actual composition of the dance.

Here two fundamental points are identified. *First*, the way in which a shared agreement as to large scale aims or aspirations, vaguely expressed, might lead to quite radical differences in what happened 'at the coal face' of delivery to pupils. Thus, the *mere* sharing of such aspirations is not a sufficient basis for joint work. *Second*, a fundamental difference of *concern* was identified. That is to say, the dance artist in concerned to make art (to some degree or other) and sees this as developmentally advantageous for pupils. In contrast, the teacher is concerned with pupils' learning, seeing engagement with the art as an appropriate 'vehicle'. Of course, such a contrast is never quite as hard and fast as I have made it seem. Its importance, though, is that both elements are integral to the *artistic* approach for dance education. We cannot realistically imagine that pupils' contributions will lead automatically to the production of artworks (see Chapter 6) — which is one reason why the notion of *master-works* has a fundamental role here, and why the dance artists were behaving appropriately in employing such *masterworks* from their repertoire. But the context *is* the educational one, and so behaviour appropriate in dealing with trained dancers is clearly inappropriate for pupils.

As an interesting side-issue, it is worth noting that the one *specific* aim in the formation of these pilot projects, the 'intention that boys be involved as fully as possible' (Briginshaw *et al.*, 1980: 19) was certainly not achieved. Although some mixed groups were taught, and boys saw performances by companies associated with the dance artist, the hoped-for concentration on the work of male pupils was not apparent in these projects. (It is worth reminding ourselves, of course, that we are here referring to some initial projects and of a considerable time ago.) Interestingly, though, one of the projects — that taking place in Havant, with Christopher Bannerman of London Contemporary Dance Theatre — consciously used a work (Robert North's *Troy Game* [1974]) as a topic of study because it was an 'exciting and athletic dance for men' (Briginshaw, *et al.*, 1980: 5): students from the London School of Contemporary Dance performed this work as part of the project.

The three projects included performances, lecture demonstrations, open rehearsals, open company classes and company members taking sessions with pupils. Further, there was some informal interaction between associated companies and pupils. But these company residences were seen as supplementing the individual work of the dance artists. Roughly, then, the work could be divided into three stages. First, a preparatory phase in which some degree of agreement as to what would happen and why was identified. Second, a company residency phase in which the work of a company with whom the identified dance artist was connected was presented in the school setting; and finally a choreography session in which the dance artist in question returned to the school and leading the students into choreography of their own, building on technique sessions.

The report by Briginshaw *et al.* clearly identifies the need for an elaborate and comprehensive preparation stage; as so often, this is an aspect easy to neglect. But determining the 'what' and 'why' for such activities is important. However, for our purposes, those questions should be answered through the remarks in the previous sections. We have here experts with an intimate knowledge of masterworks and a good grasp of technique. In this way, the broad contours for the preparatory work are laid down by the arguments presented here. The importance of the company residency is a topic which deserves far more discussion than I can give it. In essence, though, because it is explained via our concern, articulated in the previous section, with masterworks, it should include at least three elements. The first will be the presentation of such *masterworks*; second, the detailed discussion of some sections of such *masterworks* with pupils, ideally involving their learning these sections and considering how they might be expanded or how similar ideas might be used in their own dances. And third, supporting the second, the opportunity to begin learning the technique which those masterworks employ. As the listing given above makes plain, this is broadly what *did* go on, although the rationale was perhaps not clearly articulated, and not always successfully implemented. For example, in one project the value of classes for pupils presented by individual company members was questioned. Since those 'members had little teaching experience' (Briginshaw *et al.*, 1980: 25), this comment probably identifies, as we did earlier, the differential approach of dance artist and dance teacher.

The question of the place of technique in the work of the dance artist in education remains vexed. As the remarks above make explicit, the technique is not merely peripheral to the *masterworks*: it is the *medium* of those *masterworks*, the 'material-in-certain-characteristic-applications', as Cavell (1969: 211) calls it. And what can realistically be taught to absolute beginners in the relatively short period within which the dance artist will typically have contact with schools might make one hesitant about pupils ever acquiring sufficient understanding of the technique to bring that understanding to bear when they confront the masterworks. Learning technique takes time. In the projects described by Briginshaw *et al.*, one solution was to take as the group with whom the dance artists primarily worked those who already had some developed expertise in the technical aspects of dance. In any case, the dance artist's work should be seen as involving the technical only insofar as it might be thought to contribute to the understanding of the masterworks. Of course, having such experts in technique 'on the spot' may tempt teachers to run *additional* sessions simply concerned with technique. But these are *not* integral to the work of the dance artist in education, as we have been considering it here, although of course they might contribute in ways which facilitated later engagements by the dance artist. Briginshaw *et al.*

(1980: 22) introduce that question, from the Calouste Gulbenkian report *Dance Education and Training in Britain* (Gulbenkian, 1980: 50): 'It is point of debate whether classes to develop a technique of classical ballet, say, or contemporary or modern dance not only can but should be held in an ordinary school unless the school is prepared to give the necessary time on the timetable'. Recognising the *place* of such technique as it applies to the school's pupils, namely that it is there to facilitate understanding of masterworks, we may be some way towards deciding coming down on one side of that 'debate'.

Thus far I have highlighted some aspects of the work of the dance artist in education by referring specifically to the work of the pilot projects in 1980, as reported by Briginshaw *et al.* This is a way of showing how the abstract theoretical concerns which we have voiced are indeed those central to a consideration of the role of the dance artist in education, and how emergent answers from 1980 might be strengthened from a theoretical perspective by our considerations.

Dance artists and masterworks

Thus far, in this chapter, we have presented three major points. The first differentiates the role of the dance teacher in the school from the dance artist in education: insofar as those roles could be thought of as equivalent, we are simply wasting time and energy by inserting dance artists into education. The jobs could be equally well-done by our (trained) teachers! So any argument, such as mine, which wishes to urge an important place for the dance artist in education must show how that place differs from the place of the teacher. Second, we have discussed the importance, for the understanding of dance, of what we have called *masterworks*. Implicitly, the place of the dance artist in education has been explained via the notion of such artists having a *tacit* knowledge of masterworks. So the considerations earlier in this chapter (pp. 78–81) should be seen as supporting both the artistic account of dance education and the importance of the dance artist. Third, we have considered (briefly) the history of provision of dance artists for education, typified by one moment in its UK history. This has involved some (admittedly brief) consideration of the rationale *actually* offered for this practice. Thus we have seen that the differentiation required by our first point is not always observed or apparent or argued for. That is to say, the rationales actually offered for the introduction of the dance artist have often been inadequate or insufficient rationales. None of this undermines our point. Indeed, the *history* of dance artists in education is not strictly relevant to our consideration if (or to the degree to which) that history reflects a *mis-use* of those dance artists.

We have seen two related tasks for dance artists. The first concerns their input in respect of *masterworks*: in any typical case such masterworks will be the *repertoire* of the company or companies from which the dance artist originates. Second, we have acknowledged that the dance artist may have something to offer in terms of the teaching of *technique* (such as Graham technique) or, more generally, of performance skills. However, it is clear that this second aspect, that emphasising technique, should be seen as *depending* on the first, as it did when Martha Graham was constructing her technique (McDonagh, 1973: 168). For Graham evolved the technique by training dancers in the movements required for particular choreographies. In this way, as we have noted, it is the masterworks which have priority.

At this point, it is important to more explicitly connect our masterworks with the idea of understanding dance. The thought, which I have been canvassing in various forms since the mid-70s (McFee, 1976), is that it is from such masterworks that we learn what counts as *dance reasons*. That is to say, we learn what it is *relevant* to introduce as a reason in appraisal, appreciation, evaluation or such like.

The clearest way to introduce such notions returns us to the idea of a *medium*. If we ask the question 'what is the medium of dance?', we must recognise that there is no medium of dance *in the absence* of the practice of dance. As Stanley Cavell (1969: 221) puts it:

> The home of the idea of a *medium* lies in the visual arts, and it used to be informative to know that a given medium is oil, or gouache or tempera or dry point or marble...because each of these media had characteristic possibilities, an implied range of handling and result. The idea of a medium is not simply to have a physical material, but a material-in-certain-characteristic-applications.

To fully understand this notion of a *medium* as it applies to dance, it is important to recognise that it operates at two related levels, both having a dependence on the notion of a masterwork. Just what Cavell means (and why he is right) can be brought out clearly when we consider the logic of *evaluating* a particular dance movement. For when we evaluate, we in effect point to features of what is going on which we see as important or valuable — or, equally, malign — to the performance of whatever it is. To put that another way, certain things have the status of *reasons* for any judgement we make, and we would justify that judgement in terms of those reasons. For what *sorts* of thing can acquire the status of reasons? What *sorts* of features are valuable? In answering this question, we should bear in mind that the reasons at issue are *dance reasons*, that the value at issue is *dance value*. So to present reasons of, say, biomechanical value would be beside the point.

Now, how can any feature of a particular movement sequence acquire that status of a *dance reason*? The reply must be that it acquires this status by reference to what has gone before in dance — that is, to dance practice. But where do we encounter dance practice? And we encounter such practice (and learn to understand it) when we encounter masterworks.

Not, of course, that slavish adherence to practices of the past is prescribed by this recognition: the work of the revolutionary too is rendered intelligible by reference to what has happened before, against which it is a reaction. So if we ask about our appraisal of what understanding in dance is, we see it depends on dance reasons — and those in turn depend on the employment (in our coming to understand dances) of masterworks.

If, in these ways, the notion of a *medium* is crucial for our appreciation of dances, it is equally crucial in relation to the creation of dances. For learning a technique is not, merely, learning to perform certain movements. It is learning to perform them, at the least, so that in the context of a dance constructed *within* that technique, they have a certain 'emotional' value. The audience for dance in that technique — say, Graham technique — comes to understand a particular sequence of action in that technique as typically having a certain importance. Indeed, the ability of the audience to understand (or *decipher*; see *UD:* Ch. 9) the movements depends, in ways urged above, on just this relation to what that audience is familiar with. And, of course, that audience is familiar with our masterworks. It is from *them* that the audience learns the expressive potential of patterns of movement.

I am urging, then, that central to the understanding of dances is seeing the technique-elements that they involve as the *material* of dance creation: that is, seeing these as part of the *medium* (in the sense explored here) of dance. For they are the 'material-in-certain-characteristic-applications' (Cavell, 1969: 221) identified earlier as what the word 'medium' means in this context. In this way, masterworks have roles at two very clear levels. First, they operate at the level of understanding. So that making sense of works that others have choreographed depends on seeing those works in some, perhaps quite subtle, relation to our masterworks. Often this relation will be fairly easily expressed in technical terms. So that, for example, if I have a good grasp of a number of works employing Graham technique, some works by Merce Cunningham may become intelligible to me: broadly those where his technique is not so different from Graham's. And, as I spend time studying other of Cunningham's works, the degree to which they start to operate as masterworks for me may mean that, progressively, I come to understand more and more works which employ technical devices different from those with which I am familiar (McFee, 1978: Ch. 2).

But there is another level at which the notion of the masterwork has a major application for us. Imagine a dance teacher looking for *material* from which to construct dances, say for children (or equally imagine the teacher planning to allow the children choreographic freedom and wondering how best to prepare them for this adventure). Now the technical resources of masterworks plug-in to this search in a very direct way. Thus, wishing to get my pupils to consider the evocative nature of dances, I might show them the video of Martha Graham's *Lamentation* (1930). In this way, I would be introducing them to a *masterwork*, to some technical resources and also giving them potential material (building-blocks) for their own choreography. Equally, I might see the advantage in offering them the dance artist — someone who could explore segments of the repertoire with them, discuss the production values of those elements and not only teach the technical aspects but (perhaps) demonstrate them too! Here the dance artist functions as a kind of super-interactive video. Yet this is not intended to be a derogatory remark. On the contrary, it identifies exactly what the dance artist is offering us in education: it is knowledge of the repertoire plus technical expertise in demonstrating and explaining that repertoire.

The descriptions given above may generate two questions which, though related, tend in almost opposite directions. The first question is 'What has any of this has to do with education?'. That really asks both 'What educational value is being inculcated?', and 'Why can't it be done, or done to as high a standard, by the dance teacher?'. These amount to asking why the dance artist in education is desirable. The other line of interrogation asks why anything *other* than the dance artist is desirable: what, in effect, has the teacher to offer?

In fact, the response to both questions is that *we* have no real basis for answering either of them. Our philosophical investigations alone cannot determine, to take them in reverse order, why the dance artist might not do it all; although, as noted earlier (pp. 77–8), we recognise at least two different roles here, and suspect that the time taken for adequate training for each will tend to preclude adequate training in the other. Thus there may be good *practical* reasons why the scope of the dance artist is different from that of a dance teacher. Indeed, since the dance artist's value depends on a grasp of masterworks, we an imagine such a grasp being gradually attenuated (or just fading away) if that person spends all or most of his or her time out of the repertoire setting, teaching children. So, pedagogically, we recognise the important differentiation of the two roles. Moreover, we have not suggested at all that dance education consists *solely* in the interaction with repertoire and technique that the dance artist has to offer.

On the other question, the first one, again the answer is a pragmatic, pedagogic one. For, of course, it *may* be possible to deliver the understanding of repertoire and its connection with technique as offered by the dance artist, but to deliver it through some other means: for example, through intensive use of video. Again, from our *philosophical* point of view, there seems no reason to prefer one to the other. But, of course, having on-site a body who can genuinely demonstrate, who can explain, answer questions, and break the repertoire into the elements as conceived by its repertory presenters (as opposed to the divisions that the dance teacher might discern) — all of this seems highly advantageous. Thus it seems likely that a distinctive role might be developed for the dance artist. (Notice, though, it may require skills not required of someone who is solely a *dancer* in a professional company.)

Conclusion

In this chapter we have explored the notion of a dance artist in education, and the role that such a dance artist might have in dance teaching for children. Our conclusion has focused on the role of masterworks for the understanding of dance. Indeed, a satisfactory grounding in masterworks achieved in some *other* way might be a suitable alternative to the role of dance artists in education. So that one policy were might insist that one or other of these should be a part of children's dance experience (that is, of their educational experience more generally). For then I imagine that, once the calculations were done accurately, the provision of dance artists for educational purposes would be a money-saving device compared to the provision of adequate facilities for the sorts of, say, video-based investigations which would be required as an alternative. None of this is to our philosophical point. What this chapter should demonstrate is the importance, if the artistic account of dance education is adopted, of the notion of *masterworks*, and the potential role of the dance artist in education in the 'delivery' of those masterworks to pupils in schools.

Chapter 9

Understanding Dance:
the Role of Dance Criticism

Introduction

This chapter lays out an account of understanding dance, and in particular of dance criticism, which presents one aspect of our defence of the artistic account of dance education. For, as we will see, both considering the work of established critics, and learning to do dance criticism, contribute to one's coming to understand dances. As this is a topic on which I have written extensively elsewhere (*UD*: Chs 5, 6 and 7), the presentation here is intended simply as a sketch of major considerations and conclusions.

Two points should be made immediately. First, I am using the word 'criticism' in a slightly more extended use than it is sometimes given in English. As Richard Wollheim (1980b: 185) has noted, English has no general word to cover our appreciation, judgement, comment etc. on the arts — the word 'criticism' is about as close as we get. So I speak of *criticism* in this encompassing sense of the word. Second, criticism in this sense is done both formally — by professional critics such as (in the case of dance) Marcia Siegel — and also informally, by us all, when (say) in the bar during the interval in a dance programme we discuss what we have seen. So criticism, in the sense intended here, is not solely the province of the professional.

Criticism as noticing

In this work I will urge a view of criticism — sometimes called a perceptualist view (Shusterman, 1981) — which suggests that criticism should be thought of as a kind of *noticing*; the noticing of critically relevant features. This idea has a number of related aspects. First, *noticing*, like any perceptual mode, is concept-mediated: what one can *notice* depends on the concepts one has. Second, *noticing* takes us a little further than *just* seeing. If I look at a crowd of people which includes Uncle Harry, then in a sense I see Uncle Harry, but I may well not notice him. Third, *noticing* is always the noticing of *features*, in this case features of the dance. One cannot *notice* what is not *there*; but what is there may not be entirely obvious. Thus conceiving of criticism as a kind of noticing pushes our attention onto the dance under consideration, in an appropriate way. A useful illustration of this point could come from one of the multiple-figures beloved of psychologists (see figure).

Here, what we can say — for example, that it depicts a young woman with a hat or an old crone — depends upon the public features of the design; and on our *taking* each in a certain way. So that a certain mark is the line of a jaw, for example. Seeing the mark in *that* way justifies the claim that a young woman is depicted. Thus the attention is specifically *on* the design: and this would be equally so if the design were claimed to be the crone, and the mark to be part of her nose.

A fourth feature concerns *what* is to be noticed (on this model). Of course, no specification of *kinds* of item can be given — it is not a matter of looking for particular movements, say. Any general remarks one might make (such as instructions to look for line, grace, unity etc.) would be unhelpfully vague. For what precisely, say, 'unity' means in the context of a particular dance may differ from what it amounts to in respect of another dance. However, one remark, with two dimensions, can clearly help us understand what is noticed: it is that criticism is a matter of noticing *critically relevant* features. This point must be amplified by drawing a contrast between two kinds of critical relevance. The first concerns the way in which we see something *in* the work in a certain way: as when Marcia Siegel (1977: 200), discussing Martha Graham's *Deaths and Entrances* (1943), remarks that we can see 'three women trapped by their own indecisiveness and gentility. The women fondle objects that seem to suggest action, but they're unable to act'. Our attention is directed to what the women do (fondle certain objects) and we are invited to get an insight into the *detail* of the dance — to focus on, in this section, the trapping forces of indecision and gentility. So the features pointed to — the actions of the women — are critically relevant when seen in this way because they allow us insight into this section of the dance. (This also happens, too, when a formal relation is pointed out.)

The second kind of critical relevance concerns us seeing the work as a whole in a particular way. So that when Marcia Siegel tells us that Joan of Arc in Martha Graham's *Seraphic Dialogue* 'enacts her interior struggles, doubts and spiritual joy' (1977: 205), or that 'In Graham's universe, Joan wins her own beatification' (p. 206), we are invited to see the whole work in a certain way, emphasising its 'cosmic' aspect.

And of course the contrast between these two kinds of critical relevance need not be sharp. Sometimes identifying a particular feature both helps us to see the work in a certain way and to see a particular part of it in a certain way. It is this idea of *critical relevance* which will be used to rule out, as playing a part in your criticism, remarks which are *true* of particular dances but — as we might think — do not contribute to our understanding of them. So that, for example, it may well be *true* that the soloist performing Martha Graham's *Lamentation* had a boiled egg for breakfast. But so far this does not help us to see any aspect of the work in a different way or to see the work as a whole in a different way: it is not critically relevant. Perhaps one can imagine a situation in which it *was* of critical relevance: for example, when it explained the dancer's being able to do certain movements. Frankly, this might seem a little unlikely. But the major thoughts here are, first, that there *is* such a constraint on critical relevance and, second, that one should not *prescribe,* in advance of seeing an actual example, what might and what might not be of critical relevance.

A fifth factor here takes the form of what, following Richard Wollheim (1983), I spoke of as a 'restrictive proviso', which sets limits on the acceptability of any interpretation of a dance (*UD*: 139–45). The proviso is that nothing is critically relevant *merely* because it allows some change in understanding — although that is required: further, it must lead to a *correct* or *acceptable* interpretation of the dance. Thus this proviso *restricts* what might count as a genuine interpretation of a dance. Such an interpretation must be *justifiable* in terms of how the dance is understood, not simply be a *possible* way of thinking about the dance. This factor is important for two reasons. First, it means that not just *any* (seemingly) critically relevant remark will actually be so. Second, it requires us to show what are and what are not *acceptable* interpretations (in this sense) of the dance. And that takes us forward to the discussion, later in this chapter (see pp. 98–9), of the objectivity of interpretation. For, as we will see (and drawing on the discussion of institutional accounts of dance in Chapter 3), questions about the acceptability of interpretations are, at bottom, dance-critical questions.

Finally — our sixth factor — modelling criticism as a kind of *noticing* (that is, on a perceptual mode) involves us in an *extended* version of the perceptual. This point is most easily brought out in respect of literature: the verb 'to read' is not a perceptual verb at all. However, it does not seem to me wide of the mark to think of reading as involving just the kind of noticing I am describing. Applied to dance, this point means, for example, that we must accept that one *sees* relationships in dance (that is, one notices them if one has the appropriate concepts, training etc.); and that dances have *perceptual* properties in virtue of their art status which might conflict with other properties ascribable to them. For example, if we think of the *lightness* of a particular dancer, that is a kind of lightness appropriate to dance as an art — a kind of perceived lightness — and remarking on that lightness is not denying that, for example, the dancer herself weighs 130 pounds.

These six remarks take us some way towards understanding what it would mean to model criticism as a kind of noticing. I will add two further comments. The first is that, as far as is possible, this account is not intended to be revisionary: it is intended as a description of what critics presently *do*, whether or not they would *say* that this is what they do. Second, it is intended as an account of what critics *must do*, or of what they *centrally* do, leaving open the question of whether there are other things which (as a matter of fact) they do as well. So that, in contrast to some theorists (Shusterman, 1981), I *am* urging that a 'noticing-type' account of criticism should cover all the central aspects of criticism; but I accept that, for example, giving a general history of a dance may be something a critic legitimately does yet, if it has no critical relevance in the sense described above, it is not part of what that critic does *centrally*: and hence not part of what I am describing here.

Not checklists or rules

It is worth briefly putting aside two mistaken accounts of the nature of criticism since both show us something revealing (*UD*: 131–4). Sometimes criticism is conceived of as involving the use of a checklist, or set of 'criteria', in terms of which an object is appraised. It is fairly easy to see that such a model renders criticism both impossible and irrelevant. For if criticism is to be understood in this way, the checklist itself must be easy to apply.

As we have seen, however, standard features which might be on such a checklist — such as originality, or unity — may amount to something different in different cases. Thus it is not simply a matter of using the checklist as some kind of template when considering the dance: at best, the checklist provides some useful terms which one might apply in one's criticism. But then the real criticism consists in seeing how those concepts apply in *this* case. The criticism takes place *outside* the use of the checklist. Moreover, a checklist of this sort — if it is specific enough to be of any use at all — will seem to preclude originality on the part of the artist: if one has a checklist for classical ballet (imagine this happening at a particular time) then dances employing Graham technique would be obviously flawed in certain key ways (toes not pointed, for example). But this shows, of course, the inadequacy of the checklist rather than anything about the dance. And, although this is a drastic example, the same point applies in respect of *any* checklist. It represents a certain moment of thinking about the nature of the art form, rather than being something which applies across all time.

Two points must be added. First, we have seen *some* use of a checklist — as providing the sorts of general concepts under which the work might be interpreted: as we might say, as providing concepts appropriate to our noticing features of the work. So the possession of a candidate checklist might be no bad thing (for example, the one that the Assessment of Performance Unit produced: APU, 1983: 12). But it must not *function* as a checklist: one does not use it to *determine* the artistic value of the dance. Rather, it provides some helpful hints and reminders in determining that merit. Secondly, we have seen how this characteristic is, as it were, *explicit* in most checklists: they present only broad concepts, the application of which to a particular dance must be *interpreted* by the critic. Thus the model of a *fixed* set of characteristics, which one simply ticks off, does not apply. Here I am arguing, of course, against a certain *model* of criticism. That is to say, I am arguing that checklists, such as that provided by the assessment of performance unit, should not be taken *too seriously*. They are one of the tools which might be employed by a *sensitive critic* — but, I urge, that critic is simply noticing artistically relevant features.

A comparable mistake involves seeing criticism as involving the application of certain rules[1], rules for artistic merit. The simplest cases here might be those which, since Aristotle (1965: 40–51), have been drawn up in respect of tragedy: for example, that tragedies should have unity of time, place, etc. (see also Shusterman, 1981). Such rules, if we had them, would be subject to the same criticisms as applied to checklists. For *how* are those rules to be applied? What do they amount to in the case of a particular artwork? To continue with the drama example, when precisely do we have unity of time? Since this is a matter for interpretation, the rule clearly leaves considerable leeway: it does not determine what the critic must do or say. Equally, the rigorous application of such rules precludes originality or creativity. Precisely *why* is unity of time so important for a tragedy? Surely we can imagine (and today have examples of) tragedies which break this 'rule'. Thus such rules fare no better than our proposed checklists or criteria. Suitably understood, such rules might be of some *use* — they might help one focus on the artistically relevant, for example. What they would not do, of course, is provide an uncontestable basis for criticism.

There is, however, a further difficulty for the view of criticism as based on the application of rules. (As we will see, there is a broad parallel in the case of the checklist-view too.) Let us ask *why* it is thought that the *rules* are essential. One standard reply is that, without some such rule, one cannot move from one's *description* of the work to some general *evaluation* or *appreciation* of it. That is to say, it is argued that between one's noticing of certain features in the work and one's judgement of the work, there is an *inferential*[2] step. Consider a very simple case, continuing our tragedy example. Step 1: I notice that a particular play has unity of place. Step 2: I bring to mind the rule 'all tragedies must have unity of place'. Now, Step 3, I can arrive at a conclusion — in this case it may be the weak conclusion that what I have in front of me *could* be a tragedy. But nonetheless I have arrived at that conclusion by employing a factual, descriptive first step, and a general, evaluative, and rule-expressing second step (Ground, 1989: 92–3).

There are two difficulties with such a view. The first concerns the *appropriateness* of such a deductive[3] model for critical thinking (see McFee, 1990; also Davies, 1990). But the second difficulty is more fundamental. For *why* is it necessary to invoke a rule here? A standard reply would be that one needs a rule to get from the judgement that, say, the drama has unity of place to the conclusion about its possible status as a tragedy. Put more generally, the thesis would be that one must move from judgements to conclusions via rules. But if this is so, we will need not just the rule, but a rule about the implementation of that rule. And a rule about the implementation of that rule. And so on indefinitely. Thus, by its own lights, this position requires not just *one* rule for any critical judgement, but an infinite number of them. Of course, its defenders will urge that *one rule is enough*. They will say that, with one rule, we can move from our observation of the dance or drama to our conclusion. Yet when they claim that if the *other* rules are not necessary, the one that they are insisting on fares no better. If they insist we can do with *almost* no rules, we should go further and insist that we can do without *any*!

The conclusion to reach, then, is that promised: that neither a model of art criticism based on a check-list or a model based on rules will correctly account for the nature of critical activity. This conclusion should move us towards the view of criticism as noticing, as urged here.

Criticism and meaning

There remain many important questions concerning our understanding of criticism as a king of *noticing*, the noticing of artistically relevant features. Some of those will be considered in succeeding sections of this chapter. In particular, the question of the objectivity of criticism will be treated briefly (pp. 98–9). Here, I wish to turn to the *importance* of criticism. For, on some traditional views, dance criticism is seen as some kind of 'froth' on dance study, an unnecessary adjunct to the practice of dance. That view will tend to support *anti-intellectualism* in respect of dance studies, and also subjectivist claims about the priority of dance practice. It is important, therefore, that the artistic account combats such assertions.

The tool to be used here to combat such claims has two components. The first is a claim about dances as *meaningful* or *meaning-bearing*. By this I intend that dances are the sorts of things that we make sense of or understand. Indeed, this chapter (like my other book) is explicitly entitled 'understanding dance'. Moreover, one regularly hears, in discussions of dance performances, remarks such as 'I didn't understand the second piece', 'I had trouble making sense of that last section', with the implied conclusion that other parts were understood or were not problematic in these ways. So, to put that technically, I am urging that, since dances are the sorts of things we *understand* (to the degree to which we do in any practical case), and since meaning and understanding are correlative notions, it follows that dances should be thought of as meaningful or meaning-bearing.

The second prong concerns the way in which meaning is to be understood. Here I draw on a slogan from Wittgenstein (1974: 69): 'meaning is what explanation of meaning explains'. To put that another way, we should look not to fixed objects, *meanings*, but to our practice of *explaining meaning* when asked about it (*UD*: 113-4). This slogan is designed, first and foremost, to deal with meaning in respect of language. So that, perplexed by the word 'evanescent' you ask me what it means. I then offer an explanation which takes away your perplexity: I have given you the meaning of that word. Notice two characteristics here. First, such explanations occur *in response to perplexities*: I explain the meaning because you ask for it, or because you need to understand it (even if you have not yet asked). Second, the standard for adequacy (one might even say completeness: see Cavell, 1981b: 37) is that I deal with *your* perplexity. There is no suggestion that I must say *all* that I could say — far less *all* that could be said.

My proposal, then, is to use this Wittgensteinian slogan in the case of the meaning of dances. The two characteristics just noted would then apply. We would no longer think of the dance work as having some complete meaning, which a greater elaboration might pick out, and we would have a way of explaining the appeal of certain dances for me: they pose perplexities or resolve them, or some such. But what perplexities? Our answer, as one might expect (see Chapter 4), is 'perplexities in respect of life-issues'.

So I am urging that the meaning of dances is what is explained in the explanation of the meaning of dances, applying my Wittgensteinian slogan to dance. But who explains dances to us? Well, explanation in this sense was the job attributed to critics at the beginning of this chapter. So we look for the meanings of dances in the works of critics, both formal and informal. But if we wish for particular enlightenment, perhaps we will prefer the works of the formal or professional critics.

Adopting this Wittgensteinian slogan has a number of related advantages. First, it directs our attention to something public and tangible: the explanation of meaning. In this way it avoids the confusion implicit in looking for mysterious entities, *meanings*, somehow 'out there' beyond human practices. Second, it allows us to put aside what I shall call *associations* (see p. 97). Third, it makes meaning something that is made by human beings: hence something which human beings do know in typical cases, and moreover must know. The idea of forever and in principle inaccessible meanings is obviously excluded. A meaning which *could not* be explained would, on this account, be no meaning at all. That point is easy to misunderstand. For, while critics' work *typically* consists of strings of words in sentences, there is no requirement here that our explanations of meaning be *solely* in this form. They could include, for example, gestures, demonstrations and so on, as well. In this way, then, we have an account of meaning for dances which connects with human practices and makes dances inherently the kinds of things it is in principle possible to understand. Of course, that requirement for an *in principle* understanding does not take us very far: we will still need to develop skills and sensitivities in order to *actually* do the relevant understanding.

The point of this section has been to show how dance may be viewed as meaningful, and how that meaning is to be understood. We have seen the importance of dance criticism for that meaning. If this point is conceded, dance criticism is a central rather than a peripheral element in dance studies: and hence, one might think, in dance education.

The meaning of a dance

In this section I will combat two misunderstandings concerning the idea of meaning. The first is that there is *just one* meaning for any particular dance — say, Christopher Bruce's *Black Angels*. The second concerns a particular way of going *beyond* meaning for a dance into what I shall call 'association'.

It might seem that the discussion in the previous section had, as an outcome, the thought that there is just *one* meaning for a particular dance. In the case of Christopher Bruce's *Black Angels* it might even be that one thought that criticism of the dance was encapsulated in Richard Austin's excellent book *Birth of Ballet* (Austin, 1976). But this view is mistaken in at least three ways. First, and both most contentiously and most abstractly, we cannot expect critical judgement to simply stand still if we acknowledge (as we did in Chapter 4) that art in general (dance in particular) has an historical character. Second, we recognise that, as with the explanation of a word, different people may need to be told different things. Hence what is *explained* will differ in the different cases. If each of these explanations is seen as complete, we have a diversity within dance meaning. This point is contentious. Perhaps all the explanations could be somehow *added together* to produce one, THE, meaning. What seems correct in that thought is that, following literary theorists[4], it seems right to think of the meaning of the dance as its 'collected criticism'. Third, we have to consider the possibility that the explanations of dances are actually incompatible. (Consider, for example, a Lacanian feminist 'reading' of a dance and an interpretation by a more 'traditional' critic, such as Marcia Siegel.) In this case, it would *not* be possible for them to be added together, even if one wanted to. These considerations lead me, at least, to a more diffuse or pluralistic conception of the meaning of the dance.

The other area of confusion here concerns the notion of what I am calling *association*. Suppose that at a performance of a particular dance, I meet a particularly attractive and interesting woman. That dance might forever in my mind be *associated* with the woman in ways which affect what I would say about the dance. Yet those remarks are clearly not about the dance itself — they depend upon the associations I am making, associations which depend on my special circumstances of meeting the woman at that performance. It would obviously be a mistake to include such associative remarks in one's criticism. Conversely, any remarks 'convicted' of being associative in this way are for that reason not of critical relevance. The scope of associative remarks might difficult to define particularly closely. Consider, for example, the fact that a particular stager puts on *Swan Lake*. Well, if I mention it in my criticism only because I have enjoyed his work in the past, but have nothing to say in respect of *this performance*, it seems right to dismiss my remarks as mere association. If, by contrast, it is his achievements in past works which plug into this one and allow me to say something different either about the work as a whole or about some aspect of it then, by the test developed earlier, my remarks are of critical relevance: and hence are not mere association.

This, of course, is how to deal with our remarks about, say, the profit that a particular performance makes, or the stars that it encompasses. Anything which is not involved in the taking of artistic interest in the dance, but which critics say about it, is association in this sense. And that means it is not part of the meaning of the dance.

One way of putting this point would be to say that associative remarks are not remarks about *the dance itself*. Another way would be to say that associative are *external* to the dance itself. But this intrinsic/extrinsic contrast is very hard to draw (*UD*: Ch. 6). Nevertheless, it is of fundamental importance. To see this, we need only turn our attention in more detail to our key notion — the notion of explanation. For, recall, we are to explicate meaning in terms of explaining. But do some remarks genuinely constitute an explanation, and not something else? Suppose I get you to understand the meaning of a word by giving you some drug or by torturing you, or some such: have I explained that word to you? Well, I have got you to understand it (in the example as given); equally, I have not *explained* it to you. My procedure has not been a *rational* one, drawing on appropriate or relevant reasons. A danger in allowing association is that what is connected merely by association is, for these purposes, not a reason-based characteristic.

Objectivity and institutionalism

We have now arrived at a crucial point. For our account of criticism has developed in such a way as to focus our attention on the objectivity or dependability of criticism. That issue surfaced briefly earlier (p. 91), with the need for a *restrictive proviso* on our account of criticism. It is also here sharply in the need to distinguish reliably between meaning and association. There is a third way to bring out the problem, and a revealing one: it concerns the idea of *reading-into* (*UD*: Ch. 6). For one danger to be avoided in criticism is the danger of *arbitrariness* — of reading-in to a work something which is not *there*. But what is there? In the case of a dance, we have an assemblage of moving bodies, in costumes, probably to music, in a particular space, staged by a certain person or group of people, choreographed by a certain person or group of people, in a certain tradition. That is to say, we have a highly complex object. What features *precisely* does the object have? Which of them are critically relevant?

A full answer would have at least two dimensions. The first would look at the dependability of the application of our concepts. It would draw on what is sometimes called the Private Language Argument[5]. The upshot of such a consideration would be that our judgements cannot be entirely arbitrary. However, since this argument does not achieve all that we require (*UD*: 144–5), I shall not consider it here[6]. The second dimension, though, draws on ideas already introduced (in Chapter 4). Suppose that one accepts a broadly institutional account of the nature of art. That is to say, one accepts that, in order to be art-type dance, an object must receive *other-acclamation* from the Republic of Dance. If we now ask what guarantee have we for avoiding the charge of arbitrariness, our guarantee lies in the activity of the institution. It functions as an *authoritative body* in terms of our judgements of art works. In practice, this means that when one learns about dance, one does so from acknowledge examples of dance (what are sometimes called *exemplars*; see Baker & Hacker, 1980: 23–46), together with informed discussion and the like. One learns how to explain dance, how to discuss it: one learns how to go on in such discussions or arguments (Cavell, 1969: 92). And these things are learned as appropriate topics for rational debate within a critical tradition. This gives us, in effect, a guideline for dealing with the charge of arbitrariness. It suggests that any interpretation will be acceptable just in that case where informed critical theory or informed dance theory of the time takes it to be acceptable. Equally, it will be arbitrary, or involve reading-in, just in those cases where the comparable informed theory takes it to be so. In this way, then, we secure the objectivity of critical judgement.

Of course, someone who rejected the institutional account of art would not have dealt with this problem. However, at the least, they would have identified a *major problem* to be dealt with. It will not do to leave critical judgement entirely unsupported. Those who reject an institutional account of art will need to look elsewhere for such support.

Criticism and experience

It might be urged that my emphasis on *understanding* dance is misdirected. For is it not true that dance is something that we *experience*, intimately connected with our feelings: and is this not true, as it were, *first and foremost*? So the objection would be that my account is unduly rationalistic.

My reply has two parts. First, and briefest, I deny the hard-and-fast contrast between feeling or emotion and understanding implicit in the claim. Both are large areas in human experience and, while there may be *places* of contrast, a part of my general thesis is that the understanding of art is not one of them. In that way, then, my conception of the rationality of the experience of dance is — perhaps — less *rationalistic* than it might be thought to be.

The second point partly explains and partly fills-out the first. For, as we have recognised for some time, the experience is concept-mediated. Hence, *one* way of thinking about experiences — feelings, emotions, etc. — is in terms of the concepts *under which* they are experienced (and in the case of emotions, also their *objects*). So our study of feelings is incorporated simply by considering these concepts. However, the mere possession of concepts is not enough. One must be able to *mobilise* them (Wollheim, 1986: 46) in one's experience. That is to say, one has to be able to *use* one's concepts. The basic idea here will be familiar to any of those who have studies literary criticism and, having learned, say, from a teacher, the many virtues of a particular poem, still cannot *see* it as a good poem. As we might say, they cannot *notice* those features in the work for themselves. They may have the concepts, but they are unable to *mobilise* them. A study of the mobilisation of concepts would, of course, be of considerable benefit here. In its absence, we have a realistic picture of criticism simply by focusing on the concepts and letting the mobilisation take care of itself. We also have a way of explaining why, even though I can learn concepts from Marcia Siegel, my criticism of dance is less perceptive than hers: she can regularly mobilise those concepts in her experience — at best I can do it only occasionally.

A further consideration which might be raised (here briefly) also concerns the nature of rationality. It has been sometimes assumed that the power of argument is compelling in a way unrelated to the feelings of people. None-theless, there is an element of mistake in such a view. As Lewis Carroll ([1894] 1973: 1104–8) pointed out, there is nothing *compelling* to an argument beyond what someone reading can *see* as compelling. In Carroll's presentation, one character, in frustration with his opponent failing to acknowledge what he takes to be compelling arguments, urges that 'Logic would take you by the throat, and *force* you to do it' ([1894] 1973: 1107). But there is no *Logic* in this sense: there are only people's practices. And it is a fact about people (well, anyway, most people) that they can *see* arguments as compelling. It is this ability or capacity which allows us to formalise (acceptable) arguments through systems of logic. That capacity respects certain general rules or 'Logical Laws'. We do recognise, for example, that you say nothing if you contradict yourself. This can then be enshrined in a law of non-contradiction. One danger here, a danger associated with excessive rationalism, is in thinking that this 'Logical Law' takes us far beyond the practice of argument as employed by actual human beings. Our safeguard will be to restrict our claims on behalf of Logic or Reason to the actual practice of reasoning (Baker, 1988: xiv–xvii).

The upshot: criticism and dance education

The upshot of the argument in this chapter should be clear by now. It has been urged that critical thinking is central rather than peripheral to the nature of dance: it is where we go to find the *meaning* of dances (given our commitment to the Wittgensteinian slogan). As a result, dance criticism must have a *central* place in dance education. After all, we need to teach pupils to *understand* dances — and that is equivalent to teaching them dance criticism, in our wide sense of the word 'criticism'. Further, we need to teach them the concepts appropriate to such criticism: we need to teach them the kind of noticing that is criticism. To do this, we need to show them *exemplars*. That is, we need to come up with examples of dances and the associated criticism. And doing this will be bringing dance criticism as an object — say, the criticisms of Marcia Siegel and such like authors — into centre stage for dance education.

PART III

CONTRASTING ACCOUNTS

Chapter 10

Dance as 'Aestheticised Movement'

Introduction

This chapter begins Part III, in which I shall consider three positions, each running counter to the artistic account. Adopting all or any of these positions might undermine the artistic account by rejecting its central ideas of art or by robbing it of practical value: that is, by removing any sense in which it points to *kinds* of dance to be studied.

I begin that investigation by considering an attitude which — I shall argue — is commonly adopted by those with a strong, if uncritical, adherence to the importance of dance. I shall consider this view in a fairly abstract way, but will focus on three (arguable) examples of the view to avoid 'straw men'. These do represent typical varieties of the view at issue. The view concerns the nature of dance: in particular, the relationship between dance-status and educational value. The view might be briefly summarised in the slogan that dance is just *aestheticised movement*. A typical example might be the following (Hirst, 1989: 41):

> Dance is simply the art form of movement. It comes about when movement of any kind is so aestheticised that the prime intention becomes the presentation of aesthetic form.

There are clearly two related ideas in that passage. The first, with which we have no quarrel, is to emphasise the idea of *art*. The second seems more problematic: for it seems to *explain* art-status in terms of the aestheticising of movement.

It seems important to distinguish between three kinds of view here, each of which will considered later in the chapter. First, we consider the aestheticising of movement in terms of a certain *view* or *perspective* taken on movement. Second, we consider this as a concern with a special *kind* of movement: that is to say, where aestheticising *transforms* the movement. Here we should ask 'Transformed how, and into what?'. Third, we consider the view that aestheticising creates — not just dance — but a special *kind* or *type* of dance (educational dance) of particular concern to us.

In what follows I begin by considering the first two of these positions, identifying a crucial confusion between the transforming of movement and the taking of a certain view of that movement. Next I will consider the importance of such transforming: in particular, the question 'transformed into what?'. Then I will look at the implications for education of taking either of these views of the nature of dance. Finally, having considered some variants in which a broadly similar view might occur, I will look briefly at the notion of a uniquely 'educational dance'.

A crucial confusion

As we saw, Paul Hirst's explained dance *as an art form* in terms of its being 'the aestheticising of movement'. A key issue here will be *how* the expressions 'aestheticised movement' or 'the aestheticising of movement' are to be understood. Equally, these are notions with which it is easy to confuse oneself (one might even wonder if Professor Hirst played fast and loose with it; see McFee, 1989a), using whatever meaning/sense best suits one's purpose. It is important, therefore, to identify a central area of confusion. To do this, notice two kinds of cases which might be considered. The first case: I see a person sweeping in a graceful, elegant, fluid etc. way, and so I concentrate on the grace, line etc. of the movement. Now, I have lost interest in the purposive dimension of the activity: I have *aestheticised* it. So I am making an *aesthetic* judgement in respect of that bodily movement. Notice, though, that it is still sweeping: and if the room is not cleaned, it is bad sweeping, however graceful. In this case, although we are taking an aesthetic interest in the movement, it is central to our position that this is still genuine *sweeping* — in particular, that it is not dance. To put that point in the jargon of Chapter 2, we are taking an *aesthetic interest* (or a *merely* aesthetic interest) in the sweeping: we are not taking an *artistic interest* in it. Nor would it be possible to do so — since that sweeping is not an appropriate object of artistic interest. We are considering some common sweeping, not an art work.

A second case would be this: having seen the sweeping above, I decide to use sweeping as a *motif* in a dance I am making. Being literal-minded, I actually use a broom is my activity. I have aestheticised to sweeping. But now it is no longer sweeping at all. It has become dance. And this is so *even if* the stage ends up remarkably clean at the end of the activity. This second use of the term 'aestheticised' means that dance evolves in the aestheticisation of movement. In a typical case, it seems entirely appropriate to take an artistic interest in the activity just described. In this sense, we might well see dance as the aestheticising of movement. But clearly that is a very inexact way of putting the point. What goes on there is the *transformation* of the movement in question (the sweeping) into something else, namely dance. We no longer have a suitable object for aesthetic judgement or appreciation but, rather, have created an appropriate object of artistic appreciation.

Recognising these two difference accounts, each of which might be explained as 'aestheticising of movement', is recognising a fundamental problem. Each dimension could be considered independently. Asked how plausible it is to consider dance as the aestheticising of movement in the *first* of the two senses distinguished, it is easy to see that this idea has *no* plausibility whatsoever. Taking an aesthetic interest in sweeping does not make sweeping dance, any more than taking an aesthetic interest in rugby transforms that game into an art form. Indeed, our rationale for the artistic/aesthetic distinction is — in part — this kind of contrast. So, if we think of the aestheticising of movement along the lines of the first account, it will be inappropriate to regard *dance* as aestheticised movement. This point applies fairly widely. As I remarked elsewhere (*UD:* Ch. 2), taking an aesthetic interest in sport does not require 'translation' of the movement into something else. We are simply enjoying it in its context. And the criteria for success here are not aesthetic (or in the case of aesthetic sports, not wholly aesthetic; see Best, 1978a: Ch. 7). For example, the elegant Australian rugby player David Campese must score or set up tries or defend against them, etc., if he is to be successful. Success is internal to the *sport*; it is not artistic success. So we recognise that, insofar as aestheticising is equivalent to 'taking a view of' the activity, dance is *not* just aestheticised movement.

On the other hand, suitably understood, to see an activity as *dance* is indeed to 'aestheticise' it. That is to say, in our second case — where the activity is *transformed* into dance — it may be right to see this as aestheticising. This idea, though, is that it simply does not tell us enough. For now we must ask what makes the activity *dance*, rather than some *other* activity in which it is appropriate to take an aesthetic interest: for example, one of those *sports* where aesthetic interest is central (Best, 1978a: Ch. 7). In effect, we are asking 'Transformed into what?', the topic of our next section. But the transformation here must be transformation into the art form *dance*. For standard cases of *aesthetic interest* — for example our aesthetic interest in sport — does not involve transformation; moreover, it is not the sort of activity for which a central educational place is sought. If that were what one meant by the expression 'aestheticised movement' one would have lost much that is central to *my* understanding of dance; in particular there would be no need (and no place on such a conception) for the specialised movements of a dance technique.

The nature of the transformation

Suppose, in line with the second of the two cases described above, one sees movement as *transformed* into dance, and *sees* that transformation[1] in terms of aestheticisation. At one level, an adherent of the artistic account of dance education need not disagree. For now the movement becomes, in some way or other, *dance* — and its *dance* status explains its educational value or relevance. As it were, the movement of sweeping is transformed into (an element of) the art-form of dance. Then, of course, one needs to say quite a lot about art-forms. So this account by itself takes us no further. Even if we accept that *this* kind of aestheticising has the power to transform movement into dance, it still remains an open question whether (if at all) dance has any educational place. I am suggesting that one must give *some* answer to the question of what the arts in general (and dance in particular) have to offer in education. Thus *some* answer has to be given about the role of dance, if dance education is to be justified, or defended, or established. So far, speaking of dance simply as aestheticised movement is not responding on that point.

A useful way of continuing this discussion is to return to the details of the debate between Paul Hirst and myself (McFee, 1989a). My claim is that Hirst has offered no defence of dance if he has only defended dance as aestheticised movement: for, if the term 'aestheticised movement' is meant in the first sense, the value of the activity is still to be spelt out. In particular, whatever value obtains here has little or nothing to do with the *activity* of the movement itself. In contrast, if the term 'aestheticised movement' is meant in the second sense, no central (educational) value is yet articulated as residing there. We can see both these points by considering a view which contrasts with Professor Hirst's. Suppose one accepted, as Her Majesty's Inspectorate at one time seemed to (HMI, 1977), that education required experience of *the aesthetic*. Even if one interprets this as *bodily* education, gymnastics or synchronised swimming or diving will do just as well as dance: they all offer aestheticised understanding of a bodily sort. Once that point is accepted, dance education may as well pack up its tents. There can be no justification of a distinctive *dance* education if all that is required is aestheticising in that first sense. However, there is more to the issue than that. For Hirst *might* argue, in line with the remark of his quoted earlier (that dance is 'the art form of movement'; see Hirst, 1989: 41), that it is its *artistic* nature which justifies the educational place of dance. That is a way of re-stating the position of this text, so there is nothing with which to disagree. But Hirst now owes us an account of the educational relevance of the *artistic*: that will involve him saying a lot more about art, and about what makes *dance* an art form. In short, he will need to spell out the *artistic* nature of dance: in particular, he will need to say more than just that it is 'aestheticised movement'.

The implications

I wish, briefly, to record two major implications which follow from the preceding arguments. The first concerns the nature of dance. I have urged that, for educational purposes, finding dance as an *art-form* is crucial. This does something both to explain the place of dance-technique, since that is a characteristic of art-type dance, and to tie-in any justification of dance education with more general justifications of aesthetic education. By contrast, seeing dance as just another kind of *movement* (albeit as aestheticised movement) is, so far, not a way of bringing out its educational relevance at all. Worse, it offers no justification for the importance which should be placed on dance *technique*. For if the project were merely to find some movement, and aestheticise it, then — on the face of it — any movement is as good as any other. For these reasons, then, to think of dance as 'aestheticised movement' is to denigrate it. That formula says nothing interesting about dance. In particular, we have not distinguished dance from other activities in which we might with justice take an aesthetic interest.

As applied above, a second set of considerations militate against considering dance as 'aestheticised movement'. In essence, they cluster around the educational importance attributable to dance. (Of course, those who wish to deny dance any such educational importance might take succour from these matters). To see these points, ask two related questions. The first is 'What dance is to be performed?'; the second, 'Why should that dance be done?'. With the resources for answers restricted to the notion of *aestheticising*, neither question is answerable. Since any movement might be aestheticised, it follows that we cannot determine what dance should or should not be done: all looks equally plausible. Nor can we decide *why* a particular dance should be performed rather than some other, nor why any should be performed at all. If we are simply interested in movement which is *transformed* by aestheticising, we should ask ourselves why that transformation is thought important.

Again, we have an answer here, consisting in a reiteration of our artistic account. But, of course, that is another way of saying that dance is very much *more* than 'aestheticised movement' — in particular, it is an art form with all the value that the notion 'art' brings with it. (Here we have expanded our account of that value in terms of emotional education in respect of life-issues.)

Some variants

This section emphasises two theses: first, that the idea of dance as 'aestheticised movement' is not restricted to those ignorant of the history and nature of dance. So I shall cite two important theorists of dance, Betty Redfern and Peter Brinson, whose ideas *might* be interpreted in this way. I do not, of course, wish here to argue that these are *correct* readings of Redfern or Brinson. My point is to identify a way in which their writings *might* be read, and to urge that, if so read, they are mistaken. This leaves entirely open the question of whether or not this view is a *mis-reading*: my point is simply that, interpreted strictly literally, it is a plausible reading. (And, of course, it derives from my experience of how these works *have been* read by my students.) I should also add that these works were chosen for two related reasons. First, they have a certain justified currency. Second, they are better rather than worse examples from this field.

As our first example, consider a brief passage from Betty Redfern's *Dance, Art and Aesthetics*. Considering the 'great variety of forms and styles' which might occur under the general title 'dance', Redfern (1983: 6) notes: 'an aesthetic interest can extend — in principle, at least — to anything whatever, an account of such an interest does not require that it be specified in advance how a dance (say) might be classified'. This passage *could* be read to incorporate the *aesthetic interest* in reggae, disco etc. Its danger, though, is in finding a common *aesthetic* interest across dance: so that the distinctive characteristic of dance would be such an aesthetic interest. This would be a way of finding dance 'aestheticised movement'. Of course, Redfern's own account is far more subtle than this. For example, she quotes with approval Timothy Binkley urging that 'aesthetic qualities are neither a necessary nor a sufficient condition of arthood' (Redfern, 1983: 44). Nonetheless, her focus, in an important book, is on the *aesthetic* possibilities of the art form of dance: although she does not say this, it would not be unreasonable to read her account of dance in those terms. Indeed, the final chapter of the book, which discusses *aesthetic* appraisals, is partly a discussion of the art forms, but not wholly. Thus, to some readers, Redfern could appear as an advocate of the view under discussion.

A more extravagant example of the same difficulty — the difficulty that a writer may intend something quite different but be interpreted in a 'dance as aestheticised movement' fashion — occurs in respect of Peter Brinson's *Dance as Education*. The book begins with a statement of faith that 'Dancing … is part of human history, part of the history of human culture and part of the history of human communication' (Brinson, 1991: 3). Of course, it is far from clear what precisely what is intended by this. Nonetheless, the book plunges straight into a discussion of the dance as performed by the Royal Ballet (Brinson, 1991: 4) and numerous theatre companies. In this sense, Brinson offers us *no* account of the nature of dance. Nor, as we have argued, need he do so. The point, though, is that it is easy to read his later remarks about the characteristics of London Contemporary Dance, Rambert Dance Company, Royal Ballet etc. *as though* they were determined by these earlier remarks. And these earlier remarks themselves may lead inexorably to the conclusion that dance is movement in which one takes an aesthetic interest. For the very diversity of dance which Brinson (1991: 3) notes — to include 'the clog dance in Lancashire' as well as activities in 'dance halls and discos' — together with his focus on a dance culture as part of 'a popular, lively culture... forming and formed by majority taste' (Brinson, 1991: 137) will mean that what *is* dance is not readily distinguished from what is *called* dance. Asked what dance in a disco has in common with (art-type) dance for the theatre, it is easy to respond that both are movement viewed as aesthetic. Indeed, this thought is implicit in a number of places. For example, above the caption 'Other ways to dance' (Brinson, 1991: 71), we are shown Ghanaian dance being taught to school children, while the surrounding discussion centres on *kinaesthetic* understanding (*UD*: Ch. 13). But what makes this activity *dance* at all? It is movement in which an aesthetic interest is taken; and that *might* readily lead us to view dance as aestheticised movement. Indeed, if we consider later sections of Brinson's book, the temptation becomes even stronger. For Brinson (1991: 108) goes on to consider cases of 'community dance and mime', and it is easy to locate, within that idea, the thought that we have here the aestheticisation of movement drawing on community roots.

Brinson's own thinking *might* run in the opposite direction. Thus, for example, Brinson (1991: 117) writes: 'It follows that the grammar of community dance, however adapted to meet the needs of the community, will be enriched by reference to existing dance techniques and and other art forms'. Moreover, he clearly distinguishes dance from physical education on the basis that 'dance is an art and physical education is not'; he claims a distinctive *educational* importance for the arts (p. 70); and he cites with approval (p. 73) David Best's recognition of the inappropriateness of a *generic* conception of the arts, as discussed in the Appendix to Chapter 4. If he is consistent, these commitments will guarantee distinctively art-related account of dance. So careful readers of Brinson's book may not take his view to be a version of the 'dance as aestheticised movement' position. But they will be detail-conscious readers, not perhaps those who simply pick up the book as a source for an improved understanding of the concept of dance education. (We do see, though, a danger in simply *assuming* that the concept of dance is a clear one, one reason why here I have stressed the artistic character of the dance under discussion.)

The idea of educational dance

If we accept that dance is more than simply 'aestheticised movement', where does that leave us in respect of dance education? What must be acknowledged is that a much stronger account of dance will be'*required* for the recognition of the educational importance of dance. This point is significant here since some classic writing on Modern Educational Dance seems to urge that the educational relevance of dance lies in its aestheticisation of movement. For example, Joan Russell's *Modern Dance in Education* begins with a chapter on *movement*, which it refers to as 'an expressive art' (Russell, 1958: 18); while Laban's own *Modern Educational Dance* talks of the educational importance of the 'art of movement' (Laban, 1948: 7), which is taken to be synonymous with dance; and Valerie Preston's *Handbook for Modern Educational Dance* presents 'movement ideas ... [being] developed into the Art of Dance' (Preston-Dunlop, 1963: 130). In any of these cases, it is easy to see the transition from 'mere' movement to dance as one of aestheticisation.

The general conclusion in this section is that no dance is uniquely educational: a dance will only be intrinsically educational in virtue of its being (and to the extent that it is) an art. To suggest that conclusion I urge three points. The first is that, historically, the movement for *Modern Educational Dance* should be seen as an acceptable contribution to the *delivery* of dance education; as we might say, to *methods* of teaching based on child-centredness *and* a particular analysis of what was crucial in understanding dance movements. But the analysis was, at best, a secondary consideration. Giving up that analysis did not require that one give up the general teaching methods, although the details might then become more fudged. Some of this material is discussed by David Best (1985a: 66), who remarks that an emphasis on *free expression* works appropriately to remind us that 'there are attitudes to methods of teaching which can stifle individuality, imagination and a kind of self-confidence'. The educational dance movement was directed against such attitudes, both in general and specifically as they were thought to exist in the teaching of ballet and modern dance. Yet, as Best (1986: 66) notes, '*some* teaching of disciplines leads to restrictions on freedom, one does not respond by dropping *all* disciplines'. So correcting that pedagogic emphasis did not require the *abandonment* of technique for dance, in favour of the aestheticisation of movement.

The second point reiterates a consideration raised earlier: that if one urged the distinctive educational contribution of a particular kind of dance, that would itself need to be argued for. Further, any such argument would need to avoid giving a *purposive* account of dance (see Chapter 2). It is difficult to articulate an educational contribution for dance which is none-the-less intrinsic to the activity. By contrast, the artistic account draws on a general argument for the educational relevance of things artistic, and applies that argument to a specific case of dance. So that if one believed in Modern Educational Dance, for example, one would need to explain what precisely was *educational* about it.

The third point is the difficulty in giving a satisfactory answer there, if one thought of dance as aestheticised movement. To see this third point, let us return to the two cases presented initially — cases of sweeping. If we think of aestheticised movement in the first way, it can have no educational role. For the movement itself is of no significance: all that is important is how we choose to look at it — for that is what aestheticises it. Clearly this cannot be what is meant. But if we turn to the other account, we are still owed an explanation of what it is that makes the activity *dance* rather than something else. And, again, it seems unclear how this *alone* could be what generates its educational importance.

Conclusion

The conclusion to be reached from this chapter concerns our need for an explanation of the nature of dance which distinguishes it from the *merely* aestheticised, and — if such an explanation is to have educational 'bite' — it should pick-up not merely the *distinctiveness* of dance, but the *value* associated with that distinctiveness. For being different is not, of itself, any justification for a place in the school curriculum. In this vein, we have rejected the idea of dance as aestheticised movement and the idea of an 'aesthetic experience' justification for dance; as well as trampling over the artistic/aesthetic distinction, such justification will not provide a specific rationale for dance in education. For that reason, we should *hope* that position which generates it is not correct. Investigation then convinces us that this is so!

Chapter 11

Dance and Popular Culture

Introduction

To reprise, I am not claiming that artistic education exhausts dance education. The full richness of the anthropology of dance and the sociology of dance — not to mention the history of dance — is *not* of artistic concern: although it may well have a place within a 'complete' (Baker & Hacker, 1980: 78ff.) dance education. But I am urging that artistic education must be central to any dance education that wishes to avoid being swallowed by other 'disciplinary' enquiries or fields of knowledge, including physical education. For the distinctiveness of dance, from among other physical activities, lies in its being an *art form*. Further, if we couch our argument in terms of the experiences etc. of pupils, then what the arts have to offer (and dance from within the arts) is key. It *justifies* our insistence on the need for dance education.

But another source of insight is available here. For augmenting the artistic thrust is less straightforward than it might seem. For example, the key question for some anthropological investigations is 'Is this really dance?'. And this is no straightforward matter (*UD*: 284–92). So that, for example, Adrienne Kaeppler (1985: 92) comments: 'In many societies...there is no indigenous concept that can be adequately translated "dance"'. As a result, she does not write about dance *as such*, preferring to consider the 'movement dimension of separate activities' (p. 92) within the society. Another anthropologist, Spencer (1985: 38), comments: 'dance may be defined in whatever way seems most appropriate to the study of any specific situation or society'. Be this as it may in general, this cannot be the case if one's interest lies in studying *dance*, for then whether or not one is actually studying *dance* (and not something else) will be one of the points at issue. Of course, as Spencer (1985: 38) continues, 'Dance is not an entity in itself, but belongs to the wider context'. This point reiterates something noted in Chapter 2. But how that context is understood is crucial here. To claim, as for example Spencer does, that dance is a kind of ritual action is to offer (the beginnings of) an account of dance.

But insofar as we wish to concentrate on *dance* and not (for example) on *ritual* we will need some index on whether or not some activity is indeed dance. One aspect of that index will be whether or not the activity is a fit object for artistic appreciation. Or so I have been arguing. (Later sections of this chapter consider some counter-cases.) The point here is that we do not, of ourselves, have some clear understanding of what is and what is not dance *irrespective* of the purposes or uses to which the dance is put.

What is true for the anthropologist of 'dance' is equally true for the historian of dance. This point has at least two dimensions. First, if we have some evidence of a certain movement activity taking place at a certain historical time, what should lead us to call that 'dance' rather than some other name for movement activity? It is not clear what *could*: evidence as to what it *was* called simply repeats the problem. The second dimension concerns the difficulty in interpreting the historical 'evidence' that we have available to us. Some of these difficulties are raised in a clear way in the opening pages of Belinda Quirey's *May I Have the Pleasure?* (Quirey, 1976). What these difficulties for the historian and the anthropologist of dance indicate, of course, is the difficulty of making sense — as 'dance" — of an activity far removed from what we understand by dance, and from the context within which we learned to use the word 'dance'. These difficulties' — for anthropologists and historians — will be the beginnings of my counterblast to any objection to my claims about the centrality of the artistic.

However, it is worth considering a set of views of 'art-objects' which deny the genuine existence of art (as we have been understanding it), by denying artistic value. In fact, as we will see, this denial might take one of three forms, all of which consist in asserting that dance is simply a popular cultural form, with the idea of *art* being either irrelevant or pernicious. The first view, which I shall characterise as philistine, may be brought by considering a view that the conservative politician Norman Tebbitt is popularly supposed to hold in respect of art more generally. Here is Peter Fuller (1988b: 211–12) giving exposition of Tebbitt's position:

> During a public debate about whether there should be Page Three pin-ups in popular newspapers, Tebbitt made a widely reported observation to effect that middle-class people could see spicier pictures of naked women on art gallery walls, and he really could not see that there was any difference between such things and the *Sun* Page Three girl.

Such a position denies the idea of artistic value as we have been seeking to develop it. Those who 'could not see that there was a significant difference' (Fuller, 1988a: 64) between art works and pin-ups are those who deny the whole category of art. However, it is not essential to consider this position here. For denial of the whole category of art will leave us looking for some alternative justification for the place of dance in the school curriculum — given that, having progressed this far in the text, we are committed to the need for such a defence. In what follows, then, I shall consider two other positions which, although connected to the philistine one, at least seem to offer a reason to offer dance in the curriculum.

The first of these positions is that of what I shall the 'popular culture' theorist, who urges that dance has a place in education insofar as it is one example of popular culture and insofar as it is studied as such. This view will be considered in the next section. The other view, sometimes attributed in visual art to the writings of John Berger (1972: see Fuller, 1988a), is one which incorporates *a* concept of art but (one might think) a concept rather different from that developed here. We will come to that position eventually.

Popular culture: a topic for theory

Perhaps the biggest challenge to the approach to dance education adopted here — the artistic approach — comes from the thought that dance should be seen as just another part of popular culture. One advantage of the popular-culture approach, of course, is that it promises to focus equally on all of dance, rather than just concentrating on those bits which are *art*: so reggae, disco, ballroom, folk, etc., have an *equal* place. Thus we should study dance marathons (Calabria, 1976) or the tango (Salmon, 1977), to take two examples from a popular journal. We can imagine similar studies being undertaken by pupils, and we can even imagine them having a practical dimension. The point is that our interest, in such studies, lies in what we learn about the society which produces the phenomenon in question. Thus, 'the tango manifests western culture, fanciful escape into the obstruction of life…which points out human folly by means of burlesque or by intensifying incongruities' (Salmon, 1977: 865). While the dance marathon allows the observer to 'focus…on the celebration of the common man at the price of personal exploitation…' (Calabria, 1976: 67). These topics may sound like the sorts of life-issues referred to in Chapter 4, but what distinguishes one from the other is the direction of any understanding fostered. For the concern in the popular culture approach is to understand culture — as part of, or in contrast with, *society*. So what, ideally, we understand better as a result of the investigation would be the social situation in the particular time and place. That is to say, what we understand is society. Or at least something similar. In contrast, under the artistic approach, our aim is to better understand *the work of art itself*, even though doing so may/will have some bearing on life-issues.

Two thoughts are prompted. The first, perhaps betraying vested interest, urges that to see dance as *one element* of popular culture is to reduce dance education to (one element of) popular-culture education. This is to miss its unique possibilities. The second thought builds on this one. For when we see dance as part of popular culture, we miss its *physical* dimension: the health-related possibilities of dance education. I would be the last one to stress the benefits of such possibilities; I see them as, at best, 'spin-offs' of dance education, yet they are real spin-offs. They are part, one might think, of the *subsidiary* aims of education. In locating the distinctiveness of dance education, one aspect here must be its physicality (as we urged in Chapter 2). The upshot, then, is that the popular culture approach does not look promising as a way of establishing the distinctiveness of dance. (But that never was its project.)

However, there is a third related line of discussion. We should question the *specificity* of the notion of popular culture, and hence its usefulness as an analytical tool. One writer (Gibson, 1986) points out its variety by noting that just some of the elements of popular culture will include television, radio, football, horse racing, darts, pigeon racing, horror films, snooker, thriller novels, newspapers, folk-songs and pigeon fancying. He even mentions folk-dance. He then comments, surely rightly: 'The only valid generalisation about popular culture is that it is enjoyed by many and that it is undeniably potent in shaping attitudes and behaviour' (Gibson, 1986: 72). Certainly, there are popular cultural forms. And it may be a mistake to dismiss them as false consciousness (McLellan, 1986: 22–3) ensuring that subjects acquiesce in their own subjugation. This much is acceptable.

However, as Gibson notes, the attitudes of the popular culture theorist will be to encompass all facets of cultural life. Thus, it is 'expansive and analytic: television, pop-music, skin heads comprise objects of study as well as the works of Shakespeare' (Gibson, 1986: 99). So we are driven to ask if the idea of 'popular culture' really defines either an area of investigation or a set of methods for investigation. For in neither area nor methods does it seem to be separate from sociology, literary theory and studies, social history — either in theory or in practice. One might think, with justice, that popular cultural theory achieves its completeness of coverage at the expense of glossing over important distinctions: for example, between one kind of text and another. Applied to dance, will it mean treating in the same way *all* movement activities? Surely it will: as just another 'inscription' or 'form of signification' (contrast Eagleton, 1990: 334–5; 373). To repeat the point above, the cultural theorist will treat dance in whatever way he treats the rest of popular culture[1]. And that will not be desirable for dance education. (Indeed, there will be no distinctive dance education on such a theory.) How much less desirable when dance is merely one cultural form among others. Certainly this line of thought offers no promise for dance education.

The three pragmatic considerations just outlined suggest that, given the choice, the dance educator would hope that the popular culture approach is not the right way to treat dance. That antipathy on the part of the dance educator is revealing insofar as it highlights the felt need for a distinct identity for dance, if the idea of dance education is to make sense. But is the hope just expressed well-founded? I think it is. For the heart of any enquiry must be the articulation of either methods or area of study. The study of popular culture does applies methods from other areas/disciplines to a field picked out in a very general way. Of its nature, it runs across distinctions between popular cultural forms, for it is aiming to understand what Raymond Williams (1961: 65) called 'the actual life that a whole organism is there to express'. And to do so *through* understanding those forms. Now, it is certainly possible to treat dance as one such form. But two points are germane. First, identifying the topic for study as *dance,* and not something else, will not be done within this kind of analysis. For integral to the analysis is the denial of any distinctiveness to dance: it is one popular cultural form amongst others. Second, one cannot argue that there is only one way to treat dance. For just as literature has — not without a struggle — reasserted its independence of the study of written inscriptions, so the study of dance as an art form can surely (and I would say *must* surely) do the parallel thing. Indeed, one might argue for this idea in terms familiar to the theorist of popular culture, identifying the *structures of feeling* (see Gibson, 1984: 63) which characterise the artistic approach to dance study. Then dance study would *collapse* into the study of popular culture.

No doubt I have been going too quickly. It will not do to dismiss a whole line of enquiry with these few brief remarks[2]. Still, the direction of commentary is clear enough, and surely sufficient to establish at least the *possibility* of an independent dance education only by denying the commitment earlier identified to popular culture.

Popular culture and art

The issue of popular culture has, in effect, two related dimensions for dance education. The first, and perhaps most important, concerns the extent to which dances *other than* the art-type dance advocated here are suitable education vehicles. Adopting a popular culture approach offers a re-orientation of the *importance* of dance and, correspondingly, a re-assessment of *what* dance forms should be included within the curriculum. But we have seen that — insofar as we are committed to dance education, or to any distinct place for dance in the curriculum — we should reject this aspect of the popular culture approach.

The other dimension is more abstract, less dance-specific. It concerns the general *plausibility* of the account of artistic education here, by undermining the claims of art to a distinctive character: in particular, to a distinctive kind of value. In effect, this is not an argument about the *suitability* of art in education, but one about the *possibility* of art as we have been understanding it. We will consider this point before turning to our third account of the relationship between dance and popular culture.

Giving a brief account of a view of art (and hence of dance as art) which seeks to undermine the category of *art* as we have employed it involves bringing together rather disparate claims: for no-one holds this extreme view in this extreme form — at least no writer of whose work I am aware. Nonetheless, the threads of this position are apparent in widely read authors, so I will articulate the position using quotation from them. Much of this material is about art more generally, although we can be confident that its authors would apply it to dance without significant alteration. Such a position aims to demonstrate the way in which 'the cultural product ("work of art") loses its character as transcendent, universal fact, whose "greatness" is unanalysable, but somehow mysteriously and inherently present. It is seen instead as the complex product of economic, social and ideological factors' (Wolff, 1981: 139). This means, of course, that consideration must be given to the social role or roles of dance at a particular time. Thus, dance history has sometimes concerned itself with precisely where, say, dances to the music of Rameax fitted in to the court life of Louis XIV. Here the answer might draw on relevant social history, including, say, the founding of the Royal Academy of Dancing in 1661, which served both to institutionalise professional dancing masters and to produce *some* degree of standardisation in which was taught. In this way, we might locate a precise social role for these dances. Relatedly, such an account emphasises the place of such dance as an object of *domination*: as the province of the gentry rather than the peasantry, or of the wealthy rather than the poor — under the aegis of royal patronage! So the dance has a social role and a historical position. Both have historical and economic dimensions. We see the economic and social base on which dancing is constructed at that historical moment.

Two conclusions may be noted. First, if our understanding of dance is to be thus historically and economically located, it will follow that works of art such as dances are neither transcendent nor universal. Second, the roles envisaged are not in any way the kinds of *artistic* roles which we have earlier discussed. The position is stated in a usefully blunt way, as follows:

> Even when it is present in the most banal form, or when it glosses over the most profound human problems, concealing their underlying and living contradictions, mass art plays a well-defined ideological role: to keep mass man in his place, to make him feel at home in his mass being, and close the windows through which he might have captured himself a truly human world. (Vasquez, 1973: quoted Laing, 1978: 105)

Applying these ideas, we should see dance as the product of a certain kind of society — and, today, of a capitalist society — and as having certain roles to do with the palliation of protest to a dominant ideology. Of course, such a position need not operate in one wholly general way. 'Questions about the actual relationship of the economic and the ideological…are always empirical questions, whose answer requires the historical analysis of a concrete situation' (Wolff, 1981: 140). And this lesson has been explicitly learned. Thus, Ruth Katz (1983: 529) can write about 'the waltz in ideological and social perspective', and the 'appropriateness of the waltz' as elements in an argument that 'everybody dances the waltz'. But the argument there focuses on the different social expressions that the waltz represented to different groups. Yet if the nature of dance is in this way historically and culturally specific, and ideologically determined, discussions of the nature of dance as art will simply turn into discussions of the ideological values which hold the notion of art in place. These in turn will dissolve into discussions of the economic and social order within which that ideology operates. In this way, art as such finds no place in the discussion. Art works, such as dances, are simply one kind of artefact of industrial capitalism of a certain kind. Here, then, we have some reasonably sharply articulated view which denies the applicability of the notion of art.

How might that position be combatted? I shall use a simple but important argument, drawn from the writings of the late Peter Fuller. The argument begins by accepting that the account of dance, or of art more generally, just given indeed addresses *some* characteristics of dance — roughly, it is a study of the history and development of dance *production*, in the technical sense that term has in sociology (Eagleton, 1976: 2). That is to say, it is concerned with the social and historical forces which lead to the production of certain dances at certain times; and many of those forces have an implicit or explicit ideological tinge. All this, Fuller urges, we should accept as legitimate. His point, though, is that something crucial is missing from such a study, no matter how completely, thoroughly and expertly it is pursued. As Fuller (1988c: ix–x) puts it, 'I came to feel that … left-wing aesthetic theorists of the 70s … ended up with "art-shaped" holes' in their theories. The argument, then, is that such theorising leaves out something important, something which needs to be stressed; and stressing it is a way of reinstituting the concept of artistic value.

The argument itself is extremely simple. Consider any art work which is the result of many constructors. (Fuller likes to use the example of the Parthenon frieze which, so long as we are untroubled by its art-status, is a perfect example.) Notice that the work of two of this object's constructors are different: as we might say, different in quality. As Fuller (1980: 236) puts it, 'you will begin to discover that some of the sculptors who worked on the Parthenon frieze were much better than others. You will begin to see this for yourself by using your eyes. Some were just not very good at expressing their experience of, say, cloth in stone. They depicted folds in robes or drapery in rigid slots, dug into the marble like someone furrowing the surface of a cheese with a tea-spoon'. We compare their work with those others, those whose 'representations seem to have lightness, movement, and translucence, the stone breathes and floats for them' (Fuller, 1980: 236). Both were working under identical social, economic and ideological conditions — or so we can imagine. Thus, the kind of analysis envisaged earlier will simply fail to distinguish the positions of the two sculptors and hence will be inappropriate to explain the differences between their sculptures. For, and this is important, it is the *art works* that are to be explained here, not the sculptors lives. Of course, we naturally think that there is a strong relation between one and the other; and we are right (*UD*: Ch. 11). But that relation eludes the sorts of concentration on the economic and ideological postulated earlier. So we have, first, something we wish to explain (something we 'see for ourselves') and, second, a method inappropriate for that explanation. In this way, we see clearly that something important is being omitted. What is being omitted, of course, is the theoretical material we needed to explain the difference between the *craftsman* and the *artist*, as we see them represented by the two sculptors imagined.

This argument is extremely powerful. If accepted, it requires that art be understood using the concept *art*, and not in terms of some reduction of art to its sociological, economic or ideological 'components" — indeed, it is a way of showing that there is more to art than these elements. And the argument has a greater application than simply the cases that give rise to it. So that, although *it* draws on works by many hands, that it simply an argumentative device. If the concept *art* is required to understand such works, it is required to understand *all* art works. Thus, this argument from Peter Fuller ensures the employment of the concept *art*, by ensuring the independence of the notion of artistic value.

Artistic value and popular culture

To adopt the position argued thus far is to commit ourselves to a view of art which recognises what we have called *artistic value*: that is to say, not one equivalent to an account in the sociology or history of art. At this point we turn to a contrasting position mentioned at the beginning of this chapter, there associated with John Berger. An interesting recent controversy concerning visual art focuses our attention sharply on the *place* of the arts in society: hence, the place of dance. In contrast to those (broadly marxist) theorists who *dismiss* the idea of art and of artistic value — as bourgeois, ideological or some such — John Berger (1978: 703) acknowledges the importance of art and of artistic value. But he then *explains* that value (or is taken to explain it) in ways which do not, for example, distinguish art from advertising or from industrial design (Berger, 1972: 29). In this sense, his discussion of art works makes them just another popular culture manifestation. For a theorist wished to dispense with the concept 'art', this may be a suitable strategy (compare Wolff, 1981: 141). Yet if, with Berger, one wishes to do justice to the concept of art, it is not clear how one can take such a line. This takes us back, of course, to the 'philistine' view ascribed to Norman Tebbitt in the introduction to this chapter. For Berger's method of distinguishing art from advertising seems no clearer. Here is Peter Fuller (1988a: 58) again:

> According to Berger, originals and, more particularly, the places that house the originals (that is museums) had ... become in a certain sense, redundant .... These arguments came together in Berger's assertion that what he called 'publicity' or the spectacle of modern advertising — with its emphasis on 'glamour' and the desire for material goods and beautiful women — was not something quite separate from the western transition of oil painting, but rather an extension of it. Advertising was the modern version of it.

Quite explicitly, Berger urged 'Art must... serve an extra-artistic purpose' (Berger, 1969: 37; quoted Fuller, 1988b: 211), and his conception of this purpose related it to the purpose of other cultural objects. 'It is necessary to see works of art freed from all the mystique which is attached to them as property objects' (Berger, 1969; quoted Fuller, 1988b). And one might think that the indictment of Berger is complete when Fuller (1988b: 212) notes him 'pressing his point home by juxtaposing a detail from Ingres and a "girlie" pin-up'.

One question of scholarly importance would be whether or not Berger actually held the views which Fuller has been ascribing to him. I shall not consider that question directly, since it is clear that his work *might* be interpreted this way, and to some degree *has* been interpreted in this fashion. So the position may be considered independently of Berger's commitment to it.

But our consideration can be surprisingly brief. Can this position develop a distinctive art education? Could a suitably amended version produce a distinctive dance education? The answer to both these questions must be 'no'. Applied to painting, Berger's discussion of *art* and his discussion of advertising will inevitably run together — both are popular cultural forms in the sense we have been discussing them. Applied to dance, his view will treat as of equal importance dances employing Graham technique, or classical ballet, on the one hand, and the fox trot, tango and pogo on the other: all are popular culture 'objects', with their 'extra-artistic purpose'. Therefore, this position is subject to both the sets of objections raised thus far. It offers us no constructive way to fill in the 'art-shaped hole'. And it does not identify a distinctive *dance* education. In this way, it fares no better than the philistine view.

Conclusion

This chapter has combatted any attempt to explain dance education as popular cultural education by considering how each of three versions of the 'popular culture' thesis fail to do justice to dance. In particular, the following have been highlighted: the danger of philistinism; the danger of focusing onto culture and *away from* dance; the danger of leaving an 'art-shaped' hole in one's theory; and the danger of accepting *art* only to deny artistic *value*. All these dangers will avoided once we see that, whatever its place elsewhere, the 'popular cultural' approach will not serve to justify a distinctive place for dance education in the school curriculum. (And this claim might be read-into the Physical Education National Curriculum document [DES, August 1991, Appendix D, §6], as we saw in Chapter 7.)

We turn now to a related issue, offering another candidate justification for dance education.

Chapter 12

The Issue of Multi-Culturalism

Introduction

A recent video (BAALPE, 1990) made by the Physical Education Association in Britain opens with some young people performing Gujerati folk dance. Without wishing to criticise this particular video, it is easy to see how the image it presents might be confusing[1], and in two related ways. The first concerns tokenism — the thought that to have taught Gujerati folk dance is to have addressed 'their' culture. Tokenism is rightly to be rejected (see pp. 126–7). But then one must ask oneself how, if at all, the cultural values of ethnic minorities in a multi-ethnic society (such as the UK or the USA) *are* to be addressed through education. This leads to the second point, one about relevance: for, as my colleague Scott Fleming was told by a South Asian friend, Gujerati folk dance had about as much to do with *his* home life as, say, Morris dancing does for the average English person — which is to say: virtually nothing at all!

Four major issues are identified here. First, and most important in many ways, is the issue of *racism*. For clearly any education system worth the name must run counter to racist tendencies. This is a minimum requirement which the *artistic* account for dance will have to meet if it is to have any plausibility as an account of dance in education. The second issue concerns the dangers — one might even think of them as *racist* dangers — of tokenism here: of imaging that one is thinking cross-culturally or multi-culturally simply because one has an *element* of one's curriculum drawn from another culture (in this case, dance from another culture). The third issue concerns the cultural possibilities of dance: for dance used to promote cultural understanding will not *typically* be 'art-type' dance and/or will not be performed to a sufficiently high standard to satisfy the *artistic* account. And the general 'cultural expansion' account of dance is common, featuring (for example) in the Physical Education Document for the National Curriculum in the UK (DES, August 1991: Appendix D §6). Stressing this possibility for dance is (to that degree) *rejecting* the artistic account. Indeed, it will certainly involve focusing on dances *other than* those preferred by the artistic account, both as objects to be taught and objects to be considered (say, on video). Or so one might think. The fourth issue concerns the *value* content of dance, given (one might think) the *cultural dependence* of values. I will consider the issues in that order.

Racism

Any satisfactory account of the place of dance in education in a multi-ethnic society must recognise three fundamental distinctions. To fail to do so will be to ignore central concerns — in particular, issues of racism. And, as stated above, the avoidance of racism is crucial. The first distinction is between *content* and *delivery*: so that one might, for example, be presenting culturally specific material (content) but in a non-specific way (delivery). So we can imagine the teaching of dance taking place in a racially-neutral fashion, and hence the classes themselves not being racist (because the delivery was not), while nevertheless acknowledging that the *content* of the classes might focus on, and seem to privilege, the cultural heritage of one ethnic group. And, I suppose, that means to privilege it *over* the culture of another ethnic group. If this *possibility* is conceded, one concern for the teaching of dance in education is alleviated: although another is intensified. For there will be no *in principle* difficulty for the inclusion of, say, Graham-style modern American dance in the curriculum. However, there will be major questions about how such a course of study is indeed to be *delivered* (Cole, M., 1989).

The second distinction is between *multi-culturalist* and *anti-racist* responses to a multi-ethnic society. In essence, the first is an attempt to *integrate* across cultural differences by providing cultural insights from the various ethic groups. Against this strategy is set that of anti-racism, which requires a more strenuous effort to avoid any from of racism — so that there is commitment to the possibilities of positive discrimination, for example. Notice, however, that we will have satisfied the constraints of ethnicity here if we are anti-racist in the *delivery* of the material (to use the first distinction) however we stand on the material itself.

The third distinction worth noticing (Fleming, 1991: 235) is that between *personal* racism and *institutional* racism. Thus, as Abercrombie *et al.* (1984: 173) correctly recognise, racism

> may be (1) overt and individual, involving individual acts of aggression against subordinate groups or individuals, or (2) covert and institutional, involving structural relations of subordination and oppression between social groups.

As an example, notice that, just like in some sports, it seems true that there is a high proportion of Afro-Caribbean dancers in major dance companies[2]. Thus there are candidate role-models for youth. What must be avoided, of course, is an attitude which attributes this *fact* (if fact it be) to some special connection between Afro-Caribbeans and, say, rhythm, or any such. For this is simply a kind of institutional racism.

My point thus far is that, in a multi-ethnic society, avoiding racist attitudes and behaviour need have nothing to do with the *content* of the curriculum. In particular, there is nothing inherently racist about the emphasis on *art* throughout this volume.

I foresee a major objection at this point, for might there not be an *institutional* racism in the privileging in education of some form of Western ethnic dance (as Joann Kealiinohomoku, 1983, called ballet). In part, I address that question later in this chapter (pp. 131–4). However, it is worth saying something at this stage. For clarity, let us consider a culture which does *not* employ the concept 'art'. If the concept 'art' then acquires a major place in education, it will of course follow that the education is not reflecting the culture: the education does, but the culture does not, possess the concept 'art'. Still, this is another way of saying that pupils are taught a distinction (the distinction between art and other things) which they may then choose to employ in a variety of contexts. As a contribution to the Personal Enquiry conception of education (as articulated in Chapter 3), this seems relatively straightforward. Even if we ask ourselves how it stands more generally, we should conclude that there is no genuine *privileging* of one culture over another. For there is no insistence that *this* distinction be drawn universally. Rather, pupils are taught what to make of the distinction *whenever* it is drawn. Thus, urging that the concept of art has no place in certain cultures, and hence that my *artistic* approach for dance education will focus on cultures where this distinction is in place, is just another way of reinforcing the sense in which the educational value of *dance* is to be rooted in that distinction. Of course, there is no reason to think better (or worse) of cultures which lack this distinction. All we are saying is that *this* distinction explains the purpose of dance, and hence the place of a particular kind of dance, in the education system. We will need to see, of course, what other arguments might be raised for *other* dance forms. One aspect of that issue, identifying a potential difficulty, is the topic of the next section.

Tokenism

Once we understand the idea of tokenism — of seeming to think multi-culturally by including *one* example of work from another culture — we are left with a simple question: how can tokenism be avoided? And posing the question in that way makes clear that there is really only one answer to this question. Tokenism can only be avoided by giving far more of the culture at issue.

Applying this thought to dance, we see a further difficulty. For, as with the Physical Education Association video already mentioned (p. 124), much of the cultural experience of dance which is, in principle, part of a specific culture, is in fact no part of the *common* or *lived* culture (Bennett *et al.*, 1986: xi–49). Thus supplying a cultural background will be like, in the English case, supplying a cultural background appropriate to some folk-dance form such as Morris dancing. (The British alternative comedian Alexei Sayle, punning on the name of an inexpensive British car, denied that this folk activity should indeed be called *Morris* dancing any longer — instead, and following the logic that the activity is now the preserve of the middle class, he suggested *Volvo* dancing!) Moreover, to give that much cultural information is to move away from a discussion or analysis or presentation of *dance*, and into another area: that is, this is a way of dropping dance education in favour of other (no doubt valuable) aspects of the process of education. That is to say, the question of tokenism highlights a way in which, in order to satisfy the demands for a genuine cultural education, one must move *outside* our original topic, dance education.

Naturally, the aim here is not to decide between multi-culturalist and anti-racist approaches to teaching (that is, to what we have called *delivery*). Rather, my discussion is designed to operate against those who see the introduction of 'ethnic' dance (for example, Gujerati dance forms) as *itself* a blow against racism.

Consider the following description, which characterises as typical situation in which Indian dance is offered an educational place (Semple, 1990: 39):

> A dancer will visit a venue and expect to be the sole purveyor of a particular culture. The dancer will not only teach and perform, but might be asked to cook and give a brief humanities talk, in order to contextualise the workshop ... for ... the work has no chance of being contextualised if it is not placed within a whole curriculum scheme.

The point here, as Scott Fleming (1993) noted, is that it is hard to see how dance, cultural cuisine and a short talk will provide any sort of meaningful cultural context for the dance. Thus, the experience as described will typically be tokenistic.

The cultural possibilities of dance

A major difficulty lies in identifying precisely what role is being ascribed to ethnic dance: in this case, to a South-Asian dance form. For example, traditional Indian dance might be seen as a valuable expression of South Asian culture (Hargreaves, 1986: 108); moreover, as a means of developing a greater level of understanding of the culture and lifestyles of the

Indian sub-continent. To make this issue more precise, we should return to our original example, asking 'Who is the Gujerati folk dance *for*?'.

Responses to such a question might be of two major kinds. Reviewing each of them will show us the contours of the debate and, as we will see, will show how inappropriate this sort of justification is for any activity worthy of the name 'dance education'.

Asked 'Who is the Gujerati folk dance for?', a first answer might be that it is for *everyone*, to aid cultural understanding and to give a breadth to the curriculum by exploring cultures different from one's own — except for those *with* this culture, but then *they* explore another culture in the rest of curriculum programme! In order to characterise this view, we might call it *cultural expansionist*, since it emphasises an aim for the dance as giving a broad sense of 'other cultures' to its general recipients. As we saw in Chapter 7, the National Curriculum document for physical education (DES, August 1991: 75) identifies, as a focal point for dance, such a traditional/folk dance context, as well as a popular cultural/art theme: so that, for instance, 'Bhangra' and 'South Asian forms' are explicitly mentioned in the popular culture/art category, while 'some South Asian forms' appears in the traditional/folk category. So this *cultural expansionist* response is pervasive and important.

Nonetheless, this answer to our question about the place of Gujerati folk dance is problematic for four related reasons. First, it is rooted in the idea that a *cultural analysis* is the basis for an identification of what is educational (Lawton, 1989: Ch. 3). But this idea is problematic viewed as a general thesis about the curriculum: as Lawton (1975: 62) notes, its only sound basis is in the claim that 'some kinds of knowledge are superior in some meaningful way to other kinds of knowledge'. The implication, that some forms of culture are similarly superior, has been criticised by Kelly (1990: 116). We might imagine our criticism beginning from there. For we must either identify a *common* culture here, which might perhaps be done (as we shall see), or we must argue for the inherent *superiority* of one collection of cultural values over another. All in all, this conception of an educational analysis deriving from a cultural analysis is at best problematic. The point, of course, is that the idea of 'a selection from the culture' (Lawton, 1989: 19) is no more plausible as an educational basis for some kind of majority culture than it is applied to any specific instance.

However, and second, the *cultural expansionist* answer in justification of the place of Gujerati folk dance is misleading in another fundamental way: for it will perpetuate 'exoticism', on which the dance form is viewed, as it were, as one might view foreign animals in a zoo — for their interest, but not really taking them seriously. So, far from producing a shared cultural understanding, this use of Gujerati folk dance would tend to differentiate those familiar with the form from the rest of its pupil audience: it will generate the kinds of 'them-and-us' which multi-culturalism seeks to avoid.

The third point on which this *cultural expansionist* answer is problematic is one noted already: that it is simply impractical, given the time constraints of an average school curriculum. *Of course*, one might do justice to the cultural background required for a full understanding of Gujerati folk dance. But to do so would be to go far beyond what it is realistic to give *dance* education — indeed, beyond the time allowance it is realistic to give to more generalised cultural concerns. For both in its technical aspects and in terms of the myths and other cultural artefacts which support it, Gujerati folk dance would require an immense investment of staff time if it to be done in a non-tokenistic way.

The fourth consideration here is that a *cultural expansionist* answer raises questions about the *standards* by which cultural artefacts are judged: indeed, this is one dimension of our first articulated problem. We will sharpen this problem later in this chapter (pp. 131–2) but, for now, it is worth noting that the *general* version of this question is a familiar one for philosophers, associated with their discussions of relativism (see Chapter 1; *UD*: 301–9). Here Peter Winch (1973: 27–42) asks, 'Our standards or theirs?'. Of course, such questions have greater bite if we think of them as applying to the whole of one's life-style, not merely to the place of dance in one's curriculum (Winch, 1987: 194–207). Nevertheless, it is hard to see how, in any satisfactory articulation of the cultural background to Gujerati folk dance, one might not come up against myths or cultural beliefs which might themselves be challenged. We can imagine that challenge taking the form of someone objecting 'But this is unintelligible!'. As Winch (1973: 19) replies, it is essential to ask 'Unintelligible to whom?" — for clearly there are cultural groups who do not find this material unintelligible.

None of these four problems amounts to a refutation of the *cultural expansionist* answer to quertions about the place of Gujerati folk dance in education. However, each makes it less and less straightforward to insert this dance form. Taken together, they do represent a substantial difficulty. In particular, this doesn't look like the general justification for *dance*: at best, and if successful, it will generate a *whole curriculum* of cultural study! That is to say, if its arguments are successful, they generate, not a rationale for dance education, but an expanded culturalist version of the whole curriculum. I do not at this moment wish to suggest that such a conception is mistaken. At the least, it is not the conception in place and, before adopting it, we should assess its plausibility. Such an assessment will be aided by a return to our original question.

We asked earlier, 'Who is the Gujerati folk dance for?'. Our first answer, the *cultural expansionist* one, was that it was for everyone. But we have seen that this response leads to no straightforward justification for dance education. Can we offer an alternative? At this point I suggest a *cultural support* answer: that the rationale for the Gujerati folk dance is to give the 'immigrants' from South Asia (often first or second generation) a sense of cultural identity or of ethnic pride (Fleming, 1991: 230). If this answer were accepted, it would be clear how the inclusion of the Gujerati folk dance would have a multi-cultural effect in respect of the appropriate South Asian pupils, although its role for pupils with a different ethnic background would still stand in need of justification.

However, on reflection, this answer too is an inadequate one, and for four related reasons. The first, of course, concerns *tokenism*, as discussed earlier (pp. 126–7). For one cannot realistically induce any sense of cultural identity or ethnic pride with the kind of inputs imagined by, for example, Semple (as quoted above).

A second criticism, too, has already been articulated: that Gujerati folk dance is irrelevant to everyday life. For many Britons of South Asian origin, appropriate contemporary dance forms have far more to do with Black American street culture (as popularised by, say, Michael Jackson) than with forms from the Indian sub-continent. So the dance form does not automatically offer a cultural identity to those from the Indian sub-continent. Neither does it offer a step towards multi-culturalism. As my colleague Scott Fleming (1993) discovered, pupils of South-Asian background are likely to find themselves the butt of jokes if they are perceived by classmates as the *reason* why that class is 'subjected' to Gujerati folk dance — and this point is only exacerbated in any school where dance is already seen as a peripheral (or perhaps a girls-only) activity. For these reasons, then, it easy to see how Gujerati folk dance might be seen as irrelevant even by those of South Asian descent.

The third point grows from this one. For the *diversity* among South Asians must be recognised. The Indian sub-continent has a number of dance forms, and it is far from clear that any represents a *dominant* form. At best, pupils might be expected to identify with one such form — and there is no reason to suppose that that will typically be the Gujerati folk dance which, in our example, we have imagined being taught. Notice, this point is not aided by postulating the introduction of another South Asian dance form instead, for the diversity amongst those of South Asian descent means that *any* dance form will represent only a small proportion of Britons with this ethnic background. And what is true in Britain is equally true in other places.

A fourth point picks-up aspects of the second and the third, reporting some further results from the research of Scott Fleming. He found pupils with a South Asian background whose experience was not *centrally* defined by their culture — that other factors were at least as important. As a result, drawing on his own ethnographic study of a London secondary school, Fleming (1991: 235) produces a categorisation which allows that 'most individuals, most of the time, could be recognised as belonging to one of [the categories] by his general appearance and demeanour'. In particular, his categories were 'not defined to according to any religious or cultural criteria'. This is, as it were, the reverse of the second and third points above. For not merely is there a significant diversity amongst pupils with South Asian backgrounds to be taken into account, and not merely is much of the traditional culture from, say, the Indian sub-continent an irrelevance to the everyday life of such pupils, but further the *lived experience* of pupils might have little or nothing to do with their *specific* cultural background — that racism, for example, might have much less to do with the subtle distinctions that we are here noticing, and that would be required from any cultural analysis.

Privileging of Western values?

Once we accept that the teaching of dance in a multi-cultural society is unlikely to strike a major blow either *for* multi-culturalism or *against* racism, we are in a position to consider what precisely *should* be taught in schools: in particular, what might be educationally justified *as dance*, putting aside any multi-culturalist aspirations which might remain. Thus, we return to the question posed initially in this text. Rather unsurprisingly, our answer is the answer already given: that is to say, in this case too we might realistically offer the *artistic account* of the nature of dance education. Confronted with critics, our response might typically be the one articulated earlier: the value of dance as emotional education in respect of life-issues.

Faced with such an analysis, no doubt presented less baldly, I imagine two issues for debate, both to be addressed in this section. First, the critic might dispute the way in which my emphasis on the *artistic* seems to privilege the values of Western culture (broadly Western European culture) over the values of other cultures. Second, the general question, 'Whose standards?', might be raised as a related way of urging that there is no general justification for the emphasis here on the activities of (broadly Western European) dancers, choreographers and dance theorists. I shall treat each objection in turn.

The first objection focused on the way in which the *artistic* account of dance education seemed to privilege a particular set of dances, as masterworks; and those masterworks seemed to have a common origin in the culture of (roughly) Western Europe and North America. One aspect of the reply here will emphasise the need to be convinced, for any study, that what we are studying is indeed *dance* (*UD*: Ch. 14). This means, of course, ascertaining that the concept *dance* is an appropriate one to characterise the physical activity in question (for this is by no means obvious). Finding an activity designed, not merely to please the gods, but to *bring about* a certain divine activity, we might well feel that this was, for that reason, not dance: that the boundaries of dance had been exceeded. The point is simply that the topic at issue is *dance*, and that that concept can only be understood from the perspective of (roughly) Western Europe and North America. Of course, that concession still leaves open the questions of how far the dance forms of, for example, North India (such as kathak) are dance in this sense — and that will be of a piece with deciding whether or not they are art! For it is not obvious that all activities for which the best English word we can find is the word 'dance' are nonetheless dances in this sense (*UD*: 285–6); and this sense is crucial if we are to maintain the *artistic* account of dance education. For pursuing dances which are *not* art would be pursuing activities with no educational justification (as yet).

To see this point clearly, consider the objection of someone who says, 'But there are cultures where dance has a different meaning/significance than it has in yours'. My response would be, 'Of course!'. But this would simply be another way of saying that those dances were *not* art, and therefore would not be justified in a school curriculum if the artistic account of dance education were in place. In this way, we see that, as far as *dance* is concerned, there is nothing here which privileges one *culture* over another. At best, we are emphasising the concept *art*, and allowing (in principle) a place within the dance education programme to *any* dance works which are art in that sense.

But might there be works which were *art* in some other sense? The answer here must be a firm 'No'. Of course, the *word* 'art' might not be used — as, for example, in *The Womanly Art of Breastfeeding* (to give one of David Best's favourite examples). Yet the use of the word 'art' here has no bearing on whether or not the activity is *art* in the sense we are concerned with it. In the same way, the mere fact that we call certain activities *dance* does not, of itself, offer any place for them in dance education. That place must still be sought. As argued here, the justification must be centrally an artistic justification.

That leads neatly to the second issue to be discussed in this section: that concerning the 'standard' in place in our cultural understanding. Notice, first, that there is a real question here, the issue of what decisions are to be taken, given that (practically) *some* decisions are required — that one can't do everything that might be thought desirable. For example, the idea of a cultural analysis (Lawton, 1989: Ch. 3) turns out to be an analysis of *one* culture; perhaps, we might even say, of *our* culture. Such an analysis might be seen as privileging *our* culture (whatever that is).

We can begin from the 'universality' of dance. We have argued that there is something to be learned from dance — something in respect of 'life-issues'. And these life-issues matters obviously are *value* matters also. Now, they are trans-cultural just to the extent to which they are life-issues. If we find — instead — that their emphasis is restricted to some particular culture, they will still be educationally justified *to the degree* to which people participate in that culture. In the case of a multi-ethnic society, we should expect the level of that participation to be fairly high: not, of course, to the exclusion of other (cultural) values, but in addition to them. Of course, this is a discussion of dance only: we are not exploring the question of the cultural in general. So, in a different vein, no real conflict of values for the pupil exists here: what is taught is either *intelligible*, and hence its values are intelligible to that pupil, or *not intelligible*, which involves its implicit values also not being intelligible. Of course, the matter is rather more complicated. Exposure to dance teaching is intended not merely to *show* values to pupils, but to *teach* or *inculcate* those values into the pupils in question. That is what we mean in speaking of 'education of the emotions'.

At root, there is a distinction here between the values that people hold (including their cultural values), and what we might call the *language* in which such beliefs are expressed and which makes them possible (Winch, 1987: 206). What I have called the *language* is not, in that sense, a topic for discussion or for learning: it is the framework within which discussion and learning takes place. Stanley Cavell (1981a: 64) puts this point poetically when he says that 'words come to us from a distance'. He means, of course, that we *learn* to understand and to make sense of actions and events in terms we did not ourselves invent. Indeed, we might think of a culture as centrally consisting of practices learned and understood in just this way. Then there will be no hard-and-fast answer to whether or not dance of another culture is understandable. As we saw above, it will be understandable to the extent that the *language* in which it is understood is familiar to its audience, and not, to the degree which it is not.

In this respect, the difference between different *cultures* resembles the difference between groups with different levels of knowledge: with a certain knowledge of modern dance, the works of Martha Graham may be intelligible to me in the way that those of Merce Cunningham are not — but this is typically remediable, if I see more of Cunningham's work, learn about it through reading and perhaps practical activity, and reflect on its properties, structural and otherwise. In the end, there may be a limit to what I can learn. That limit may be set partly by my *other* value commitments, partly by the degree to which I am genuinely able to mobilise key concepts in my experiences, and no doubt a number of other factors. The point, though, is twofold: first, there is no *in principle* bar to my coming to understand the dance of Merce Cunningham; but, second, there may be a considerable number of *in practice* difficulties to be overcome. We find ourselves in this situation with respect to dance education. Of course, differing cultural backgrounds may make it extremely difficult for pupils to grasp key concepts, and to mobilise them in their experience. Certain dances build-in values, myths, stories (and musical values) which may be alien to some pupils. But this is not an all-or-nothing business. These will be alien to different degrees across a typical class of pupils. In this way, we see how understanding dances is not incompatible with significant cultural differences, and even with those differences being strongly connected to values.

A further issue is worth noting: that there is a difference between a value commitment, for example, to the sanctity of life, and the *upshot* of that commitment — that is to say, what it will mean in a specific case. This is another way in which apparently different values may amount to the same thing, while apparently similar values may amount to disparate things. In a familiar day-to-day example here, suppose the sanctity of life applies not to all human beings, as we see them, but to all the *really human* — so that, for example, some classical Greek states did not count the killing of 'barbarians' (that is, those from states outside Greece) as murder. Equally, we can imagine that the accounts of their lives given to Christopher Bruce by South American natives, accounts which stimulated him to create *Ghost Dances,* meant something rather different to them than they did to Bruce, the 'sophisticated' Westerner. This identifies a further point. For the *dance*, as Bruce constructed it, may still be open to various kinds of reading, but the root sensibility behind the work is a sensibility geared to the notion of art. That is one reason why the work is eminently suitable to have a role in dance and education.

Conclusion

The main conclusion to be reached from this chapter is the difficulty of doing justice to dance viewed *as a cultural vehicle.* This conception of dance, first, asks too much of our understanding, requiring us to enter deeply into the culture from which the dance emanates; second, and more practically, it requires too much time on, say, the school curriculum to be plausible. If such a justification were offered for the place of dance in education, it would lead to the demise of dance. Therefore the suggestion implicit in the argument of this chapter is that such a justification be given up, or at best attenuated. If this point is accepted, much of the rhetoric sometimes produced around a multi-culturalist conception of dance is seen for what it is. Consider for example Peter Brinson (1991: 181) writing:

> The UK today is a multi-cultural and multi-racial society within this world. Consequently its educational system must serve the particular needs of such a society and equip young people to live within it.

Reading such a claim correctly is recognising that it is *not* a recipe for Gujerati folk dance in schools in a tokenistic way, and nor is it a recipe for the inclusion of vast cultural studies programmes as a means to supplement the Gujerati folk dance. Rather, it is a question of drawing what is best from the lived experience of those in a contemporary culture.

This point leads naturally on to another, best introduced via an example. Consider Picasso's use of African masks, for example in *Les Demoiselles d'Avignon* (1907). One might argue that the masks from which Picasso began were not art, because they were constructed in a culture which lacked the concept *art*, and/or because they had primary purposes other than artistic ones. Yet *Picasso's* use of them circumvents any question of *their* art status. The works he takes as leading him forward are not required themselves to be art works. Indeed, all that is at issue is the art status of Picasso's *own works*. That is not affected, however we decide on the art status of the masks. To apply, there may well be pieces of African dance, or South Indian dance movements, which might constructively be integrated into the technical range of contemporary dance creation in this country[3]. That offers an area of cultural richness to the contemporary choreographer, but it says nothing one way or another about the discussion of this chapter. Indeed, an example makes the point quite sharply. William Louther produced a powerful and original dance, *Vesalii Icones* (1973), drawing on the anatomical illustrations of Vesalius: but that does not automatically make Louther's dance a biological exploration. In this way, then, one can see how nothing argued here runs counter to a use of 'ethnic' material in dance composition, or indeed for the integration of ideas with origins in other cultures into contemporary dance choreography. But all these possibilities are not, of themselves, contributions to multi-cultural education.

It must be acknowledged that this chapter represents simply a sketch of a very complex area. But it includes enough elaboration to work against regular *misconceptions*: in particular, misconceived justifications of (and also hopes for) the role of dance in education. It is a success if it simply puts aside the misconceptions.

PART IV

CURRICULUM MATTERS

Chapter 13

Aims, Objectives and Processes

Introduction

This chapter is built on a number of commitments already established earlier in this text:

- given its basis in the work of Stenhouse[1], it is not surprising to find that there is not an *objectives* model for the curriculum at work in this text: more specifically, there is not a *behavioural* objectives model (Carr, 1984);

- given, too, remarks in Chapter 3 about the value-aims of education — aims internal to the practice of teaching and learning — it is not surprising that the aims of dance education are conceived of as *internal* to dance education;

- finally, and again, given the direction of Stenhouse's writings, it is unsurprising if a *process* model for the curriculum as a whole, and for dance curriculum in particular, is put forward.

A key constraint to be taken up in more detail (applied to dance) in Chapter 15 is that educational activities must be theorised in a way which allows us to determine — at least in principle — if education has occurred, or if teaching has been successful. I shall call this a constraint concerning *accountability*. In the simplest case, *if* one had a list of *aims* for education and a list of *objectives* which derived in a clear way from those aims, and *if* one could determine if the objectives had been satisfied (for example, through assessment), one would have a way of deciding — in principle — if the aims had been met: therefore, if the teaching had been a success. In this way, one's teaching would be *accountable*. Just to be clear on the terminology, we can say that the meeting of aims must be — in principle — *open to evaluation*: not, of course, that one directly assesses whether or not aims have been met. Assessment should, on such a model, tell you if the *objectives* are being satisfied; and either that in itself guarantees that the aims are met, or one has some additional means of arriving at this guarantee.

The argument for accountability as a *requirement* in education is a simple one. For, first, teaching is an *important* business, because children are important, both in themselves and as the future of a nation and the world (to put it grandly). Second, teaching is typically paid for by ordinary people, say, through taxation. Third, children, as pupils, are vulnerable. These three considerations — and there may be more — combine to suggest an overwhelming need to determine whether or not teaching and learning (and more generally education) have taken place. It is a 'legitimate interest' (Homan, 1991: 65–67). Of course, one does not expect always *always* be able to decide in practice whether or not teaching has taken place. Rather, one does not have *educational* aims if one could not, in principle, know if those 'aims' had been met. Such aims are not aims for *education*, whatever else they are. An example explains. If I *aim* to induce in my pupils a life-long commitment to, say, a concern with health, it follows that no amount of evidence could prove that I had succeeded — short, that is, of checking pupils until their dying days! As a result, this cannot be an *aim* for my teaching: at best, it might be a vague aspiration of mine (compare Kirk, 1986: 169–173). With this clarification, we can return to a fundamental question concerning the nature of dance education: how are we to conceptualise the curriculum in general and the dance curriculum in particular? Our answer will follow Stenhouse down the path of a *process* model.

Rejecting an 'objectives' model

One part of any answer concerning the conceptualisation of the curriculum must involve rejecting a prevalent 'objectives' model of the curriculum: and, for brevity, I will here consider only a simplified version of that, from Tyler's original work[2]. This will allow consideration of Eisner's elaboration, employing the idea of *expressive* objectives — an idea with some currency in aesthetic education. Further, it will allow some consideration of David Carr's discussion of the specific place of behavioural objectives in dance education.

Tyler (1949) considered four questions fundamental for any curriculum:

1. What educational purposes should the school seek to attain?
2. What educational experiences can be provided that are likely to attain these purposes?
3. How can these educational experiences be effectively organised?
4. How can we determine whether these purposes are attained?

The thrust of these questions may be put schematically in the following simple model (Lawton, 1989: 11):

Aims and objectives
↓
Content
↓
Organisation
↓
Evaluation

For Tyler, such a model would help to clarify possible answers to questions about the objectives of particular programmes, or even of particular teaching sessions. He felt that general statements of what one was attempting — for example, 'I am trying to produce a well-rounded personality' (Lawton, 1989: 13) — do not allow us to see precisely what the desired goal is, and therefore do not make plain *precisely* how a particular kind of teaching might contribute to that goal. Whatever Tyler himself intended, his work was used to suggest that the *objectives to be specified* should be behavioural objectives. So these objectives would specify how a pupil was *to behave* by the end of a particular session of teaching: they should specify the behaviour of the pupil and the context of that behaviour. And the more specifically the objections could be stated, the better chance one had of decided whether or they had been fulfilled.

In effect, criticisms of the *behavioural objectives* conception of the curriculum have been of broadly two kinds, putting aside those to do with the practicalities of implementing this kind of system. The first kind have focused, unflatteringly, on the crude model of psychology on which this *behavioural objectives* approach is founded. As we will see, this kind of criticism, applied to the teaching of dance, is found in the writing of David Carr. The other criticism, though, has rejected the whole conception of education in terms of a set of outcomes (satisfied objectives) which were essentially detached from the *process* which gave rise to them. This criticism has two related dimensions. The first, largely due to Stenhouse, rejected the suggestion that 'objectives' could usefully be stated in terms of changes to students' behaviour — rather, they should be specified in terms of activities for the teacher. As we saw in Chapter 3, part of Stenhouse's argument here was that teachers *would not* always know exactly what response was an appropriate one. As will be recalled, Stenhouse reminds us that the *successful* piece of work may be the one which surprises us, rather than the one we expected. It follows, of course, that we could not have specified in advance what that student would produce: that is, after all, the nature of the unexpected.

All of the above could be read as an objection to the word 'objective' — and indeed Stenhouse (1983: 81) did write 'I prefer intended learning outcomes'. But it is far more than that. This brings us to its second aspect. For Stenhouse did not merely think it inappropriate to focus on behavioural outcomes for students, he also thought it *essential* to focus on the practice of 'delivering' material: that is to say, on 'a process rather than an output model' (Stenhouse, 1983: 82). Again, this position is neatly summarise by Elliott (1991: 51), when he speaks of his position as 'in opposition to the development of a curriculum technology which stressed the *prespecification* of *measurable learning outcomes*'. That is to say, Elliott was advocating a *process* model of the curriculum by identifying three related, but mistaken, characteristics of alternative views of the curriculum. The first is the idea of a curriculum *technology*, represented by the 'rational planning' model (Elliott, 1991: 135–6), of which Tyler may be taken as representative. Second, such a technology would stress 'measurable learning outcomes' (objectives) where the word 'measurable' leads us to infer that these are intended as *behavioural* objectives. (For further consideration, see Stenhouse, 1983: 81–2.) Finally, Elliott objects to 'prespecification': the idea that such objectives could be specified in advance of the teaching, and hence *independently* of the practice. In this sense, the objectives are viewed as 'technical ends' (Elliott, 1991: 51). In contrast, we will urge, with Elliott and Stenhouse, that educational values cannot be defined *independently of*, and *prior to*, the practice of teaching. This will be a reiteration and expression of our position from Chapter 3.

In defence of a *process* account of the curriculum, Stenhouse (1975: 95) makes essentially the same point:

> The process model is essentially a critical model, not a marking model. It can never be *directed* towards an examination *as an objective* without loss of quality, since the standards of the examination then override the standards imminent in the subject.

Putting that in our language, if we have a way of specifying *what is required* (say, for an examination) prior to and independently of a particular practice ('the standards imminent in the subject') then we are focusing not on what is required, but on what we can reasonably manage or assess. This is an important general point, some of whose implications will be taken up later, for, as Stenhouse (1975: 95) goes on to lament, 'examinations are so important in our society'.

However we sort out that matter, and its associated concern with accountability in education, we must recognise that an 'objectives' model is separating the educational outcomes from the practice. In Chapter 3 we agreed not to adopt this conception. But there is a particular reason why enthusiasts for dance should follow that line. As we saw in Chapter 4, giving an account of the *value* of dance is giving an account of its *intrinsic* value: it is not something we could specify *independently* of the dance itself. Thus, a conception of education such as Stenhouse's fits very naturally with the nature of dance as we have been articulating it. These considerations, then. should lead one away from an objectives model. To reinforce them, we return to the other line of criticism.

The other objection to the objectives 'model' derived from its commitment to mistaken models of the person (*UD*: 52–6). David Carr's discussion is of particular use to us here, since it is both clear and directed to the specific case of the teaching of dance. Carr (1984) imagines student-teachers (perhaps with a physical education background) faced with the prospect of teaching dance. One response by such students might be to teach, say, the national dance of a particular country, as being a more straightforward task than teaching 'creative' dance. If asked, such students might well respond that they could know in advance if the lesson had been a success because they could specify in advance what they wished the pupils to be able to do: namely, they wished them to be able to perform a certain sequence of movements, to a certain rhythm, with a certain music, in a certain order, and so on. That is to say, they might be able to give a *behavioural* specification of what was required — and perhaps this would be true in contrast to what was possible for the'creative' dance. But, as Carr points out, such students are misleading themselves. If the reproduction of certain *movements* were all that was required, then of course the students' specification would be quite accurate. But *that* specification could be fulfilled by androids (robots with human shapes) or by apes. That is to say, this sort of specification does not really pick out the subjects as *people* at all, and hence does not treat them as people. As Carr (1984: 74) puts it, such an attitude has reduced the dance to 'a sequence of colourless movements'. (Here Carr is respecting the movement/action contrast which we drew in Chapter 2.) Thus, seeing the activities in *that* way is not seeing them as *human* activities at all. Instead, as Carr insists, one must recognise how human activities have specific purposes imbedded in them — in this case, these might well be artistic purposes. Indeed, that is what it means to think of these as *human* activities. To claim that apes or automata were dancing would be to ascribe those (artistic) purposes to them. But, as we saw, to be able to *perform* an action it is required that, at least in principle, one be able to *intend* to perform that action. And for our apes, or for our automata, this is clearly problematic. Apes are not really candidates here (see Sparshott, 1988: 217–20). Equally, the case of the automata — say, the dancing androids — is at best a highly problematic one (see Searle, 1984: 57–70). The point, of course, is that we are recognising a dance as *something other* than just a sequence of movements. But in doing so, we also recognise that some ways of characterising those sequences of movements will therefore *not* be ways of describing or characterising dances. Thus, to set *behavioural* objectives, in the manner of our imagined student-teachers, is to set objectives which are not related to *dance* at all: at best, we have moved to another realm — a realm shared with apes and machines.

The conclusion to be reached, of course, is that an 'objectives' model of the curriculum is inappropriate at the least for the attribution of a distinctive dance education. But could an alternative model be found, one which fares better?

If, as urged here, an 'objectives' model of the curriculum is inappropriate for dance education (or artistic education more generally), this in turn sheds light on a project of Elliot Eisner's, 'to complement, not to replace' (Eisner, 1972: 156) the idea of an instructional objective. Our position is that the notion of an objective in this sense is misguided — that it needs to be rejected not modified. Eisner (1972: 156) says of the term 'expressive objective' that it 'describes an encounter the student is to have'. Seen one way, there is nothing here with which to disagree. Eisner is making at least two important points. First, artistic education must be seen as involving *at least* the pupil's training in the skills and the techniques essential in the expression; and, to some degree or other, we might imagine the specification of expected learning outcomes for these. Second, the pupil is intended to *manipulate* the medium of expression in ways which the teacher cannot predict with any certainty. These are certainly the kinds of expectations that our typical dance teacher would be entertaining.

But should they be termed *objectives* at all? We cannot think of them as *behavioural* objectives: since, as Carr has shown us, they are not behavioural in that sense. Rather, they are action-related or person-related, since they are *artistic* 'objectives'. Moreover, it will be odd to think of them as *objectives* when we cannot specify, even in principle, the intended outcome — or, at best, can only specify it as a vague aspiration that pupils become masters of the material in question. If this point is accepted, the force in using the word 'objectives' is entirely dissipated: we are not, in that sense, answering Tyler's questions at all any longer. I conclude, therefore, that an 'objectives' model of the curriculum will not take us very far when we are thinking about dance education.

The nature of the process model

At the heart of the model articulated and rejected in the previous section is the view of 'education as a linear process' (Kelly, 1990: 59): education was thought of as leading from aims to outcomes whose achievement can then be evaluated. Our contrast, drawn from Stenhouse, was with a *process* model. This model has sought to ascribe a central role to the teacher, and to teaching, in any activity which could genuinely be classified as *educational*. As we have urged (in Chapter 3) the values of education must be internally connected to the practice of teaching. Thus any attempt to specify those values, or any aspect of them (such as the aspect appropriate as the aims of particular course), cannot ignore teaching. So, contrary to a phrase in common use in educational circles, teaching is is not merely the *delivery* of a curriculum specified independently of teaching; rather, it is the *realisation* of an activity with in-built value aspects.

Much of general importance follows from the adoption of a *process* view of the curriculum although, as we shall see, its implications should not be unfamiliar to those engaged in dance teaching — even if they would not put the matter in quite this way. Two features in particular are relevant. First, giving up the 'behavioural objectives' conception of student learning outcomes means that precisely *what* pupils achieve cannot be completely prespecified. In effect, we no longer think of education as primarily concerned with the learning of *established facts* or *established patterns of movement*, but rather with enabling pupils to discover facts for themselves, and with the exploration of movement forms. Hence the focus both in teaching and in assessment must be on 'the intrinsic qualities of being' (Elliott, 1991: 10) which pupils manifest through their activity. As Elliott continues, 'The manifestation of such qualities can be described and judged, but not standardised or measured'. So much, then, for the kinds of previously articulated 'standards' mentioned in Chapter 7! Second, and in the same vein, teaching becomes both an *enabling* activity in respect of pupil development, and a moderating one in terms of pupil success. Both of these characteristics are commonly employed by dance teachers: they regularly exploit the possibilities of pupils exploring composition through the building up of small dance-like activities, perhaps from given 'building blocks' drawn from a technique or from a masterwork. They do not know in advance what pupils will do; but they are capable of recognising quality products here, and of helping pupils towards such products. Further, their job is to *enable*, perhaps by suggesting new movements or new possibilities; but also to *correct* if pupils perform badly.

Employing such a *process* model for the curriculum does not require that teachers somehow 'look into the minds' of pupils: what is being judged in assessment, just like what is being considered by teachers in classes as a basis for enabling or other kinds of help, is what pupils *do*. In this sense, it would not be mistaken to claim here a concern with *products* (*UD*: 279–80) — the point, though, is that these are not products which could be pre-specified! To put the matter figuratively, concerning myself with the *process* of choreography might well take the form of paying close attention to the differential *products* of my pupils in weeks 1, 2, 3 and so on of the course. That is to say, I am not trying to use material which is somehow arcane or unavailable to public scrutiny. Indeed, my concern is with what the pupils do (including what they say) in the class. But, as will be obvious, this is not equivalent to my setting behavioural objectives.

It is no part of my task here to provide a full exposition and defence of a process conception of the curriculum. That would require a work of a very different character, and some such works exist (for example Elliott, 1991). But seeing how a process model of the curriculum would operate, and recognising some of its demands, we are in a position to investigate particular examples of curriculum planning; and, following the general principles of this work, I shall use as an example later in this chapter (pp. 149–50) the National Curriculum in the United Kingdom. Before that, though, it is worth remarking on one aspect of a process model of fundamental importance for the adoption of such a model: the weight it places on the professionalism of teachers.

The importance of professionalism

On the process model, satisfactory pupil activity must be recognised, in the classroom, by the teachers, since we cannot *pre-specify* the behaviours to be required of pupils. In this way, the process model emphasises the importance of teachers. Another way of putting this point, a more revealing one, would say that it emphasises teacher *professionalism*. In this way, the work of Stenhouse 'invited teachers to research a problem of curricular action rather than offer them curriculum prescriptions' (Simons, 1988: 87). For the role of the teacher in developing a curriculum could no longer be treated simply in terms of the *delivery* of that curriculum; hence, it could not be reduced simply to putting in place previously specified activity-targets. Rather, the teacher's role involved coming to recognise what were and what were not appropriate behaviours in the particular context of that class. This point is important for us for two related reasons. First, it emphasises the 'open-endedness' of the teacher's role, thereby giving due weight to the teacher as *informed observer*. Stenhouse himself was very clear on this point. Developing a curriculum was, on this conception, not a matter of explicitly articulating a series of standards to be achieved or criteria to be met. Rather, it was 'conceived as a probe through which to explore and test hypotheses and not as a recommendation to be adopted' (Stenhouse, 1975: 125). This will mean that success in a particular lesson or a particular course will be judged at least primarily from the perspective of the teachers. Applied to dance teaching, the importance of informed observation of lessons and of courses is stressed: such a conclusion obviously coheres well with the view of the objectivity of dance appreciation developed in Chapter 1, and (as we shall see) extended in Chapter 15.

Second, emphasising teacher professionalism has very important implications for *theory* in relation to teaching, and associatedly the whole idea of *research* into teaching. In this chapter, I will say something about the theory/practice considerations, and consider some implications for research into dance teaching in Chapter 16. As Elliott (1991: 45) has noted: 'Teachers often feel threatened by theory'. The nature of that *feeling of threat* is important here. For teachers regularly see themselves as practitioners, centrally concerned with *action*. Often, they regard themselves as naive, needing other 'experts' to explain to them what it is they *should really* be doing. As we will see, the process conception should move us away from this mistaken view of the teacher: but to advance in that direction we should first note (from Elliott) three related major elements in that feeling of threat. The first is that theory is seen as the product of a group of *outsiders* who 'claim to be experts in generating valid knowledge about educational practices' (Elliott, 1991: 45). So theory is seen as the product of people who have some techniques, methods, or procedures *other than* those of the teacher which they apply from some detached, neutral position. Second, and relatedly, theory is seen as essentially involving *generalisation* across specific circumstances. Since theory should apply (it is assumed) to *all* contexts of practice, the *specific* experience of teachers in their classrooms or studios is not an adequate basis for generating knowledge (or so it seems). Theory for teachers must be theory for *all* teachers: and this can be daunting, since what teachers *really know* obviously turns on their own experience. Third, theory is seen as building on (and hence building-in) some ideal of society or the human individual. That is to say, the *justification* of theory lies outside the scope of the teacher's ordinary experience. This is one reason why theory can be seen as the produce of 'expert' opinion.

Of course, the theorising of practical knowledge is important. We need to bring to bear on our experience concepts which have a wider application than simply that experience. We need to challenge established ways of looking at teaching situations; in particular, the assumption that what is happening in a particular teaching context is somehow *obvious*. That is to say, we need to find ways of being surprised by the everyday. And theory can help us there. For one possible achievement of theory is to render problematic the taken-for-granted (Biott, 1984: 71). So some generalised rejection of *all* theory is mistaken. For example, some of the abstract theory of, say, Antonio Gramsci (Anderson, 1976) can be very revealing if we consider power relations in societies. In particular, it can render problematic — in a constructive way — the negotiation of power between, for example, men and women. In this way, it can lead us away from either facile acceptance of patriarchy or from equally facile dismissal of *every* social feature as the product of patriarchy (Hargreaves, 1992). Here is one example, then, where a more general theory might impact on our understanding of the educational.

Nonetheless, giving weight to the teacher (the teacher-as-researcher, as Stenhouse would put it) reinforces the theoretical possibilities that begin from the teacher's own practice. Such a move towards an enquiry-based view of knowledge will certainly involve us in rejecting the thought that there is some *privileged* way of knowing and, with it, the thought that understanding teaching is the *monopoly* of outsiders. Further, it should warn us against trying to achieve unwarranted scope, or the unwarranted *limitation* of scope, in our enquiries. Discussing what goes on in my classroom or my studio is not *obviously* of general significance, but neither is it *obviously* of significance only for me. Moreover, emphasis on the professional responsibilities of the *teacher* in this way will move us away from reliance on mechanistic procedures for enquiry, such as questionnaire instruments or psychometric tests or Systematic Observation schedules.

Taken together, these remarks emphasise three points. The first is the idea of *craft-knowledge*: a kind of knowledge arrived at by doing something rather than reading about it. Craft-knowledge, of course, will then be investigated through an investigation of the practices central to the profession in question (Brown & McIntyre, 1986). We will return to this idea in Chapter 16. Second, and related, is the idea of teaching and research as *practices*; that is to say, social activities with their own normative rules. As a result, it is sensible to at least consider the teaching situation as a collaboration with pupils and colleagues. Again, this idea has a direct application to dance teaching: we readily acknowledge that choreographic responsibilities can be given to pupils, in appropriate circumstances, and that other pupils (and perhaps teachers) can learn from this experience. The third point involves seeing teaching as essentially *emancipatory*: that is, as empowering the taught. This should involve both giving the taught a feeling of mastery or control of the learning, and freeing the teachers from *established* ways of seeing. Again, this is a complex idea. It would be easy to misunderstand it and hence to slide into a subjectivism which prioritised pupil activity such that teachers could not, under any circumstances, be seen to *correct*. As noted earlier, such a notion is self-contradictory. But in any case, it is not what is being urged here. Consonant with our Personal Enquiry account of education, we see general goal of education as providing self-determination for pupils. So it becomes essential that they *go beyond* their teachers, but not necessarily in ways that their teachers find unrecognisable. These three points are fundamental for an adequate understanding of teacher professionalism: they ground any understanding of what kinds of processes and procedures enable the teacher to help pupils towards the attainment of self-determination (Kelly, 1990: 121)[3].

Discussing the general position of teachers in curriculum theory, Kelly (1990: 125) remarks on 'the scope...[British] teachers have enjoyed in their curriculum practice'. As he goes on the record, 'A common curriculum framed in terms of principles and processes would not take away that scope: indeed, it would demand a full exercise of it'. That is to say, such a curriculum would require well-informed, well-trained and well-motivated teachers, knowledgeable in their fields. Although these requirements may seem idealistic, they are not unreasonable to expect of educationalists, given the general importance of education. It is now worth asking about the degree to which the National Curriculum in the UK does indeed adopt a *process model* of the curriculum; and also the degree to which teachers have been (or will be) given the kinds of scope and responsibility which (with Kelly) we have recognised are essential within any satisfactory process model.

Physical education and dance in the National Curriculum: a process model?

Following the general policy in this text, I wish to make the rather abstract remarks about process models in the curriculum more explicit by taking as an example the National Curriculum document for physical education in the UK, focusing of course on aspects concerning dance education. It is important to notice that this document merely indicates recommended programmes of study in a fairly sketchy way[4]. Hence, although I read it strictly literally, it is unrealistic to expect that it deal with *all* eventualities, nor that it was intended to do so.

Looking at what the documents present to describe what pupils *must* be able to do at the end of each Key Stage, we find a collection of fairly general suggestions which might be treated quite differently in different classes, where the individual needs of pupils and the individual areas of expertise of teachers might be given full reign. There is still an emphasis on the giving of opportunities, on responding, yet the emphasis on being guided and on selection of content by teachers as well as pupils has not disappeared. Again, nothing here need lead one away from taking this as a process model of the curriculum. In fact, dance fares a little better than other activities. For example, it is suggested that by the end of Key Stage 2, pupils should be able to show that they can 'swim at least 25 meters' (DES, August 1991: 19). In contrast to the dance remarks, this is clearly a product-directed target. There is doubtless room to argue about the degree to which the National Curriculum in the UK as a whole is built on *product* lines (Kelly, 1990), and the degree to which the physical education proposals do and do not adhere to that model *because* of their relation to a more general structure. None of that is centrally to our point. The intention here is simply to show how, as articulated in the documentation under consideration, the prospect for dance education might be *understood* in process terms, with the additional implication that it *should* be so understood.

Here the point about the professionalism of teachers becomes crucial. For the remarks do not in general determine *what* a pupil shall do, nor even what achievements of the pupils shall be measured (though some of this is available in other documents from the National Curriculum Council).

This identifies two clear mistakes which might be made. On the one hand, it might be assumed that such brief statements, as it were, did one's curriculum planning for one. In this way, a teacher might attempt to structure classes taking these statements as objectives. I am suggesting, though, that this would be a recipe for bad teaching. These statements are designed to give a direction to the teacher, but not to replace standard lesson planning. On the other hand, one might build-up sets of *behavioural objectives* which translated these remarks into precise behaviours — prespecified, and then duly integrated into one's lesson planning. The first mistake would be to do, really, *no* planning; while the second would involve planning of the *wrong* sort!

As earlier, there is a similar mixture of concern with the guiding hand of the teacher who, for example, will *set* the dance and the exploratory activity of the pupil, who will perform it with appropriate *style*. Moreover, these suggestions are developmentally related to the previous ones. We have moved from simply making dances with beginnings, middles and ends through making such dances using improvisation and exploration to the communication of meanings and idea drawing on appropriate techniques. In a sense, the developmental progression is straightforward — which is not to say that it would be in the teaching context!

Furthermore, satisfaction of the requirement that pupils 'develop and use appropriate techniques and styles to communicate meanings and ideas' (DES, August 1991, §8.76: 33) could amount to a considerable number of different things. For example, alone or in conjunction with a dance artist in education (see Chapter 8), I might draw on *masterworks* to give pupils insight to the structuring of dances, the technical requirements of those dances, and the expressive potentials of those technical elements. Equally, I might focus on dance as it appears in, say, some modern musical: imagine that it was a musical with a jazz base. This might provide material for the construction of dances — and lest it be thought that such dances could not concern themselves with the communication of 'meanings and ideas' (DES, August 1991, §8.76: 33), we should remind ourselves of the many art works which do just this: for example, Christopher Bruce's use of tap in *Swan Song* (1989). Equally, the creation of works to 'communicate meanings and ideas' might be largely exploratory, as long as pupils have a sufficient grasp of compositional principles, and of performance skills (what might otherwise be called *technique*). That is to say, the *realisation* of this particular target might be very different, as might be the methods by which teachers went about ensuring its attainment. As a result, teachers must make individual judgements as to their own strengths and those of particular pupils. These different methods are held together, of course, by a common direction: they are concerned with the making of dances in order 'to communicate meanings and ideas' — which I take to be *broadly* equivalent to the communication-potential of our art-type dance.

This a way of *reading* the documentation allows scope for the varied responses characteristic of good dance teaching. Also, though, we see the kinds of argument which would need to be in place if such teaching is to be justified. That is to say, if the two mistakes identified earlier are to be avoided, teachers must be clear that the work they are involved in will not be treated in a *product* fashion by, say, some external moderator. And they must be prepared to give thoughtful and rational, rather than effusive, justifications for their practice. In this sense, identifying the demands of a *process* model for the curriculum is providing the dance teacher with suitable material for an elaborated account of established dance practice.

Of course, I have been discussing a set of *recommendations*: but that is quite satisfactory for our purposes here. They illustrate how a variety of aspirations for dance might, suitably understood, be treated as the centre-piece of a *process* model for the dance curriculum. Unless an *explicitly* 'out-comes' model of the curriculum is produced, it may always be possible to interpret the dance curriculum in this 'process' way. But if that interpretation is not shared with 'the powers that be' — for example, external moderators — the net effect will be the production of *what is taken for* vague objectives. So this discussion highlights the need for a consistent *reading* of any proposals, agreed among key participants.

Some thoughts on aims and accountability

Thus far, this chapter has sought to explain a *process* model of the curriculum, contrasting it with an *objectives* model, and to see such a model in the remarks on dance in the National Curriculum proposal for Physical Education. This investigation has, in effect, led in a circle. I introduced it by noting the need to have clear *aims* for one's teaching, aims which could be evaluated, in order that teaching be accountable[5]. If one is using an *objectives* model, it is clear when one's objectives are fulfilled; further, if such objectives are appropriately related to course aims, evaluation of the course should demonstrate that those aims are fulfilled simply by demonstrating that the objectives have been. Dropping this use of objectives is, in effect, removing that line of justification. The whole purpose of this chapter was to lay-out lines of justification for activities arguably centre stage in dance education. As noted initially, a course of study will *not* be accountable if all it can offer are vague aspirations, whose satisfaction is not amenable to course evaluations.

The heart of my response (which I take to be Stenhouse's) is to focus on the *teacher*, in two ways. First, as we have emphasised in Chapter 3, the practice of teaching should be seen as having the *value-notion* education as its 'end'. As Elliott put it, 'What makes teaching an educational practice is not simply the quality of its educational outcomes, but the manifestation within the practice itself of certain qualities which constitute it as an educational process, capable of fostering *educational outcomes* in terms of student learning' (Elliott, 1991: 50 quoted Chapter 3). If this is right, then satisfaction of our educational aims will be *integral* or *internal* to the process of teaching. That is to say, successful teaching will be *visible* to the informed and attentive teacher. Thus, an emphasis on the internal nature of the value of education means that success in education can only be judged accurately by teachers. Second, the success of teachers could not be evaluated totally independently: rather, self-evaluation would be essential, an investigation of the *practice* of teaching which would be integral both to a proper understanding of what had achieved for pupils, and, relatedly, of the success of one's methods.

Put this way, two major difficulties are identified. First, that this emphasis on the teacher might raise questions about objectivity; second, pressures *external* to the teaching situation (pressures such as the demands of employers, but equally of externally-occurring examinations), might seem to privilege the acquisition of product-based 'facts' over educational processes. Stenhouse was profoundly aware of both difficulties. As quoted earlier, 'The process model is essentially a critical model, not a marking model. It can never be *directed* towards an examination as an objective without loss of quality, since the standards of the examination then override the standards imminent in the subject…. Unfortunately examinations are so important in our society that….' (Stenhouse, 1975: 95). I leave it to readers to fill in what goes after the 'that…' in the quotation: but clearly Stenhouse is there voicing a worry about the public character of educational standards.

These two worries can only be answered by reasserting the professionalism of the teacher. But such a reaffirmation is no longer unproblematic in the way that it was. In an engaging article, Dennis Lawton (1981: 111) remarks: 'Throughout the 1940s and 50s it could comfortably be assumed that, not only was education "a good thing", but also that it was in safe hands'. Here, the hands in question were those of 'educationists'. That consensus about both the value of education and the safeness of educationalists hands can no longer be assumed. There has been a 'loss of faith' in *both* these dimensions. First, it is no longer taken for granted that education is 'a good thing' — the question of the *relevance* of education is being raised. People are asked to explain *education for what?*. This might be taken as generating just the kind of *external* standards for education which Stenhouse rightly deplored. Second, it is no longer *taken for granted* that curriculum matters are best left in the hands of the educational establishment. The key idea here was 'taken for granted'. That is, it might still be true, but now it needed to be proved, shown or demonstrated. These threads come together in calls for 'accountability'. If education becomes accountable — say, to parents and/or to industry — then the people to whom it is accountable are bound to have an understanding of the *value* of education since it will be value *for them*; it will no longer be in the hands of those who, it might be thought, have a *vested interest* in education, Thus both the public nature of the *value* of education and the objectivity of the educationalists perspective might be challenged. As Lawton (1981: 123) expressed it, when speaking of the relationship between education and the rest of society, 'the metaphor has changed from a partnership to accountability'. It does seem as though education, especially education paid for by the state, should be *in some way* answerable to the needs of, say, the national economy.

There are two related lines of response here, neither particularly strong when viewed by their opponents. Our first response is that the value of education is an *internal* one — broadly, what was once called 'liberal education'. Similarly, the second reply not only emphasises the importance of personal development, rather than the acquisition of 'facts', but also urges that judgements of success and failure be left primarily in the hands of teachers. Both can sound like replies of those with vested interests in preserving their own power, position or (even) employment: further, they can seem insular, or 'ivory tower'. And these points seem reinforced when our argument is for a subject-area such as dance, which has no obvious practical relevance. But these judgements are misplaced. For the argument turns on whether or not there is an *alternative* here: our position has been that *only* this constitutes a route for education. So that one might, for example, produce *training* in another way — but is training what is required? In particular (as we asked in Chapter 6), is it plausible to expect such training to be of *lasting* value in a world of rapid technological change? So our replies amount to claiming that only education can produce the kinds of flexibility of mind required by society (today or any day): and that — as we have seen — education *necessarily* places weight on the informed judgements of teachers.

Conclusion

This chapter has argued quite generally for a *process* conception of the curriculum, urging that such a conception readily coheres with the Personal Enquiry conception developed earlier; and that it has an especial resonance for dance education. With this in mind, some brief remarks about the way in which the National Curriculum Proposal for Physical Education in the UK might be read in this light, and exemplified both the possibilities and some of the dangers in this way of thinking. The outcome has been a curriculum model which allows room for arguments for the distinctive place of dance education.

Chapter 14

Dance Teaching and Dance Practice

Introduction

This chapter addresses two related but distinct questions. The majority of the chapter concerns the relation between the *self-legislation* which (as argued in Chapter 3 and elsewhere) is crucial for education, and the accountability and assessability (as recorded in Chapter 13) which are crucial for genuine teaching strategies, at least in principle. It will be argued that one can be 'child-centred' *without* sliding into the 'anything goes' situation which is both characteristic of subjectivism and a result of consistent application of many principles of 'movement education' (Russell, 1958: 80–1): that the *artistic* account of dance education provides a specific line of defence against such a slide into subjectivism.

The chapter concludes with a recognition that, while a *logical priority* ordering of material in the artistic account will obviously prioritise the art-based, the *practical priority* in teaching dance might well begin elsewhere. Indeed, a satisfactory induction of pupils into the art of dance (that is, satisfaction of the artistic account of dance education) may even *require* that this occur. The general thrust here is towards a *realistic* appraisal of the relationship between methods of *teaching dance* (as a part of dance education in schools) and the conceptual structure within which that teaching is to be understood. For one should neither claim that pedagogical issues are of *no* relevance (see especially Chapter 16 on craft knowledge) nor that they *determine* the conceptual direction of the investigation. Indeed, a crucial point to record here is the difference between the *logical ordering* of material in the artistic account and the *practical ordering* for teaching: for example, one doesn't necessarily *start* with art (any more than one starts, in teaching a particular set of skills in, say, rugby union, with the developed version of those skills as they appear at present in the achievements of the Australian David Campese, except when one uses him as an example).

Teaching dance: some general constraints

Let us begin with some generalities about teaching, applied to dance in educational contexts. Five factors, at the least, might constrain the practice of teaching dance in the school setting. The first concerns the point of that teaching. The teacher must see this lesson, or this programme of study, as part of a larger educational aim or aspiration. We have already dealt with this point in respect of dance by locating the central aspiration for dance education in our artistic account. Such an account might be augmented by the recognition of a general ground rule, of a kind suggested by David Carr (1978: 70):

> as knowing how to perform a given task is a matter of knowing what strategies and procedures to adopt to execute a given plan or purpose, practical knowledge is, therefore, at least to this extent, an exercise of human rationality.

This means that we should see, through dance teaching, the exercise of 'practical reason'. And expect such practical reason to be demonstrated through the lessons.

As a second factor, the methods of delivery of the dance programme and its point should be in accord. Our artistic account will here emphasise two major concerns. First, we have recognised (in Chapter 8) the importance of masterworks for understanding, a point we will return to later in this chapter. This connection with masterworks is centrally important because it ties our lessons to the history and traditions of the art form. In this way, it is of a piece with our artistic account. Second, it must be acknowledged that not *every* piece of *every* lesson can be explicitly directed towards the construction or understanding of art: that would be neither a realistic aspiration nor one likely in parallel cases such as the teaching of music or of visual art. So we must discuss the relationship of the general aspiration (with its *artistic* direction) to the delivery of *other* elements of content.

A third factor concerns the *morality* of methods of teaching. This simply elaborates a *crucial* aspect of the second point: it is one way in which the methods of delivery must be appropriate. Three concerns might be identified. First, given our Personal Enquiry conception of education, respect for persons must be paramount. Second, given our emphasis on understanding, the degree to which strongly *directed* teaching methods are appropriate must be questioned, for such methods will tend to produce those able to 'parrot' the views of teachers rather than those with understanding. Third, the values of the dance lesson should be its intrinsic values although, of course, it may be important to also emphasise its extrinsic values to pupils — for example, its health and fitness, or social, benefits.

A fourth factor will concern the effectiveness of methods of delivery. Having identified an appropriate aspiration, and located methods relative to that point, and moreover moral methods, we make no progress if those methods are not going to be *effective*. This is clearly a crucial matter, but not something on which a text such as this to comment extensively. In part, the *how* of delivery is a matter for teachers' personal choices on the basis of what works for them. In addition, it will be appropriately tempered by what they have learned in training, and therefore by examples of good practice. Teachers will clearly need a wide variety of teaching strategies. However, it is worth paying some attention to how teachers might learn the possible *variety* of such methods, how they both plan classes drawing on such knowledge and analyse their work in terms of it. This will be the topic of the fourth section of this chapter, on methods of analysis.

Finally, a constraining factor here will be the possibility of assessment of pupils' work (for example, for examination purposes[1]). In addition, it will be important to give attention to methods of evaluating course delivery, and educational success. This is the topic of Chapter 15, and can therefore be put aside here.

It follows from these five constraints, then, that we should further comment on the kinds of understanding appropriate for the artistic account of dance education, and hence some of the methods appropriate in delivery. Further, we should discuss the morality of those methods: in particular, their relation to the question of the 'child-centredness' or otherwise of dance education. This will be the topic of the fifth section of this chapter, on free expression and subjectivism.

Masterworks and understanding (again)

One question which has bedevilled dance education has concerned the place, or otherwise, of the teaching of dance techniques, such as Graham technique. The constraints articulated in the previous section give us a straightforward way to characterise each side of that debate. Those who argue *for* the crucial place of such technique are effectively trying to do justice to the *artistic* nature of the aspirations of dance education, while those who argue *against* the essential place of such technique are attempting to be true to the 'respect for persons' idea, by focusing on the supposed diminution of children's creativity that detailed technique learning might imply, and also the reduction of class time for such creativity which giving appropriate time to technique learning would entail. But this debate is misplaced. As we will see, there is no theoretical reason why the aspirations of both sides might not be met, at least in principle: just how the constraints of time imposed by school timetabling are overcome is another matter. Throughout this chapter, therefore, I shall urge the importance of the *artistic* dimension, pointing out some of its implications for teaching, while in the fifth section I shall focus on child-centred teaching methodologies, and their importance.

The point here could be introduced by imagining one sort of (heated) discussion which might take place concerning the importance of Laban's choreutics. As Thornton (1971: 56) noted, Laban himself defined choreutics as 'the art, or the science, dealing with the analysis and synthesis of movement', and activity which 'embraces the various applications of movement to work, education and art, as well as to regenerative processes in the widest sense'. Thornton (1971: 56) calls it 'the most exhaustive and most technical study of the moving body in space which has yet been produced'. Suppose, for the moment, that all this is granted: still, how does this relate to dance education? In particular, should choreutics be included in, say, the training of dance educators? Given the assumption that we have made, choreutics will obviously have a place if it is viewed as an *analysis* of movement patterns and movement activity in spatial terms. A question, though, might be the degree to which choreutics is a suitable tool for *composition*; in particular, might it be an *alternative* to, say, the study of masterworks? In fact, the answer is relatively straightforward. Our very general account of choreutics emphasises the two features crucial to such an answer. First, choreutics is a general analysis of movement; as such, it is not *uniquely* suitable for the construction of art works — one of the strengths of such wholly general analytical tools (and notations such as Labanotation are also in this category, as we saw in Chapter 2) lies exactly in their ability to apply more widely than simply to dance (*UD*: 61). Secondly, while it makes sense to move from the study of, say, Martha Graham technique to making Graham-type dances of one's own, it makes no sense — on a parallel — to imagine making choreutic-type dances of one's own. Insofar as choreutics *is* a wholly general analytical tool, it *could* be applied in the analysis of any dance, and therefore *could* be useful to a choreographer wishing to use, say, Graham technique to make a dance. That is to say, one might gain either clarity or inspiration from choreutic analysis, or from planning dances in terms of the sorts of 'harmonies' that choreutics identifies. But these gains might feature in my Graham-technique dance! The answer to the question posed earlier is a resounding 'no': analytical tools such as choreutics are inappropriate as *alternatives* to the study of masterworks, combined with the techniques within which those masterworks are constructed.

A partial parallel here, as often, come from language. Choreutics stands roughly in the same role for dance as, say, Chomsky's generative grammar does for language (Lyons, 1970: 132–6). Knowing generative grammar will not ensure that I make satisfactory sentences, although it will help me to analyse candidate 'sentences' offered by others. Moreover, if I am interested in sentence construction, knowing generative grammar might well give me an additional source of insight to draw on. But it will not give me an understanding of either *words*, the root-meaning units, nor the capacity to recognise which sentences *work* or *make sense*. Indeed, Chomsky's work recognises that the final arbiter for sentence adequacy must be the views of native speakers (Lyons, 1970: 39–40). The points from generative grammar apply directly to choreutics. We need to learn the 'words" — that is, meaning-units — which are provided through the technique. (Although, of course, there is no exact equivalent here in movement terms for *words*; see *UD*: 117–18). Moreover, we need to understand the sorts of meaning-giving structure which apply in respect of that technique: and we learn this in part through the study of our masterworks (*UD*: 203–13).

Lest this discussion be misunderstood, notice two further points. First, this discussion highlights a *strength* of general analytical tools such as choreutics, as well as a limitation. Second, there is nothing in this discussion which depends on its being *choreutics* that I have chosen to discuss. Any tool designed to apply to *all* movement, and therefore have application to *all* movement, will be comparably deficient once applied solely within the confines of dance.

Moreover, the examples of both composition and technique given here are not in any way authoritative in this respect. The point is simply that *technique* and *masterwork* are crucial concepts: that we cannot teach dance to any level without teaching these to at least *some* level. Without them, we simply have nothing which is *dance*. As we saw in Chapter 8, mere *movement* is not the medium of dance in this sense, any more than sound is the medium of spoken language. So any programme of study must give attention to these key concepts if it is to do justice to the point of dance and to relate methods of delivery to that point, with the important proviso that precisely *how* this is done will be in the gift of teachers. Additionally, such teachers will be informed spectators of dance, whose presentation of choreographic structures brings with it the emphasis on understanding dance so crucial within dance education (as argued in Chapter 9).

Methods of analysis of dance teaching?

The fourth of our constraints (see pp. 155–6) concerned the *effectiveness* of methods of the delivery of dance education. As noted there, this work has relatively little to say on such a topic. However, there is one particular way in which such teaching *is* brought within the ambit of the sorts of analysis practiced here. For teaching and learning are not simply something which *may* occur in lessons. As we saw in Chapter 13, the idea of teaching is *crucial* to our conception of educational value. In this vein, the document *The Curriculum From 5–16* (HMI, 1985: 10–11) comments favourably (strongly) on the 'influence of learning activities and teaching styles on what is learned and how well it is learned.... Active learning, and a sense of purpose and success, enhance pupils' enjoyment, interest, confidence and sense of personal worth; passive learning and inappropriate styles can lead to frustration and failure'. Thus the *how* of teaching is seen to be important not only for its effectiveness, but also for, at root, the *what* of delivery.

To make the succeeding discussion more concrete, I will take, as an example, a widely employed taxonomy of teaching styles from Mosston and Ashworth (1986). However, it would be inappropriate to discuss in detail this Spectrum of Teaching Styles, or to comment on the general effectiveness of any or all such styles. Instead, we question the precise purposes of such a taxonomy.

At its heart, Mosston's Spectrum of Teaching Styles involves a classification of 'styles' of teaching from a *Command* style (style A) through *Discovery* to *Self-teaching* (style J and beyond). It is accepted that, in any particular lesson, a number of such styles might be used, and that a number are required (perhaps all) in order that the full range of aims and objectives for physical education be met. It is implied, also, that all or most of the styles have application to all areas of physical education and, for these purposes, dance education will count under this heading (in line with our discussions in Chapter 7). Then, for each style, we are led through its identification and some detailed comments on its implementation and importance, under the following headings (Mosston & Ashworth, 1986: 10–11):

1.　the objectives of the style
2.　the anatomy of the style
3.　the implementation
4.　the implications of the style
5.　selecting and designing the subject matter
6.　style-specific comments
7.　the development channels
8.　examples of subject matter.

Suppose, therefore, that we have such a taxonomy before us, clearly identifying both the nature of each style, the possible purposes of each style, and the educational advantages of each style; moreover, the taxonomy builds-in remarks about the need to employ more than one style both in a programme of study and within a lesson. Now, what precise uses might such a taxonomy have? I shall consider two answers, both of which are current in discussions of taxonomies of teaching styles more generally, not merely that of Mosston. The first uses the taxonomy simply as an aid to the planning of teaching. That is to say, having the taxonomy allows me to plan what I am going to do (in terms of content or material) in strict relation to *how* I am going to do it. In this way, I will be able both to ensure that I am not presenting my teaching in only *one* way (and in particular that I am not simply using a very directed or *command* style only), but also to ensure that the pupils are taking responsibility for their own learning. This will be a way of drawing on the general educational aims of my teaching. Furthermore, taking such an analytical approach to one's teaching (and in particular to the preparation of one's teaching) will itself allow the refining of that teaching. Thus, if I wish to teach a particular element from Graham technique using Mosston's style C (Reciprocal Teaching), I must have planned *what* pupils are to learn, and broken-down that material so that its key teaching points can be observed by one pupil who can then correct another. This might be effective in the ways that advocates of the use of teaching styles envisage, for example in developing pupils' communication skills, skills of observing and analysing, awareness of others, and the opportunity to give feedback. It may also be very helpful for *me* as teacher to be obliged to decide what are appropriate 'chunks' of material to be worked by pupils in this way, what are key observation points and key teaching points for my pupils engaged in the reciprocal teaching, and so on. So this kind of analytical approach to one's own teaching is very likely to be helpful, especially as it will readily allow a developmental focus: teaching similar material to a class of a different age *may* require a quite different approach. And having to think-through, say, the points to be emphasised in Reciprocal Teaching may make me more fully aware of that fact.

I conclude, therefore, that this sort of approach may be extremely valuable as a teaching aid; and one area of development for dance education could be an elaboration of a taxonomy of this sort *specifically* applied to dance, and more particularly to dance under our *artistic* account.

This brings us to the other option. For a taxonomy such as Mosston's might also be suggested as an analysis of teaching: the sort of thing which might be presented in lesson planning, and looked-for by tutors during teaching practice. Again, this has much to recommend it while we think of it as an *aid* to teaching. Sometimes, though, it might be thought of rather as if it classified *the* ways of understanding teaching. But, as with basic movements taxonomies, there is a danger in thinking that only *one* way of classifying teaching is accurate.

There are three major considerations here. The first concerns the arbitrary nature of *any* taxonomy. In the play 'Toad of Toad Hall' the jury is made up of a number of rabbits and 'another kind of rabbit': in this case, a weasel wearing a hat with long ears. It is easy to think that such a taxonomy, which turns weasels into rabbits, is just mistaken — which, in that context, it is! But that is not to say that the taxonomy that we *presently* use, or one which some use, is *the only* or *the best* taxonomy. Two examples illustrate this point. Ask how many colours there are of a paint salesman and he will answer differently depending upon which paint company he works for. There are simply a number

of different ways of drawing up a taxonomy of colours, and different companies have chosen different ones. But neither is right or wrong: the only
question concerns which taxonomy is most *useful* to you, given the rooms you
wish to paint. Similarly, the driving instructor who assures me that there is only
one occasion on which I should use my mirror (namely, when changing speed
or direction) is disputing my claim that there are a large number of such cases
(for example, when approaching traffic lights, when pulling out, when turning,
etc.). But the dispute is not one on which he is absolutely right, and I am
absolutely wrong, or vice versa. Rather, we decide for what purpose the question occurs. In the context of the driving test, it may well be appropriate to give
the driving instructor's answer. But that does not guarantee the *priority* of his
taxonomy over mine. The point, then, is simply that taxonomies should be
judged by their completeness and their usefulness. If we grant that a particular
taxonomy of teaching styles, such as Mosston's, is complete, it remains to
consider simply how *useful* it is.

A second consideration builds on a particular example. Suppose that I am
teaching dance as part of my training to be a dance teacher, and my supervisor
notices that my lesson doesn't fit neatly into Mosston's taxonomy. What might
be said? In fact, two parallel answers spring to mind: first, that the lesson does
really fit, because the taxonomy is a *spectrum* — the issue is just *where* on the
spectrum to place this particular lesson fitted. Second, it might be concluded
that the lesson did *really* fit, because its first 20 minutes were in *this* style, the
next 20 minutes in *that* style, etc. But either answer implies prior, unshakeable
and *explicit* commitment to the taxonomy. The question is not really 'does
lesson X fit the taxonomy?', but rather '*how* does lesson X fit the taxonomy?'.
The assumption here is that any lesson *must* fit the taxonomy in some way or
other. Of course, there is nothing problematic about this, so long as it is not
used as an assessment tool, nor allowed to dominate research into teaching
styles. That is to say, such a taxonomy, however *useful*, should always be
recognised as just one taxonomy amongst many, even if it were both dominant
in training and of proven usefulness. At any time, an equally or more useful
taxonomy might be constructed. So our second point draws on the first. Since
taxonomies are arbitrary, nothing but a prior commitment to a particular
taxonomy will allow one to say that a specific lesson *must* fit within that
taxonomy; but this is no criticism of either lesson or taxonomy.

The third consideration may also be introduced with an example. Imagine,
as in the case above, that the lesson during my teaching practice is judged not
to fit into, say, Mosston's taxonomy: I have been using none of the styles in the
spectrum nor any combination of them. Perhaps the reason my lesson doesn't
fit is that it is a *bad* lesson: moreover, bad for that reason. But now the
taxonomy has acquired a different role. We are no longer using the taxonomy
to *classify* the lessons: we are using it as a basis for *judging* them. Here the

taxonomy of particular styles is being used in *almost* the same exclusive way
as in the example above, but with an additional evaluative dimension. So that,
it is urged, the *reason* my lesson is bad is that it is not founded on Mosston's
teaching taxonomy. In this case, something is slightly amiss. If Mosston's
taxonomy of styles is of *good* teaching only, it follows that it is not, for that
reason, a taxonomy of *teaching*. Here we are returning to a point, made in the
section above, about general analytical frameworks. A strength of such
frameworks is that they apply *across the board*, to a variety of disparate
situations. We are identifying, then, a *misuse* of this kind of taxonomy.

This section has urged the advantages of a taxonomy of teaching styles
for the elaborations of successful techniques for dance education, although it
has not looked to other, equally productive strategies with which effective
teaching might be encouraged — for example, the study of good practice.
However, it has raised a number of difficulties in the potential overextension
of the claims of such analyses. In this way, we have looked at some of the
considerations which relate to the production of effective methods, one of our
constraints mentioned earlier (p. 156).

Free-expression and subjectivism

If, by the discussion earlier in this chapter (pp. 156–8), we have a clear focus
through to the artistic account of dance education, and if, by the discussion in
the previous section, we have at least begun to analyse appropriately methods
of delivery of our material (with the understanding that such methods may well
shape the material), there is still much to say on the question of delivery.
In particular, we have already identified the need to build-in respect for
persons, and to give due weight to 'free-expression'. That is to say, since
education is (on the Personal Enquiry conception) a matter of encouraging self-
determination, it follows that heavily-directed teaching methods will be
inappropriate. Of course, considerations of the kind raised in the previous
section will in any case militate against the exclusive use of one teaching style,
once we have a taxonomy which makes choices apparent to us. Nonetheless,
there remains an important issue, which is best introduced via an example of a
misconception about the nature of dance understanding and dance teaching.

As Betty Redfern has noted in more than one place (Redfern, 1979: 12;
1986: 82), the Department of Education and Science publication *Movement:
Physical Education in the Primary Years* claimed 'Every child can dance. The
sharpness of his sense and the intensity of his reactions frequently demand
immediate expression' (DES, 1972: 44). All that is required, on this account, to
turn the child's movement into dance is that is 'becomes clearly defined'. If
one truly believed this, the job of the dancer teacher would simply consist in
finding ways to facilitate the child's 'spontaneous expression' (DES, 1972: 44)

becoming 'clearly defined'. In fact, this claim is clearly open to interpretation in two contrasting ways relevant here. First, the claim that all children *can* dance may be simply an acknowledgement of the *possibilities* for children, and perhaps a statement of an aspect of the *entitlement curriculum* for children: none are to be excluded. In this sense, dance is within the *province* of all children, but no assumptions are imported about what they can or will do. Our artistic account could well begin from just this point. Since all children *can* dance, in this sense, our task would consist in *actualising* the possibility of their dancing, through leading them to an understanding of dance which draws on its *artistic* nature, and which therefore brings with it the sorts of concern with technique, composition and appreciation that might be encountered through a discussion of masterworks. Thus, briefly, we move from what sounds like a grand claim to *our* programme for dance education.

However, this is not the way that claim *was* interpreted, not surprisingly, given the rest of that paragraph, as quoted above. The assumption, rather, was that children need only to be left to their own devices for dances to issue forth, with the 'teacher' there simply so that the 'spontaneous expression' could be disciplined. This sounds like a recipe for a 'do what you like' version of free-expression.The thought might be that any alternative would involve the stifling of pupils creativity.

This version is important for us to contest, and for two reasons. The first, most obvious and most important, is its irreducible subjectivism. Believing that at the centre of a dance lesson is a process of free-expression *understood in this way* is tantamount to claiming that 'anything goes'. The teacher's input can never be seen as correcting or directing the pupil: to do so would be to impinge on the pupil's creativity. Second, this view of the dance lesson is deeply unhelpful. If it were true, there would be literally nothing that dance teachers could usefully do. At best, their job would consist in providing a fruitful environment to encourage pupils, complete with suitable stimuli such as music or poems or whatever, and preventing interference from outside influences — in my imagination some kind of uncreative Rottweiler! Notice, though, that there is absolutely nothing educational in any of this. If this is the dance teacher's role, then there are not dance *teachers* in the education system.

Luckily, this position is clearly misguided. As often, the parallel with education through other art forms makes the point exactly. We do not expect children to be able to write poetry unless we give them suitable building-blocks for poetry: not only words and sentence structures, but poetic forms. Of course, one such poetic form may be *free verse*, but a child who does not know what free verse is is *not* a child writing free verse. Similarly, we wish children to make *music* rather than noise. This is achieved by giving them some understanding of what makes a sound structure into music. Of course, in later life, they may come to learn that the principles they have been taught have not been rigorously adhered to by, say, Pierre Boulez; nonetheless they have been taught a framework which *facilitates* the production of music. This, then, must be the model for dance education too. This simply reiterates a point recurring throughout this text: that the making of dances requires more than just the performing of certain movements. At the least, those movements be correctly explained, drawing on dance *reasons*, and that means that the person who *sets*, or the one who *performs*, the movements must have access to such reasons, at least in principle. So my dance lesson is not structured by an unyielding commitment to the child's creativity. Rather, it is structured by the needs of the child to learn what dance is, and what dance *as an art* is, at least eventually.

David Best (1979) posed the standard dilemma in a clear way: 'Free expression or the teaching of technique?'. As Best argued in that article (see also Best, 1985a Ch. 5) and as we have seen, this contrast is spurious. In order that there be *any* expression, free or otherwise, those doing the expressing must have sufficient technical resources both to understand what they are doing (at least in principle) and for what they are doing to be understandable by its audience (with the same proviso). The elements of a technique (for example Graham technique) simply represent *one* such requirement satisfied: they provide one set of 'building blocks' for the making of intelligible dances. But intellegibility requires that the *whole* be structured also. For the teacher, the requirement here involves pupils coming to *learn* what such structuring involves. One way, of course, will be through the study of masterworks; another through introductory compositions of their own making. This *is* free-expression, in that pupils are making works of their own, engagement with which might involve life-issues perplexities of theirs: they are not being directed in these ways, even when themes, techniques and motifs are *set* by a teacher. The pupils have an understanding of the sorts of techniques and structure which *allow* such expression. Of course, this is an alternative to the subjectivist model on which children are simply left free to do *whatever* they wish. Instead, pupils' learning experiences are structured, which gives the teacher a crucial role. But that structuring is to *facilitate* artistic expression, free-expression in this sense, not to inhibit or preclude it.

David Best (1985a: 77–78) uses an example from poetry to illustrate exactly this point. Some pupils' poems were, and some were not, vivid, as recognised by a writer-in-residence. What he was seeing, as Best correctly recognises, was the children's creativity: he was making sense of their achievement as poems. But this required that the works be *structured* in ways which made them poems. They were not, say, simply shopping lists, even though both shopping lists and poems do not typically use the whole line on a piece of paper. This example also highlights a related factor, the fifth identified earlier (p. 156). For if, in this way, the pupils' achievements can be objectively rated, there is the possibility of course assessment: and, if we build in certain assumptions about the relationship between teaching and pupil success, the possibility for the evaluation of course delivery. Thus, clarifying this point has led us to recognise the importance of *both* free-expression and the teaching of technique.

Logical priorities?

Much of our argument thus far has concerned itself with, as it were, the 'upper end' of the pupils' dance experience, with their art-making and art-appreciating. Clearly, not all dance education in schools can operate in this way, for at least two reasons. First, not all classes will be so *directly* seen in relation to our *artistic account*. Second, not all developmental stages of understanding in children make a focus on such products and practices appropriate. Put bluntly, the sorts of conceptual engagement and intrinsic value which, as we have seen, are integral to the notion of art may not be within the conceptual grasp of pupils in their first years in schools. As a result, it must be recognised that much of what goes on in dance education will have an artistic direction only at infinity, as it were. That is to say, that will be the goal or aspiration of the dance education programme, rather than its day-to-day rationale.

Here we return to the crucial distinction drawn in the first section of this chapter, between the *logical* ordering of the material as given by the artistic account and the *practical* ordering of that material. This distinction impinges in three particular ways. The first concerns the way in which, for younger pupils, it will be necessary to present elements which, later, may build-up into suitable building blocks for artistic composition and appreciation: that is to say, one does not *begin* with such elements but, as it were, with their precursors. Indeed, a model for this kind of analysis might be found in the Key Stage targets for the UK National Curriculum. In Key Stage 1, pupils were simply to 'experience, and be guided towards, making dances with clear beginnings, middles and ends' (DES, August 1991, §8.40: 29); while, in Key Stage 2, such dances were to involve 'improvising/exploring, selecting and refining content, and sometimes incorporating work from other aspects of the curriculum...' (DES, August 1991, §8.56: 30). Those are the beginnings of an appropriately developmental conception of suitable material for dance teaching to pupils of different ages. So the first thrust is *developmental*. A second thrust is *pragmatic*. If we accept that, while pupils are capable, in principle, of doing A or B, that they must do A *before* they can do B (or that doing B after having done A will improve their doing of it), we have a second reason for structuring our material, also simply operating at the practical level. For, in this example, there might be no *logical* reason why A should precede B — they might, for example, be unrelated elements. Nonetheless, the experienced teacher might have decided that, as a general rule, the doing of A tended to facilitate the doing of B, or some such. In this way, even though there is no *logical* reason for preferring activity A before activity B in terms of the subject itself, nonetheless there is the pragmatic reason. A clear example comes from elementary ballet teaching — since there we have a precise repertoire of named activities. I might prefer to teach the ability to land lightly after a jump (*ballon*) before a particular kind of jump (for example, an *assemblé*). This would not be because one could not teach in another order, but because one saw *pragmatic* virtue in teaching in this order. What is true of the relatively fixed 'moves' of ballet applies equally to the teaching of less determinate dance-structures.

Neither the developmental nor the pragmatic cases, however, takes us to the heart of the problem here. That arises only in our third case, where the practical priority *reverses* the logical priority. A clear way to introduce this point is via a notion which, a few years ago, was important in the training of dance and physical education teachers: the idea of *movement education*.

Drawing, perhaps, on work in Basic Design in visual art (Thistlewood, 1981), theorists concluded that the movement patterns in dance (and also those of other activities in the physical education curriculum) depended on *underlying* movement patterns. Therefore, at the level of *logical priority*, the agents must master the underlying patterns before they could reasonably be expected to master those patterns of activity which *depended on* the underlying ones: in our case, before they could be expected to actually perform dance movements. If this were simply a thesis which picked up the *developmental* thrust mentioned above, it would be unproblematic. We accept that dance education begins with induction into material not, perhaps, *strictly* dance, but which nonetheless represents a building block for dance. However, the thesis for 'Basic Movement' could be taken more substantially than this. Thus the point could be insisted upon not just for *children* beginning in dance, but as a fundamental for dance education in higher education. (And again, this would be on a parallel with the Basic Design movement in visual art education, where Basic Design was an element in the training of art students; see Thistlewood, 1981: 34–36.) In this vein, it was urged that one could study *human movement* as such, rather than this or that kind of human movement. And license for this thesis was sought in the work of, among others, Laban (Preston-Dunlop, 1963: vi).

This idea rests on a large confusion: the confusion arising from the way in which abstraction can produce logical priority by producing shared necessary conditions, and be interpreted in terms of temporal priority or learning priority. To put that more simply, the shared features of movement education were not in fact *logically prior* in the sense of needing to be mastered by all wishing to engage in dance activity: rather, these features were understood or derived from such activities by *analysis*. One can never perform human movement: one can only perform *this* movement, or *that* movement (say, dance, or sumo wrestling, or gymnastics). Of course, if there were in fact underlying principles common to dance (of a certain type), sumo wrestling and gymnastics, then *in a sense* one would have to master those principles before one could master any of the activities. But one learns to master the principles by simply mastering the activities. So, at the level of logical priority, the apparent need for *basic movement* was in fact an illusion.

My point here is a much simpler one: that the relationship between logical priority and practical teaching priority is by no means straightforward. In particular, we should not assume that knowing one is knowing the other. If this point is accepted, it follows that the kinds of analysis of activity which issue from, say, a taxonomy such as Mosston's (see pp. 159–62) may well turn out to be revealing. They may well show us an *effective* ordering of our material, and suggest *effective* modes of delivery. But these reflections should prevent us from making two mistakes. First, we will not assume that because, say, modern dance and Olympic gymnastics have something in common that that 'something' must be taught before either of them is, nor that the place to begin teaching dance is with something *obviously* not dance. That, of course, remains an open question, to be resolved incorporating both the developmental and the pragmatic thrusts articulated above.

Conclusion

This chapter has focused on the relation between the *analysis* of dance and the *teaching* of dance. It has put aside major misconceptions about the power of taxonomies of teaching (and of movement) and elaborated the rejection of subjectivism by showing that a commitment to free-expression is not un-avoidably subjectivist. Many of its positive conclusions may be familiar: they represent the current *practice* of dance teachers. This is as it should be. the aim here has been to argue for the *need* for arguments in support of such practice, and to begin assembling such arguments.

Chapter 15

Accountability and Assessment in Dance Education

The issues

Two related thoughts prompt the concern with educational *accountability* which is the focus of this chapter, and those thoughts in turn identify three major issues. The first thought derives from our rejection of subjectivism (see pp. 2–5): that is, of the claim that dances cannot be assessed. As recent text rightly to claimed, 'assessment should play a critical part in any educational process' (Murphy & Torrance, 1988: 7). For if one believes — or hopes, or plans — that learning is taking place in a particular context, one can always ask if this is indeed so. And if we cannot, by any manner of means, answer such a question (even in principle) we must concede that no learning is actually taking place. Thus, assessment is important. This highlights the first two areas of importance: first, assessment is important for accountability. That is, asked if teaching is being successful, we answer in terms of the satisfaction of our aims (or some such). Of course, what is being actually assessed in the classroom, say through performances, exams and the like, will be the satisfaction of our *objectives* (or some such: see Chapter 13). Nevertheless, we should find ways of moving from assessment through course evaluation to the satisfaction of course aims. Furthermore, and the second kind of importance, the public character of assessment is fundamental for any claims to (academic) status by dance study, and hence any (academic) argument for the place of dance in education. As we will see, finding a satisfactory understanding of the place of assessment in dance education, a satisfactory *method* (or methods) of assessment, and a satisfactory means of moving from such assessments — via course evaluation — to a consideration of the satisfaction of aims, all represent vexed questions. These are questions dance education must address. Yet it is easy to not do so if we imagine that the answers to such questions are already before us, either handed down from the mountain or delivered by our political masters.

This, then, is our first practical thought about accountability. Also, such assessment need not concern itself *solely* with the artistic, since it has been acknowledged that there is more to dance education than this. Yet artistic education must play an important role as the object of assessment since it represents the uniqueness of dance education (or so we have argued). Further, such an emphasis on the artistic dimension might also be expected to have *some* implications for course content, implications suggested earlier but beyond the direct concern of a text such as this. Yet this idea of the importance of assessment leads directly to the second thought. For what is implied here may differ fairly substantially from has hitherto gone under the name of 'educational assessment' (I mean, of course, what theorists have described as 'educational assessment' — what I have in mind conforms exactly to what has gone on in very many classrooms). For the virtues of dance education as I have described them throughout this text clearly lie in areas where humans can recognised those virtues — value areas — but without being able to *state* (in a non-truistic way) how they do this recognition. Asked under what concepts this recognition takes place, they must reply, first, that these are *artistic* concepts; and second, that — since both the acquisition and employment of these concepts requires learning — these are concepts *mobilised* (Wollheim, 1986: 46) in the understanding, a matter which can be achieved more or less well. Thus any assessment must rest on the judgement of informed spectators.

This leads directly to the third and final area of importance. For we should not imagine that such an emphasis on the judgements of informed spectators is a kind of retreat from the objectivity of assessment. Rather, it clarifies for us the *focus* of any assessment which could actually approach what dance has to offer. Seeing it as our focus should concentrate our minds towards ensuring that it is *indeed* what our assessment assesses. (My experience from another direction suggests that *explicit* recognition in course design of the sorts of 'skills' which have always been at the heart of that discipline's teaching and learning will inflect that teaching and learning in a positive way.) My suggestion, then, is for a kind of dance assessment based on the 'skills' of understanding which, as I have argued throughout this text, should be the focus of dance education.

This may seem an unoriginal suggestion. It is interesting at the present time that such a method cannot easily yield up 'regular national tests' (Simon, 1988: 124), at least if we continue to think of these in terms of pencil-and-paper tests, or check-lists of 'criteria', or of age-related benchmarks of 'criteria-referenced' testing. For, to assess *understanding* we will need, not a check-list of performances to be achieved, but people who *understand* in what that understanding consists; and we will find our 'objectivity' through them.

Thus, in summary, this chapter addresses the need for accountability, the requirements for a public character for assessment, and the objectivity of such assessment, as I suggest it might be performed.

Assessment and accountability: the issues

Three major areas concern us directly. The first two are wholly general: they are, first, the need that any assessment be *appropriate* to what is taught and, second, that teaching be recognised as *normative* in the sense that pupils might, if things go well, end up knowing or understanding more as a result of the teaching. These two points must then be applied to our particular case, and that creates a third issue since that application to dance education is by no means unproblematic.

The first idea, it will be recalled, is that assessment must be appropriate. This point is easily seen via the following anecdote, based on a particular comedian's stage show (*UD*: 5–6). The curtain opens on a lamp post shedding a puddle of light and the comedian walking round in the puddle of light, looking down. A stranger enters, bumps into the comedian, and asks what the comedian is doing. The comedian replies that he is searching for a coin. The stranger agrees to help, and now both walk around in the puddle of light, heads down. After a while of fruitless searching, the stranger stops the comedian, and asks him 'Are you sure this is where you dropped the coin?'. The comedian replies 'No, I dropped the coin out there', pointing into the darkness, 'but I'm searching here, because this is where the light is'. That sense of searching 'where the light is" — of assessing what is readily assessed — must be avoided in any realistic assessment. An actual example from physical education further illustrates the point. We might acknowledge that, for example, the kinds of understanding required to play basketball were not well represented by, say, one's ability to do a lay-up shot. Nevertheless, one might assess pupils in terms of their ability to do the lay-up shot — scoring them with a mark in terms of the number of achievements in, say, ten attempts — because this test could readily be performed. This is an example of an *inappropriate* assessment procedure. We would hope for an assessment procedure for dance which was not inappropriate.

There is an additional complexity here, for sometimes the inappropriateness is less obvious. In the halcyon days when educational theorists believed in IQ tests, it was thought realistic to assess the intelligence of pupils using such tests. We now know that such a procedure is at best dubious, and perhaps wholly inappropriate: that there either *may not be* or *definitely is not* some general capacity which such tests examine (Simon, 1985: 106–26) Thus, the use of IQ tests is an *inappropriate* method of assessing intelligence, but its inappropriateness may be hard to determine. I mention this lest anyone imagine that finding a satisfactory assessment procedure for dance is somehow straightforward.

The second general characteristic of relevance here concerns the issue of *normativity*, a notion introduced earlier in this work. In this context, it amounts simply to urging that what goes on cannot be *purely* a matter of pupils doing whatever they want. Put very crudely, the teacher must be able to say 'this is wrong', at least in principle, if there is to be a substantial claim to be teaching whatever the *this* is. Of course, for pedagogic reasons, it may well be that one *never says* this, that doing so would give pupils the wrong impression. Nonetheless, the intention will be to lead them away from a particular way of proceeding since that way is at least unproductive and possibly (or probably) wrong.

An example makes this point. A pupil who claims that the Battle of Hastings was in 1068 might be told that she is mistaken: equally, pedagogic concerns may lead one rather to ask how she came to this view and to lead her through a chain of looking at historical sources, finally arriving at her own recognition that she was mistaken. In either case, the possibility of your *teaching* concerning the Battle of Hastings is that, for these purposes, certain responses are appropriate and certain are inappropriate. Thus, one might accept a child-centred methodology for teaching, without accepting it as an account of the subject. *What* is taught is disciplined (in both senses of the word[1]) but *how* it is delivered is another matter. As I have been urging, this is a wholly general point. To see it in a different context, consider the difference between uttering sounds and speaking words. Using a word allows one to use the *wrong* word on a particular occasion, or to use a word *incorrectly*: that is to say, word-using is normative. And this is a crucial feature of the idea of words as *meaningful*. By contrast, uttering sounds is something one simply does or doesn't do. Sounds may be pleasing or not: but they can never be right, in the sense in which words can. The general point to be made here, then, is that assessment is essential since the possibility of assessment is built into the *normativity* of the activity, which is our second point: further, by our first, that assessment must be appropriate.

Applying these two points to dance education leads to our third consideration. We must, of course, accept the variety of elements within an appropriate dance-education curriculum. Thus, dance-history might well be assessed through the composition of essays, which clearly allows the normative procedures to get a hold: these essays can be good and bad, at the least, in the way in which other essays on historical subjects are. This point might apply quite widely within dance study. However there are central planks of dance study for which *this* form of public assessment is not readily available. For technical competence, or for choreographic competence, it seems impossible that the understanding to be located there could be examined in, say, a pencil-and-paper way. Indeed, it seems clear that the understanding manifest in such activities must be explored through the observation an informed audience. This, in a sense, a problem which we must come to soon (pp. 177–9): that concerned with the objectivity, or otherwise, of appraisal of dance *when it takes place* in this 'looking and seeing' way.

An example: the TGAT report

This discussion may be framed, and made more concrete, by a consideration of some of the remarks on assessment and accountability produced by the Task Group on Assessment and Testing (TGAT, 1987) in respect of the National Curriculum in the UK. The report, produced by a group headed by Professor Paul Black of King's College, London at Christmas 1987, became the basis for educational policy, as manifested in the National Curriculum. The report identifies some characteristics as we have: 'Promoting children's learning is a principle aim of schools. Assessment lies at the heart of this process' (TGAT, 1987: paras. 2 and 3). Given that assessment is clearly an essential part of the teacher's job, what help could be given to teachers? And if, as at that time, teachers regularly used standardised tests to help them, 'what sort of national scheme could be set up which would build on the best practice and make it the norm?' (Maclure, 1988: 11). In effect, the TGAT report gave priority to four criteria: (1) assessment results should be *criterion-referenced*; (2) they should be formative; (3) they should be calibrated or *moderated*; (4) assessment should relate to progression. (A great many general considerations might be raised concerning the place of assessment in the National Curriculum in the UK; see Kelly, 1990: Ch. 4; Lawton, 1989: Ch. 7.) In general, though, the intention was to build on existing assessment procedures and practices — to improve them where necessary — but to make as few fundamental changes as possible. In the case of dance education, however, this is somewhat more problematic. Examinations which has been in place for some time in other subjects — for example, the GCE A-level and GCSE (see Ch. 14, n. 1) — were much less established in the case of dance. However, comment on these four criteria from the perspective of dance in education, partly exploring and partly considering the criteria, will provide us with concrete examples of assessment principles.

The selection of criterion-referenced measurement for the National Curriculum represents an interesting choice. A criterion-referenced test examines whether a student has or has not reached the criterion or specified level of achievement (Murphy & Torrance, 1988: 90–1). The intention, then, is that test scores depend on the specifying of an *absolute standard of quality* independent of scores achieved by other students. Such a conception seems preferable to, for example, a *norm-referenced* measurement, where it is agreed in advance that, say, 33% of students will reach a certain grade and so on: that is to say, preferable to a pattern of grades is worked out in advance and replicated (perhaps with minor adjustments) in each successive time the examination is conducted. Such a norm-referenced system, used at one time in many A-level subjects, does no justice to either the differential achievements of one student compared to another in a different year, since they may both receive the same grade; nor to the similarity between work of two students which, by being in separate years, might achieve different grades for exactly the same work. Thus there is clearly something positive to be said for a criterion-referenced system.

However, applied to dance studies, criterion-referencing represents three major problems. First, the difficulty in specifying the kinds of criteria to be employed here, given (i) that the testing must take place through a broadly observational process; and (ii) that what is being tested is knowledge and, more importantly, understanding. Neither of these lends itself to the kind of unambiguous definition which makes putting a criterion-reference into place straightforward. The National Curriculum for physical education (DES, August 1991: 19) has, among the statements in respect of Key Stage 2 (for 11-year old pupils) that such pupils be able to 'swim at least 25 metres'. This represents a sensible object for a criterion-referenced test. It will be easy to see whether appropriate pupils at that age can indeed swim the 25 metres. However, and in common with much else in the physical education pro-gramme, it is difficult to imagine any comparable 'mark' to be met which would be appropriate for dance.

A second difficulty for criterion-referencing in dance education follows from this one. If we succeed in creating a criterion which most people can achieve, we have not demonstrated very much about our teaching when pupils do indeed achieve it. On the other hand, if we set a criterion which few achieve, again, the scale of their lack of success will not help us very much with the question of accountability. For, in this second case, our planning incorporates certain levels of failure, and at best might be judged when that level of failure is exceeded. Set the criterion too low, and virtually everyone passes — which tells you nothing. In particular, it does not seem at all diagnostic. Set it too high and virtually nobody passes — with the same outcome. So such criterion-referencing will be very complex if it is indeed to satisfy the requirement for accountability.

A third difficulty for criterion-referenced assessment applied to dance runs in roughly the opposite direction. In line with ideas from Stenhouse (see Chapter 3), we value the ability of pupils to *surprise* us. It will be difficult to reflect that capacity for being surprised in our criteria. For instructional objectives must be written in as precise a way as possible to allow for reliable criterion-referenced measures. It will not do to simply include vague state-ments about creativity or originality, for example. But if we do not, it may be very difficult for us to reflect what we recognise as educationally valuable in dance education. None of these three alone represents an insuperable difficulty for the production of criterion-referenced assessment for dance in education. Together, though, they represent a large task which requires energy and commitment as well as time if it is to be done satisfactorily. Here, too, it is important to notice that the guidance given by, for example, the physical education document (DES, August 1991) for the National Curriculum is just that: guidance. It is certainly nothing like the whole answer.

The second criteria articulated by the TGAT report was that assessment results should be *formative*, providing information which would be useful when deciding how pupils' learning may be taken forward. This is clearly an admirable intention. However, as has been recognised (Lawton, 1989: 54), the system is also *summative* for 16-year olds (Key Stage 4), since it is taken to provide a comprehensive overall picture of the achievements of any pupil at the end of their period of statutory schooling. Clearly, though, the idea of formative assessment is closely related to that of assessment as criterion-referenced. When I see how my pupils are succeeding, and not succeeding, at the criterion-referenced tests, I need also to have ways of recognising, preferably from the results of those tests, what to do next for those pupils — in particular, what to do next for those who are not succeeding. Thus taking seriously this criterion would also involve us in the careful writing of detailed criterion statements.

Further, TGAT recommended that assessments should be calibrated or *moderated*. If we think of the process of moderation as 'bringing individual judgements into line with general standards' (Lawton, 1989: 57) we recognise two dimensions here. First, moderation should certainly be seen as *controlling* for aberrations from those standards brought about by individual teachers' preferences or areas of knowledge, for example, 'the well-known "halo" effect — a tendency to think that pupils "good" in one area will be generally "good"' (Lawton, 1989: 57). So meetings which agreed that a certain child was achieving a certain criterion (in the criterion-referenced test), or more generally was arriving at a certain grade, would have the effect of insuring that the same grade amounted to the same thing in whatever place it was awarded. Second, the use of moderation should communicate to teachers clearer ideas of general standards, and hence of their own work in relation to such standards. So the moderation process would have the effect of acting as staff development for the teachers concerned.

Applied to physical education, this idea of moderation is clearly essential. As was already in place in some of the examinations in dance in the UK (Williams, 1986), a moderation procedure is particularly important when the best that can be given as specification of what to look for depends on the expertise and experience of the observers.

In this way, the question of moderation brings with it, in a way very appropriate for dance in education, a justified dependence on the work of the teacher: in particular, the teacher as arbiter or assessor. Like Helen Simons (1988: 78), I am 'committed to the notion that self-direction by accountable professionals offers the best hope of continuous improvement in the educational experience offered to children in schools': in particular, I am sure that this is crucial for an adequate dance education in schools. And if asked to tie that commitment into the present position of, say, the National Curriculum, I should do so by emphasising what it means in respect of *moderation procedures*.

In this context, the TGAT report (1987: para. 72) considered three ways in which such moderation might standardly be achieved. The first was a *reference test*, an external instrument sent to the whole population of pupils being tested by their teachers. As this has little obvious application for dance education I shall simply consider the other two. The second alternative was *moderation by inspection*. As the name implies, the suggestions was that grading in schools be made by some external moderator, whose information about the school might be incomplete in ways that were *important* to the assessment. Finally, TGAT considered *group moderation*, emphasising communication through the exchanges of samples at meetings with other teachers. This approach is at present used by, for example, the GCSE. Group moderation allows examiners to clarify the objectives of the programme of study and the basis of their own judgements. As the TGAT report notes, it is 'the only one of the three moderation methods which would enable the professional judgements of teachers to inform the development of the National Curriculum' (TGAT, 1987: para. 72). As I have suggested, this method is both the one that most naturally applies in the case of dance, and the one presently in place. Moreover, such a concern with the importance of the *teacher* was echoed in responses to the TGAT report. Such responses resulted in the first of three supplementary reports (TGAT, 1988) in which 'the use of externally prescribed tests and of teachers' own assessments, combined through effective moderation pro-cedures' is agreed as the best method of securing standards and improving learning as well as enhancing professional skills (see Lawton, 1989: 63).

The final criterion from the TGAT report is that assessment should relate to *progression*. There are three related issues associated with the notion of progression. The first concerns progression through the *material* in the course or in the discipline. In this way, we might wish to see the work of students increasing in complexity, as their understanding deepens. Second, we must relate progression to *development*: so that what is asked of pupils is realistic in terms of their intellectual and emotional maturation (Gallahue, 1982: Ch. 3). Third, progression must take account of the differential starting point of pupils. And, as the TGAT report rightly recommends each of these aspects should be considered in the framing of assessment. For, if we must do Y in order to do Z, it may be that that renders assessment of Y unnecessary once we are assessing Z. Equally, any assessment must be appropriate for the capacities of the pupils: the programmes of study must be *realistic* — and that may well affect what might be asked of them at a particular level. Finally, it is important that assessment reflect the *possibility* of challenge to those either gifted in the area or who begin with some previous understanding or experience for some other reason.

Methods of testing

Thus far, we have recognised the general importance of assessment for accountability, and considered, as an example, the TGAT report's suggestions concerning the nature of assessment. What can we say specifically about assessment for dance? One strategy which might be profitable will be the detailed scrutiny of the actual syllabus for some dance examinations (for instance, A-level). But the danger there is in getting bogged-down in the details of the particular case. So, instead, I shall comment on four general characteristics of any method of treating appropriate for dance in education.

First, it must be rooted in 'looking and seeing': that is, in the recognitional powers of informed observers. This idea has been explored throughout this chapter, and its objectivity is the topic of the next section. Notice, too, that it can readily be related to progression, and can be formative and moderated. For its relationship to progression and its formative character may be learned as observers become *informed*, while moderation might well be a key part of such learning. However, this kind of assessment does not lend itself to criterion-referencing. It is this context that David Best (1990a: 10a) suggests that what is put forward be *called* targets (and hence criterion-referenced) even though they were really just guidelines for informed observers (perhaps helpful with the moderation process: see pp. 174–5).

Second, any assessment appropriate to dance in education must focus on its artistic character, and do so in order to explore its contribution to *understanding*. This is not to deny the potential importance of, say, dance history or the anthropology of dance. Rather, it is to insist — as we have seen — that they cannot be the basis for a distinctive dance education. So our testing must centre on pupils' *understanding* as it is manifest in the artistic activity: in particular, we might expect what they say and do in responding to dance to be of importance here. This is another place where *masterworks* (see pp. 78–81) could be crucial. We can imagine videos of (sections of) such masterworks being employed as part of the examination process. It might also be possible to conduct at least some of this assessment in pen-and-paper terms, which facilitates moderation. Just *how* this would be managed is an important practical question. But seeing this as the target may direct attention appropriately.

The third characteristic grows from this one (and picks-up an earlier idea; see p. 67): that the pupils choreographic 'productions' will typically not be artworks. So what is their role in assessment? Our answer is of a piece with our 'process' conception of the curriculum. For in these productions we see the level of understanding reached by pupils. That understanding takes place in a *context* provided by (genuine) artworks — say, our masterworks. Indeed, without a background of such works, it would be impossible to see the dance products as manifesting *understanding* at all. It is important not to mis-understand this point: for the dance works are not *signs* or *symptoms* of the understanding: rather, they are *internally* related to it (see Chapter 3).

Finally, and fourth, this point reinforces the importance of practical participation in dance, both as a pedagogic tool for teaching dance-under-standing and as a resource for making such understanding manifest. As we saw (Chapter 6), one clear way of demonstrating understanding may be through participation. This point has a negative corollary, though: teachers must not focus exclusively on this one way of making manifest one's understanding. Indeed, the appropriate weighting of practical performance here may make it rather *less* crucial than it sometimes been assumed. For example, if this is right, it will be inappropriate to award marks (or anything similar) for a performance *as such*. The assessment should depend on understanding, and be tailored to allow the requisite understanding to be demonstrated.

In these ways, any 'methods of testing' appropriate for dance in education will provide accountability and will respect (some of) the TGAT criteria. But will the testing be objective? We now turn to that question.

The objectivity of appraisal

Implicit in all that has gone before is the commitment to the acceptability of evaluation/appraisal of dance based (roughly) on 'looking and seeing' dance, at least of that 'looking and seeing' is done by informed observers. It is important to raise four points at this stage in explanation and supplementation of this commitment.

First, the evaluation/appraisal could not be done in some other way; so this is not a 'second best' method of appraisal. Again, a parallel may be helpful. At present, the evaluation of diving as a sport involves judges observing the dive. But commentators often remark on the amount of splash the diver produces entering the water as though that were indicative of the quality of the dive. Suppose, for a moment, that this were true, and that we had an advanced and totally accurate splash-meter. Would this be preferable to (that aspect) of the observation of the informed judges? If we conclude that it *would* be preferable, we are saying that — to this degree — the observation of the judges is simply the best we can have, not what we really want. But the size of the splash is actually irrelevant. We are interested in the *look* of the dive: that must be the basis of any assessment of it. Of course there may well be a correlation between elegance of dive and volume of water splashed. In this example, the judgement of the informed observer represents not just the best possible, in the sense of the best we can manage, but rather the best there could possibly be. This is equally true for dance education. Since observation of artistic value for dance is the only way of directly coming to understand that value, this is a procedure that we *must* adopt.

The second point is to emphasise that, contrary to what is sometimes assumed, such judgements are perfectly public and shareable. Being public and shareable in this sense is the same as being objective: that this is what the word 'objective' means in this context (*UD*: 32). Nonetheless, that is not a point that I wish to dwell on. But this point is built on three related considerations, all of which should be familiar by now. The first, on a parallel with the *look* of things (*UD*: 33–5), is that the artistic merit of a particular dance is public and shareable; the mere fact that it depends on the perceptual powers of humans does not preclude its being public and shareable. The mere fact that *some* people are colour-blind, and hence cannot tell that a piece of white paper with a red light shined on it *looks* red, does nothing to undermine the perfectly public character of the *red look* of such a piece of paper. Indeed, we would not be able to identify them as colour-blind (that is, as having some kind of deviant perception) if the standard perception were not uncontroversial. So we should conclude that there is no reason here for doubting the public nature of judgements when the making of those judgements involves the discriminatory powers of people. The second consideration follows from this one. For when one pupil complains that my judging of his dance is a *biased* judging, or when another complains that my assessment of her is *prejudiced*, they are implicitly conceding the point about the public and shared character of the judgements at issue. To accuse me of bias is, in effect, to say that I am doing *badly* something which, but for my bias, I might do *well*. Equally, somebody who was *not* prejudiced might see this student's work with a clarity that I lack. In both cases, my blinkered condition is contrasted with a standard, un-blinkered condition. Thus these accusations make manifest our commitment to the idea that assessment here is not *necessarily* biased or *necessarily* prejudiced: that it is only accidentally or contingently so, in ways in principle remediable. Thus, again, the point to recognise is that there is no bar here to the making of public and shareable judgements — the sorts of judgements which might be exploited in successful moderation of assessment.

Another consideration here draws on the multiple figures from psychology, as discussed in Chapter 9, there employed to illustrate that something which was public and shareable, a particular design, might nonetheless be seen in more than one way. Or, to put that point the other way round, the most important characteristic was that there were ways of *mis-perceiving* the object, or seeing it wrong! Again, this central point follows from our earlier discussions about the importance of concepts in perception. That discussion emphasised how one might, through the mobilising of inappropriate concepts in one's experience, misperceive an object. The clearest example here might be of taking birdsong to be music (or music to be birdsong), which would be to misperceive it. For these reasons, we should accept that our evaluation and appraisal of dances is public and shareable evaluation, even though it is centrally on 'looking and seeing'.

The third point might be introduced by asking the question 'Is such evaluation/appraisal objective?'. Our answering thought will be 'Who cares!'. That is to say, the issues here are about publicity, and hence about amenability to rational argument. So that, in seeing our judgements of dances as public and shareable, we are also seeing them as matters around which debate and discussion is possible. And it is debate and discussion, or more generally rationality, which matters for accountability and for assessment which is open to moderation. So our third point is to recognise that the word 'objective' is not what is at issue here: that all we want from objectivity is guaranteed if one has public, shareable judgements, open to rational consideration.

The fourth point, and the final one, picks up the relationship between such public, shareable and rational judgements and the question of testing. I am urging that assessment for *key* aspects of dance in education will be done through 'looking and seeing' by informed observers: and those informed observers will typically be trained teachers. In effect, there are three aspects to this answer. The first, articulated in the points made above, is that the judgements are public and shareable. The second, implicit here although explicit in Chapter 9, is that such judgements represent appropriate evaluations for dance works. In part, our argument here might draw on our institutional conception of the nature of art (Chapter 9; *UD*: 71–81): artistic value is an art-critical matter, and such judgements are examples of art criticism in this sense. Third, and perhaps most important, the judgements are made by people who understand not merely *dance*, but also the way in which the performance of certain dance movements manifests *understanding* — in that sense, they are knowledgeable not merely about dance, but also about education. This conception of the dance educator as having a fundamental role is important in this text in at least two ways. First, suitably filled out, it is part of our differentiation of the dance teacher from the dance artist in education (see Chapter 8). Moreover, this emphasis on a unique role for the dance educator poses an important question, again one central to the progression of the argument here. For how are such educators trained? In what does their training consist? In Chapter 16 I shall argue that central to an understanding of that training will be the idea of a *reflective practitioner,* with its associated view of the nature of knowledge and understanding.

Conclusion

This chapter has defended the objectivity of assessment in dance, and has explored some appropriate methods for such testing, within constraints such as those laid-down by the TGAT report. Its overall aim was both the emphasise the connection between assessment and accountability and to consider how such accountability for dance education might be secured. This last aspect has two elements. First, the focus (in assessment) on understanding means that — if performed correctly — the assessment *guaranteed* that pupils had gained understanding: thus, the degree to which they did would be a measure of success in teaching. In this way, courses could be monitored. Second, course monitoring would allow *explanation* of relative successes, so as to avoid a crude, mechanistic model of the relation between teaching and understanding. What has also been emphasised, of course, is the dependence of this process on the judgements of informed observers (that is, of teachers). In this way, accountability *is* dependent on teacher-professionalism.

Chapter 16

Reflective Practice and Dance Research

Dance research and dance study

The strategy of this chapter is to consider first the nature of dance research and then to say something about research into dance education, with some remarks about the inter-relation of these two. That will lead us naturally into a greater elaboration of the topic here, that view of the dance educator as *reflective practitioner* noted at the end of the previous chapter.

Dance studies should be seen as fulfilling two fundamental principles (Baker, 1977: 24; *UD*: 313–14). These are (a) the autonomy of artistic enquiry: that the concepts and statements used in our discussion of the arts are not logically equivalent to any non-artistic concepts or statements; (b) the reality of artistic enquiry — that it is possible to give genuine explanations of the concepts and statements used in discussion of dance. These two principles, which resemble those which might be articulated for an enquiry such as jurisprudence, focus on 'the increase of understanding, not of knowledge; the generation of new insight, not the discovery of new facts' (Baker, 1977: 24). These principles are fundamental just because, without them, dance study would collapse into some other study — for example, study of the biology of dancers, or the economics of arts activity, or the sociology of the 'consumption' of dances — or would be reducible to some other activity. Our discussion of the artistic character of dance serves both to distinguish the arts from other areas of human experience and also to distinguish dance from within the arts. In this way, the concepts that we use to understand dances are importantly different from (although not unconnected with) concepts we use in other places. Like other art forms, dances have a crucial connection with life-issues (see Chapter 4). Moreover, this condition works in a negative way, since things other than art forms may have a connection with life-issues, but nothing which lacks this connection can be an art form. Additionally, the connection of a particular work with its peculiar *life-issues* will be unique to that work.

A second point is that dance study is not exhausted by so-called disciplinary perspectives on dance: that is to say, that there is a need for *dance research* and not just research which is essentially history or sociology taking dance simply as its subject. Of course, the distinction here may be a rather subtle one. If one's concern is really with *dance* but given the discipline of one's historical investigation, one may well be doing dance research in just this sense. My aim, though, is to insist that there is research into the art form *itself* and not merely into its history, consumption, or the physiology required for its delivery. While not exhaustive, certainly a major element of this research will be philosophical in character.

Third, there is the need here for dance research to learn from cases of research in other areas, and especially research in music. At present, dance studies has at best an *emergent* articulation of key issues: the issues are not yet articulated. In musicology, for example, it seems that there is agreement as to what some *issues* are. For example, there are issues concerned with the appropriateness of 'authentic performance' (Kivy, 1988). Of course, there isn't a universally agreed answer, but there is a question universally accepted (well, by all but a few cranks — who may turn out to be the heroes: see McFee, 1980b). So articulation of *issues* or *questions* is crucial: it underscores Toulmin's account of the *disciplinary* (Toulmin, 1972: 262; Cavell, 1981b: 269). There is a need for dance research to model itself on research about the arts: for example, into art writing through its relation to understanding art (or art-understanding).

Finally, such research in dance is important, but also of importance will be research into dance *teaching*, not least because (as argued in Chapter 15) satisfactory dance education places considerable weight on the understanding and expertise of such teachers.

The four points above articulate both some limitations as well as some possibilities for dance research. It is important, though, to notice that this is not just research as defined by, for example, both the Roith (1990) report and by the Council for National Academic Awards in the UK in terms of 'related activities': that is, as I have been describing it, dance research does *not* involve the creation of dances. To be more precise, it may well involve the use of reconstruction in coming to understand dances and therefore bringing those dances into being. But, since the notion is centrally of the *reconstruction* of something previously existent, it is not creation in that sense. Of course, this position is not intended as a way of denigrating creation, but rather of making the necessary distinctions between different activities. Students of dance may, for some purposes, be creators of dances, but that activity should be seen as importantly from the activities of dance scholars. We might think here of the kind of 'product development' which takes place in the Research and Development sections of large companies. In this sense, R & D is not research.

Of course, this view of research is not universally adopted. Some authors write of research *for* a painting or a dance, and also of research *in/through* a painting or a dance. On my account, neither is genuinely research. If I am 'researching' *for* my dance, I am gathering information or experience or stimuli or some such which I will be building into my dance. But this is not a rational procedure of the accretion of knowledge and understanding: not a procedure with an *independent* methodology. Indeed, if we study the works of those who have attempted to treat it in this way, we find either that they have given up in despair, or that their work is stultified by it. Equally, to see my actual dance as research (and hence to think of myself as researching *through* the dance) is to confuse different ways of coming to understand. In a parallel case, we might well accept that Jane Austin or Shakespeare presented a considerable amount of material manifesting understanding of the human mind. But that did not make either of them psychologists. What they were doing was informal, non-disciplinary, and therefore not research — however informative it turned out to be.

Reflective practice: a view of practical knowledge

As we have seen, many issues relate to the nature of dance research, most of which are not *uniquely* related to research in dance education. One area which, as we argued, *is* crucial for dance education will be research into the nature of dance teaching. To introduce such a question it is useful to say something briefly about Donald Schön's notion of the *reflective practitioner* (Schön, 1983; Schön, 1987). Some, for example Elliott (1991: 50), have explicitly claimed that the sorts of reflection on the relationship between process and practices which justify the expression 'reflective practice' are what, Elliott says, 'others, including myself, have termed *action research*'. Among the virtues of the expression 'reflective practice', 'reflective practitioner' are *first* (and unlike Stenhouse's 'teacher-as-researcher'; see Stenhouse, 1975: Ch. 10) the scope is *obviously* wider than just teachers; while *second* (and unlike 'action research'; see Carr & Kemmis, 1986: Ch. 7), the question of *how*, if at all, it is research does not immediately arise.

I take it as axiomatic that the term 'reflective practice' means what Schön takes it to mean. At the centre of Schön's strategy are three related ideas: the *first* is an opposition to technical rationality: 'Technical rationality is an epistemology of practice derived from positivist philosophy' (Schön, 1987: 3). The *second* idea is a regard for *practice* as embodying both *knowledge* (notice Schön's use of the expression 'epistemology of practice' above) and the *solution* to problems: 'competent practitioners usually know more than they can say' (Schön, 1987: vii). This emphasis on practice is why is makes sense to 'turn the problem upside down' (Schön, 1987: 12) by taking *practice* as a basis for theory, rather than vice versa. The *third* idea is a view of knowledge: 'an epistemology of practice based on reflection-in-action' (Schön, 1987: xii).

Each of these three ideas has an important bearing on our topic, although the third is the most important. For the aim is to see *reflective practice* as a knowledge-generating activity: and hence to see the extent to which it is (and to which it is not) a *research* activity. Let us consider each feature in turn. The ideal of technical rationality[1] should be a familiar one. As Schön (1983: 165) points out, it rests on three dichotomies — each of which is to be undermined or rejected. The *first* is a separation of means from ends. This allows us to conceive of a process whose *objective* can be specified *independently* of the means of achieving it, and whose effectiveness can be measured as 'effectiveness in achieving a pre-established objective' (Schön, 1983: 165). [This aspect is at the root of Stenhouse's (1983: 81–2) criticism of an 'objectives' output model of the curriculum — see Chapter 13.] *Second*, there is a separation of research from practice. This takes us into our second general aspect — but it also imports (as a model for rigour) 'the method of controlled experiment' (Schön, 1983: 165).Yet such a method has no clear place in the work of the researcher aiming to understand *practices*. *Third*, there is a separation of knowing from doing, which makes action 'only a kind of implementation' (Schön, 1983: 165), rather than an integral part of the process of knowing. In general, an emphasis on technical rationality treats difficulties which arise in the practice of, for example, the craft of teaching as *problems* where the *form* of a *solution* is clearly known: all that is wanted is the means to that solution. In contrast, Schön (1983: 15–16) insists: 'The situations of practice are not problems to be solved but problematic situations characterised by uncertainly, disorder, and indeterminacy'.

The emphasis on *practices* is equally central to Schön's position. The idea is, first, that such practices embody *knowledge*, despite being 'a process we can deliver without being able to say what we are doing' (Schön, 1987: 31). The knowledge is 'knowing-in-action' (Schön, 1987: 23); and, for Schön (1987: 33), 'a professional's knowing-in-action is embedded in the socially and institutionally structured context shared by a community of practitioners'. Moreover, this practical competence can transcend the *mere* ability to perform the task — it can become *reflective*: 'a skilled performer can integrate reflection-in-action into the smooth performance of an ongoing task' (Schön, 1987: 29). So the practices are important *both* as embodying knowledge (knowledge-in-action) and as embodying reflection (reflection-in-action). Schön (1987: 40 fn.) offers two central comments on this picture. The first concerns its in-built flexibility and responsiveness: 'competent professional practitioners often have the capacity to generate new knowing-in-action through reflection-in-action undertaken in the indeterminate zones of practice'. However, it is a mistake, Schön (1987: 40 fn) insists, and rightly, to confuse *practical knowledge* (or, as we will call it, *craft-knowledge*) with what is sometimes put under that heading: 'the knowing-in-action characteristic of competent practitioners in a professional field is not the same as the professional knowledge taught in the schools; in any given case, the relationship between the two kinds of knowledge should be treated as an open question'. These two ideas — opposition to technical rationality and emphasis on practice — come together when we turn to the third idea, and begin to articulate Schön's view on the nature of knowledge.

At the centre of Schön's notion of *reflective practice* is a view about *knowledge* (and a related view about *understanding*): that knowledge is *essentially* connected with action and with practice, rather than peripherally or accidentally so connected. Now, this may be arguable as an account of *most* (or even *all*) knowledge. However, for our purposes, it may usefully be restricted to knowledge in those social institutions we are calling *practices* (Pettit, 1980: 5–6). [Of course, if natural science were a practice in this sense, its knowledge too would be analysed in this way. But it is no part of my strategy to insist that science is such a practice[2].] This view of knowledge is one way of articulating the *craft-knowledge* idea[3]. As Sally Brown and Donald McIntyre (1986: 36) express it, applied to teaching, such knowledge is:

i.   imbedded in, and tacitly guiding the teachers' every day actions in the class room;

ii.   derived from practical experience rather than formal training;

iii. seldom made explicit;

iv.   related to the intuitive, spontaneous and routine aspects of teaching rather than to the more reflective and thoughtful activities in which teachers may engage at other times;

v.   reflected in the 'core professionalism' of teachers and their 'theories in use' rather than their 'extended professionalism' and 'espoused theories'.

This view of knowledge has three related characteristics of particular relevance here. First, it locates the knowledge through *what is done*, through the practice. In this way, the knowledge is not some set of abstract propositions connected at best *causally* with the practice. Rather, it is central to it. As Wittgenstein[4] was fond of quoting from Goethe, 'In the beginning was the deed'. Of course, the knowledge *could* perhaps be expressed propositionally: but that was not its central expression. (In *this* respect, at least, it resembled Ryle's *knowing how* to do something; see Ryle, 1949: Ch. 2.)

A second key feature comes out when we see that, since this knowledge is *internally* connected to a practice, it cannot be treated as a mere outcome or end of that practice: that is to say, it cannot be treated in terms of 'instrumental rationality' (Carr & Kemmis, 1986: 131; 151) or 'technical rationality'. In this respect, then, some of the insight from Critical Theory is incorporated: and Critical Theory is relevant here since some theorists of action research, for example Carr & Kemmis (1986), have seen such ideas as central to any satisfactory account of research of this kind.

Two features in particular are retained. The first is a 'rejection of "naturalness"' as Gibson (1986: 4) states it. Since no *social* facts are value-neutral, there is no *neutral* descriptive standpoint from which to survey them. So there is a rejection of the possibility of a neutral, 'scientific' viewpoint. Second, there is a rejection of the concentration on the technical — on *means*, that is, rather than *ends*. Gibson offers a clear example, in the Secretary of State for Education's resistance to the inclusion, within A-level physics, of consideration of 'the social applications of science':

> Instrumental rationality demands that A-level students, future scientists, should not concern themselves with the social consequences of their activities, with the implications of nuclear power or pollution. (Gibson, 1986: 8)

Here, the emphasis is on science as means to an otherwise-specifiable end, conceived of from some neutral perspective, as though this were *obvious*; and with no discussion of the question '*why*'. On such a view, *what is learned* is separated from *how* and *why* in ways quite contrary to our concern with the *internal* relations between knowledge and practice. Equally, we might reflect on the ways in which *teaching* and *learning* might be conceptualised: to think of a *fixed* curriculum which would be *delivered* by teachers might well be to adopt a perspective of instrumental rationality. But to do so is just to ignore connections between the *aim* of teaching (namely, education) and the *practice* of teaching. In short, it is to deny the relevance of *craft-knowledge*. And I have suggested the inappropriateness of such a denial.

As a result, if we learn enough about a certain practice (for example teaching) to see it as *embodying* or *constituting* a certain craft-knowledge, there is no *further* step to decide the direction of possible change. It is not *hypothetical* (in Aristotle's sense[5]): it is not a matter of doing this *if* one wants a certain outcome. For understanding the practice is understanding that a certain outcome — namely, education — is the essential aim of that practice, properly conceived.

The third noteworthy feature of this view of knowledge is that it lends itself to a *knowledge of values*: that it undermines *one* distinction between objects of knowledge (facts) and values (see Putnam, 1990: 142–62). For knowledge can then be *internally* related to those values which function as the 'ends' of practices. Again, perhaps not *all* knowledge is like this; but of this model of knowledge has *any* place (that is, if it is a *partial* picture of *some* knowledge) it follows that knowledge is quite different from its portrayal in, for example, a pure propositional form by Hirst (1974: Ch. 3, 4, 5), Peters (1966: 53-5) and others (for example, Dearden, 1968: 61-4).

Of course, my *concern* with the nature of a satisfactory account of research into the *practice of dance teaching* derives from my dissatisfaction with *my* side of discussions on these topics with students considering such 'action research' methodologies — mainly, with a view to using them in investigating their own practice. For them, *problems* about how this activity is research at all are immediate, in one of two ways. Either the student, having been taught to be appropriately critical of research methods, finds the grand *claims* of 'action research' unpalatable; or, convinced of the effectiveness of the methods *from the first person perspective* (that is, from his/her own work), the student wishes to write a justification of that choice of research-paradigm. In either case, the student will need to defend (or to consider the defences) of action research as a style of research. And either of these situations might be intensified if the student wished to *integrate* the action research material into material drawn from quantitative research, into, say, a multi-method 'paradigm'.

So questions of degree of *generalisability* will be fundamental. Again, Schön (1983: 129) offers the beginnings of an answer: for it is fundamental to the idea of *reflective practice* that 'the practitioner approaches the practice problem as a unique case'. Hence any response must acknowledge this uniqueness. Indeed, it is sometimes urged in discussion of field research in the social sciences that — since each situation is unique — there is a major issue about generalisability.

But the model of *reflective practice* takes this point as central or integral, rather than a hurdle to be overcome. And for two reasons. First, the concentration on *practices* removes the possibility of serious use of a 'model of controlled experiment' (Schön, 1983: 144). If our aim is to understand the knowledge (in particular, the *values*) that hold in place the habits of teachers, we cannot expect to investigate that knowledge by *removing* the teachers from the situations in which the knowledge is implicit. For the knowledge would only be displayed in those situations. To expect to proceed by *removing* the teachers from the *practice* would be to deny that this is *craft-knowledge at all*. Second, the uniqueness is *not* such as to preclude *some* generalising. As Schön (1983: 137) puts it (and the point is a commonsense one), it is a matter of 'bringing past experience to bear on a unique situation'. This is something with which, at the everyday level, we are all familiar. To do this *reflectively* is for the practitioner to see the unique situation *as* falling under the aspect of his '*repertoire* of examples, images, understandings and actions' (Schön, 1983:

138). So the unique *situation* is understood, explained and *acted*-in by bringing to bear concepts (etc.) built-into one's practice.

At this stage, the fine detail of the problem is perhaps clear. For how do we turn the understanding into action? How can it be that research-knowledge is internally connected to action?

Schön's answer is confusingly expressed, but its contours are both clear and plausible. He puts the point by including in his account an element he calls '*hypothesis testing*' (Schön, 1983: 146–7). Now, it would clearly be less confusing to reserve the word 'hypothesis' for its original home, in controlled experimentation. Still, the point (having a tentative claim which is then subject to testing) is an appropriate one. So let us stick with the word 'hypothesis'. Schön's idea is that the practitioner *reframes* the situation, bringing *craft-knowledge* to bear, and that 'the practitioner's reframing of the problem of the situation carries with it hypotheses about the situation' (Schön, 1983: 148). So, in this sense, the hypothesis is not (or need not be) explicitly formulated. And if it is formulated, it will be expressed rather as a candidate *way of characterising* the situation. Yet the point of it all is to find a more revealing way to characterise the situation: and the practitioner explores whether or not that way *is* more revealing by acting *as though* it were. It is in this sense that the 'practitioner's hypothesis-testing consists of moves that change the phenomenon to make the hypothesis fit' (Schön, 1983: 149). Now we see how the research *knowledge* issues-in action.

However, two of our major problems are intensified. For, first, we have seen that there is no *method* for the construction of the 'hypotheses'. Rather, the practitioner just draws on personal experience and that of others — and does so *reflectively*! But that is not a method or strategy. Second, the potential conservatism of the position is apparent. For practitioners *may* look no further than their *own* practice: in particular, there is no express directive to look at good practice.

But is this research?

I imagine that, at this stage, an objector might inquire whether or not an investigation into reflective practice, or into the craft-knowledge of the reflective practitioner, was indeed *research*. And this point turns, at least in part, on the view of knowledge that such a conception of 'research' brings with it. To some degree, therefore, we are combating it by recognising that the conception of a *reflective practitioner* brings with it a revised view of knowledge. Moreover, one part of the problem is resolved when one jettisons the (positivist) demand for a certain kind of 'scientific' model for research or for research-knowledge (Carr & Kemmis, 1986: Ch. 2, also 118–22). This point is widely accepted; there are kinds of research *other than* that conducted by natural science. And an additional dimension of the problem disappears when one recognises that not all natural science works in the way the positivist describes — although that is not a point I will pursue here (see Kuhn, 1970; Feyerabend, 1978).

However, even with these concessions, the precise nature of research into practice remains unclear. One way to bring out the unclarity is to ask how the *practice* of what we are calling 'action research' is to be understood as *research*: that is, as the practice of seeking to answer 'why?' questions by gathering original knowledge and/or understanding in relation to some problem (a crude account of research: on 'why?' questions, see Phillips & Pugh, 1987: 42–6). For what makes the *outcome* of the action research process knowledge?

It must be accepted that this problem comes about because the *data* of the action research process is typically reports of words and actions: but what makes our discussions of these reports trustworthy? What makes them *quality data*?

Two possible answers here are, first, that there is some *internal validation* process as part of the method(s) of action research (the example often given is the process of 'triangulation'; see Elliott, 1976: 300–304) or, second, that there is a *theoretical* justification for the procedure — in particular, that its justification lies in Habermas's discussion of the Ideal Speech Situation (ISS) (Carr & Kemmis, 1986: 141–4). It will be acknowledged, of course, that either of these kinds of validation might back-fire or go wrong. But if used *properly* (their adherents urge) they are plausible. Broadly, then, these constitute an appeal to some kind of structurally-guaranteed 'validity' of method, or some external, theoretical guarantee. But the first is an extremely doubtful path (as I have urged elsewhere: see McFee, 1992b). So that even its one-time defenders now urge 'triangulation ... is not so much a technique for monitoring, as a more general method for bringing different kinds of evidence into some relationship with each other...' (Elliott, 1991: 82). The point here, of course, is that *this* account of triangulation employs it in the *generation* of data, not in deciding its soundness. Hence it cannot answer the problem raised above. Indeed, Carr & Kemmis (1986: 191), having recognised this point, construe the work of Elliott and others *in terms* of their own theoretical underpinning: that is, they invoke Habermas. But this technique (the second strategy) is equally problematic. Habermas's work is not only of extreme complexity (and hence unavailable to most teachers who might seek to engage in collaborative action research), it is also problematic in its own right. Its assumptions about the nature of language, of truth and of the workings of society are all eminently contestable[6]. Indeed, if one feature of the 'action research' literature on which its opponents focus (for example Gibson, 1986: 164) is 'the facile acceptance of Habermas' ideal speech situation', other features have been its cliqueishness, its anti-individualism and its 'neglect of the social factors which affect group processes of deliberation' (Gibson, 1986: 164) — and these are features *also* criticised in respect of Habermas's work more generally (see, for example, Pettit, 1980: 27–28; 182–183).

If we conclude that neither of these two ways of dealing with the problem are acceptable, and yet the problem is real enough (even if sketched here unduly impressionistically), we are left looking for other ways of answering that problem. But we have moved forward on three fronts:

First, we have identified one of the tasks to be undertaken — the fuller articulation of the 'reflective practice' picture of knowledge. And this should include, of course, discussion of how (if at all) other accounts of knowledge fit-in with, or conflict with, this one. Moreover, we have implicitly identified a disciplinary base for that enquiry: it is philosophy.

Second, we have seen why research of this kind is appropriately titled 'action research' insofar as it is *research* (that is, 'why?'-question knowledge-gathering) into *action*; and because it could/should have action as its outcome. So it is not a specific sort of research ('research as praxis' — see Lather, 1986) so much as research with a specific *target*: namely, practices.

Third, we have recognised that research into this kind of activity must not be expected to meet natural scientific criteria of 'reliability' or 'validity' — indeed, that to aim to do so would be to alter the *target* of one's research.

We also gain insight into the ways action research has been misunder-stood — into the ways our 'problem' is generated, as it were. The confusions arise, I am suggesting, for three related reasons. First, because it is research into a particular kind of practice; that is, one in which there is craft-knowledge. Second, because it is research based on a particular model of knowledge (especially one allowing the *possibility* of craft-knowledge). Finally, because it is research with *action* as outcome: the knowledge is *practical* knowledge, manifested in and through action. In all of these ways it differs from familiar idealisations of knowledge as propositional, abstract and theoretical. So preparation for action research requires, at the least, a re-orientation of views of knowledge.

Dance teacher as practitioner

The argument of this chapter to date leads us to two major points. The first requires our justification of the claims of the dance teacher to be a *reflective practitioner* in Schön's sense; the second asks what, in practical terms, the investigation of reflective practice amounts to. It is easier to answer the second of these questions. For our answer simply consists in saying that one takes a reputable action research primer, for example Elliott's (1991: Ch. 6) and works through the stages it describes. In this sense one is returning to the origins of this sort of research into practice, to Lewin's model (Lewin,

1952) and to its descendants. It is not essential here to run through each of these steps. Two aspects in particular are integral to the technique and dependent on our analysis of the nature of knowledge. The first concerns the techniques and methods for gathering evidence (Elliott, 1991: 77–83). The second involves the elaboration and implementation of the 'action plan'. For integral to 'action research' is 'a self-reflective spiral of cycles of planning, observing, reflecting' (Carr & Kemmis, 1986: 184), where the action researcher makes a number of such loops of planning, acting, observing and reflecting. But we have nothing special to say on these *practical* topics.

On the task of identifying the dance teacher as reflective practitioner, there are two matters to be addressed directly. The first, and most important, is the degree to which we can explain dance education as a *practice* in the sense articulated earlier. In fact, this is relatively straightforward. Dance itself is a collection of *normative* actions, where success in the practice is defined *institutionally* (that is, via an authoritative body: Baker & Hacker, 1984a: 272–3). And, as we have seen (*UD*: 84–6), success in dance *teaching* is ultimately to be understood as success relative to *artistic* aspirations, for that is the root of the artistic account. So dance education is a *practice* in the appropriate sense. The second matter concerns the extent to which dance educators possess the kind of *craft-knowledge* which might be investigated by viewing dance educators as reflective practitioners. As Schön (1987: 65–9) argued, reflection-in-action is central to the design process. At first, this point is exemplified through an actual case of design. Then it is generalised. Thus Schön (1987: 175) remarks, 'Musical performance is a kind of designing'.

Two preliminary points should be noted, taking us back to our commitment to Schön's account of reflective practice. First, Schön's discussion is of professions *other* than teaching. So it is less obvious that teachers are (or can be) reflective practitioners than some commentators have assumed. Second, musical performers are, for Schön, a good example of the kinds of professionals who can be reflective practitioners: thus, given the affinities between dance and music (both are performing arts), the extension to dancers seems natural. Moreover, Schön (1987: 182–201) explicitly considers the case of teaching music by using a *masterwork*: the pianist, Franz, teaches both a particular musical work (Schubert's *Wanderer Fantasy* Opus 15) and musical understanding more generally. So here too the comparison with dance is promising.

Moving on, we notice the task of the dance educator as constrained in just the ways Schön (1987: 208–15) suggests. For pupils must undergo *induction into craft-knowledge* which, for teachers, requires that their own craft-knowledge include that of teacher as well as dancer. The pupils must be led to grasp both the designing of performance and the performance of design. (For Schön [1987: p.210] a key question is whether these points apply more widely than to the performing arts: for us, it is sufficient that they do apply to those arts.) From the teacher's perspective, this induction process must respect at least two principles: first, it must recognise phases (perhaps developmental phases) so that pupils need X before Y; second, it must operate flexibly — we teach Y before X, in some circumstances, but only by leaving-out Z. (Here I have in mind pupils in accelerated music schools, where the breadth of education can sometimes be sacrificed to the requirements of musical excellence.) As Schön notes, this can be accomplished in a number of ways. For example, one teacher 'taught generically, by demonstration and imitation (Schön, 1987: 214), making no attempt to account for the indivi-duality of this or that student. Contrast the pianist, Franz, with his student, Amnon: 'Franz ... responded continually to the specific strengths and weaknesses of Amnon's efforts at imitation, moving with reciprocal imme-diacy through cycles of demonstration, imitation and criticism' (Schön, 1987: 214–15). The point is that either or both might be suitable ways forward for a particular student with a particular teacher. Our investigation takes us into cases: but these cases unfold the values of the practitioners and, ultimately, of the *practices*.

The upshot of following-through Schön's discussion of the teaching of music is to see two related areas for dance research: for both dancer and dance teacher will be reflective practitioners, in the sense articulated here. Of course, it would be wrong to suggest that no research previously undertaken fitted this mold. However, none that I know of does so *explicitly*: and explicitness is essential if one requirement is a reformed view of knowledge, as urged earlier (p. 190). It would be equally mistaken to predict what such an investigation might yield. I suggest only that it offers a promising research route, both for dance education and for dance study more generally. For we are invited to show what we can do, rather than just telling what we can say.

Conclusion

This chapter has argued that one profitable direction for dance research might be into the *craft-knowledge* both of dancer and of dance teacher. It is argued that such research must be based on a revised conception of knowledge, that implicit in treating the dance teacher (and dancer) as reflective practitioner, in Donald Schön's sense. Although the outcomes of such research cannot, of course, be predicted, it is promising not least because it gives due weight to the *doings* of dancers and dance teachers, as indicative of the values which hold such practices in place.

Chapter 17

Conclusion

Introduction

Towards the end of *Understanding Dance*, I mentioned what was there called 'an attractive picture of the nature of dance in education' (*UD*: 314): that thinking of dance in terms of its *artistic possibilities* was both fruitful and revealing. This book has attempted to make good that claim by articulating the educational aspects of that thesis in more detail. With this in mind, the discussion is illustrated with concrete material from, for example, the National Curriculum proposals in the United Kingdom. Moreover, I have included material not *directly* concerned with dance as such: material on educational theory. Also present is a conception of knowledge and understanding which, while consonant with that explored in *Understanding Dance,* is distinctive in being inflected towards the study of — and in particular research in — dance teaching. I hope that this picture is attractive to its readers, even though much of it is unfashionable, running counter to directions within current educational thinking (especially in the UK).

However, there are a number of issues which readers might have *expected* to find here, but which are absent: some, as articulated in the Preface and Chapter One, are excluded as not falling within my disciplinary ambit — that is, as not being philosophical matters. In particular, there is little here about the *practicalities* of teaching dance. Not that such issues are not both important and problematic: rather, they remain issues for another occasion (and perhaps another author). Moreover, the discussion would profit both from being less abstractly framed and from having actual examples from dance works and from dance teaching. Achieving the first of these would certainly require a different author: my mind has an abstract turn. Achieving the second would require a longer book, and perhaps also one where each *example* had to be justified as appropriate for dance in education. I have preferred to leave this task to the knowledge and discrimination of the dance teachers who, I hope, will be the primary readers of this text. Further, there is very little on the philosophical underpinning of the position. Yet some of that is in *Understanding Dance*, much of it is not crucial (and is hinted at in works referred to), and any of it would serve to make this text still more abstract.

An omission recorded: the post-post

The omission of one issue, though, is important. There is nothing here about post-modernism, or about post-structuralist dance, or about post-modern dance. This omission is deliberate, and is explained by four related concerns of mine. The first point, and perhaps the most important, is that questions about the nature of *post-modern* dance are not uppermost in the concerns of the dance teacher working in schools. It may well be, from time to time, that such a teacher is vexed about the nature of post-modern dance as a personal issue; it may even be the case that the visit of some post-modern to a local theatre may lead to productive discussion with pupils around this topic. Nonetheless, it did not seem to me crucial as such. The second point is partly an expansion of this one. For a teacher, faced with the need to discuss post-modern dance either with pupils or with an 'internal' self, is not short of useful material. For example, Joyce Sherlock (1989) offers a thoughtful discussion of the place of dance study in post modern culture, illustrated through a relatively detailed reading of Christopher Bruce's *Ghost Dances* (1981), while David Hughes (1990) offers some remarks on the nature of post-structuralist dance, which suggests, among other things, that the terms 'deconstruction' and 'post-structuralism' are 'loosely interchangeable' (Hughes, 1990: 30). Moreover, there are useful collections on post-modern culture (Foster, 1985), and perceptive discussions of post-modernism (Norris and Benjamin, 1988). In this way, the teacher has access to material which could be used to structure thought about the nature of the post-modern.

In spite of this useful material, however, my third point concerns the difficulty in deciding precisely which category to consider: 'post-structuralist', 'post-modernist', or what? Further, should one be thinking about 'post-modern *dance*', or about post-modern *culture*, with dance merely one manifestation: that is, are we talking about a kind of dance, or a cultural condition? It seems to me that either answer is possible, but neither is profound.

For Lyotard (1984: xxiii), the term 'modern' — and, by extension, 'post-modern" — designate 'any science which ...': that is to say, the term applies to what Lyotard calls *science*, and what we might call investigations into knowledge and understanding. If this is how the term 'post-modern' is to be understood[1], it follows that there can be no post-modern dance (in this sense).

Of course, the illusion of a *post-modern* dance might come about because the manner of understanding the project of (modern) dance could become altered as a result of the change in the nature of knowledge. So that it is intelligible to think of modern dance as *progressing* while we think of science (and knowledge-gathering more generally) as progressing. But 'post-modern science ... is theorising its evolution as discontinuous, catastrophic, non-rectifiable and paradoxical' (Lyotard, 1984: 60). That is, Lyotard sees this 'not as a repudiation of a bad account of science but as indicating a recent change in the nature of science' (Rorty, 1991a: 166). We can imagine a dance form which was itself as *discontinuous* from the past of dance in a similar way.

However, there is something decidedly odd about this version of the character of post-modern dance. Two related questions bring out the oddity. First, what makes this activity *dance*? Second, what project of *modernity* does such dance transcend? In answer to the first, we notice that the movement-activity must be justified as dance — and this will involve appeal to dance-movements, and to explanations using *dance-reasons* (see pp. 85–6; *UD*: 253). So post-modern dance is not escaping dance of the past: rather, it is one way of rebelling against such dance. But rebels are understood by reference to that they rebel against! In this sense, calling dance 'post-modern' is a polemical stance, rejecting the *answers* that might previously have been given to questions about the nature of dance. Yet rejecting the answer is accepting the *question*.

On the second question, we see that the project of modernity encompasses just the sorts of rejection of the past at issue here. For modernism 'the relation between the present practice of an enterprise and the history of that enterprise ... has become problematic' (Cavell, 1969: xix). Moreover, as Cavell continues, 'the repudiation of the past has a transformed significance'. In respect of painting, Cavell (1979b: 109) asks us to see 'modernist painting as an *acknowledging* of its conditions'. More completely:

> Whatever painting may be about, modernist painting is about *painting*, about what it means to use a limited two-dimensional surface in ways establishing the coherence and interest we demand of art. ... The problems of composition are no longer irrelevant to the audience of art when the solution to a compositional problem has become identical with the aesthetic result itself. (Cavell, 1969: 207)

Despite its oracular ring (McFee, 1980a), this view indicates how a concern with the nature of the artistic enterprise itself — with its 'conditions' in Cavell's term — is characteristic of modernism of this sort. And yet that is exactly the kind of *risky* concern with its own nature characteristic of so-called post-modern dance: for, in its practice, it is centrally concerned with the borderlines between dance and non-dance, with what (if anything) makes a movement sequence dance. This seems a reaffirmation of, not an extension beyond, the project of modernity.

These three reasons, then, explain why I have not explored the post-modern or post-structuralist: that it is not the main concern of dance teachers, that relevant material is to hand, and that the *notion* of the postmodern was not clear.

My fourth point concerns the problematic character of standard post-modernist theorising. Put roughly, it is just a new kind of subjectivism, with all the failings of the old kind. Insofar as this charge is appropriate, one can simply dismiss these post-isms as subjectivist. I will not, of course, here attempt to demonstrate that point. The inordinate amount of time, and detailed textual reference, needed to do so has required that I exclude it from this work — or at least, that is one reason! But if we are aware of the kinds of objection to subjectivism canvassed throughout this text, we are unlikely to be taken in by at least *some* of the cruder presentations of post-modernist thinking.

Of course, if the thesis were, instead, that post-modern *dance* was the topic (which seems to be Hughes' view in some places) the issue would be a different one. We would need to ask what, precisely, the characteristics of this form of dance are — how does it resemble, and how does it differ from, other things we recognise as dance? Of course, this is an interesting topic. But it is a topic within dance criticism. It is exactly on a par with deciding the characteristics of, say, Romantic Ballet, the one additional difficulty being that one is making the judgements of broadly contemporary works. Thus, the distinctiveness of post-modern dance is a distinctiveness *within* the framework articulated thus far. Indeed, interestingly, the volume of *Dance Theatre Journal* which includes Hughes' piece also includes a review of DV8 offering 'physical theatre'. I have no difficulty in thinking that this is *dance*, however we prefer to sub-classify it. So I have little need of further theses concerning *kinds* of dance in the current scene, at least beyond sub-divisions offered me by major critics.

Concluding Summary

Where have we arrived in this text? Six main areas of discussion have yielded informative remarks, which may be summarised as follows.

• *The Artistic Account of Dance Education*

This view builds on the artistic/aesthetic distinction to find the justification of dance in its artistic possibilities. First summarised in Chapter 5, we have expanded and explored this account. In particular, we have defended it as an *adequate* account (because it explained the educational distinctiveness of dance in both its *educational* and its *distinctive* dimensions); as *preferable* to other candidates — not least because they fail to explain the educational; and as providing the *centre*, although not the totality, of the dance curriculum in schools.

- *The Project for Research*

The key characteristic has been to locate a *dance* research, rather than one depending on disciplinary perspectives on dance (history of dance, sociology of dance etc.). We have suggested one avenue here, building on Schön's notion of the *reflective practitioner*. That notion seems fruitful for research into the craft-knowledge of the dance teacher, but also of the dancer.

- *Dance Understanding*

An important element in the account of dance education was the weight given to dance as a vehicle for understanding, inherited from the associated account of dance as such. So that if, with Adshead (1981), we were to take choreography, performance and critical appreciation as basic concepts for dance as an area of academic study, we would justify their several places by reference to their contribution to dance understanding, and to understanding more generally.

- *Constraints on Assessment for Dance in Education*

In a climate of increasing enthusiasm for assessment, we have laid-out some constraints on any pattern of assessment appropriate to dance in education (while not ignoring the advantages of — indeed the absolute requirement for — some such assessment). This has been one way of emphasising the importance of the teacher in dance education: in particular, the understanding and professionalism of the teacher.

- *A View of Education and of the Curriculum*

Throughout, a Personal Enquiry conception of education and a 'process' model of the curriculum have been employed. Although some arguments for these positions have been given, chiefly negatively (against competing views), it cannot be claimed that either has been established in this text. However, and first, for both positions the suitability of and compatibility with the artistic account of dance education has been demonstrated. Second, this promises to be a fruitful area of general education research (if a currently unfashionable one), and an area with a clear impact on the nature of dance education.

• *Against Subjectivism in Dance Education*

Seen in one way, this has not been a topic in this text at all. I rejected subjectivism in Chapter One, and have merely reiterated that rejection throughout. Seen another way, though, the whole text is part of the polemic against subjectivism. It highlights the numerous places where the temptation to subjectivism is presented to the dance educator. At each stage, it is important to see how the subjectivist position undermines the claims to understanding, to learning, to art-status, or all of these!

If this collection of conclusions is accepted, suitably filled-out by the detailed discussion, this text will have achieved a major aim: the educational distinctiveness will have been demonstrated. Yet, if my *questions* are recognised as the appropriate questions to be asking, this text will also have fulfilled another aim — even if my answers are rejected. And, in doing so, it will have clarified (some of) what are and what are not issues for the academic study of dance.

And finally

A reader might have hoped for an account, in a few lines, of the concept of dance education. Such a reader might be puzzled that a book-length discussion *still* has not come-up with such an account. But that thought misses the point in three important ways. First, we have an account of dance education: the *artistic account*. It makes plain what is central, what peripheral, in the thinking on dance education. Moreover, it makes explicit both key distinctions (such as the artistic/aesthetic distinction) and important assumptions — such as those concerning the nature of education. Second, the elaboration here is too brief to deal with all the issues posed by this account. Some desirable ways of expanding the account have been eschewed to avoid lengthening this text. Third, the project here is to answer *standard* perplexities of those concerned with dance education. As such, it requires an overview (Baker, 1991: 58–61), working one by one through such perplexities. That is how I have proceeded here.

The emotional origin of this book is my profound commitment to the importance of dance (indeed, of the arts more generally), and especially its educational importance. The practical origin of the book, as reported in the Preface, was my being invited to hold forth on this topic, in the context of the National Curriculum in the UK. I have found myself wanting to expand on what I said initially and to further explore the topic. But the intellectual origins of this book are imbedded in a further set of commitments of mine: philosophical commitments. As recorded in section 1, this text has had very little to say on these commitment — and rightly so, given its intended audience. Yet the untangling of some of the philosophically-demanding lines which lead from dance education (and, in my thinking, typically lead into the philosophy of Wittgenstein) is an important task, not unconnected with a more complete account of dance as an academic discipline.

To end on a personal note, I do not imagine that I will be writing on dance in the near future, although I have a number of projects not completed — for example, one concerning expressionism in dance, another concerning the nature of dance notation. The commitments which motivated this book are as strong as ever. But it is time for others to make what they will of the ideas.

PART V

SUPPLEMENTARY ESSAYS

Supplementary Essay 1:

Truth, Dance Education and the 'Postmodern Condition'

Preamble

This essay is an expanded version, with specific reference to dance, of a paper (McFee, 1998) initially composed for a volume on art education. But that paper drew on other writings of mine (especially McFee, 1996) — and some presentations — so this version effectively reinstates that earlier discussion. I have maintained the direct connection to arts *education*.

The discussion came about because, in CDE, I had written as though I had a clear refutation of postmodernism but either it did not fit in that book or there was no space to include it. Invitations to expand on these points — especially from colleagues at University of Surrey: Roehampton (as it now is) — led me to reconsider the brief remarks offered in CDE, although without withdrawing them. There (CDE: 194-6) I raised four concerns about postmodernism:

(a)   '.... questions about the nature of *post-modern* dance are not uppermost in the concerns of the dance teacher working in schools'.

(b)   'a teacher .... is not short of useful material' on postmodernism and postmodern dance.

(c)   '.... should one be thinking about 'post-modern *dance*', or about post-modern *culture*'.

(d)   '.... the problematic character of standard post-modernist theorising ....[as] just a new kind of subjectivism'.

In a sense, the discussion here elaborates these points. But I saw how the drawing of some distinctions here might be useful: a full understanding would necessarily not only contrast postmodernism with postmodern dance but would show how what had been called 'post-modern dance' (for example, by Sally Banes, 1987) was better seen as modernist (as Banes, too, came to recognise[1]). As she puts the point, we might choose 'to call sixties and seventies post-modern dance *post-modern* and dub eighties new dance post-modernist' (Banes, 1987: xv). Notice that, like CDE, Banes still hyphenates the term. Indeed, the expression 'postmodernism' did not occur in CDE, since I too tended to hyphenate: but that fashion has moved on.

To begin, let us ask: Is there a specific problem here for arts education, which connects it to (roughly) problems of *understanding*, or making sense of, postmodern art? Thus suppose a writer characterised art's 'postmodern condition' in terms of 'irony, parody, displacement, complexity, eclecticism...' (Jenks, 1986: 15). Or, more bluntly, claimed that for art: 'Truth has been replaced by the twins "Relativity" and "Legitimation"' (Burgin, 1986: 49). What should we make of this? On the face of it, both comments imply that remarks ('criticism'[2]) about artworks cannot be true or false. Would this undermine the very possibility of *arts education*, by controverting any application of the idea of *truth* to art? Then, however education is explained, arts education will not involve development of understanding, since truth and understanding are related. In part, the threats to arts education are familiar; and have been met — *subjectivism* (understood as the doctrine that 'anything goes', that there are no wrong 'answers': *UD*: 21-38) and *relativism* (understood as the possibility that two people in genuine disagreement might both be right: *UD*: 301-09).

What precisely is being urged by such thinkers: what *counts* as postmodernism here? If the answer turns on particular stylistic features of *art*, that will raise a set of issues for arts education different from those raised if the answer relates to more general features of our capacity to understand artworks. So there are two[3] *key* issues: the (supposed) threat to arts education is a product either, first, of postmodern *art* providing a specific challenge to the *stability* of claims to artistic knowledge, by importing an eclecticism destructive of unity within artworks[4] or by undermining those artistic traditions constitutive of the 'stability' of the idea of the artistic. Or, second, of difficulties arising from of the state of contemporary society ('the postmodern condition') or the interventions of theorists of postmodernism.

The essay initially addresses postmodern art, and then comments on the specific claims of dance, before offering an account of arts education that has learned from postmodernist concerns. For the challenge of postmodernism is not *all* foolishness — although its relativist/subjectivist pretensions are! First, postmodernists rightly urge that a widely employed conception of knowledge is not sustainable — but this is nothing new: a tradition in British philosophy[5] gave, in effect, the same answer to these concerns as an *enlightened* (or rectified) postmodernism. Second, the postmodernist attack on *logocentrism* too has a point: namely, that a widespread conception of *rationality* is mistaken — and this is crucial in defending the rationality of artistic judgement.

The challenge of postmodern art

Might the 'postmodern condition' (or postmodernism) *within* the arts —

postmodern art, if you like[6] — undermine art's educational position? Even if the arts *had* an educative role at some point in their various histories, perhaps that time has passed. Perhaps the arts should no longer be regarded as *uncontentiously* educational (or, perhaps, *exposure* to the arts be no longer viewed in this way). Hence arts education might have gone wrong in three further ways: first, social changes (etc.) might be such that art has lost its educative power — I shall not consider this bleak option: second, contemporary (?) art might lack the educative power of art of previous periods; and, third, mere *exposure* to the arts might no longer be enough for educational purposes. As we shall see (on the third point), *mere* exposure to the arts was *never* enough; but our view of the arts obscured this fact when people *theorised* about art education — in *practice*, it was always implicitly conceded.

Eclecticism and understanding

To sustain the second of these claims, one might either argue about examples ('What is educative about seeing such-and-such a work by Damien Hirst?') or try to identify some particular characteristic of contemporary art which renders it problematic. And, if the specific culprit were *postmodern* art, one might focus on its *eclecticism*. For perhaps the postmodern attitude here is 'a thoroughgoing mixing up of categories' (Crowther, 1993: 94).

Yet why should eclecticism make understanding difficult? For example, one can make sense of a 'unity' achieved through humour and pastiche. But understanding a pastiche essentially involves recognising that it is a pastiche: and therefore understanding it against the background of what is familiar — even if the familiar is being treated ironically. The only difference is the range of sources that might be employed: just knowing about, say, dance of the past will not suffice. For some dances by Lea Anderson, for example, a knowledge of films ('...one of Astaire's and Rogers's most famous dances': Mackrell, 1992: 130) or of advertisements might be essential. But such knowledge is likely to be quite widespread: it is not obvious that eclecticism necessarily precludes understanding.

Of course, what is required in order to understand postmodern artworks will be specific to that work (and that artform): it will be case-by-case[7]. The distinctiveness of postmodern art is then *within* a familiar framework, provided by our understanding other artworks (to the degree that we do), learned as we learned to understand other artworks.

Given that theoretical point, our practical concerns as theorists of arts education are both with what we can understand and with what concepts are mobilised in doing so (plus how we came by or learned them).

But this cannot be quite right. For modernist art is not well understood. Much of the public view of art of, say, the twentieth century (in fact, of art in general) is either philistine[8] or out-dated, or both — still trying to come to terms with the innovations of the painting of Picasso from 1908 or the dance of Martha Graham of 1930. How can this audience hope to make sense of contemporary works that take Picasso and/or Graham as starting points for innovation? Or even works regarding Picasso or Graham as too far *in the past* to even be treated in this way?

Of course, there is no ready reply to such a difficulty. Our *hope* must be that a widening of interest in art, in combination with arts education (and possibly motivated by it), will overcome the problem. But, from a *theoretical* or *conceptual* point of view, we know *what* is needed even if we cannot see how it is to be achieved.

Loss of traditions?

Now we are approaching a second issue concerning the 'stability' of the idea of the artistic, in a 'world' of loss of tradition (see Cavell, 1969: 202). But there is no general answer. As Stanley Cavell (1969: 219) notes, 'The trouble is that the genuine article [of art] .... really does challenge the art of which it is the inheritor and voice'. Rather, we should recognise that, for modernism, 'the relation between the present practice of an enterprise and the history of that enterprise ... has become problematic' (Cavell, 1969:164).

On this characterisation, the project of modernism can be contested only, first, by retreating to the past, by turning to a time when the medium of art (in that artform) was uncontentious — generating archaic forms, which may not be intelligible; or, second, by disputing the relevance of the project: that is, denying the very possibility of art. (This cannot be a live option for an arts educator.) Anything else is just a (*polemical*: Cavell, 1969: 221) way of *answering* the project, by providing an implicit answer where doing such-and-such does indeed constitute a way to make art. Suppose, for example, we accept that '[t]he post-modern choreographers of the 1960s and 1970s saw their work as part of a continuing debate about the nature and function of theatrical dance' (Banes, 1987: xxv). Then these choreographers were centrally engaged with the project of modernity, which has a developed critical discourse. And understanding them is no more difficult (and no easier!) than coming to grasp and apply that critical discourse elsewhere. So both worries have been addressed/answered.

Of course, this response is rooted in contrasting our response to artworks (where the idea of a *critical discourse* makes sense) with our response to other objects in which we take an aesthetic interest (where it does not): that, as it were, there is a key difference *because* we are considering artworks.

Here it might be questioned whether we *should* think (in this way) of the interest we take in *art* as importantly importantly *different from* our other aesthetic interests? (And a parallel question could be asked about aesthetic experience.) Or whether engagement with art is simply a (non-cognitive) response like that involved with, say, beauty in nature? Here, we should make two points. First, and practically, treating these kinds of interest as importantly alike requires different arguments to justify arts education since, on the face of it, non-art aesthetic interest could be found in appreciating the grace and line of the radiators that heat the school, the melodious singing of birds in the school's playground, the design of the wallpaper, and so on. In short, there would be no *obvious* place for a concern with *art*; neither with its making, nor straightforwardly with its appreciating. For why privilege one source of aesthetic pleasure over others?

Such a conclusion is very destructive of the claims of aesthetic education. To avoid it, we must introduce our second point: that is to continue distinguishing the concern with art (both its making and its understanding) from the rest of aesthetic interest; and doing so in a way that is educationally relevant, stressing the cognitive dimension of the arts. And this is just to restate the importance of the artistic/aesthetic contrast (see CDE: 17–18; and Supplementary Essay 3)

As we have seen, meaning (or intending) of the sort relevant to artistic understanding has a *history* — what can be *meant* depends both on the history of the form up to the point of one's so meaning (including being in revolution against such history) and on the 'narrative'[9] that might be appropriately given in explaining what the work *meant*. This ensures what Jerrold Levinson (1996: 152) calls an 'intentional connection to preceding art, however provisionally identified'. Hence we value art *differently* from the ways we value other aesthetic objects, such as natural beauty, the decorative, or designed objects (the Ferrari). One may contrast the (varied) interest taken in art with the (equally diffuse) interest taken in *other* things in which we take an aesthetic interest — indeed, the *educational* distinctiveness of art depends on such a contrast.

Now, we do *draw* the distinction in 'real life', without having a good way to *mark* that distinction in words — we often use the term 'aesthetic' to capture our interest both in the art *and* in the Ferrari, and we use the word 'art' in other than the 'fine art' sense: for instance[10], there is a book entitled *The Womanly Art of Breast-feeding*. So respecting this distinction is quite difficult — we typically use exactly the same forms of words on both sides of the contrast.

The solution is to adopt a *technical* distinction, reserving the words 'art', 'artistic' and the like for our concern with 'fine art', and using the term 'aesthetic' and its relatives only for the other concerns — for natural beauty, the fountain, the firework display, and the Ferrari. This distinction is *artificial*: we do and we must draw it — but we do not typically mark it using these words.

Intermezzo: the 'other side of the coin'

The possibility of *artistic knowledge* is central: knowledge *manifest* in art, that is, rather than knowledge *of* art (or, worse, of art history). For only through artistic knowledge in *this* sense could art claim to be intrinsically educational in its own right (that is, not as history etc.). And education has a clear connection to understanding. What is *true* (and hence can be known) and what can be understood are connected.

The educational status of the arts was, at one time, regularly assailed by contrasting arts with sciences. Judgements of the arts differ from, for instance, judgements made in the natural sciences, such as physics or chemistry. But the differences are not in terms of their public character, their amenability to discussion, or their commitment to truth. They are no more *necessarily* subjective than many other judgements.

When education was explained in terms of *forms of knowledge*[11], acknowledging the arts' educational value required bringing them within that framework[12] — arguing that artistic knowledge was actually propositional, despite appearances to the contrary (for example, Hirst, 1974: 152-64); or that the artistic amounted to knowledge of *a different kind* (Peters, 1966: 158-9). And even giving up a 'forms of knowledge' analysis for the educational, its adherents discussed the arts in suitably *cognitivist* terms.

Such a view recognises that art is a human construction. But, as Lyotard (1984: xxiii)[13] notes, having recognised that we speak and judge as 'the contingent historical selves we find ourselves to be' (Rorty, 1991: 214), why should such (historically-rooted and contingent) judgements carry any weight for others (much less be compelling on them)? Rather (Lyotard thinks) we should deny any single discourse the right to judge others on its terms: all discourses are equal! Faced with a search for some tribunal of Pure Reason, Lyotard asks, 'What language do the judges speak?'. Any answer *seems* to import arbitrariness into the heart of human judgement — and hence artistic judgement.

As traditionally viewed, scientific description of the world around us has a reductive tendency, treating colours as optical effects, sensations and emotions as brain-states, etc., etc. So are there *really* red post boxes, blue cars, toothaches, depressions and loves? These seem contingent features of our contemporary account of the world; and natural science seems to offer a preferable alternative — a view of how the world *is*, abstracted from any particular historical or cultural position: the View from Nowhere (compare Nagel, 1986).

In denying such reductionism, theses such as Lyotard's *appear* to commit *some* defenders of postmodernist thinking to attacks on the concept of truth. Given that there are no 'metanarratives' (Lyotard, 1984: xxiii), no overarching explanatory frameworks, the model of knowledge based on the (supposed) qualities of scientific knowledge is undermined by the postmodernist tendency to claim science as just another 'narrative': that is, as just one description among many, with no further claim to authority. Thus, for example, Putnam (1992) and Luntley (1995) couch the challenge of postmodernism in terms central to science. In part, this recognises a general (and agreed) characteristic of science: namely, the *inherently* changeability of the 'truths' of science and technology, in a world where theories can change.

Further, it might be thought that '[o]nly descriptions of the world can be true or false' (Rorty, 1989: 5). Then, 'it is difficult to think of the world as deciding between ... ' (Rorty, 1989: 5) alternative descriptions of events, once these are seen as *whole* ways of describing: 'the jargon of Newton versus that of Aristotle' (Rorty, 1989: 5), for example. But then 'socialisation, and thus historical circumstance, goes all the way down ... there is nothing 'beneath' socialisation or prior to history which is definitory of the human' (Rorty, 1989: xiii). Thus, someone might think, 'Truth cannot be out there ... because sentences cannot so exist, or be out there' (Rorty, 1989: 5). This can seem to imply that truth is 'free-floating', tantamount to claiming that there is no truth.

In this way, postmodern theories give a new piquancy to issues raised earlier — other areas are now subject to critiques familiar in respect of the arts. The very possibility of truth (and, importantly, of knowledge and understanding) seems under threat *generally*: one issue is *now* whether *science* can meet the standards formerly ascribed to it (the standards used in 'arts bashing'), where this is part of a general attack on the *idea* of knowledge or understanding — or even of truth.

From the fact that language has no foundation in the 'facts' of the world, it *seems* to follow that all truth claims are ultimately arbitrary, which undermines the notion of truth[14]. There was *not* 'one right answer', but the conclusion that *anything goes* simply does not follow. Such theorising assumes (mistakenly) that what is not *independently* 'legitimated' is thereby guaranteed to be arbitrary. Yet, from a rejection of the search for 'universal commensuration in a final vocabulary' (Rorty, 1979: 368), nothing follows about issues of objectivity.

However, a worrying response to a recognition of differences between arts and sciences has been to embrace that difference. This most damaging error comes from the friends rather than the detractors of arts education. Beginning from a mistaken picture of scientific knowledge, it typically insists that the arts contribute in education 'the other side of the coin' to what is contributed by the sciences. So the educational place of the arts is justified by *contrasting* what the sciences have to offer with the 'babble and rhapsody' and the 'profound acts of liberation' (Abbs, 1991: 112) of the arts — but since the sciences offer objective knowledge, it is easy for the arts to be relegated to offering something *not* objective and *not* (really) knowledge. Yet, as we have seen, any inference from the objectivity of science to the subjectivity of the arts is unsound.

'Aesthetic education in an age of postmodernism'

Other views of objectivity might be offered. But *this* one shows why artistic judgements cannot be *dismissed* as subjective, and connects with the human capacity to make artistic judgements: it is, in an apt expression Putnam (1990: 210) attributes to David Wiggins, 'objective humanly speaking'. And this is all the objectivity arts education requires.

In rooting objectivity in *human* capacities, this account might seem insufficient for (the possibility of) artistic knowledge: does it not conflate what is *true* (and hence knowable) with what humans *think* or *believe*? Recognition that there is no external perspective is only worrying if our account of reason or of truth would thereby be undermined: but why should that be? Those knowledgeable about an artform recognise ways of articulating *relevant* reasons here — that is, of clarifying relevance — allowing the identification of a certain claim as a *reason* in the context of the artform under discussion: as being an *artistic reason*, as we might say.

This account has made plain some of the attractions of postmodernism, although putting them more soberly: the idea of the 'objective humanly speaking' and the *fishes'-eye* view of truth (UD: 307). Applied to arts education, rejection of the requirement for 'one right answer' should militate against the assumption of 'one right reading' for artworks.

Moreover, our judgements have an historical character (McFee, 1992b; 1995). As Gordon Baker and Peter Hacker (1984c: 4) put it, 'We cannot return the apples from the Tree of the Knowledge of History ... Though we know the Impressionists were outrageous revolutionaries in the theory and practice of painting, we can no longer *see* them as outrageous'. But these are facts about what it is to see the Impressionists as part of an on-going tradition, where later events shape how *we* can make sense of the past. So we have an account which both tolerates and explains diversity within a framework of rational constraint.

Rationality and appreciation

Notice the logical peculiarity in suggesting that 'the postmodern condition' requires new conceptualisations of (for example: Lyotard, 1984: 60) knowledge or science. For this suggests, not the identification of a *mistaken* view previously held, but a new situation, a 'condition' where the whole idea of knowledge or of science *can*, and perhaps *must*, be understood differently. So (on this view) the old account *was* accurate, but *no longer* is.

But, if there were, at one time, arguments for (or against) some view of the nature of (say) science, surely they are arguments *now*. And if there are *now* counter-arguments, there were such arguments then — even if they wouldn't easily be urged! For instance, if later changes in social understanding or scientific theory make us doubt the explanatory adequacy of some 'metanarrative', we are surely just seeing that it was *always* false (in its full generality) but that the area of its falsity wasn't *clear* previously.

No doubt there are problems about 'our' understanding of the world; perhaps our account of rationality *is* flawed. Yet these '...require not only rational reconstruction but criticism. But criticism requires argument, not the abandonment of argument' (Putnam, 1992: 130). The reply to attacks on 'logocentrism' (Norris, 1987: 28) is that, if we need to modify *our* account of rationality, we cannot do without *some* such account — since we will need criticism to motivate and to direct any modification. Indeed, as Putnam (1992: 124) urges, 'the collapse of a certain picture of the world, and of conceptions of representation and truth that went with that picture of the world, is very far from being a collapse of the notions of representation and truth'. Finding that a certain metaphysical picture is *now* bankrupt is (typically) a way of noting that, for all its apparent successes, it was *always* bankrupt: that its 'successes' are indeed only apparent (and probably best explained in some other way).

A considered response from within arts education to the 'challenge' of postmodernism, then, would involve, first, arguments against subjectivism/relativism previously deployed in arts education — issues that have always arisen; second, emphasis on artistic appreciation is something *done* — as it were, *done* first, and *explained* afterwards (sketched briefly: above); third, bringing out how, in learning artistic appreciation, we learn to become *competent judges*. The third of these is our chief topic here.

A full reply should also indicate that the 'cognitive dimension' of art imports reference to what humans characteristically find valuable, to what may be called *life-issues* or *life-situations* (*UD*: 173-90; CDE: 41-7); and that the ability to make informed artistic judgements (central to arts education) involves not merely what one knows (one's *cognitive stock*: Wollheim, 1993: 134) but also one's ability to mobilise that cognitive stock (those concepts) in one's experience of works of art: thus artistic appreciation has both cognitive and affective dimensions (see McFee, 1997 esp. 34; McFee, 2001a esp. 160; Supplementary Essay 3).

Arts education and competent judges

It might *seem* that judging, say, the Picasso a masterpiece can be analysed as, first, thinking/knowing *certain things* about it — such knowledge being 'motivationally inert' (Price, 1988: 87); then, second, valuing those *things*. In this way, critics might agree about the facts of the matter but differ in the evaluation of the artwork in question.

Such a view is mistaken, in ways relevant to artistic (aesthetic) education, first, by being misguided in general as an account of action[15]; and, second, in under-rating the degree to which artistic judgement is a kind of action.

This second point recognises the fundamental role — for arts education — of training in artistic judgement, understood via two slogans (McFee, 2001b: 100–104):

> *Arts education is learning to see.*
> *Arts education is leaning to value.*

For learning to *see* the work of art in question appropriately is learning what to see as *valuable* in it (or how to see it as valuable); and hence learning to value it — although I may rebel against what I have learned! We are here describing a person learning to be a *competent judge* in respect in matters artistic (sometimes in relation to some particular artform, sometimes more generally).

So someone failing to understand an artwork may be *misperceiving* that work, failing to mobilise *appropriate* concepts (or *categories*: Walton, 1987) in his/her perception of the work. And that amounts to both a failure to *understand* the work appropriately and a failure to *appreciate* it appropriately. When I treat the music by Messian *as though* it were genuine birdsong, I misperceive it by applying the wrong *category*; but I also mis-value it — since the *normativity* that follows from recognising it as art (rather than as *merely* aesthetic: CDE: 17-18) would be inappropriate to birdsong. If, instead, I treat it as *tonal* music, I import *a* normativity alright — but my judgements will be inappropriate *to the Messian* (even if heart-felt!) And hence my valuing of it will also be inappropriate.

However, learning to *see* the artworks as valuable (and to see certain features of the works as *reasons* for my judgements) is engaging with the narrative of art history in respect of that artform. For if my judgement of that artwork is to be explained or justified to others, reference must be made to the history and development of the artform in question — perhaps referring to a revolution against traditional ways of working in that form. For only in this way am I connecting my claims for *this* work to what is acknowledged as valuable from *other* works — and hence to artistic value!

This section emphases the role, in *understanding* art (and hence in *learning* to understand art), of *competent judges*: that the idea of art as meaning-bearing (or of art's having a 'cognitive dimension') depends on the *possibility* of creatures able to recognise such meaning. The possibility of competent judges, therefore, is a conceptual requirement for any artistic judgement at all, a precondition for what is 'objective humanly speaking'. Such competent judges will, at least typically, be those who informed humans *regard* as competent: the role involves being an *informed* and *sensitive* spectator of art (typically, in a certain artform), possessing appropriate *cognitive stock*, and able to *mobilise* that stock in one's experience of artwork.

The account of *artistic knowledge* and of the place of *competent judges* in arts understanding (and hence arts education) given here exploits the insights *behind* postmodernism to clarify the nature of arts education, without accepting the excesses of some theorists of postmodernism: in particular, there is no real concession to subjectivism or relativism, no weakening of the commitment to the ideal of *truth*.

The rationality of artistic understanding

What model for coming to understand artworks has been developing here? This view (Ground, 1989: 93) recognises that we do and must bring to such appreciation a large amount of knowledge, a substantial cognitive stock. Further, since that knowledge draws on the narratives of art history in the relevant artforms, it includes knowledge of other artworks (and perhaps other works by the artist under consideration): we are familiar with the appropriate *category of art*. The appreciation then takes the form of perceiving the work (looking at the painting, hearing the music, etc.) in the light of such understanding: it is perceptual rather than inferential, a species of noticing (*UD*: 138-47: CDE: 89-92) — given suitable conditions and knowledge, people have the capacity for such understanding of art because they have the capacity to perceive artworks. As Wollheim (1993: 142) puts it, 'perception of the arts *is* ... the process of understanding the work of art'. But, of course, this is merely a precondition for such understanding, since neither the *sensitivity* nor the *informed-ness* required is guaranteed. So the view is *perceptualist* in the quite strong sense *both* that what is required for artistic appreciation is a human power or capacity[16] (although this is only a prerequisite for artistic appreciation) *and* that there is nothing more to understanding here than perception, once the idea of perceiving is understood with appropriate richness.

Of course, art appreciation must operate through 'perceptual engagement' (seeing, hearing) with the work(s): your judgement of the work must relate to what you see in it, not to what you have been told is there. Still, such engagement may usefully be supplemented by discussion, drawing parallels, etc.: so, although appreciation is centrally perceptual, the spectator's perceptual judgements (and his/her taste) can be 'influenced' — just as well for arts educators! This is one way in which we should regard appreciation as rational.

Given my concepts and my ability to mobilise those concepts in my experience of art (as both my concepts and my powers are at *that* instant), I not only *see* a particular artwork in that certain way, but *judge* it that way (or *appreciate* it that way).

Certainly my appreciation of an artwork can change: I can regard a work differently, or an 'insight' of yesterday can seem insubstantial or misconceived today, and so on. But here I am mobilising different concepts in my appreciation of that work — and this would be explicable to some degree. For example, it might be 'explained' either by my acquiring new concepts or by my becoming able to mobilise different concepts in my experience of the work. And, of course, the first of these might involve my *bringing to bear* concepts not previously brought to bear — perhaps because of, say, the re-hanging of a familiar picture or because of other things I'd seen/heard: other narratives I'd *found* relevant.

Moreover, our coming to understand artworks (to the degree that one can) must be 'one step at a time'; hence some steps may prove impossible for a particular person. If I cannot see that a particular artwork has a certain property, despite your best efforts, there is nothing more that you can do that will guarantee my coming either to see the work as you suggest or to value the work in that way. (In this way, the situation resembles that of the person who cannot see the 'old woman' aspect of the multiple-figure: you can point out its characteristics in a variety of ways, but ultimately I must see it for myself.)

Since it is 'one step at a time', there may be some steps I cannot take: that is, some concepts I either cannot acquire or cannot mobilise in my experience of this work of art (perhaps of art generally). For me, that artwork will be a closed book (again, like the multiple figure). And this in turn might be explained: for instance, by reference to other knowledge or other valuing of mine. For example, I am an admirer of the minimal (say, Rothko) and have no time for the sentimental (say, Holman Hunt). Now, we might expect me to find the transition from my understanding of the dances of Martha Graham to those of Merce Cunningham to be an easy one to make. And we might explain its facility in terms of my avowed admiration for the minimal, viewing Merce as *more* minimal than Martha. (And a converse explanation for my difficulties in coming to grips with sentimental choreographers.)

Equally, faced with a spectator/student who has reached his 'last step', the arts educator will employ two basic strategies — of pointing to features of *this* work that (at present) the spectator/student does not see in the appropriate way, and of offering theoretical 'chat' to *explain* seeing the work in that way, with the discourse drawing on what the spectator/student *does* view appropriately. Either of these strategies may be augmented by looking at *other* works too: for at the centre of both strategies is the suggestion that *this* be seen in a way one already sees *that*. It is as *case-by-case* procedure in precisely this sense (Compare McFee, 1978 Ch 2).

Recall that the postmodernist critic claimed that the model of a purely deductive rationality was unsustainable. Without arguing this matter in detail (compare McFee, 1990), the aim has been to concede that point; but to insist, by contrast, that there is a perfectly good model of rationality that *does* apply here — where *here* is, especially, the domain of arts education and artistic judgement. And that model is the *case-by-case* one.

Our strategy here (in respect of rationality) parallels that in respect of truth/knowledge claims: the theorist of postmodernism was *right* to urge that a certain typical, traditional or dominant model is unworkable. What does *not* follow, of course, was that rationality lacks 'bite' here. And our explanatory tool has been the rationality of criticism, combined with our insights into the *knowledge*-base implicit in the *practice* both of criticism and of the teaching of artistic judgment.

Making postmodern art

Similar responses apply in respect of the making of art. For here too the issue of understandability is paramount. For instance, the problem of unity is common problem in most artworks, especially once the desire to break with traditional forms is embraced. As one case, consider the problems encountered by Morton Feldman (1926–), who embarked on an 'abstract sonic adventure' (Brindle, 1975: 129) designed 'to destroy conventional musical continuity' (Brindle, 1975: 126). So a typical piece of his for solo piano, *Intermission 6* (1953^{17}), consists of a few sheets of score, with the pianist choosing which order to play them in, instructed that (having moved onto the next sheet) he cannot go back. Such works provide opportunities for *huge* variations between performances.

But (a) a particular pianist will typically play through the pages in the same (or roughly the same) order. So, in *practice* (or in *reality*), performances by this pianist *do not* differ radically; (b) the selection of chords that form the score of works in this mode tend to be fairly similar. So that the performances are rather 'samey': each work in this style resembles the others — an *experienced* unity which the works actually lack? (and are expressly intended by Feldman to lack) — *we* are supplying both these kinds of unity.

And, of course, even in extreme cases (such as Feldman's), this process of striving for the new is *not* a 'denial of tradition' but a *polemical* answer to questions about the role of tradition (which is as true for postmodern art as it was for artistic modernism).

Moreover, we should recognise artworks as occurring only in a background (where appropriate) of the re-performing, restoring, reviewing (etc.) of those artworks (and see Supplementary Essay 3). This was part of what was meant when I wrote of the need to justify the movement-activity *as dance* — using *dance-reasons* (CDE: 84-87; *UD*: 253).

> We would need to ask what, precisely, the characteristics of this form of dance are — how does it resemble, and how does it differ from, other things we recognise as dance? Of course, this is .... a topic within dancecriticism. It is exactly on a par with deciding the characteristics of, say, Romantic Ballet, the one additional difficulty being that one is making the judgements of broadly contemporary works. (CDE: 196)

It is what, above, I characterised in terms of the 'narratives' of dance with which one is familiar.

Example: postmodern dance and narrative

As a typical account of a particular work from the modernist 'phase' of postmodern dance, consider the following, for Yvonne Rainer's *Trio A*: 'There is no story, character, attitude or action that the movement can be correlated to: thus, *Trio A* forgoes all the traditional narrative devices ...' (Carroll, 1981: 100). Indeed, we might agree with Adrian Stokes (1935: 105) that one aspect of modernism in ballet involved the replacement of narrative based on 'mimed action', so that 'the action of a modern ballet is expressed in the dancing itself'. But there are two key points here: first, that does not mean that the narrative element is necessarily absent from such dances — rather, its artistic irrelevance is being urged. And, second, these are not the works at issue.

For postmodern dance, then, the situation is different than that Stokes describes. As Banes (1987: xxix) notes, 'the narrative, whose death seemed a certainty in the sixties and seventies, has been reborn in the eighties'. Yet agreeing that some postmodern dances have a narrative element does not require that a similar attitude be taken to narrative: instead, a different attitude, one more difficult to characterise, is reflected in the narrative element.

One symptom is that characterisations become inceasingly theoretised: such dances 'are different from modern dance ... because in important ways the present the nondance information (i.e. plot, character, situation) rather than represent it. They are not seamless theatrical illusions ... ' (Banes, 1987: xxxi). But if, for example, we think that Ian Spink's *Dead Flight* (1980) 'suggested some influence of Pina Bausch' (Jordan, 1992: 187), we are reminded that there are various kinds of theatrical illusions. Equally, we might take Spink's *De Gas* (1981) to be 'theatrical' (Jordan, 1992: 189) or notice the 'raw theatricality' of DV8[18] without mistaking either for the narrative works of previous generations. Moreover, as a comparison of critical description of performances of DV8[19] may illustrate, there are various ways of invoking narrative. Consider, first:

> ... the eight women waited for an agonisingly long time for their lovers, who never showed up. The, when eight men finally appeared, the women set out to pursue them, chasing them up and down the stage, hobbled by their high heels and tight dresses.

This is a straightforward story, posing for the audience questions about 'the ways in which women bind themselves to men' (Mackrell, 1992: 124). Then, second:

> The atmosphere is charged with the desires and demands of clutching hands and convulsed bodies. The dancers portray, from one moment to the next, childish ineptitude and acrobatic virtuosity as they progress and regress through their personal emotional experience.

No hint there of story-telling or a story line as such; yet there is, as the critic noted, 'a social and psychological agenda'. That means that the understanding of this work can draw on what we know of psychological odysseys, and see this dance as depicting some such. Certainly this is not easily treated as the sort of dance dismissed by DV8 in the manifesto for lacking :personal and social commitments' (Mackrell, 1992: 127). So we see that not all works are committed to narratives and that such commitments may be difficult both to identify and to gauge.

Of course, narrative is one way to offer unity: and, as we have seen, a difficulty is to experience the unity of such works. In fact, the difficult lies partly in the fact that we have no guarantee of what will or will not be readily experienced as unified — and hence as a unity. Before turning to that topic, however, it is worth putting aside two other considerations, both of which raise problems for the idea of arts education be disputing that the kind of understanding offered here — if it is — could (in principle) yield knowledge.

Postmodern dance and (the possibility of) understanding

We have already stressed that the model for reasoning and rationality deployed here operates case-by-case (and see below). Moreover, we have seen that such 'reasoning' (that is, critical commentary) must be rooted in features of the dances themselves (compare Supplementary Essay 3). Thus, in summary, we come to understand danceworks:

- 'one step at a time'; hence some steps may prove impossible for a particular person;
- through 'perceptual engagement' (seeing, hearing) with the work(s);
- supplemented by discussion, drawing parallels etc.

By these lights, can postmodern danceworks be understood? The answer must be: 'to the degree that these three conditions are met'. In this way, we see the distinctiveness of postmodern dance as *within* a familiar framework, provided by our understanding dances (to the degree that we do), learned as we learned to understand other dances.

What then might seem the specific problems here in respect of postmodern dance? To repeat three: first, it might be thought that its understanding was problematic because it was 'revolutionary' — but, first, this 'revolutionary-ness' is common to many periods and genres of art; and, second, it is always understood by *reference* to tradition … *and* other views have been evolutionary.

Then, second, if the postmodern attitude here were indeed 'a thoroughgoing mixing up of categories' (Crowther, 1993: 94), this might be thought to generate a confusing eclecticism. But we should recognise 'unity' (and such like) as abstract concepts, given substance in concrete instances: we cannot really say in advance of an example what will or will not count as unified. Thus, for instance, contemporary tragedies regularly do not maintain Aristotle's categories for the 'unity' of time and place, but are unities nonetheless, for Aristotle's comments were (in fact) simply guidelines for tragedy-writing, drawn from past tragedy-successes, rather than conditions to be met by any unity.

Third, the 'irony' supposedly prevalent in postmodernist works seems to pose a problem or raise an issue. For 'irony' of this sort must be recognised as such: if we fail to recognise it, we will have misunderstood. But, just as a pastiche essentially involves recognising that it is a pastiche, and therefore understanding it against the background of what is familiar, the same is true of the ironic. So, there is a problem here, but a familiar one. For, as Cavell, 1969: 219) perceptively notes of art in general, '[t]he trouble is that the genuine article [of art] .... really does challenge the art of which it is the inheritor and voice'. And that is one reason why, as recorded above, the 'general public' is often slow to accept the innovations of (its) contemporary art. In this respect, we might see a second, related difficulty for postmodern dance since, as Banes (1987: xiii) records, 'the early post-modern choreographers ...[were] ... both bearers and critics of two separate dance traditions'. So an audience that merely grasped one of these traditions would still fail to understand the works. But that is merely to acknowledge that the *real* background to works must be understood. And that has always been a condition of a suitably sensitive criticism.

Postmodernism in art might be characterised in terms of a break with project of modernity. But notice that we are, in effect, recognising two ways of contesting the project of modernism:

• Retreating to the past — drawing on previous model of artistic success, rather than the contemporary ones. But this attitude is readily understood.

• Disputing relevance of the project: that is, denying art. But that is simply a way to reinstate the 'art-shaped hole' (CDE: 120-23; *UD*: 294-7) in one's account — one is no longer discussing what is distinctive of art. And this cannot be a suitable strategy for an aesthetician or an art-educator. So neither option is really viable. And anything else is just a (polemical) way of answering the project of modernity, since it grants the intelligibility (or answerability to reason) of one's fabrications — such as one's dances.

Conclusion

Suppose that the positive positions developed above are adopted: suppose, further, that the response to postmodern art is of the right order — where does that leave arts teachers? In particular, have the insights into knowledge in general, practical knowledge and rationality clarified the position of the teacher? If such a clarification has taken place, our confrontation with postmodern theorising is justified.

First, I have shown how objections to the very idea of arts education might be met, stressing the possibility of artistic knowledge. And that should imply that a more generous account of *knowledge* is required. If today we see knowledge *in general* as *more* than (or *other* than) propositional knowledge — at least, for educational purposes — that is tantamount to treating other areas as we were once inclined to treat the aesthetic.

How plausible is it to *deny* that such practical knowledge as teachers employ *is* knowledge, once simplistic views of knowledge are put aside? Yet, if it *is* knowledge, then (to repeat) knowledge is not as is sometimes thought.

Of course, its value could be denied; but surely not by anyone (outside Her Majesty's Government [hereafter 'HMG']) with a commitment to teachers: successive Governments in the UK have seemed convinced that what cannot be stated, first, cannot be knowledge (*propositional* knowledge is prioritised), and, second, cannot form the basis for assessment — that is, there is no place for 'looking and seeing' by *informed* observers. Hence *artistic knowledge* would be impossible. A further objection would be to the term 'informed': there are no 'experts' here, no 'safe hands'[20]. For if there were experts (and especially if they were *teachers*), HMG might have to consult them on educational policy.

No doubt the scientific credentials of education seem doubtful (compare Standish, 1995: 272). But this reflects on the equation of knowledge with that provided by science. We need a revised account, *not* taking scientific knowledge as our central case, if we are to do justice to the full range of knowledge.

Second, we have seen how arts teachers are typically custodians of artistic knowledge; they are the *competent judges* in matters artistic whose existence is guaranteed by the very possibility of artistic meaning, or of the arts having a cognitive dimension. And we have recognised the centrality of that dimension to any justification of the arts in education, a fact having crucial impact in respect of accountability (and assessment) in arts education. For it means, of course, that teachers are indeed *experts* here, with the kind of *knowledge-in-action* which cannot be readily written down (by them or anyone else) but which the employ in practice: they are precisely the kind of experts whose possibility or existence HMG (in its previous incarnation at least) was at pains to deny. And since this position developed from our giving postmodernists their due, it might well be a picture of arts education in an age of postmodernism.

This view has three (related) major consequences: first, it creates an essential role for arts teachers in assessment — although this is news only to some theorists, since arts teachers themselves have both always known it and always practised it (at least when out of the spotlight of, say, the more idiotic demands of the National Curriculum in England and Wales[21]). Second, it provides an account of the *objectivity* of the judgements of such teachers (at least in principle[22]) sufficient to sustain the requirements of accountability in arts education. In doing so, and third, it highlights the sense in which arts teachers are the most important resource of arts education. This seems to me a very suitable outcome of this investigation, even if an unsurprising one.

Supplementary Essay 2:

Dance-Identity and Understanding

Preamble

This essay is a slightly extended version of one presented to the Society for Dance Research in London, on 27th Feb. 1993, and subsequently published in *Dance Research*. It applies some morals from the discussion in UD to a specific question, but it also illustrates how these issues are of importance to practitioners. This version includes brief comments on another problem for my picture of dance.

Its primary importance lies in connecting the theoretical issues from philosophy to practical questions for dancers, suggesting that one can confront the practical question more clearly once one sees what is (and what is not) at stake.

Inevitably, there is some overlap with the body of CDE and with the other Supplementary Essays. In particular, the importance of the artistic/aesthetic contrast — stressed here — is yet more explicit in Supplementary Essay 3, and in the Introduction to the Enlarged Edition.

Introduction

Was that *Swan Lake* I saw you at last night? In asking this question I intend to raise an issue which — though a technical issue in philosophy — is revealing in respect of the nature of dance, and of the character of our understanding of dances. My strategy will be first of all to lay out the background to this issue, identifying the kind of philosophical problem it represents (a problem concerning identity), and a number of background assumptions. Then, in the second part, I will consider three difficulties, the resolution of which should at least begin to help us to appreciate the nature of dance understanding.

Before doing so, however, it is worth recognising the interest of this question. The point at issue is whether the dance performance you attended last night was indeed *Swan Lake*, or whether it was some other dance. And this is an important question since this cannot in general be an open question, for two related reasons. Put extremely bluntly, first, the dancers must be told what to do (and what not to do) on a particular occasion: and what they do will be fundamental in determining whether or not the performance was indeed one of *Swan Lake*. Second, critics must understand what critical canons to bring to bear on that performance, what categories of art (Walton, 1978) are the appropriate ones here. And what applies to professional or formal critics applies equally to the rest of us when we come to make sense of a particular performance.

Identity questions

In philosophy the sorts of issue we are considering here are called (numerical) identity questions: that is, questions asking 'Is this the very same object as that?'. For example, is the person receiving the Nobel prize for peace the very same person as the schoolboy who bullied me all those years ago? Notice that we are asking if it is *the very same one*, not merely something similar. Notice, too, that — as in this case — we do not resolve the question by looking for total similarity: the receiver of the Peace Prize might be tall and bald, while the schoolboy was short and with hair. So, at its crudest, an identity question has the form 'Is object A (identified at some particular time) the very same F as object B (identified at some other time)?'. In our case we already know what the F stands for: it is 'dance' or 'work of art' — more precisely, it is both of these.

Dance as art

It is important to recognise that, in framing our identity question as I just have, I have imported the assumption that dance works are works of art, or, at least, that the dance works in which we are interested here are works of art. This brings with it three important related ideas.

    The first factor is a fundamental distinction — drawn clearly, in one version, by David Best (1992c: 165; see *UD*: 42-4; CDE: 17-18) — between artistic judgement and appreciation (our judgement of works of art) and aesthetic judgement and appreciation (our judgement of natural beauty, of fountains and firework displays — perhaps better called merely aesthetic judgement). Applied to dance, this [technical] artistic/aesthetic distinction means that not all dance will be considered — only that which is art: and further, that when considered, it is considered as dance and not, for example, as movement (see Carr, 1987; *UD*: 52-65; CDE: 12-14). Both the detail and the importance of this distinction were stressed in CDE. (For some additional thoughts, see also Supplementary Essay 3.)

The second point here is a view of the nature of art. For seeing dance as an art form requires that at least something be said about the nature of art. The model or account of art that I employ is an institutional one, in a technical sense, after the style of *the Republic of Art* (Diffey, 1991: 39-52). The central thought here is — in general terms — that something is art if the right people say it is art. We should recognise, first, that the process of objects being/ becoming art should best be thought of in two stages. In the first stage, the work is offered as art: we can call this stage 'self-election' — someone puts an object forward as art. The second stage might be called 'other-acclamation', and amounts, roughly, to that work being accepted by others. In the specific case of dance, this 'republic' will be composed of choreographers, producers, dance theatre owners and so on, and (in particular) other dance-critics and dance-theorists. Any movement sequence put forward as dance (self-election) and accepted by others (other-acclamation by the republic) is indeed a dance. Notice, too, that the other-acclamation operates through an authoritative body (Baker & Hacker, 1984a: 258-9).

Our third point, by way of 'ground rule', stresses (again) the objectivity of artistic judgement. For it is also important to recognise that artistic judgement and appreciation (using the distinction drawn above) is public and shareable, at least in principle. That is to say, it does not imply the 'anything goes' of subjectivism. It is a central thrust of all my work that subjectivism in dance study is to be rejected: that notions of reason and rationality have a purchase here. (See *UD*: 21-38 for further discussion.)

Dance as performing art

Speaking of dance as a performing art is appealing, implicitly, to a contrast between visual and performing arts[1], leading naturally to two important points concerning the nature of the performing arts. First, the idea of a performing art implies the possibility of a number of performances, each of which is the artwork. Second, the work of art is encountered only when one attends a performance, for only then is the work instantiated[2]. So this contrast tells us something important about performance. In contrast to visual arts, such as painting and sculpture, which are atemporal, performing arts like dance take time — not just in the trivial sense that it takes time to see or experience them, but in the more profound sense that they centrally involve *events*, which are in the flow of time, occurring at a particular moment. Moreover, visual arts are fixed after their creation[3], whereas performing arts are inherently under-determined by their creation: they must be brought into completeness — as the title suggests — by performing them. And this point is crucial since it makes clear that there is necessarily a (conceptual) role for the performer(s) here, although we must explore the nature of that role.

Dance as multiple art

Recognising dance as a performing art is recognising its evanescence. As dance critic Marcia Siegel (1972: 1) notes, 'Dance exists at a perpetual vanishing point. At the moment of its creation it is gone'. But, having accepted the transience of dance in this sense, we must still acknowledge its permanence: that the very same dance can be re-performed at some later date. But that fact itself must be explained. To do so, we must first consider the arts more generally, rehearsing familiar considerations (CDE: 20–21).

For the purposes of our discussion, works of art can be divided into two classes, the first kind to be called *particular objects* and the second kind *multiples* (see Wollheim, 1973: 256). Typical of the first sort will be paintings: for example, the *Mona Lisa*. Typical of the second will be novels (for example, James Joyce's *Ulysses*) but also music and dances.

To see the *Mona Lisa* (an example of a work of the particular object sort) I must confront a particular physical object, a particular pigment-covered canvas currently in the Louvre in Paris. But this is not so for works of the multiple sort. For *Ulysses* or *Swan Lake* may be encountered in many places at once: we will have the very same work of art in circumstance in which we do not have the same physical object or collections of them. For example, *Swan Lake* could be performed simultaneously in London and in New York. Notice that we are not saying that, in the case of multiples, these are works of the same *sort* in different places. Rather, they are the very same work of art. The Bodley Head *Ulysses* and the Penguin *Ulysses* are the very same novel, the same work of art. And, typically, novels, pieces of music and dance are art of the multiple kind[4].

Recall (CDE: p. 20) that the performance of *Swan Lake* in London typically differs from that in New York, having a different cast, being performed on stages differing in size, and with the producer (possibly) emphasising different characteristics, perhaps to suit the dancers in his cast. So that one can have the very same work of art in some multiple art form without having an indistinguishable work of art.

Type/token analysis

I propose, at this stage, to introduce a way of talking about the multiple arts, although this way of talking has implications for our study of works of art themselves — implications not always recognised (contrast Redfern, 1983: 19). As earlier (CDE: 20; see *UD*: 90–93), the technical device used is a distinction between types and tokens, where the token is the specific object in front of me and the type is the general object. For example, in the case of the Union Jack flag, the token is a piece of cloth that I am holding. But this is no more, and no less, the Union Jack than, say, the one on The Palace of Westminster. The Union Jack (in the type-sense) is an abstract object.

This type/token language provides us with a clear way of talking about works of art that are multiples. We can have a discussion of one sort about *Swan Lake* — the dance in the abstract, as it were — and another discussion about a particular performance (token of that type).

At least two important features from the type/token distinction will carry over to the discussion of multiples, if that way of talking is to be used. First, the type is an abstract object — one never confronts the type directly. Second, all tokens are equally important, all are equally the type. Thus no individual text of Joyce's *Ulysses* is uniquely the novel itself. Each is as much (or as little) the work of art as any other. In particular, the novel is not uniquely instantiated in the version that Joyce himself wrote by hand (supposing that he did this). Each token is equally a token: the hand-written token no more so than the printed ones. Those not prepared to regard the work in this way cannot use the type/token contrast to characterise it. To apply, using the type/token analysis will preclude thinking that a particular performance — say, that staged by the choreographer — is somehow more central than any other performance[5].

It is important to recall here that performances will differ in detail. It follows that what philosophers speak of as the identity of our artwork cannot require indistinguishability. When we talk about *Swan Lake* and not about a particular performance, we must recognise that certain features of the work will be under-determined — not all the features of the performance will be required by the dance itself: performances could differ in these respects without becoming tokens of a different type. Since there can be these differences between performances, it follows that the work itself cannot be determinate on whatever are those 'changeable' features.

This is not a matter of mere academic interest. The answers to such questions must be determinate — at least in principle. If it were in principle impossible to answer these questions, whether or not two performances were of the same dance would be simply a 'matter of opinion'. And that leads to a quite unacceptable subjectivism.

So we have an answer to our identity-question: performance A is a performance of the same dance (same work of art) as performance B if it is a token of the same type. But this is a purely formal answer, for we do not (yet) see how the type 'constrains' its tokens.

Most of the points thus far are relatively uncontentious, at least as far as their broad direction is concerned. One might dispute my account of the nature of art (replacing it with one's own) or my use of the artistic/aesthetic contrast. But a broad concern with dance as a performing art brings with it most of the conclusions drawn thus far. The big exception, as I implied, is my use of the type/token distinction: one might feel that this was not an appropriate tool here.

Two points follow. First, one might still need another tool, or set of them, to characterise the relationship(s) between the abstract object and the performance. Second, that relationship must be describable in ways that emphasise the authority of the dancework itself: that one can fail to perform a particular work — this being our bulwark against subjectivism. With these points in mind, let us attempt to put some flesh on the formal bones.

The thesis of notationality

There is clearly a need to explain how the abstract object is related to a particular performance. Moreover, it is necessary to show how to relate two performances together; and to accommodate differences in performance. If not, we will be in the 'anything goes' position characteristic of subjectivism. We have made some progress in describing the events under discussion by employing our type/token distinction. However, we cannot offer a general account of how the type/token relationship serves to constrain the tokens, so as to subsume them under the type. I suggest, though, that our practical concerns here are at least clarified by the *Thesis of Notationality* (see CDE: 21).

Multiple arts can be made in at least two ways. What we are describing is how one sets about creating the type; but, since the type is an abstract object, one cannot make the type directly, as it were. First, one can make the type by producing a token, as in the case of novels. Producing a token of the work — say, the hand-written token — allows the creation of other tokens of the same type. It also provides a test for whether or not putative tokens are really tokens of that type. For they must 'conform' to that original token in a relevant way. Similarly, in dance, one might 'push around' the bodies of particular dancers in order to create one's token: or, indeed, whatever other kinds of interchange the choreographer chooses in making his dance-work. The key idea is that he makes the work by making a performance of it. This first construction of the dance (through performance) allows successive performances of it, and so on[6]. And these will be other tokens of the same type The second way one can make the token is by making a recipe or mechanism for producing tokens. In the case of music or dance one might write a score. The score then serves as a recipe: following it correctly generates that particular piece of music — from a musical score — or of dance, if it is a movement-notation score. That is, following the recipe allows one to create tokens of that type.

But for dance (as for music) typically one can create the type in either of the ways described above: I can work with the dancers or I can write the score. So that, for example, Christopher Bruce did make *Black Angels* by directing Zoltan Imre and Lucy Burge and the rest[7], but it is not entirely fanciful to imagine a choreographer bringing that dance into being by writing a score. And it is a characteristic of performing arts that they can be made in either of these ways.

Suppose we made the type by making a token (that is, by actually performing). Now, our achievement is that, from this performance, other performances can be generated: the performance the choreographer extracts from his dancers, in composing the work, serves as a kind of example. The importance of this 'example' is that its existence has created the type, the dance-work itself. But not all of the features of that 'example', that performance, are equally important in deciding — for some later performance — whether or not it is a performance of our newly-made dance: the example under-determines the dance. So we must know, or learn, which of the features of that 'example' performance are the crucial ones in respect of whether or not a particular performance at another time is of that work of art: which features are decisive in respect of work-identify.

Of course, if we make the dance (the type) by writing a score in our movement notation, then again the score allows us to make other tokens of that type, other performances of that dance[8]. And since the dance could be made by making the score. Hence the score could be used to resolve questions about work-identity. Thus, although the type of the dance could be made in either of the ways described above, the second of these — using the score — is, to some extent, preferable, for two reasons. First, creating a dance by creating a token leaves the underlying future of the dance uncertain. It can be performed again, but such repetitions will depend on the memories of the people involved — the choreographer, the dancers, and so on[9]. Clearly, it is unsatisfactory for the continued existence of dance works to depend in this way on recollection, especially if those works are to be thought important. If we are to have permanent dance works of art at any level of complexity, we should prefer to have scores for those works[10].

Second, having composed the dance by writing a score for that dance, any dance which conforms to my score, and which is seen as dance, will be a token of that type: in creating a recipe, I specify which of its features are the crucial ones. By contrast, creating the dance, the type, by creating a token may leave open which of the features of this particular dance-performance are crucial to other dances if they are to be tokens of the same type. So the sorting out identity-matters for performing arts will be facilitated if types within those arts are (or anyway can be) created by the making of recipes or mechanisms: that is, scores. And this conclusion cannot be any more threatening for dance than its parallel would be for music — where it is a commonplace.

Of course, in respect of the creation of any particular work, just this dance could have been created directly, by creating a token of that type. Yet this fact cannot be decisive, for the possibility of its employment is central to the ability to create works of performing art such as dance[11]. Even though the notation for that art form need not have been employed in the creation of a particular work, we could have made just that work by creating a score or mechanism. And this fact reinforces that sense of the work itself as an abstract object: that is to say, we can recognise the dance (the type) as importantly like the notation. And our aim here was to understand how the type operates to constrain its tokens.

Of course, dances at present are very often, perhaps even always, made by making a particular token. My discussion, though, is directed to showing that fact as uninformative concerning the nature of dances. By contrast, the possibility of making the type by making the score offers a useful insight into the character of performing arts by suggesting a relationship between the type and the notated score.

Our problem lies in finding constraints under which performance A will be a token of the same type-F as performance B. My thought is that these constraints might be seen as provided by the *score*. So one might express a *Thesis of Notationality* in roughly the following way:

> *Performance A and performance B are performances of the same work of art (in any performing art) just in case both satisfy or instantiate some particular 'text' in a notation agreed by the knowledgeable in the art form to an adequate notation for that form.*

Such a thesis makes the notation important, just because it allows us to describe (even if only in principle) whether or not the object in question is a token of a particular type.

Of course, this represents an idealisation since many dance works are not, or were not, notated at all. The Thesis of Notationality will only be of practical help when there is an authoritative score: only then can we determine in practice whether two performances do or do not conform to the score. But that thesis is designed to make explicit (in a practical way) the constraints from the type. So we should see authentic performances as constrained in line with it even when there are no actual scores[12].

Yet consider a time when there was no established system of notation, and hence no 'texts' recognised as authoritative by those knowledgeable about dance. Should we conclude that, since there were no authoritative scores, adherence to the Thesis of Notationality would preclude works counting as being re-performed? Such a conclusion would be unwarranted, for three reasons. First, the Thesis of Notationality addresses the question of whether two performances are of the same work, and answers in terms of their relation to a score. That is, we can only use the idea of Notationality to determine (given that we have a score for a particular work) whether or not two performances are of that work. If there were no score, applying the Thesis of Notationality would give no result: there would be no 'text' to which the performances did or did not conform. The objection, therefore, takes the scope of the Thesis of Notationality to be greater than it is. Second, an emphasis on Notationality is designed to bring out an underlying characteristic of a performing art such as dance, deriving from the possibilities of the creation of dances. And those possibilities remain even if there were not appropriate notation systems: as we might say, dance is notational[13]. Finally, the Thesis of Notationality should be seen in its specificity: it is being advanced today, when we have such notation systems and can imagine any dance as in principle notatable. We should conclude, therefore, that the impact of Notationality, although slight, advances our appreciation of the way the dance-type constrains its tokens.

In respect of the Thesis of Notationality, three points are of central importance. First, Notationality does not, as it stands, guarantee that the performance under consideration is indeed a dance[14]. So the Thesis of Notationality does not give us a way of determining absolutely whether or not a particular performance is a token of the same type as another performance. The notation is only a movement notation, after all. But it does offer us a (defeasible) necessary condition for dance identity[15].

The second point introduces a complexity of the Thesis of Notationality. For that thesis places a certain weight on the particular notation system in question. A different notation system would have taken as crucial different features of the dance, so that movements which satisfy a Benesh score might not satisfy a Labanotation score, and vice versa. In response, we can only urge that reputable notation systems alone count here: that those who are knowledgeable about the art form decide what is and what is not reputable.

The third point is that anyone who rejected the Thesis of Notationality would need some other 'mechanism' for providing constraints on possible performance which are to preserve 'same-work' continuity, and on possible interpretations of such works. For it is unacceptable to conclude that it is in general an open question whether or not performance A is the very same dance as performance B. We must not concede this to be a matter for individual decision, or a subjective matter, for to do so is to rob dance of all importance (in ways discussed throughout CDE). No doubt there are borderline and problem cases here. But it must be possible for the relevant considerations to be articulated, even if we cannot always arrive at a satisfactory conclusion. If the Thesis of Notationality is accepted, one has a way of accommodating the difficulties mentioned above. The notation under-determines the performance: yet it still constrains it. This is exactly what is required if subjectivism is to be avoided.

Problem case 1: Re-choreography

The type/token distinction does not of itself decide what is to count as a token of what. There is a difficult borderline between re-staging a dance and re-choreographing it to produce a different dance. In some Nureyev productions, for instance, it is difficult to say with certainty whether he has re-staged or re-choreographed. For example, it is recognised that, in his staging of 19th-century works such as *Swan Lake*, Nureyev 'has been at pains to reassert the place of the male dancer in these ballerina-vehicles' (Brinson and Crisp, 1980: 244). We have simply recognised the difficulty in deciding, in a practical case, whether a particular performance is or is not a performance of a particular type. We have recognised re-choreography as leading to a different work of art its tokens are tokens of a different type. What this case throws up is the degree to which we can (or cannot) in practice recognise when we have an example of re-choreography. The Thesis of Notationality may not help us here. That Nureyev made certain changes may well mean that his work no longer satisfies a particular notation for *Swan Lake* — but here we have two alternatives. One would be to suggest that we have indeed a piece of re-choreography here. But the other alternative would be to doubt the appropriateness of the notation. And nothing said here will allow us to decide between these alternatives[16].

Problem case 2: 'New interpretation'

A different problem arises with a work such as Mats Ek's *Swan Lake* (1987). When Judith Mackrell presented this ballet (in the series 'Dancemakers', BBC2, 1990), she spoke of this as 'a version of *Swan Lake*', as 'updating', and as a 'new interpretation' which 'retold' the story. It is important to recognise that this is most certainly a different art work: not merely is the choreography different, but there are also differences in the story line and in the music. (For example, some music was specially written for the suite of national dances.) One might wonder why this work has anything to do with *Swan Lake* (in the Petipa and Ivanov version). Is it really to be described, as Ek himself said, as simply the use of 'a new dramatic "language"'?

     This case is revealing in two important, and related, ways. First it allows us to recognise the difference(s) between different 'tellings' of the same tale: that works of art with the same story may still be radically different works of art. The absurdity of supposing something different is brought out by Betty Redfern (1979: 18). If one thought otherwise, she notes:

> There would be no need to see, for example, Martha Graham's *Night Journey*, since we could get the same experience by listening to Stravinsky's *Oedipus Rex*, and neither of them need really have bothered since Sophocles already 'said' it all in *Oedipus Tyrannus* centuries before.

So it is important to recognise the diversity which is possible within a background set, in this case, by elements of music and story.

     The second point, though, runs in a different direction. For making sense of Ek's ballet will involve relating it to previous work in two ways. First, there will be connections to Ek's other work, and to the tradition in which he choreographs. Second, there will be a relation to a *romantic ballet* tradition, whose conventions he is certainly playing with (for example, in his 'dumpy' swans, some of whom are male).

In fact this point has a general importance (compare McFee 1992b): for it emphasises the degree to which any interpretative understanding of any dance depends on the tradition within which the work was created and has been understood — even when in rebellion against such traditions — where this tradition should be seen, first, as integral to any satisfactory 'making sense' of the dance and, second, as operating both as a 'wider' tradition within which the work is created and as a 'narrower' tradition formed (roughly) by the artist's other works[17].

A problem with type/token analyses

It is easy to become mesmerised by the minor differences between performances of the very same work: that we can have one dress-rehearsal for a whole week of performances shows that such differences need not be crucial. For, of course, performances will differ in detail. So its being *the very same artwork* cannot require indistinguishability. In this way, focus on *Swan Lake* (rather than on a particular performance) recognises certain features of the work as under-determined — not all the features of a particular performance will be *required* by the dance itself: so performances could differ in these respects without becoming tokens of a different type. Since there can be these differences between performances, and yet they still be performances of that very same dancework, the work itself cannot be determinate on whatever are those 'changeable' features.

In this way, and for roughly these reasons, I have urged the employment of Peirce's *type/token* distinction, with performances as *tokens* of a dancework *type* (*UD*: 90-97)[18]. And our two cases (above) clarify when these difference might be germane. But there are another set of abstract problems, best brought out by thinking in more detail about the role of the performers. For, in an idealised case, what the performer does is to bring that dancework to completeness by *performing* it: but this performance will inevitably differ from others, not least because (typically) he/she gives the work a personal 'twist', emphasising (slightly) different aspects of it. Recognition that there is an *it* here, distinct from any performance, is crucial for the idea of performing art. Therefore, if we consider a dance performed on Tuesday and on Wednesday, there will be differences: and *some* of theses differences will be differences in what I have called *performer's interpretation*.

In the case under consideration, the performance on Tuesday night and that on Wednesday night are (essentially?) performances of the same work: that is not the issue here. Now I am recognising three (related) situations: first, that some (practical) cases *will be* performances of such-and-such a work — say, *Swan Lake*. I take this to be agreed on all sides: and it is these *I* am calling tokens of the same type. Second, some cases clearly *will not* be the same work (despite similarities: Mats Ek uses the music and a *version* of the story). Third, some cases will be border-line or contentious: what do we make of Nureyev's re-staging (McFee 1994b: 30-31) — is it re-choreography? And what about Matthew Bourne's *Swan Lake* with 'a radical gender twist' (Mackrell 1997: 32)? Is the performances of either of these really *Swan Lake*? There need be no answers to such questions, apart from that given (implicitly or explicitly) by the practices of the Republic of Dance (*UD*: 71-4); and therefore as mutable as such things are. (Indeed, we could usefully consider when such an issue might arise.) Certainly, we should not assume/expect that there *must* be such an answer: and I take *that* to have been the essentialist view here. For saying that two performances of the same dancework have *something* — the type — *in common* need be nothing more than a manner of speaking (*a façon de parler*): as we might note that all games are games, to use Wittgenstein's famous example — nothing need turn on this.

After all, there is no suggestion here that all *dances* have something in common — that is, it is not the claim that the term 'dance' could be defined, or that there are necessary and sufficient conditions of dance-hood. So the debate is unlike one where, say, it is asked what all tables have in common. Instead, the claim is a much weaker one: that not *anything* could count as a performance of *Swan Lake*, even if we cannot say precisely what would and what would not (in the abstract) — that (concrete) performances are 'constrained' by the (abstract) *type*.

The argument *for* some sort of 'constraint' here really has three motivations (already sketched). First, and negatively, it is a rejection of the 'anything goes' of subjectivism — the thought (to which I will return shortly) is that not just *anything* could count as a performance of *Swan Lake*. Second, this is a case of *unity-and-difference*: that there is one specific artwork, *Swan Lake*, here — in the jargon (Scruton 1997: 101), this is a discussion of *numerical identity*[19]. So the case differs from, say, that of tables, where each is a table (of the same kind) *without* the implication of there being only *one* table: at best, this discussion of tables would turn on qualitative identity. (And the same is true of our different beetroots [Carr's example].) Here, in the important case where *this* performance differs from *that* one, both are performances *of the same work* — this point must surely be granted (indeed recognised to occur very regularly) by any who accept the possibility of performing arts, where the artform is a multiple (*UD*: 88-90). So granting that they are the same work does not imply that they do not differ. Thus there is a reason to refer, at least sometimes, to the work 'underlying' various performances (of it): hence, to refer to the *type*-artwork. And, as above, if we rehearse on Monday and perform on Tuesday and Wednesday, for *which* performance was the Monday event a rehearsal? If we answer 'both' (as we must) we highlight the sense in which there is just *one* artwork here (*UD*: 93) — one rehearsal can (simultaneously?) be a rehearsal for more than one performance.

Third, the 'constraint' referred to above is not a *practical* one: it means only that if someone wants to stage *Swan Lake*, the resulting performance will be constrained. In effect, this will recognise the difference (sketched above) between *re-staging* (which gives a performance of the *same* dancework, tokens of the *same* type: arguably, Nureyev's *Swan Lake*) and *re-choreography* (which gives performances of a *different* dance work, tokens of a different type: say, Mats Ek's *Swan Lake*). Of course, the details of this boundary will be contestable. As earlier, what are we to make of Matthew Bourne's all-male Swan Lake, with its 'radical gender twist' (Mackrell 1997: 32)? A *critical* debate (as I think of it, a debate *within* the Republic of Dance; see *UD*: 71–4) might be located around just this point. But, in recognising it, we acknowledge the (possible) distinction between two dances, both called 'Swan Lake', with (largely) the same music and similarities of story-line, and so on: all we dispute is *where* this boundary falls in practice, one group arguing that Bourne's is a work *different* from the Ivanov and Petipa (a token of a *different* type) while the others dispute this claim.

Next, notice that no-one ever suggested that just *anything* could count as a performance of *Swan Lake*: typical suggestions for constraints would be provided by its having to be a *movement-sequence*; its having to be a *dance*; its employing *certain music*, and perhaps a certain *narrative thrust*. Any of these might be missing or attenuated in a particular case (within [arguably] limits of re-staging, short of re-choreography), but an 'object', even an art-object, which lacked *them all* would not be *Swan Lake* — indeed, it would not even be a dance! (Lest this seem too prescriptive, we might additionally concede that a choreographer might even succeed in getting round these constraints — but it would require a complex critical story, drawing on yet other features of dances valued by the Republic of Dance.)

Finally, the considerations given above suggest that — if the type/token language is rejected — some alternative must be proposed (*UD*: 98-9) since we will continue to treat dance as a multiple artform; and that any alternative too would have implications, which must then be analysed. Equally, any practical problems it posed, or practicalities it suggested, would need investigation. So, at the least, there is a useable insight here in identifying the need for some descriptive framework, since issues about the relation of performance to dancework arise regularly.

Further, one feature of the identity of artworks fits at best awkwardly with the type/token treatment: namely, that each performance is *the very same artwork*, not merely one of the same kind — there is numerical identity here.

In contrast, examples typically used to illustrate the type/token contrast (say, national flags or words) are not cases where numerical identity (in contrast to qualitative identity) makes sense. For example, the five-word sentence 'My cat ate your cat' employs five *token*-words and only four *type*-words, because the word 'cat' occurs twice. If we imagine someone speaking this sentence (utterance) or writing it (inscription), there are accordingly either two utterances or two inscriptions of the word 'cat'. But it seems odd to puzzle further if there are one or two *words*, since we know that both utterances/ inscriptions of 'cat' are tokens of the type-word. It makes no sense to ask if the first and second occurrences of the word 'cat' are occurrences of *numerically identical* or *numerically distinct* words, although they are clearly different utterances or inscriptions. Yet just this contrast must make sense for dance performances: if there is only one dance work (say, *Swan Lake*) 'in the offing', its status as *the artwork* guarantees that any performances of it instantiate *that very* artwork, despite differences between performances (see later). But the type/token language — well-suited to the discussion of words and flags — has no obvious way to accommodate this (compare Meskin, 1999: 46-48).

The type/token contrast is centrally a *way of talking* about artworks that are multiples, a way which permits us to distinguish talk about the art-object from talk about 'its' performances (or instantiations)[20]. Of course, first (as we have seen above, and recognised; see *UD*: 90-92), this jargon has certain implications: for instance, that the type is an abstract object, and that all tokens of that type are *equally* tokens (there are no privileged tokens). The suitability of such implications to the analysis of dance must be investigated. And, if these implications did not hold for dance works, this would be an inappropriate way to talk about them. Second, it is a highly abstract way of characterising the relation between dancework and performance — as such, it is hard to see its 'teeth'. For this reason, any practical implications to this way of talking (beyond those, noted above, that attend this way of conceptualising danceworks) must be located by finding a practical correlate of the type: this is what my *Thesis of Notationality* (above; also *UD*: 97-98) is designed to do.

Performer's interpretation

The remarks thus far have attempted to address the identity questions insofar as they related to the performance of the work. However, equally relevant will be considerations relating to the understanding of that work — and, as we will see, identity issues and those concerning understanding come together. For one way of posing questions about the identity conditions for dances is to ask how the abstract object, the dance, is related to a particular performance: and a typical reply would focus on the idea of interpretation. It is natural to speak of *interpretations* of artworks: but *what* is being interpreted in these interpretations? Here we are investigating how the work itself provides constraints on understanding (for example on criticism); how inappropriate interpretations are to be ruled-out. For this is another place where the issue turns on the authority of the dance-work.

The term 'interpretation' is used in two quite distinct senses here. The first, typified by a critic's interpretation of a particular dance, characteristically consists of a string of sentences discussing the structure and value of the work in question: that is, it will usually be composed of *words*. This is 'critic's interpretation'. But also we speak of interpretation when considering a pianist's rendering of a piano piece — say, Pollini's interpretation of Schoenberg's *Six Little Piano Pieces Opus 19*. Here interpretation typically consists in some set of actions performed, or, as we might say, in producing that object in which the witnessable work consists (see Urmson, 1976: 243). For dance, it consists in performing (at least) movements of the body. So the word 'interpretation' amounts to two quite different things here. The second sort — performer's interpretation — is unique to the performing arts, while there are critic-type interpretations of all works of art. As a result, any problems we have in understanding the idea of critic's interpretation — or in seeing the basis of such interpretation, or its relevance — are equally problems for *all* the arts, as much in respect of painting or sculpture as in respect of dance or music. The issues to be addressed here concerned how to make the interpretation an interpretation of that *particular* work of art, and no other, and how to rule-out inappropriate interpretations. In the case of the performing arts, these problems can now be seen to have two dimensions, since they apply not only to critic's interpretation — a difficulty shared with other art forms — but also to performer's interpretation.

It is tempting to assume that there are answers in terms of some 'firm' or uncontentious details of dances, some 'facts of the matter' to which any critic's interpretation has to conform, and which must be part of any performer's interpretation. Such a line of thought should be rejected for two related reasons. First, it is impossible, even in principle, to genuinely confront dance-works uninterpreted: for to take an artistic interest (see above) in any work of art is – one might say — to interpret it (in the 'critic's interpretation' sense). There can be no 'facts of the matter' different from interpretations while we are considering the objects in questions as objects of artistic interest. So any (critical) description of the work is essentially interpretive to some degree (the first point). The second point is this: when one witnesses a work in the performing arts, it is already a performer's interpretation, and hence it alone cannot answer for us questions about the grounds from which such interpretations begin.

Nevertheless, this consideration does show us something useful, by allowing us to put aside one aspect of our difficulty. For, once the performer's interpretation is completed, the work of art in one of the performing arts (such as dance) can be seen as determinate. Hence it is in the same position as a work of the particular object sort, or a non-performing work of the multiple sort, such as a work of literature. Each has a physical instantiation which is then the subject of critic's interpretation. And such critical interpretation will draw on the traditions and conventions of that artform. If this is broadly right, we can turn our attention to the *performer's interpretation*.

What, then, are the constraints on performer's interpretation? Since we employ the type-token contrast, we might reply — as I noted in *Understanding Dance* — that the constraints on whether or not one particular performance of *Swan Lake* (Tuesday's) is a token of the same type as another particular performance of *Swan Lake* (Wednesday's) were constraints provided by the type, by its features. But we have recognised two key problems with such an answer. First, the (metaphysical) language of types and tokens did not provide us with practical constraints on the tokens. Second, the type under-determines performances — so, within what we acknowledge as the same dance, a variety of perceptible differences are quite acceptable: indeed, such are to be expected in performing arts. All-in-all, we have no idea what features the type will offer for us, what practical constraints it imposes. So my suggestion has been to recognise that the constraint on performance as actually provided by the notation or by some notation-equivalent. It is in this sense that Notationality is so fundamental a feature.

We can usefully take the Thesis of Notationality as providing the potential constraint on performance interpretation: the performer's interpretation must satisfy that notation. And any performer's interpretation which fails to do so is therefore an inappropriate or incorrect interpretation. But two aspects of this conclusion are worth noting, to avoid misunderstanding. First, it is central to the position here that the works in any performing art — such as dance — are under-determined by their notations just as they are under-determined at their creation: they are only brought to determinacy by performance. It is in this sense that works in the performing arts come as a recipe, as it were, with a note attached saying 'and now perform it'. And that amounts to the instruction to produce a performer's interpretation. Second, the adequacy or otherwise of the systems of movement-notation employed is itself a crucial issue here (although one for another occasion). For asking whether or not a particular dance-performance conforms to a score is exactly like asking if a particular perform-ance of a play conforms to the text: there are various ways of conforming to a text — differing in various ways, and more and less satisfactory.

A major point throughout has been that scores under-determine the features of the work. Nevertheless, they offer a way of understanding the regulation of possible lines of fulfilment. So there are varieties of unacceptable responses to that score. It is in this way that the authority of the dance itself is emphasised. In this sense, any such unacceptable 'performance' does not satisfy/fulfil the score at all — such performances do not generate tokens of the particular type. Indeed, this is what is meant by calling them 'unacceptable': they are 'beyond the pale' for that work. This in turn indicates the degree to which the performer's interpretation is circumscribed by the features of the dance itself. Thus we should think of the relation between type (that is, abstract object) and token (that is, performance) as mediated through the routes to that performance: through the various ways of realising that score, which is to say, again, through the performer's interpretation.

A virtue of this way of construing the relation between abstract object and performance is that it highlights an interesting ambiguity in the term 'interpretation' in this context, one that has been pernicious to the understanding of the nature of dance. For what one sees is that, while the critic's interpretation is a thing (say, a collection of words, spoken or written), the performer's interpretation is not — at least, not on the fairly everyday sense of the word 'thing' meant here: rather, the performer's interpretation is visible in the subtle differences between various performances — that is, those with different performer's interpretations. The use of the same word, 'interpretation', in both contexts has generated confusion by suggesting that what is true of one kind of interpretation would be true of the other. But this, as we have seen, is to misunderstand.

Sharpe's problem

A revealing problem for accounts such as the one given here was posed by Bob Sharpe (1979), in a discussion of musical performance — from which we can begin. In effect, there are two related difficulties. First, in the case of Pollini's performance of the Schoenberg *Six Little Piano Pieces Opus 19*, we have, as it were, three 'objects' for analysis, not two: for we have the artwork and the performance on a particular Tuesday night, but also (we might think) Pollini's interpretation of that work, which Tuesday's performance instantiates better than Wednesday's, and so on: call this 'Pollini's (general) interpretation'.

The second problem comes about because — for Sharpe — a type/token analysis implies interchangeability of corresponding elements of tokens: he urges that this is true of flags, but not of performances of musical works (or of dance-works) if the type is seen as the abstract artwork. And this second point is crucial because it helps us to decide how to apply the type/token contrast: the performances will permit interchangeability of corresponding elements without (radical) loss of coherence (Sharpe urges) among different instantiations of the same performer's (general) interpretation. So that Pollini's interpretation of *Six Little Piano Pieces Opus 19* as he performed it on Wednesday night would still have been a 'unity' if he had played the sixth piece, the piece dedicated to Mahler, in the way that he did play it on Tuesday night. But the coherence would have been lost if another performer's (general) interpretation of the sixth piece — say, Glen Gould's — were substituted. As a result, we should think of the performance as the token with the performer's (general) interpretation as type. And this will be important because authentic performances are instantiations of the type.

Now, this second difficulty (and the answer it suggests to the first) result from two misunderstandings: first, the type/token relation lacks the supposed characteristic — one cannot in general substitute, say, corresponding corners of Union Jacks, if their sizes are radically different. Rather, as with the musical example, one can do so if they are broadly similar, or to the degree that they are, and if not, not. But large differences are permissible between tokens of the same type — differences of size for flags, for example. Second, the performer's (general) interpretation, the supposed type on the new account, is an abstract object — but one which operates relative to another (yet more abstract?) object, the work of art itself; but no account of the relationship between them has been given. So this account leaves one open to problems of a kind it poses for us: how to relate together the various 'objects' of analysis. But if we give-up Sharpe's conclusion from his second problem, we no longer have an argument for his conclusion to the first.

What does this mean for the first problem? How are we to handle the bewildering variety of 'objects' of analysis thus generated? To sketch a reply, three points are essential. First, in the absence of an argument, there is no reason to adopt Sharpe's view. Second, we are working within a commitment to use a type/token analysis *somewhere*: this is something we and Sharpe are agreed about. Third, recall that we are talking of tokens (performances) which — even for Sharpe — are of *the same work of art*: that is, they are not 'beyond the pale', into re-choreography (or its musical equivalent). So they are 'constrained' in whatever way constrains work-identity. This suggests that we should continue to treat the artwork itself (which does the 'constraining') as the type: what then is the token? Clearly, it cannot be the performer's (general) interpretation since, as noted above, that is another abstract object. Indeed, the only candidate here is the performance (given that a type/token analysis is to be maintained) since only the performance is a 'concrete' object, actually encountered.

But that appears to leave no (logical) 'room' for an account of the performer's (general) interpretation. However, this appearance is deceptive, for the performer's (general) interpretation is really just an abstraction from the performer's interpretations as realised in performance: that is, the performances (perhaps supplemented by discussions). In this way, it should be recognised as arrived-at backwards, as it were, from performances. Thus the performer's (general) interpretation is no more than a route to the performer's interpretation, the token.

Of course, for some purposes, we may choose to collect performances in that way — it may be revealing to do so if it shows us patterns in the creative lives of such performers. So it may be clarifying to know that this is Pollini's Schoenberg or Nureyev's *Swan Lake*: that may help us to be clear on the appropriate critical (or analytical) concepts to bring to bear. But — in my example at least — these are still simply tokens of the (artwork) type.

Conclusion

A sub-text throughout this paper has been that the philosophical 'moves' it employs are revealing in respect of the nature of dance: that a consideration of identity-questions for dance-works can offer insight into the understanding of dance. Seeing dance as appropriate for a type/token analysis (whatever the details of that analysis) already leads us away from misconceptions arising from an over-weighting of particular performances: differences in perform-ances are compatible with the performances being tokens of the same type. Moreover, recognition the subsequent need for an account of how the type constrains its tokens in this case also represents a (potentially) productive re-orientation of research effort. In this area, the Thesis of Notationality offers both a model for what might be sought, and a 'Aunt Sally' for the missiles of others. But to resolve such difficulties is to engage in philosophy; so any refutation of my detailed claims constitutes a triumph of my underlying aim!

Similarly, the distinction between performer's interpretation and critic's interpretation can provide a way of separating-out our tasks — for, while the importance of critic's interpretations may differ from artform to artform, the possibility of (indeed, the necessity for) such interpretations is common to all artforms. And recognising that may allow the placing of due weight on the performer's interpretation in the analysis of performing arts. Moreover, my discussion of Sharpe's problem is of a piece with this general concern. For it emphasises the need to treat the performer's interpretation as the route from artwork (abstract/type) to performance (concrete/token). Here too the disputing of my conclusions is engaging in philosophical reflection.

Supplementary Essay 3:

Art, Audience and Understanding — the Case of Dance

Preamble

This Essay combines ideas from two publications (McFee, 2003a; McFee, 2003b), which focus in more detail on both the distinctiveness and the public (or shareable) character of our understanding of art. The assumption here is that we speak the truth when we urge that certain dances have certain properties — and then the Essay tries to articulate what follows from this assumption. (In a language popular in philosophy generally, the position is *realist* about artistic properties; but it recognises their response-reliance as a crucial feature of such properties.) Some of the sections are more technical than much of this work — and may usefully be skimmed.

For reasons that should become apparent (and consonant with the direction of CDE), my attention here is primarily to those dances that are (also?) artworks. There is less here explicitly about *dance* than I should have liked — fewer dance examples, as it were — because fundamental to my concerns here are features or properties which (I will urge) are *shared* by artworks. So many of my examples *here* are drawn from the other arts.

Introduction

It might be urged that many texts in aesthetics — and specifically my *Understanding Dance* — focus on the cognitive properties of artworks (in my case, danceworks) at the expense of the experiential properties of those works. This criticism has some justice: but a fuller answer to it should begin by explaining that such an emphasis on the cognitive is warranted *partly* by the more general — and misleading — emphasis on the experiencing of artworks. For what is distinctive of artworks (if one had to choose just one thing) is their invocation of artistic concepts: that is to say, to take an artistic interest in a particular object is to regard it under a certain battery of concepts (and to be right so to do, when it *is* an artwork) — thereby introducing the *artistic/ aesthetic* contrast (as below). Since this feature is widely ignored or missed, it makes sense to emphasise it. And doing so will work against the sort of over-emphasis on the sensuous to which, say, Arthur Danto was responding when he stressed, as two features characteristic of artworks[1], their *aboutness*[2] and their *embodiment*. But, as we shall see, this stress does not preclude giving *due* weight to the sensuous properties of artworks. For, as Peter Kivy[3] once put the point: 'To describe something in artistic terms *is* to *describe it*; but it is to savour it at the same time: to run it over your tongue and lick your lips; to "investigate" its pleasurable possibilities'.

Since attention to the cognitive was never intended (at least in my writing) to *preclude* giving such due weight to the sensuous, it is important, before coming to the case of dance, to plot some of the contours of both the cognitive dimensions of art and its affective dimension, viewed quite generally. So we will highlight experiential elements both within the cognitive capacities and implicit in (some) artistic properties. We will also recognise the importance of the experiential aspect of artistic meaning.

Part of my thesis here is precisely that (for philosophical aesthetics) nothing can usefully be said about the nature of dance *experience* as such. Rather, we must learn, first, to characterise artistic properties — and especially artistic meaning — by recognising their *embodiment* (hence, their essential sensuousness); second, to recognise differences in concepts (and powers and capacities) which ground the claims to different experiences.

But there is also a strong connection here to the idea that art in general — and dance in particular — necessarily has an *audience*: so the discussion will also make this issue central.

Meaning and the artistic

I begin from the fact, familiar through this work, that our appreciation, judgement (etc.) of artworks differs in important ways from our appreciation, judgement (etc.) of all the other things in which we take an aesthetic interest, even though both might be characterised in terms of a concern with grace, line, and so on — or their opposites. That is, I begin from an *artistic/aesthetic* distinction (*UD*: 42-4; 168-82; CDE: 17-18). And, although I acknowledge the diversity *within* the aesthetic side of this contrast[4], our interest here lies in *artistic* appreciation, *artistic* judgement, and so on, since we have recognised that as an assumption of the account of dance education offered here.

Asked to *motivate* this contrast between artistic and aesthetic, I would (first) point to the difference in our interest in the great painting and in the wallpaper on the wall on which it hangs — that we value each (in a non-monetary way) but that we do so differently; we would not, say, *confuse* one with the other without misleading ourselves. Then (second), having made out the distinction for one artform, I would urge it quite generally. Thus the grace of the roadsweeper (or the gymnast) should be contrasted with that of the dancer: to this degree at least, art-status should be seen as *transfigurational* (Danto, 1981; *UD*: 51-2). Further, I would indicate how artistic appreciation, artistic judgement (etc.) locates the artwork in question in the history and traditions of artmaking and art-appreciating in the artform (and, perhaps, that *genre*, etc.). So this is one place where a failure to know or understand counts against one's possibilities of making (genuine) artistic judgements — that is, judgements *true* of the artworks before one.

The first corollary (of the artistic/aesthetic contrast) concerns the equivocality of predicates ascribing properties to artworks and otherwise: that one's calling a painting, say, *gaudy* will amount to something different when one recognises that the painting *is* an artwork from what it amounted to when one mistook the gaudy object for, say, wallpaper.

The key case here, of course, concerns the term 'beauty': if I (mis)take something for an artwork, and find it beautiful, my now coming to recognise that it is *not* an artwork will *not* leave that judgement unaffected — rather, it will affect the judgement 'not by raising or lowering that judgement, but by knocking it sideways' (Wollheim, 1993: 174): even if I continue to regard the object as beautiful, its beauty will amount to something different. So one cannot *just* say, 'Well, OK, it is not art but I still find it beautiful'; for what one meant by the term 'beauty' is implicated — hence the 'still' ('I *still* find it beautiful') is unjustified! [Those theorists who do not accept this do not, in *my* view, really acknowledge the artistic/aesthetic contrast.]

A second corollary of the artistic/aesthetic contrast (and one explored previously: CDE: 17) is virtually the converse of this one: that to take an artwork for a (merely) aesthetic object is to *mis*take it, to misperceive it. One kind of misperception would be taking an artwork in a way that *couldn't* or *didn't* treat it as an artwork: hearing the atonal music as though it were birdsong. Or again, as though it were *poor* tonal music (missing the category). A similar kind of misperception would beset those ignorant of the conventions etc. of that artform: just as David Best (1978: 115; 1992c: 171), although knowing nothing of Indian Dance, is entranced by the quality of movement in Ram Gopal's dance — while recognising that he is unable to treat it as art. As a result, applications of predicates to non-art that could also be (centrally?) applicable to artworks will always amount to something different in that use (if appropriate = true).

The third corollary grows from these two: that artworks have a kind of value (of a non-monetary kind) not [in principle] shareable with (mere) aesthetic objects — this kind of value is not easy to characterise, of course: but, as a first shot, we might talk of the kind of *meaning* appropriate to artworks. To see the object (say, the dance) as an art-object (not a [mere] aesthetic object) *just is* to ascribe this sort of meaning.

To be clear: my aim here is not to *limit* the realm of what is (or could be) art — much less to impose some narrow limit on it (*pace* Korsmeyer, 1999: 103; Shusterman, 1992: 18-21). But I *am* urging that, if someone argues that such-and-such is *art*, that person is thereby committed to find such-and-such *valuable* in ways typical of art[5]: that is why the person insists on the term 'art'! And thereby committed to contrasting the (appropriate) perception of such-and-such *as art* with the *misperception* of it as merely aesthetic — that is, as being graceful etc. etc. (or its opposites) but *only* in the manner of the wallpaper in our earlier example, not of the painting. So in these cases too the artistic/aesthetic distinction will be fundamental.

Further, a consequence of my position will be that an object or practice might be *mistaken* for art; that its grace, etc., might lead someone to take it for art, but be wrong so to do — although, in any particular case, whether or not this were so might be at best arguable. Yet notice that it wouldn't be for, say, American Ghost Dances, if the description of them I quote in *Understanding Dance* (*UD*: 286: quotation from Spencer, 1985: 2) were correct; namely, as having 'the very specific ... purpose of restoring lost lands and traditions'. For, whatever the purpose of dance, it is not this! So accepting this characterisation of the Ghost Dances is accepting the (negative) conclusion: these are not artworks. Hence, someone urging that these *were* indeed artworks must be contesting some aspects of that description.

That artworks (such as dances) can be *misperceived* either as merely aesthetic or in an inappropriate category identifies a quite general constraint here: for, in treating the artworks — in virtue of *being* artworks — as amenable to kinds of *misunderstanding*, it recognises them as objects of understanding. Danto characterises this feature by speaking of the *aboutness* of artworks. What we take from Danto here includes the *transformative* effect of art-status: that the artwork acquires *artistic* properties — and this distinguishes it from its 'non-art' cousins. In a similar way, a graceful action might simply be my walking, or part of my gymnastic floorwork, or part of my dance: but these are not equivalent actions — that it is dance (when it is) *transforms*, or trans
figures, that action. So the thought is that an object's being an artwork necessarily plays a role in our appreciation of it — that it makes a difference because art-status permits us to see the *object* (especially when a physical object, such as a painting) as embodying meaning, an idea that only makes sense for artworks (not for the [merely] aesthetic).

Moreover, when (say) the action of the roadsweeper is transfigured, there is a clear sense in which it *is* changed — a set of properties is acquired — and a sense in which it is not: the patterns of muscular movement, say, might be the same. And this tells us something about the nature of the new properties, by stressing their connection to the audience for them: roughly, to say that a movement pattern becomes *transfigured* into a part of a dance is to say that we can (and should) now see the movement pattern that way, just as the transfiguration of sounds into music (the creation of tones, rather than mere sounds: Scruton, 1997: 18) means that they are heard differently — and this is what their being different consists in!

Danto's gallery

This idea could be elaborated by reference to Danto's 'gallery of indiscernibles': here objects indistinguishable to (say) visual inspection (we could not tell their photographs apart, say) might be a number of different *things*. Some elements from the catalogue, all of which are comprised of a canvas with a painted square of red pigment, are:

(a) 'a minimalist exemplar of geometrical art ... [entitled] ... "Red Square"' (Danto, 1981: 1);

(b) 'a still-life executed by an embittered disciple of Matisse, called "Red Table Cloth"' (p. 1);

(c) 'a canvas grounded in red lead, upon which, had he lived to execute it, Giorgione would have painted his unrealized masterpiece "Conversazione Sacra"'(p. 1): here, I imagine the preparation done by workers in the studio — this *would have* become an artwork, although presently it is not;

(d) 'a surface painted ... in red lead' (p. 1): although Danto does not explain this, I image its being a kind of window blind, the red pigment being especially suitable in a certain climate. As with (c) above, Danto would call this a 'real thing': we can adopt this terminology.

And, of course, any of these objects ('real' or artwork) might be mistaken for any other ('real' or artwork).

As we have seen, these *are* different: different things can (truly) be said of each — and one can misperceive any of them by (mis-) taking it for another one, or treating one as though it were another (if these are different modes of misperception). Now, since these cases *are* different, it follows both that we should be wary of treating them in the same way, and that at least *some* cases of treating them in the same way will involve misperception.

Further, the 'transfiguration' into artwork is important just because it brings with it a critical vocabulary of the kind appropriate to art — the kind of *artistic valuing* from which we began! For that is precisely what the artworks [(a) and (b)] both have, and the 'real things' lack; moreover, this is a clear way of articulating one way artworks differ — a different critical vocabulary is appropriate to each, since each has a place in a different 'narrative' of art-history, or in a different tradition: what we have characterised as a different *category of art* applies to each. And a different critical discourse follows.

At least in some moods, Danto seems to say that *sensuous* properties (as I am calling them) are artistically irrelevant, since two objects indistinguishable in purely sensuous terms might still be, say, one artwork and one 'real thing'. Hence 'the eye is of no value whatever in distinguishing art from non-art' (Danto, 1994: 7). But his difficulty arises from a commitment to the sort of *essentialism* that seeks necessary and sufficient conditions for (in this case) arthood. But the properties of artworks — although transfigured — do not fail to be sensuous merely by being crucially the properties *of artworks*. Indeed, this is my point about the 'equivocal' character of such properties. Rather, the artistic/aesthetic contrast must work against a *crude* view of sensuousness by emphasising the cognitive dimension in (even?) *some* aesthetic appreciations[6]. In fact, even (for instance) *seeing red* might be thought of in conceptual terms: then (some) failures of perception here might be explained in terms of the lacking of the cognitive stock.

Mobilising concepts in one's experience

However, this point can be over-stressed. For instance, discussion of the nature of criticism can be conducted in terms of the *cognitive stock* appropriate for criticism: that is, the critic's powers are treated (exclusively?) in terms of what he/she *knows*. This procedure is, of course, warranted by fact that the charge of misperception can be sustained by pointing to the employment, in the perception, of inappropriate concepts. Yet that does not do enough to characterise what can go wrong — and even less so what can go right — when critics confront artworks. For example, if the perceptiveness of any perceptive critic of art were just a matter of the *cognitive stock* (of what the critic *knew*), the distance between him/her and us would become remediable, at least in principle: we could all acquire that cognitive stock, and with it that critical perceptiveness. That this is obviously not true should make us hesitate here.

So however revealing this talk can be, it leaves out something crucial. In this vein, Wollheim (1986: 48) speaks of 'the concepts ... the spectator has and mobilises': hence a crucial additional idea is of *mobilising concepts in one's experience*. The phenomenon referred to (the need identified) is familiar, I imagine, to anyone who has been taught a critical vocabulary for poetry but, at first, cannot see that this vocabulary informs the understanding of the poem — and then, quite suddenly, it does: the person can now mobilise those concepts in the appreciation of the poem. But talk of artistic appreciation requiring that *artistic concepts* be 'mobilised in one's experience' employs the *term of art* as another way of stating the problem (or a part of the problem) about expressiveness. For the work must be *found* expressive, by *me*, on the basis of *my* observation (etc.). So the expressiveness of (for example) the painting depends (minimally) on the possibility of creatures who can *respond* to it, finding it expressive.

Identifying the requirement for *mobilisation*, then, basically explains why there might be misfires here: and, even then, it really says no more than *that* the person cannot bring the concepts to bear — it does nothing to explain why this should be. To put that the other way round, the contributions of *cognitive stock* and *mobilising in one's experience* as differential explanations of failures to make sense of artworks: 'He lacks the requisite cognitive stock', 'She has the concepts, but cannot mobilise them in her experience'. More exactly, these are diagnoses of relevance to aesthetic education: 'He needs to learn more about ...' (and then some filling about cognitive stock; locating the work in its appropriate tradition, for example); 'She needs to be helped to see *these* artworks in ways we know she can see others', say — roughly as someone unable to see one aspect of a multiple-figure might be helped[7].

But, in Danto's gallery of indiscernibles, it is effectively denied that the physical properties of a particular artwork need be unique to it: rather, the same red square of pigment on a canvas could amount to any of a number of objects, some artworks, others not. Yet Danto is here trying to 'break the hold' of a certain misconception of the role of perceptually-immediate properties — they are not *all* that makes an object either the artwork it is (rather than some other) or an artwork at all!

For this reason, we should recognise the feature Danto was (correctly) identifying: that the meaning of the artwork must be (uniquely[8]) instantiated in the work itself, rather than completely expressible in terms *detached* from the work. In the dance example, only *dance*, and only *this* dance, offers me this (precise) insight. So one cannot (even) say what *I* have learned. For, if I could, I would (therefore) be able to 'express' the insight detached from the dance itself (especially from the sensuous properties of the dance). But then those sensuous properties would seem irrelevant. No, what I learn is not (completely) expressible in some other form. And this is what his stress on the (necessary) *embodiment* of artistic *aboutness* is designed to secure. Of course, this feature can be over-stated: the content of very many artworks might be expressible as, say, 'man's inhumanity to man' — clearly suitable for Picasso's *Guernica* but equally for Wilfred Owen's poem 'Dulce et decorum est'. Still, these works are not equivalent: nor could they be correctly taken to be. So their 'aboutness' will be distinguishable; and in just the ways Danto-esque talk of 'essential embodiment' sustains.

The point about sensuousness is sometimes put by saying that *all* that an artwork means or says cannot be expressed in another way, neither in another artwork nor in a non-art fashion; or that it cannot be paraphrased *without remainder*. The thought here is a good one, and need not mislead. But the expression is not helpful, as it may suggest a *finite totality* of meaning or 'aboutness' here — an *all* that could be reached (in principle). Yet we are not committed to that idea (see McFee, 2000: 122–3). Rather, the conception of the contextualism of meaning employed here works against any such assumption; for there seems no obvious *finite totality* of contexts.

Moreover, the conclusion that artworks are not in this way 'paraphrasable' is not an empirical discovery about them, based on considering lots of cases and trying hard to render them into another form, either art or non-art. Instead, it reflects a commitment on our part, an element of the conception of art at work here. For, if two art-objects (say) did have *completely* the same meaning, such that we could say, correctly, 'if you cannot get one, get the other — they amount to *exactly* the same thing'[9], that would offer us a basis for regarding these as instantiations of one artwork, rather than as separable works. And our argument for this conclusion could begin from reflection on authorship: if the first work is by Smith, and she has embodied the relevant 'aboutness', the second work (by Jones) will simply be a copy of Smith's — or another instantiation of it — if that second work is (otherwise) indistinguishable (for artistic purposes) from the first[10]. And, of course, we precisely do treat in this way works with obvious relations one with another: thus aspects of Picasso's painting 'inspire' Wallace Stevens to write his poem 'The Man with the Blue Guitar', which in turn prompts a David Hockney volume of illustrations. But the Stevens and Hockney are clearly different works of art, amounting to something different — and that is *guaranteed* by their being different embodiments. Yet, in turn, it *guarantees* a different 'aboutness' (or meaning) for each.

In fact, although the requirements for *embodiment* and '*aboutness*' seem like the articulation of two positive conditions to be met by any putative artwork, they are more revealingly viewed as negative conditions, two ways of explaining failures of artistic endeavour (or properties of non-art objects): such-and-such report is not an artwork because, although it is certainly *about* something (namely, the road accident), that aboutness is not *embodied* in the object. And we see this by recognising that changes in the object would not change that aboutness; and that this is no flaw in the object: whereas finding that the embodiment of an art-object could be changed without its 'aboutness' changing would typically be identifying a flaw in it[11]. Equally, a piece of road-sweeping (or an Olympic ice-dance performance[12]) would consist of something — it would be embodied, in that sense. But we could not see it embodying *meaning*: it necessarily lacks 'aboutness'; and hence is not an artwork. Thus sensuousness (and hence embodiment) as a feature of artistic meaning (a) picks up a similarity to *and* a difference from (mere) aesthetic judgement, one often invoked as a characteristic of the (wider: see *UD*: 39–42) *aesthetic* and (b) seems crucial to the kind of facts that some artistic facts (like others — for instance, colour facts) are!

This second concern picks up a further element of our relation to sensuousness: the response-reliance of artistic facts (discussed below). It also averts to a third interest, one which — in introducing a sensuous dimension — makes this position not a *pure* cognitivist one: the need to mobilise (in one's experience of whatever artworks) the appropriate concepts and categories. And this, too, we have seen is best treated as a negative condition — as a way of explaining failures to understand. Here, we should acknowledge that this very *general* possibility of understanding (or of meaning, as artworks embody it) is another way of talking about the *publicity* of artworks; of those works necessarily having the *possibility* of an audience, since they are *possible* objects of misunderstanding.

So, this account of art *builds-in* the idea of artworks as objects of understanding (in principle); and hence the idea of an audience for art. As Stanley Cavell (1969: xxvii) puts it, 'It is tautological that art has, is meant to have, an audience, however small or special. The ways in which it sometimes hides from its audience, or baffles it, only confirms this'. If this were right, it would be crucial to characterise artistic appreciation so as to essentially *include* a third-person perspective, the perspective of the audience. This idea has numerous consequences: if we think, say, of *research* in the arts as a contribution to knowledge or understanding, it identifies *whose* knowledge or understanding is at issue — that it should be the knowledge or understanding of the audience! And we will return to this feature once we have said a little more about audiences, communication and meaning[13].

Here I offer a fairly thin and abstract discussion — with too few dance examples — of what this might mean for how (if at all) dance might be taken as 'a primary source of understanding': hence of the degree to which, if at all, 'dance ... could inform the language and methods of thinkers'[14]. My own thought is that one cannot locate the relevant *possibilities* of dance unless one locates them as *artistic* possibilities; and that this, in turn, has consequences for who can learn what (or know what) from whom. And the emphasis on *audiences* will be crucial if we were tempted to locate such possibilities within, say, dancers or choreographers.

The place of understanding

To properly make out the connection between intention and understand-ability requires one to reshape, perhaps simultaneously, one's account of artistic judgement (as based on what is *known*) and one's view of how an artist might fail to contribute what is then taken from a particular work. For example, suppose someone[15] offers an account of Matthew Bourne's *Swan Lake* (1995), with its 'radical gender twist ... [in which] ... Odette became a male Swan and Odile a louche freebooter', an account that stresses Bourne's use of Freudian ideas: we should not reject such an account *simply* because Bourne tells us that he did not think of it nor, even, that he has never read Freud! He might have forgotten, or have picked up Freudian ideas in other ways. But we should *reject* (or at least modify extensively — in terms of 'precursors', perhaps) a similar account of the Ivanov and Petipa *Swan Lake* (1895): since Ivanov and Petipa *predate* Freud, they cannot be seen as drawing on his *ideas* — at best, there might be Freudian *themes* at work. Roughly, that they could not *intend* to refer to Freud's ideas guarantees that they *do* not. Yet the fact that Bourne did not *explicitly* plan to draw on Freud does not have the same implication.

In effect, the two conditions here mirror more general constraints; *mere* intending is not enough ('wishing cannot make it so'), since one must achieve (to some degree) what is intended, while the *mere* fact that one could *justify* a certain account of an object (by reference to public features *claimed*[16] for it) does not make that account of the object *true*: one is not thereby *justified* in so understanding it! So one central topic for a longer paper here — to which we will return briefly — concerns what is *there* in an artwork ... what its properties or features are. So there is a relevance to both (a) the *communicative* nature of art and (b) *intention* to communicate here: central to artistic judgement is the recognition of another's view (key for communication) and of that view as *meant* (key for intention)

These are two aspects of one point. For the idea of *communication* is (essentially) related to that of *meaning*, as Best (1978: 139-40; *UD*: 243-4) has shown. Indeed, any 'learning' not so based in (at least *implied*) intention could not figure as a contribution to *meaning*: as when my boss learns from my yawning that I am bored by/at the meeting — the very last thing I'd hoped for! There is no (genuine) communication here, and no meaning, just because my behaviour lacks both the required kind of *intention* and (therefore?) anything *specific* to communicate. These fit together: there cannot be anything to communicate (since nothing was intended) and we can infer from the lack of intention that there is no 'message' to be communicated (or to fail to be communicated, or to misfire in communication, etc.). For it makes no sense to think of some *asserting* with absolutely no communicative intention[17]. Moreover, the requirement here that what I do or say be *intelligible* is crucial: to say that there is no *audience* for my work just *is* to say that it does not communicate. So that one cannot really distinguish the commitment to meaning/communication from the commitment to intention.

However, these represent two ways that there might be misfires. For there might be something learned which (while not real or genuine communication: Best, 1978: 140; *UD*: 244) is nevertheless *there* [I really *am* bored at the meeting, and my boss finds out]; equally, what is *intended* may not be realised [I *mean* to make a dance masterpiece, but ...]. So, for both — first — determining what is *intended* and what is *communicated* amounts to one determination; and — second — the recognition of *failures* of artistic achievement might be localised (for particular artworks in particular contexts) as amounting to *either* failures of intention *or* failures of communication: thus, as explicable in terms of this contrast.

Now, we are not here trying to identify some set of conditions individually necessary and jointly sufficient: rather (and positively), the thought is that useful generalisations would invoke (among other criteria) the meaning-bearing dimension of artworks; further, as often, the point is most readily seen by considering the *negative* case: that, while no set of conditions would be sufficient to guarantee that such-and-such *was* an artwork, it is possible to reject the art-status (or artistic claims) of some works if they fail these key tests.

So one importance of this meaning-bearing (or communicative) dimension is that it permits the rejection of certain works as failing this communicative intention (however conceived). Thus I will dismiss, as not bearing on meaning, (purely) accidental features — except where the decision to use them is clear (as with aleatory composition: Cage, Cunningham, etc.). That is, 'intentional' here is not equivalent to 'intended', in the sense in which prior planning or thinking-through might be implied. Rather, action (say, walking) *is* intentional unless ... where some 'recognised head of exception' fills the blank. So that actions will always be intentional unless ...; and a context of art-making and art-understanding means that the implications of these too will be intentional unless ....[18]

Now, we might ask about the research done by artists — the sense in which it could be knowledge-generating in the way in which, say, (successful) academic work is. Suppose I learn about, say, the limitations of my (antique) physiology by — for instance — experimentation: I try to do things and then ... well, some may prove beyond me in fatal ways (kinds of sub-aqua or sky-diving, perhaps) but even some of the activities with less risk may tell me what I can (and cannot) do. My question here is: why should anyone (else) care? Again, we might list some of those with vested interests of various sorts (my wife, my boss, the doctors I might sue for negligence, etc.) but, for all of *these*, their specific relation to *me* is both what justifies their interest and what redeems it — they are not interested in my activity divorced from their (varied) interests in *me* as a (specific) person.

Concern with art is not self-directed

As a slight digression, I would like to rehearse (*again*: see *UD*: 175-7) the contrast here with F. H. Bradley's insight into the non-specific concern with art — yes, it must be *this* artwork that I am making sense of — this *particular* work (with *its* sensuous properties), and not some other — but my concern is not self-directed (or, to the degree that it is, is not a concern with *art*).

But Bradley's work (especially on art) is not given the attention it deserves in contemporary philosophy[19]. Further, the article (Bradley, 1934) to which I am referring — not published until after his death, although written in 1912 — is *not* pre-figured in his other works: and so may not be read even by readers of Bradley, not in themselves a large group.

Two features of Bradley's argument are relevant to us: the first concerns the *manner* of Bradley's treatment of cases of — arguably — the *misuse* of art as pornographic (his example is from science); the second turns on the way Bradley's discussion emphasises the *generality* to the connection between art and value, a generality not shared by the pornographic.

On that first point, Bradley's tool, in respect of scientific interest in the sexual, is the accusation of *misperception*: in itself, such a scientific interest in the sexual is 'not libidinous' (Bradley, 1934: 621). But it can become so. Adolescents are regularly supposed (by film-makers, at least) to use biology texts as erotica — yet then, as Bradley (1934: 621) notes, 'as so used, they certainly ... have ceased to be scientific'. These texts would then have been misperceived — treated as erotica *even though* they were science. In confronting the second issue — the one about the *generality* of art's value — Bradley enquires about the characteristics of *proper* treatment of beauty in the pictorial arts. Consider, say, a painted nude: why is it beautiful and not pornographic? Well, if my interest in the painting treated it as pornography, that interest must centrally be *my* interest, based on my personal reactions to that painting: the essence of pornography is the *private* immediacy of its impact. He correctly infers, from the possibility of pornography, a general constraint on art. So, if my concern for — say — *this nude* is genuine (artistic) interest in beauty, it cannot be simply a *personal* or *private* concern. Since art is 'always outside of and above and beyond any mere personal feelings' (Bradley, 1934: 261), he rightly concludes that artistic value is not subjective: art's problems are not purely mine[20]. So only if these really are *life*-issues (as opposed to *my* issues) can my engagement with them be of a kind appropriate to art.

But Bradley (1934: 621) recognises his idealisation of the situation. He says, 'There are times ... where at least in the case of certain persons art fails to achieve its end, and then may in consequence merely disturb and excite. ... But here assuredly, so far and to this extent, we have not to do with genuine art'. His point, of course, is that these persons are no longer able to take an *artistic* interest in the work: rather, they will misperceive it.

In treating art in a way which lets its 'problems' become *purely* mine[21], I am on a slippery slope to sentimentalism, or to pornography, or .... Anyway, away from art. Here is Bradley (1934: 622–3) again, discussing our reaction to a poem of Tennyson's:

> … if your ideas and emotions stray beyond the vision of Fatima's passionate heart and burning flesh, if they begin to wander and turn to a mere something in yourself — it is because you have lost hold of the poetry. The beauty which transported you beyond your private being, and which held and purified your individual feelings, has vanished.

So art viewed as art cannot find a response in purely personal concerns.

If we ask 'Why not?', Bradley (1934: 623) again offers the right answer in a clear fashion. With art, 'We have everywhere … the impersonal direction and set of the interest. We are absorbed not in ourselves but by an object before our minds'. Yet what does the term 'impersonal' mean in this context? Since my appreciation of an artwork must not depend on my *specific* relation to it — thereby ruling out, of course, my economic interest in it (say) — whatever reason I have for my appreciation must be generalisable. As Kant[22] put it, 'it must contain a ground of delight for everyone'. But the artwork obviously has some hold on *our* attention, for otherwise why should *we* attend to it? Thus it connects with feelings, if not just with our personal ones. So the term 'impersonal' amounts to 'human': that is, about humankind, not just about me. For this is the upshot of the Humean Challenge used elsewhere (*UD*: 150-2; 176-7): we would not accept as art something with no connection with human thought and feeling[23].

In effect, then, Bradley (1934: 620; 621) charges that the *personalisation* implicit in the taking of pornographic interest is one feature which precludes that interest being (simultaneously) *artistic* interest. Here the 'failings' of the work taken as pornography are clearly visible as a failure on the part of the audience: as a *consequence* of (or as a *kind* of) misperception.

Yet, as Bradley (1934: 624) notes, an artist may not succeed, in just *this* respect — she or he 'may have failed to keep the [sexual] detail duly subordinate .... It may remain no longer bound to the service of the artistic purpose'. As Bradley (1934: 624) accurately remarks, '[s]uch a result … is due not to art but to art's failure'. The object has failed to be art, despite the artist's aim. And any argument[24] which urges that the *appropriate* (that is, non-misperception) response to a work is as personal or as pornographic is *thereby* an argument for the work's not being art (or an argument against its being art, if these are different).

As Bradley (1934: 626 note) was well aware, merely to have tried one's best is not enough:

> The writer or painter who has aimed at his highest, and done his best to reach it, is justified … morally, whatever he has done or failed to do. But he is justified only as a man and as to his own conscience, and his actual work may not be justified aesthetically or morally.

Rather, what has been achieved depends (as we might both suspect and hope) on what one has actually *made*.

Is taking an artwork as pornography definitely misperception (rather than, say, another legitimate way of perceiving the object)? Yes, because it cannot sustain the (relative) *universality* of artistic interest. So it would be focusing, at best, on *my* issues, rather than on *life*-issues. To see it that way is not to see an *artwork*.

That is *not* to urge that nothing could be said here. Recall artworks misperceived under *aesthetic* concepts. For instance, Norman Tebbit, a politician from Mrs. Thatcher's government, claiming 'that middle-class people could see spicier pictures of naked women on art gallery walls' (Fuller, 1988b: 211; quoted CDE: 115) than photographs of 'topless' women in a British national newspaper, *The Sun*. Those who 'cannot see that there was a significant difference' (Fuller, 1988a: 64) between artworks and pin-ups are denying the idea of artistic value as I have been seeking to develop it. But, notice, there is something to the work seen in this way. Just as the not-understood 'poem' is still beautiful, so *might* the girls (as photographed) be. So these *are* ways of taking the object in question: it *can be* an object of aesthetic interest (as anything — or almost anything — can). But, since this is (mere) *aesthetic* interest, and not *artistic* interest, it precisely lacks the life-issues connection. And that accords with our pre-theoretical conclusion here.

Audience

The point of the detour was to highlight a connection of artistic appreciation (and artistic value) to the *possibility* of [at least] some audience for art wider than me personally. If acknowledged, this conclusion has a number of implications for dance-understanding and communication: I will spend the rest of my time on three of them, dealing fairly quickly with two (in this section).

The first implication — which might be put in terms of the notion of *address* — concerns the sense in which the *specifics* of an audience are implied: of course, levels of knowledge and sensitivity are required for any artistic appreciation (I must have the relevant concepts, and be able to mobilise them in my appreciation of the work at issue — and such concepts may draw on the history and traditions of the artform, etc.). But, since the relevant interest *in art* is more general, no more specific audience can be addressed. Schoenberg (1975: 124) famously said, 'if it is art, it is not for all, and if it is for all, then it is not art'. Yet, if art is not 'for everyone', this is only because some may lack the relevant understanding, while others cannot mobilise that understanding in their appreciation — but both of these are mere practical difficulties, akin to not having learned to subtract. So no *specific* audience can be required[25].

A second implication may be drawn out by returning to the idea of research by artists (say, by choreographers). If the 'research' from the artist isn't knowledge-generating (in principle), it will be hard to see how there is anything to communicate. (I take the communication of artistic 'meaning' as necessarily a (potential) feature of artworks, without taking such meaning to be necessarily 'translatable'. Indeed, that is Cavell's point, in the passage quoted earlier.) So, for instance, suppose I draw a series of studies of, for example, *hands* as a prelude to painting the hands in one of my masterpieces: now, exactly what has been learned, and who has learned it? The answer to the second question is easier: *I* have learned it — indeed, on most readings[26], there is no implication here that *you* do not already know whatever it is that *I* learn (which is why the same explorations, with the same or similar results, are undertaken by generations of art students). But can the 'it' I learn be usefully put in some other way? (What have I *learned* that I did not know?) Many writers — with justice — doubt that such 'information' can be presented propositionally[27].

In the dance example, they might urge that only *dance*, and only *this* dance, offers me this (precise) insight. So one cannot (even) say what *I* have learned. For, if I could, I would (therefore) be able to 'express' the insight detached from the dance itself (especially from the sensuous properties of the dance). But then those sensuous properties would seem irrelevant. No, what I learn is not (completely) expressible in some other form.

Yet the relevant question here might be: why should anyone (else) *care* what I have learned? Now, this would be a *silly* question if what I had learned was readily communicable (in principle) in some non-dance form: but, if that were so, the benefit would lie in the 'what' that was learned. But then the dance itself would be of *lesser* importance — important only as a vehicle! We should be glad to find this view mistaken. Equally, if the 'what' is only communicable through the dance, it is distinctly odd — indeed, nothing more than a verbal point — to insist that I (alone) know or understand it: on the contrary, very many people can (in principle) understand the dance — whether or not any actually do — and *what* is understood is a perfectly public phenomenon; namely, the dance.

What would it *be* for the importance of dance to reside in what it offered to dancers (or, worse, to choreographers)? The kind of self-absorbed judgement this might amount to would be a rejection of the *value* of dance (as of the other arts) because it would preclude, in principle, access to that value for any but (its) dancers … and that is to deny the *necessary* 'publicity' (in principle) of value[28] — of course, lack of certain knowledge and understanding may render defunct one's judgement of certain objects; but (as we saw) this is merely a 'practical elitism' (*UD*: 159-60) — only those with certain knowledge can understand, say, propositions of nuclear physics and, even though not *necessarily* beyond others, the time taken to acquire *this* knowledge and understanding (in typical cases: contrast J. S. Mill, but even he had a nervous breakdown) will preclude one *also* learning (for instance) advanced evolutionary biology, etc.

So a key part of the importance, for me, of dance's art-status is that it is *because* a certain dance is an artwork that it has the (real[29]) meaning that it has. But failing to regard it as art would militate against just that meaning. If successful, such a line of argument would make dance no more revealing than, say, gymnastic floorwork or ice-dance — aesthetically-compelling sports/physical activities, but not art (see Best 1978: 121-2; Best 1992c: 180). [To understand why is to turn on its head the previous arguments: for the 'life-issues' connection I have urged (*UD*: 179-82; McFee, 1999: 171) is little more than a way of reflecting the importance to human life that artworks have in many/most societies or cultures or civilisations (where they occur).]

Artistic properties are response-reliant

I turn now to a third implication of the audience for art : namely, that what I encounter in artistic appreciation are *features* or *properties* of the work. But, if so, the *possibility* of these features or properties will depend on the powers and capacities of creatures (us!) suitable to recognise them. Further, they will include meaning-properties and value-properties: is that plausible? I will urge that it is.

It is sometimes claimed that what I see, in seeing a dance, or what I understand, in understanding one, is an *interpretation* of that dance. Although mistaken, this view can be revealing (compare McFee, 1999: 159-65), so its brief discussion can take us forward. Using the term 'interpretation' here suggests (at least to me) something detached (or at least detachable) from the artwork. And we have seen that such a conception of artistic meaning should be rejected. For it is only when one sees a meaning-bearing object, in this sense, that one sees an artwork. So we cannot detach the meaning from the artwork (and still be left with an artwork).

Notice, here, three key features: first, I do not typically take *my* view of a dance or a piece of music to be an *interpretation* of the piece (or to reflect such an interpretation): rather, (for me) my view is just an acknowledgement of the *features of the work* — that is how I see it! Relatedly, I will describe my view (literal and otherwise) of an artwork as an *interpretation* of that work *only* when I (explicitly) recognise other views — and recognise that they (too?) are answerable to the perceptible features of the work. And this is *more* than just my recognising that artworks may (typically) be viewed differently. For (and second) a key part of the 'seeing' (etc.) here involves seeing (or trying/aiming to see) the *artistic* features/properties of the object — seeing it as an artwork:

that is, as (say) a sculpture and not (just) a block of marble. We might bring out
the point with a three-fold contrast between:

    (a) the artistic properties of the sculpture;
    (b) the 'designed' properties of some polished stone; and
    (c) the 'natural' features of a meteorite.

If what we say of the object is all compatible with its being naturally occurring
(the meteorite), then none of *those* features are its artistically-relevant features:
certainly, they cannot be intended or meant — hence, cannot be involved in
what (earlier) I called 'genuine communication'. And if, for instance, I were to
mistake a meteorite for a Henry Moore sculpture — suppose they are indistinguishable, if you like[30] — I would then be claiming that what are actually the
wholly *natural* properties of the meteorite should be seen as intended,
meaningful, etc. (I will see *design* where there is none.) And these comments
will say what is *false* of the meteorite: such concepts cannot possibly have
application in this case. Treating it as an artwork will involve mis-ascribing
artistic concepts to it. But even if the features are designed (as in the polished
rock), that they are the features of *this particular* rock, and that the designing
was by *this particular* individual (or group), will operate differently from the
features of our sculpture. Here again, treating it as an artwork would involve
mis-ascribing artistic concepts to it. So different things will be true of each
(even when we cannot tell them apart purely visually)[31]. In a similar way, a
graceful action might simply be my walking, or be part of my gymnastic
floorwork, or be part of my dance: but these are not equivalent actions — that
it is dance (when it is) *transforms* [or transfigures: Danto, 1981] that action.

    The point, of course, is the connection between the art-status of the work
and the properties ascribed to it — someone who said that all art objects were
essentially interpreted (have I said this? See *UD*: 84-5) could just be making
that point. But this is a pretty weak or trivial sense of the term 'interpretation'.

    The real issue for us here concerns what features the (so-called) 'inter-
pretation' ascribes to the work: that they must be *artistic* features (since it is an
artwork) — so that there are other features which, while they might truly be
ascribable, will be either artistically irrelevant (because relating to, say, the
material condition of the work) or even false of the artwork: the dancer is light
(*UD*: 219) — despite weighing so-and-so pounds! Further, such features will
reflect how I see the work: for instance, what I value in it.

    As the third aspect, I argue (McFee 1992b; McFee 1995) that the features
or properties of artworks can *change* over time, especially the work's meaning-
related features; and that change can amount to *no more* than a change in how
the work in question is appropriately viewed — so not as a result of, say,
discolouration. (I am a 'forward retroactivist': see Levinson, 1990: 197; 1996:
243; McFee 1992b; McFee 1995.) But, again, this is only badly described as a
change in *interpretation* — my point might be put (as above) by saying that the

properties of the work change. And such properties come about when, say, the artwork becomes recognised as a precursor of such-and-such (for example, Kafka[32]); and therefore amenable to 'analysis' using concepts drawn from the understanding of so-and-so (Kafka).

Finding that a work admits of one or more *interpretation* is (for me) not equivalent to confronting different works — as (according to Sharpe) Margolis's *constructivism* would have it. At any one time, the issue is: what are the *features* of the work (when it is appropriately viewed as art)? And the *answer* to such a question will typically be determinate at any one time.

We see here an intersection between what I have called (*UD*: 100-01) 'critic's interpretation' and 'performer's interpretation' — a performer's interpretation can subtly alter the features of the work (that is, of that performance-token). Pollini's interpretation (a performer's interpretation) of, say, Schoenberg's *Opus 19* 'changes' some of that work's features by, as it were, stressing some at the expense of others. So key features of the work can be changed as a result of one (performer's) interpretation being endorsed — especially if it becomes 'the' way to play that piece; as certain acting performances are taken, for a time, as *definitive* (*UD*: 94).

But, moreover, the changes in the work's properties (especially the meaning-properties) which result from later artistic activities may change what the work is *like*: that is, (literally) what it resembles … for they may suggest different comparisons.

As a useful parallel[33], consider the case of someone I like but who you do not, and where (for the life of me) I cannot see *why* you do not like this person. What you say in describing the person seems accurate enough: how can you fail to regard that person well? But you do! Surely the features which we agree the person has *justify* my liking and leave mysterious your *lack* of liking. But, of course, much turns on the *perspective* you take of the features described. That is why this model (from Sharpe) of the person we like, where we cannot see (for the life of us) why others do not, is very useful here — it identifies a dispute about what the *properties* of that person really are (what is true of him/her); and may result in an intractable dispute.

In a sense, then, we are acknowledging some of the *contours* of the idea of artistic meaning, or of what is understood when one understands an artwork (such as a dance or a piece of music[34].). But we are also noting how *features* of, say, the dance (or what is *true* of it) are not independent of the nature of our concerns with it; and these concerns characteristically include value-concerns. And so these contours of artistic meaning suggest ways of connecting artistic meaning — with its appeal to value — both to more general questions of the relevance of art (when or where it occurs) and to an idea John Wisdom puts so eloquently, 'revealing anew the familiar from life' (see Wisdom, 1953: 224).

If the art-object did not bear on what *humans* valued, then (by definition?)

humans couldn't find it valuable. So, while there is no *specific* content required here for art-status (it does not have to be 'about' beauty, truth or God, for instance) — although there may be some negative ones (pornographic concerns may be excluded, say), there is *some* content[35], given by the possibility of human valuing. Thus the upshot is to place artistic meaning in two fairly specific contexts: first, one provided by human valuing as it is manifest in human responses to objects or situations — this is what motivates (slightly mistakenly: see Carroll, 1999: 171) the connection of art to emotion; second, a context offering conceptual transformation (*UD*: 168-70) — as when Jesus transformed the concept of *adultery* (one of Wisdom's favourite cases) by getting his listeners to treat as adultery even looking lustfully *in one's heart* at another's wife. Notice that this is a transformation of what we see when we look at a certain scene: to use an example from Ian Ground[36], when the flaired jeans one had admired cease (for you) to *look* 'cool'.

Response-Reliance

This connects to the parallel between artistic value and secondary qualities such as colour (as articulated by McDowell (1998), among others): that both secondary qualities and artistic value are *seen* or *recognised*; and such recognition is central to there *being* either. So that, for example, '[a] secondary quality is a property the ascription of which to an object is not adequately understood except as true, if it is true, in virtue of the objects disposition to present a certain sort of perceptual appearance' (McDowell 1998: 133). Roughly, to be a green object requires, at least on some occasions, *looking* green. There are, in effect, two points being urged simultaneously: or, better, two elements to the position. My stress here is [first] on the *direct perception* of [second] *both* (a) colour and (b) value (see Putnam, 1999: 21-41; 128-30). If you are an 'error theorist' (like Mackie [1977: 15], who seeks to deny that values are ' ... part of the fabric of the world'), you will likely regard both as not perceptible. Rather, they will turn out to be gilding, staining, etc. (in a Humean fashion). And so one part of the argument here will be a thesis about the nature of *properties* or *features* (in the world): not merely are they truth-involving — which I would certainly urge for both colour and value — but they are in *some* sense accessible to all. This last point might even be put in terms of the *universality* of genuine properties; or in terms of their *lack* of dependence on the powers and capacities of audiences. Clearly, both colour and value would (plausibly) fail this test.

The difficulty, here, is to see why these characteristics, on this reading, *must* be taken as definitive of (genuine) properties[37]. Instead, our conclusion will be roughly that of Thomas Reid ([1815] 1969: 755):

> ... that there is no solid foundation for ... [this view] when applied to
> the secondary qualities of body; and the same arguments show equally,
> that it has no solid foundation when applied to the beauty of objects,
> or to any of those qualities that are perceived by a good taste.

Like Reid, I aim to treat these two kinds of properties roughly symmetrically. Notice that colours will uncontentiously require powers of observers: as we said, roughly, to be green in colour involves at least the possibility of appearing green to some observer in some circumstances. And we must acknowledge that the recognition of moral action, or of virtue, or of artistic excellence, requires knowledge on the part of the recogniser. Are these reasons to doubt that colour and value are (genuine) properties? As Reid points out, the kind of commonsense reflected in ordinary language *does* take, say, the colours of objects to be features of those objects. So, rather than being a difficulty to be met here, this aspect of both colour-properties and value-properties just seems a fact to be acknowledged. And that, in turn, points to a powerful duality within such properties. Thus Reid ([1815] 1969: 754) effectively highlights one central issue: 'This excellence [of an air in music] is not in me; it is in the music. But the pleasure it gives is not in the music; it is in me'. For clearly the property (or whatever) that we ascribe requires *both* the characteristics of the object and the powers and capacities of the audience. The correct way to characterise the issue, therefore, is as concerning the nature of such properties. And notice how such properties — applied to artworks, such as dances — *guarantee* their own audience: for, without the audience, we might reasonably claim there is no property!

But this duality (or audience-involving character) is merely one aspect asserted here: the other concerns the *direct perception* of the contested kinds of properties. Until recently, the intrinsic attractiveness of such a view — roughly, I see red objects when I look at red objects, etc. — has been overshadowed by an apparently fatal objection: that I might *mistake* for a red object something not in fact red. Then it was urged that there *must* be something in common between my seeing the *genuinely* red object and my seeming to see such an object; something *seen* in common. (And one way forward would be the introduction of red *qualia* or sense-data for redness.)

Recently, though, an attractive alternative (sometimes called *disjunctivism*) has been put forward by McDowell and Putnam (among others). Here, I do no more than endorse it as one way — one I find generally congenial — of defusing what could seem like a substantial challenge. So, from the fact that I said I saw roses on the wall here, I might with justice urge, 'Either I really saw a wall covered with roses, or it seemed to me as if I saw a wall covered with roses' (Putnam, 1999: 129 [who attributes the view to McDowell]). But must one believe that there is, as it were, some common factor shared by both cases?

If so, it will be hard to attribute the colour to the roses (when there *are* roses), since that very colour seemed 'present' without the roses. And that is one way to dispute this 'disjunctive' position.

Now, note that this would be a peculiar argument form to offer here. For, as Putnam (1999: 27-8) notes:

> even if cases of dreaming, illusion, etc. *were* perceptions of something non-physical, and the experience of someone who dreams *were* more or less like a 'veridical experience' of, say, Harvard's Memorial Hall ... there is simply no argument that the object of the veridical experience cannot be the Memorial Hall itself.

But, moreover, I will take myself to be seeing the roses unless there is a basis (a 'doubt-or-denial' condition; see *UD*: 34) to suggest the 'seems' locution. And I will fall back on that second locution when you dispute my right to the other, giving (apparently) good reasons — and then we go on to see whether that 'doubt-or-denial' condition is rooted in the 'public domain' or in my idiosyncrasies[38].

The emphasis here is not on *perception* as such (which generates all the problems about perceptual *modes* for literature[39]), but on *recognition*; and in particular the recognition of value. This will import directly a variety of points about perception just noted (and see *UD*: 130–47) since we see the artistic value (etc.) in terms of a specific perceptual modality (or set of them). And, without this direct perceptual confrontation, we are not approaching the artwork — as cases where we deny that so-and-so is making artistic judgements of such-and-such a work because he/she has not seen it. So, while we may need to both see and hear dances — say, if they essentially involve music — *these* and *just* these are the requisite modalities[40].

Meaning, (social) significance and privacy

Thus far I have tried — as it were positively — first, to show the sense in which *artistic* meaning is the only distinctive sort that could apply to dance. Of course, dance could have *associations* or *social significance*, as any human activity might: so that, say, a *social significance* of Picasso's *Guernica* might include its being designed for *that* wall, of *that* pavilion; and then the government that had commissioned it falling to Franco's fascists before the painting's exhibition — where none of these elements bears on, say, how it looks (and hence on whether or not it is a great artwork). So these are *not* the work's meaning-features. Moreover, and second, to show how artistic meaning imports reference to an *audience*, both by highlighting that the concerns of art cannot be mine alone and because what is meant must be accessible (in principle) to understanding.

Once we recognise that there cannot be a *logical* bar to understanding particular artworks (say, dances), we are still left with familiar practical difficulties about what I know, and how well, and so on. For these will affect what I can in fact understand. And this may explain why some dance works (say) remain a closed book to some people. But, once (in turn) we recognise our role — as audience — through the response-reliance of artistic properties, there remains an obligation on us to do our best to *actually* understand (and be understood); and on the other — say, the choreographer — to make the work as plain as he or she can for us. And these seem like logical (as well as moral) obligations on both sides — at least, for artist and audience.

Moreover, we can make these obligations increasingly concrete (if still abstract), in terms introduced earlier. For my part, as audience, I should prepare myself by acquiring the battery of concepts and categories (the *cognitive stock*: Wollheim, 1993: 134) relevant for your dancework. This might involve my learning about the history and traditions of dance-making and dance-understanding in the relevant forms, which might be done both theoretically (by going to dance history classes, say) and practically — by watching and discussing dances. Further, I should endeavour to learn to *mobilise* that cognitive stock in my appreciation of danceworks: again, we can see how experience of watching and discussing dances might help here — although, of course, there is no *guarantee* for my so learning to mobilise these concepts (and hence for my being able to understand your danceworks). We might summarise by saying that I attempt to become part of the *audience* for your work, a *competent judge* in respect of it (see McFee 2001b; also Travis 1989: 47 ff.)

Your part (as choreographer) seems equally straightforward, described in the abstract: you must make dances that I *can* understand! And, of course, that does not mean that no *work* is required on my part (we have already sketched such work) nor that all of it relate specifically to *this* dance[41]; but simply that you do what you *can* to make the dance accessible to *its* audience, without compromising your 'integrity' — we have already noted that, since it is an artwork (*ex hypothesi*), it *has* an audience. So you *might* think some elaborate programme notes helped; or you might run classes in which you described and illustrated the structural relations between aspects of your dance. Or, again, you might think that the dance was so clear in itself, and its relation to the past of dance so transparent (therefore, I will not miss it), that no such strategies were necessary. You might even be right: although I would be willing to bet a *small* sum that chatting to the audience about your *past* work might still be helpful (in setting-up appropriate expectations, perhaps) — and that getting them to see the work *again* might also be beneficial. Indeed, these are just the sorts of devices we might expect more generally to aid understanding; and hence to develop an audience for future work.

Dance-understanding

It might *seem* that dance offers something *special* here, since the bodily movements of *dancers* share qualities with bodily movements of others — in particular, of the audience. And it can seem self-evident that such bodily movement can be expressive, and so on. So the *general* experiences of the audience might seem to offer some specific insight for dance.

But this is mistaken, primarily in failing to do justice to the transformative power of dance-status, in three ways. First, there is nothing in the recognition of artistic meaning that requires this kind of 'shared-ness': the expressiveness of (say) painting — and hence the experience of painting (as art) — is not similarly dependent on shared properties.

Then, second, a mistaken view of communication operates here (see above, and *UD*: 243-4). As we saw, the idea of *communication* is (essentially) related to that of *meaning*. There is no (genuine) communication when my boss learns from my yawning that I am bored by/at the meeting, and no meaning, just because my behaviour lacks both the required kind of *intention* and (therefore?) anything *specific* to communicate. And, recall, these represent two kinds of misfires: something genuinely *there* might be learned, although not real or genuine communication (Best, 1978: 140; *UD*: 244 — I really *am* bored at the meeting, and my boss finds out); equally, what is *intended* may not be realised (I *mean* to make a dance masterpiece, but ...). So the yawning case, say, cannot involve genuine communication because the intention to communicate (present in, say, 'hand-languages') is not present there; and such 'communication' lacks the sort of expressiveness (etc.) appropriate for art/dance. Or, to put that the other way, the meaning of danceworks is not (just) the meaning of movements.

Moreover, and third, the idea of some specific modality here — such as kinaesthetic sense (*UD*: 264-73) — also cannot account for genuine artistic experience of danceworks: our access to them, as appreciators or experiencers of them, is via the projective sensory modalities (sight, hearing: see *UD*: 266).

As one way to bring out the issue, ask where the *experience* of dance is located. In the muscles, joints, etc.? No — but for reasons of two different kinds: that this is mistaken as an account of the experience of movement (Anscombe, 1981: 71; and compare PI p. 185); and that the idea of giving (precise[42]) location for *any* experiences is misguided. The appreciative response to *all* art — for example, to painting — can be as much a response of the whole person as anything: in particular, nothing *specific* here about the bodily nature of dance makes the spectator's role more (or less) bodily. Of course, what one is looking *at* (or listening *to*) includes bodies in motion, at least in typical cases. But, to make *appropriate* sense of them (to not misperceive them), I must recognise (experience!) them as *dances* — and this means experience them *transfigured*. If what I see is simply movement, I cannot be appreciating the dance because I am not *experiencing* the dance — any more than the person whose attention to a music performance is entirely circumscribed by its financial implications can be truly experiencing the music, even though he sits through the sounds!

As often, it has been helpful to begin our thinking about dance from our thinking about other performing arts, and especially music — as we have seen! Here, though, there is a key difference (of an ontological sort) between the position of dancer and musician[43]. For, at least in typical cases, the musician *produces* 'just those things of which the witnessable work consists' (Urmson, 1976: 243), while the dancer's actions *instantiate* the dance. Yet what we learn is the irrelevance of the dancer's perspective on the dance: for what is minimally required of the dancer is just *dancing* — thereby instantiating (or bringing into existence) the *dance*. In typical cases, we take dancing *with understanding* to be preferable to (better than) dancing lacking understanding. But these cannot be simply the same *dancing* in the two cases: rather, dancing with understanding is dancing (subtly) different from dancing without understanding[44] — if we call the difference 'imperceptible', we are completely wrong; for we *have* perceived it, even if we cannot readily say how! And what we require of the dancers is just that *dancing*, where our explanation of it need not be revealing — as we might follow Wittgenstein in saying, 'in the beginning was the deed' (quoting Goethe; OC §402; PO: 395).

In fact, these differences reinforce (for some thinkers[45]) the inappropriateness of an appeal to dancers' *experience*: the 'internal' or 'bodily' character of dancers' experience makes it even less suitable as a model of attention to the work *as a whole* than that of musicians, who at least produce sounds 'out there', available aurally both to the producer or to other musicians. (This is Scruton's [1997: 456[46]] point: that the central musical experience is one of *hearing*, with sounds as 'secondary objects' [Scruton, 1997: 7] rather than secondary qualities.)

Moreover, how might the experience of, say, *this* dance be contrasted with the experience of *that*? As is widely recognised[47], this cannot be revealingly done in terms of some distinctive 'feel' here. Rather, the difference for philosophical purposes is located in what is experienced: that is, the difference lies in the *intentional object* (Scruton 1997: 227-8; McFee 1997: 37) of that experience. As we might put it, the experience is of the *intentional object* of that experience (and hence only characterisable via discussion of that *intentional object* [which, here, is the dance work]). Once this is granted, it (again) focuses philosophical interest back onto works themselves, rather than onto differential *experiences* of them. For one can only understand the second difference in terms of the first!

Indeed, this fact is clear once we recognise the different experiences of a cricket match offered by watching, say, a wicket being taken and (re-) watching that wicket on an action-replay screen. (Were these not distinguishable, we would have no [sporting] reason to go to matches, nor reason to watch the players rather than the 'big screen' when we were there.) For, while the *experience* is different, in what ways? To answer here will return us to the *intentional objects* of those experiences. For the intentional object of experience *of the dance* must be the dance; not something else — in particular, it must count as an instantiation of the dance (a performance of it), not a recording of that dance. And one feature which drives us in the direction is the role of *real-time* as one characteristic (among many) distinguishing these experiences as of *performances*. For it seems right that typically, for genuine performances, 'the sounds [for dance, the movements] to which the audience attends are sequenced and co-ordinated by human performers in real-time, in the presence of an audience, for that audience' (Gracyk, 1997: 140). And the actions of dancers (in typical dances) are performed in real-time, in just this way. Thus, for dance (if less reliably for music), 'the appreciation of a performance includes evaluation of these actions' (Gracyk, 1997: 140).

Recording: An Ontological Issue?

In this light, then, I shall address the application to dance of an argument (about music) which asks whether the hearing of a recording is 'a superior mode of access to music' (Gracyk, 1997: 148). In considering the tentative 'yes' answer, Ted Gracyk deploys two main strategies: first, to imagine the experience of the recorded music supplemented by skillfully recorded (video) versions of, say, the pianist's playing — what (of artistic significance) is then missing? The second strategy is to imagine what would be lacking from a world in which there were recordings but no live performances (in particular, from the artistic life of such a world). If the answer is 'nothing', or only events of social (rather than artistic) significance, Gracyk could conclude that performances[48] have no artistic role beyond that filled by recordings.

For Gracyk, one issue seems to be (roughly) how one could get the same *experience* as attending a concert, or an experience equivalent for artistic purposes. Indeed, he explains 'aesthetic experience' (by which, in context, he means our artistic experience) as 'the rewards of grasping a musical work under a particular interpretation as it unfolds in a series of sounds to which one listens attentively' (Gracyk, 1997: 100 note[49]). So the emphasis for him is on equivalent *experience*. As we have seen, that is not *our* question: rather, for us, the question is one about *replicating* (or, better, instantiating) the features of the dance work. For, as Gracyk (1997: 142) recognises, 'the sounds heard during normal playback offer either a reproduction or a representation of its *performance*'. Whatever we say for music, for dance we can note that neither reproductions (say, of painting) nor representations (of those paintings) are artworks; and that what we need here is that our access be to the *works itself* — to its properties or features.

Of course, one problem here concerns the 'open-ness' of the 'properties of the work', given the variety of ways those properties might be instantiated in different performances. But that is just a fact about the properties of abstract objects such as dances; and need not detain us unduly here.

The question of recording, though, seems a key question for dance, since much of the study of dance today begins from dance on video. (Indeed, it is the question of whether, in seeing videos, one is *genuinely* seeing the dances themselves — the artworks.) Moreover, one should not be too idealistic here: we agree that my grandson beats me at *chess*, even though I give him a Queen advantage. In *that* context, though not in all, this counts as playing chess. In a similar vein, in some contexts, I *have* been watching *Swan Lake* even though all I have seen is the video. (After all, I certainly have not been watching some *other* dance!) But, for most discussions in philosophical aesthetics, this would *not* count as experiencing the dance work — and part of the reason here is that (in watching the video) I *cannot* be experiencing some of the work's crucial artistic features/properties; hence, there are elements of the work's *meaning* which are *logically* beyond comprehension on that basis — they are necessarily lacking from what can be watched on video (although this may still be a lot better than nothing!).

So what are the features/properties of a dancework, properly seen (that is, the work's *artistic* features)? We are used to the idea that one might study an artwork with attention to something less that the properties of the work itself. As Wollheim (1986: 11) notes, tartly, 'Since the days of the great Heinrich Wölfflin, art-historians have tended to identify the objects of their enquiry with those properties of a painting which a good slide preserves'. But we typically recognise these as *second-best*, used for want of access to works themselves. What makes this problematic for music is the suggestion that music is just organised sound; then the CD, say, (in providing access to the relevant organised sound) might seem to provide access to the artwork. Here, Gracyk (1997: 148) concludes, 'I am not claiming that recordings are, on balance, a superior mode of access to music'. But he is claiming, at least implicitly, that recordings are one mode of access to the music itself (although he rehearses some reason to doubt this — basically, that it is not a performance: see Gracyk, 1997: 140): and that is, if not an ontological claim, at least a claim with ontological implications.

This is not the place to debate that ontology: at the least, it is far less plausible for dance just because of the physicality of (typical) dances — it is easier to point to features the recordings of dances lack. Indeed, if we doubt the idea of *just* having recording for dance, it is partly because we cannot even imagine how that thesis might be applied to dance. (Those who claim that dance is 'just movement' are making a polemical point: *UD*: 253; Cavell 1969: 221.)

Of course, such an emphasis on recording would minimise the impact of individual virtuosity on the part of performers. But it is important to recognise (as Gracyk [1997: 144-5] does) that virtuosity as such is not the issue: and for two reasons, reflecting the different claims of virtuosity. We cannot see the *artistic* value of virtuosity for its own sake — what Belinda Quirey (1976: 122) dismissed as 'circus tricks' (and see Rhees, 1969: 136 re. the 'trapeze artist'). Like tongue-twisters, such virtuosity for its own sake is not an artistic virtue. Nevertheless, certain virtuoso performances can become famous; and acquire — for a while — a notoriety as *the* (ideal) way to, for instance, perform a certain role. We hear, in reviews and from friends, about the height of the jumps or the degree of the leg extensions, as though they were essential features of the dancer's dramatic characterisation (or whatever). (Currently, Sylvie Guillem might fit this bill.) And, of course, this kind of gusto can undeniably make dance performances more vivid; more likely to stick in one's memory. But, to the degree that one's attention is captivated by this virtuosity, it is not on central artistic features of the dance before one. The 'interpretative' virtuosity of the performer (seen through this 'performer's interpretation'; see *UD*: 100-101) gives us reason to attend to his/her performance as *different* from others — but, of course, that interpretation could be recorded (as we might think Pollini's interpretation of Schoenberg's piano music has). So that this reason *alone* will not motivate attention to performances rather than recordings, since it seems capable of appearing in recordings.

Second, this other kind of virtuosity — the one plainly of artistic relevance — is an interpretive one which 'makes greater demands on a performer's understanding than the sorts of skills most often associated with virtuosity' (Thomas Mark, quoted Gracyk, 1997: 144). Here the difficulty can lie in performing the work *as a unity*: as with some music[50], one such difficulty is apparent in the complexity of performing *ensemble* — of fitting together with the other dancers when there is no clear, overarching relation (such as unison or canon) between your movements and theirs. But virtuosity of this sort — unlike the 'circus tricks' variety — will not bring rapturous applause from uninformed audiences. Rather, it will involve the thoughtful, intelligent performance of the work. Indeed, we might not even regard this as virtuosity, although it is both clearly craft-skill of the highest order and the province of the few among dancers, as elsewhere.

Performance Traditions and Traditions of Performance

It is worth reflecting on the abiding appeal of particular artworks — the sort of thing sometimes (with some justice) enshrined in the idea of a *test of time*. For, in urging the value of artworks, we are urging their enduring value. But how is this to be explained? One way points to the possibility of continually 'finding something new' in a particular artwork: we might characterise this in terms of (subtly) different critics' interpretations of those works. And, of course, this applies (when it does) across the arts. But performing arts have an additional set of possibilities here. Thus we might take differences in performances as crucial to the abiding appeal of performing arts. And such differences might be of two sorts: first, differences of 'performer's interpretation', as when Pollini's Schoenberg *Opus 19* differs from Glen Gould's; or, second, differences in performances as such, as when Pollini plays *opus 19* with slightly different emphasis today compared with yesterday, although both are *his* performer's interpretation. (Very often, performances will differ in both ways — although typical audiences will be most aware of one aspect or other.)

But the parallel, applied to dance, may be more revealing. For dance performances generally offer these differences each time: for we may see the same dance, in the same performer's interpretation, but with different dancers, and on a performance-area of a different size (or even a wholly different type — as I saw William Louther dance his solo masterpiece *Vesalii Icones* (1970[51]) under a proscenium arch and 'in the round'). Hence work in the performing arts has a kind of inexhaustibility additional to that of the other arts. But it would be a mistake to treat all such cases as ones where the audience is just spotting mistakes, or waiting for errors of virtuosity — so these are not of the 'crash and burn' type that Gracyk (1997: 144–5) imagines, but of the *intelligent* (and hence reasoned) re-doing. Two points here: first, the arts as such do not need such 're-doing', but it is a feature of typical performing arts — it follows from the possibility of seeing the very same artwork at different times and in different places. Second, the idea that it is *reasoned* here gives importance guidance. For we cannot see such reasoning as entirely the province of one dancer or stager. Rather, the thought of 'reason' here points to (and highlights the importance of) two aspects of 'skill': what might be called both a *performance tradition* and a *tradition of performance*.

Of course, these are really only separable for analytical purposes — by the first I mean that performers require appropriate skills in order to perform particular works; and especially works of the past. Begin here by thinking about *dance techniques* (such as Graham technique) which, while they constitute bodily conditioning and the 'inculcating [of] certain fairly specific bodily skills' (*UD*: 201), also involve the learning (or, at least, acquisition) of a 'vocabulary' of movements appropriate for dances created using those techniques. In this sense, then, Marcia Siegel (1972: 107) is right to speak of 'technique-as-aesthetic'. Those of us who watch performances by dancers in training, and by poorly trained dancers, become adept at noting when this is missing: in the lack of appropriate bodily tension for such-and-such, or the lack of a 'feel' for this choreography — for me, the second most clearly manifest in Nureyev's dancing of Graham dances (see Siegel, 1979: 202; Croce, 1978: 162; *UD*: 203). Moreover, the history of most techniques — coming from the requirements of specific dances for the companies concerned (*UD*: 205) — reflects this connection between technique and dance-character. And, even if the training of dancers is no longer built on specific techniques such as these, that training still involves their learning to perform the patterns of movement appropriate to particular dances. (One fear, at least on the part of old fogies such as me, is that what is learned is inadequate to perform dances of the past — if so, this would be a flaw in training; and criticisable as such!) On this model, though, dancers undergo a kind of apprenticeship, in which they learn two (or two-and-a-half) crafts: they undergo the bodily training and are inducted into the understanding of the movements (and the dances) that result — and they may in this way gain insight into choreographic processes (although they need not [so this is the 'half']). All this is what I am calling a *performance tradition*: dancers learn to perform, and to understand in a dancerly way, dances. And that, of course, allows the performances of dances of the past in what I earlier called a 'reasoned' way: that is, in *new* performers' interpretations (*UD*: 100-01). Without such a tradition, there would be no-one capable of performing certain dances; and so, even if the dances were 'preserved' (say, in notated form), they could not be danced. Just such a *performance tradition* would be threatened if attention to recordings replaced attention to dances. (Interestingly, the substance of Gracyk's position seems to assume the continuation of a performance tradition — part of what he means by a 'craft tradition': Gracyk, 1997: 144[52].)

But there is another aspect of performance which needs to be ensured (although, as above, the contrast can really only be drawn for analytical purposes), and that I call a *tradition of performance*. By this I mean that an audience of 'competent judges' (McFee, 2001b: 104-08) for dance works is required; and such an audience would require to understand these works through experience of them *as performed*. It would also embody the contemporary understanding of how the works should (typically) be performed — an understanding that later stagers might contest profitably in making new versions of particular (extant) dances, and one to which choreographers could respond (as Mats Ek does, in his comic traducings of the typical expectations of classical ballet: say, in his *Swan Lake* [1987]). Such traditions form a background here (part of 'the lay of the artworld'; Noël Carroll, 2001: 91) which permits the choices made to be *reasoned* choices, defensible (in principle) in discussion. Without such a tradition, 'however small and special' (Cavell, 1969: xxvii), choices here could only be arbitrary.

To bring out some of these issues, let us ask: does the performance tradition for, say, the current Royal Ballet dancers overlap sufficiently with those of (say) Paul Taylor or Ashton to permit the dancers to perform these choreographers' works? Suppose that it does not (see Challis, 1999). The case in point suggests that the *performance tradition* required for these works either was never part of the training regime for these dancers (Taylor) or has ceased to be (Ashton) — because, say, a British style of ballet performance, with its 'emotional depth' has been replaced by a Russian style, with its 'formal precision' (quoted Challis, 1999: 147, both quotes). The outcome in the most extreme case would, of course, be to render the performances (and hence the works) unintelligible to a knowledgeable audience: in the less extreme case, this audience would just struggle to understand. An example familiar to some might be the unclarity of works as experienced in, say, some choreographic competitions, where the performance skill of dancers is insufficient (or inappropriate) in ways that make it difficult to see *the dance* (through these performances). Similarly Rhees (1969: 159) speaks of 'the way in which a piece of music may remain uninteresting until you hear it played by a really good pianist'. So these difficulties have a direct bearing on dance experience, for the identification of *dance meaning* through such experience would remain problematic.

Here, too, the audience needs to be able to recognise (at least) when dancers fail to instantiate a particular choreography[53]. And that will require both a *performance tradition*, as just noted, but also a *tradition of performance* which permits (a) the audience to distinguish interesting and valuable difference from mere mistake, and (b) the impact of 'posterity' to lead to a revision of that judgement. For a 'knowledgeable audience' just is one that can distinguish originality from mere novelty (is Matthew Bourne's *Swan Lake* [1995] really doing anything new at the level of artistic meaning?); and can find the continuity within trivial changes.

The upshot here: the *experience* of dance has such traditions implicit within it. I do not mean, of course, that these traditions must be part of what the audience must know, if that means that all audience members must be able to recite the history, and so on, to us. Rather, the knowledge might well be acquired *other* than as a kind of book-learning (it almost always will be for dancers), and be manifest in action and in intelligent attention.

Conclusion

We have noted how the capacity to 'see' artistic properties (and hence artistic values) in an artwork might be thought about: we have seen its dependence on various conceptual masteries (that is, on one's cognitive stock) — even though this is not *all* that is involved. Many of our points, applying these insights to dance, have been negative: it is *not* built on empathy or a kinaesthetic sense; it does *not* require that one be (or think like, or feel like) a dancer — all these are incoherent requirements. And, while there is clearly *something* which 'connects' the possibility of dance to the reality of movement for most of us, this is a long way from a usable insight, because of the *transfigurational* aspect of art-status (see above; Danto, 1981) — and hence of dance: what we see as dances are crucially different from any movements we encounter elsewhere. (If they resemble anything, it is the gestures of 'hand-languages' such as ASL or Pagett, or the conventional gestures of the hitch-hiker — these at least are intentional communication, even if typically lacking the expressive element associated with embodiment.)

The upshot is that a philosophical investigation of dance experience will not, productively, discuss *how* (or, worse, *if*) such experience is central to artistic appreciation of dance; nor can it attend to the *nature* of such experience (as though it had *one* nature). For, first, we recognise that one cannot really appreciate dances unless one has first-hand *experience* of them, and unless one finds them powerful (or otherwise) on the basis of that experience. Further, the *experience* here is centrally that of the audience of dance. Second, experiences are not helpfully characterised in terms of their distinctive 'feel' (part of what Wollheim [1984: 38; 42-5] calls their 'phenomenology') because the only exact characterisation of the experience is in terms of the *concepts* under which the experience takes place (the concepts *mobilised* in that experience) — exploring these concepts *is* exploring the experience. Third, while the experience is not exhausted by this focus on concepts, that is the part that can be examined. In particular, discussing 'mobilisation-conditions' is really a positive-sounding version of the 'recognised heads of exception' to claims to critical appreciation.

It might seem that these points, which could be made for the appreciation of any artform, must require modification when applied to dance. But we have seen that this is not so; and for three related reasons. First, the appropriate perspective here is the perspective of the audience — and this is equally true for all artforms; second, the audience for dance is as much a visual and/or aural audience as the audience for painting or for music (respectively) — dance offers nothing special here. In particular, artistic experience of dance does not require one to experience dance other than perceptually (for example, kinaesthesis is not required; see *UD*: 264-73). Third, the distinctive experience of dancers is a quite separate topic; and not one we would expect to be very revealing, given the variety within dancers, within dances, and within the perspectives on a particular dance afforded to each dancer — the solo dancer knows all of the dance 'from the inside' (at least, all of the movement of the dance[54]) while one member of a group has that perspective only on his/her piece of the dance; and that may not be a *useful* perspective from which to take in the dance as a whole! (Certainly, we should readily grant the parallel points for, say, musicians in an orchestra — although (as we saw earlier:) their relation to the music differs from the dancers' relation to the dance.)

My target, throughout, has been a certain conception of the *meaning*, *importance* and *value* of danceworks — and, in particular, that conception as it applies to *meaning*. I have urged the crucial character here of *artistic meaning*, discussing aspects of its relation to an audience, while highlighting how confrontation with artworks might be revelatory for that audience. (A fuller discussion would say a lot more about such revelation.)

I have been arguing, in effect, that art-status builds-in certain constraints concerning intelligibility. But it is crucial here — especially if we think for a moment about the *making* of dances — to recognise that this was a *logical* or *in principle* requirement: it says nothing about the extent, or otherwise, of the audience in question.

This, in turn, is important in two respects: first, in terms of creativity or development, there is no suggestion here that an *established* audience is required (there may or may not be such an audience). In particular, there is no requirement for the *repetition* of previous intelligibility (again this may or may not occur) — although the presence of dance techniques, and their inter-relations (for example, the way Cunningham technique grows from Graham), will tend to strengthen the explicit connection to the past of dance. Second, and relatedly, artworks may need to 'create the taste' by which they are then valued. So that my choreography may be thought *safe* if I draw extensively on the forms etc. of the past, or *radical but intelligible* if I challenge the past aesthetic in clear ways, or *powerfully challenging* if, say, a whole genre is contested. These represent some of the ways of making intelligible dance-works, works that can have (or acquire) an audience. Hence these are ways of making art. Yet they also highlight a way of *failing* to make art; namely, by lacking an audience. Of course, I may wait for the judgement — that is, the audience — of posterity: and/or I can work to create the taste that gives my work an audience — the kind of PR job by which, say, T. S. Eliot's critical writings developed critical categories, and a critical sensibility, that was then applied to his own poetry. But I cannot rest content that just *I* understand it (unless that is a coded way of waiting for posterity). For if the work is not art in anybody's eyes — if it permanently lacks an audience — then it is not art. In this case, too, it lacks meaning (of the kind discussed here). And that is a salutary possibility.

Notes

PREFACE

1   Ludwig Wittgenstein (1889 — 1951) was an Austrian who became professor of philosophy at Cambridge. An elementary but trustworthy introduction to his work is Kenny, 1973; a more detailed account is Hacker, 1986. Any thorough study must begin with the 3–volume commentary on Wittgenstein's major work, *Philosophical Investigations* (1953): Baker & Hacker, 1980; Baker & Hacker, 1985; Hacker, 1990. [(2004): there is now a fourth volume!]

For an understanding of Wittgenstein's importance and of how to interpret his works, see Baker, 1986; Baker, 1988; and Baker, 1991. The importance of Gordon Baker's work on Wittgenstein for my own would be difficult to over-stress. [(2004) See especially his later writings, such as Baker, 1998.]

CHAPTER 1

1   The word 'object' is here used rather as in the expression 'direct object' in grammar. In this sense, dances as well as paintings count as objects (Anscombe, 1981a: 3–11).
2   Consistency is a crucial notion in any argument. If one simultaneously says that something is true and that it is not true (which is what it means to fail to be consistent) one is not really saying anything. As a result, to find inconsistency in a position is to find that position flawed (Shaw, 1981: 32–34).
3   (2004) This account was written as the details of the National Curriculum for England and Wales were being finalised. Since then, the National Curriculum has undergone various modifications. However, the alterations are not germane here: the structure remains (broadly) subject-based, in four Key Stages, organised so as to permit assessment and also (teaching) accountability. Similarly, dance retains its place within physical education; and is available at the advanced level (A-level). In these ways, the changes

in the *detail* have no bearing on the points made throughout this work: indeed, it is consonant with the project of philosophy that the chosen example is from the *past* of education, since this highlights that the points are general ones (hence, applicable within other curricular structures), rather than depending on the minutiae of a particular curriculum.

4   On this point, see Carr (1987: 344): 'Choreography just *is* the art of making dances ... whereas drama is rather more than just the creation of acts of thespianism. Dance, then, appears to be directly connected with action and performance in a way that drama is not'.

CHAPTER 2

1   To understand the (technical) ideas of necessary and sufficient conditions, consider the case of a triangle. Triangles are (a) plane figures, (b) with three straight sides, (c) completely bounded by those sides. Each of these conditions is *necessary*, in that when any is not satisfied we do not have a triangle. If, say, condition (a) fails, the figure is three-dimensional; if condition (b) fails, the figure could be a square or some such; without satisfying condition (c), the figure might be a kind of open box. So a figure lacking any of these conditions is definitely not a triangle. Equally, the conditions are jointly *sufficient*: any figure which fulfils all three conditions is definitely a triangle. We can see this point by imagining a fourth condition, say, that the sides were of equal length. It is apparent that this condition is too strict: it rules out, for example, right-angle triangles. Taken together, necessary and sufficient conditions comprise a definition.

Notice that satisfaction of a necessary condition for triangle-hood does not make a figure a triangle: squares too are plane figures, for example. Moreover, sufficient conditions might not be necessary (although they are in this case). A sufficient for being an author might be to have published a book: all who have published books are authors. But there are other authors too. Hence writing a book might be a necessary condition of authorhood here, while publication would be a sufficient condition.

2   The words 'movement' and 'action' are here used in a way traditional in philosophy (*UD*: 52–8), in which actions are what people do, explained in terms of reasons, motives and the like, while movements are explained causally as changes in human bodies. Thus most actions will also comprise movements, but insofar as we are looking at them as the product of human design should be thought of as human action and explained accordingly.

3   (2004) See Supplementary Essay 3 for further detail on the artistic/aesthetic contrast, including some more of its implications. As was urged in the Introduction to the Expanded Edition, this contrast is fundamental to all the thinking on (philosophical) aesthetics here. In stressing the importance of

the contrast, the distinctive character of my version of it should also be recognised — in contrast to, for example, Korsmeyer, 1977.

4   The terminology of types and tokens derives from the American philosopher C.S. Peirce (Ayer, 1968: 147–9). Further discussion of this topic, also using the flag example, may be found in Wollheim (1980a: §§35–36; 74–84).

5   On necessary conditions, see note 1 of this Chapter. It is important, though, to recognise that I am here urging something slightly weaker, which might be called a *normally* necessary condition (Baker, 1977: 43–56); I am urging the *defeasibility* of this relation (see *UD*: 61–3). Defeasibility, though a technical idea, is familiar from the law, where *contract* is a defeasible notion in just the sense intended here.

6   (2004) For some amplification, especially in respect of the practical upshot of this discussion, see Supplementary Essay 2. A fuller investigation would show how consideration of identity-conditions for danceworks relates to the (artistic) character of dances — what other might call *the essence of dance.*

CHAPTER 3

1   These views may each be traced back to a Latin root, the first to *educo, educare* meaning to bring up or rear; the second to *educo, educere* meaning to lead out. See Peters, 1966: 36–7.

2   The words 'primary' and 'secondary' have certain associations for teachers in Britain. Best puns on these meanings, partly because he suspects that the primary qualities of education are best represented in the UK by primary education. I prefer not to use these words.

3   This whole section has a major debt to Winch, 1987: 177–8. Some of the discussion of Cavell (as well as the general thrust) is his.

4   For a discussion of such possibilities, see Hare, 1972.

5   The key notion here is of the *intentionality* of emotions, by which is meant the way in which love is always love *of*, desire always desire *for*, and so on. See Anscombe, 1981a: 3–11; Kenny, 1963: 60–62.

6   (2004) This discussion employs a restricted use of the term 'practice': but the idea of *practices* is much deployed at present, often with reference to ideas attributed to Alaistair MacIntyre. For two related discussions, suggesting some limitations of some of these ways of proceeding, see McFee, 2004a: 73–83 esp. 77–82; McFee, 2004b.

7   What is being emphasised here is what, later, we will refer to as *normativity*. See *UD*: 81–83; 307–308.

CHAPTER 4

1   In probably the best book on Hume's philosophy, Barry Stroud (1977: 21) refers to 'a typical Humean challenge': the point is that, while Hume cannot prove what he is urging, he gives reason to doubt that any counter-example to his claim will be found, and suggests how to respond to putative counter-examples. For a more negative analysis of the method of challenge, see Flew (1961: 25ff).
2   The discussion of institutional accounts of art here owes a great debt to the works of Terry Diffey — especially Diffey (1969). This whole account of institutionalism is broadly Diffey's.
3   In this case, 'the Greeks didn't have a word for it': that is, they had no word which *distinguished*, for example, art from craft or art-making from craft-making. Hence they did not have the concept *art*. It follows that they could not *intend* to make art, and hence could not make art. See *UD*: 284–92.

CHAPTER 6

1   (2004) In referring to the craft-knowledge (or craft-understanding) as 'not describable in detail', the text might seem to imply that we do not (yet) know *all* about it. But, actually, it is highlighting a bigger issue; namely, that there can be no *all* here, no finite totality: see McFee 2000: 117–123.

CHAPTER 7

1   I derive this idea from some lectures and unpublished writings of Gill Burke which argue that only an intrinsic aim for physical education can satisfy the demands of such an aim. See also her paper (as Gill Westhorpe), Westhorpe, 1974.
2   This document was selected as giving a clear presentation of a moment in the development of the National Curriculum for physical education in the UK. As such, it is a suitable example for our purposes. Of course, some of its recommendations will be/have been modified by succeeding legislation.
3   Dance is also discussed in the document (DES, August 1991) in the following places: 11–12 about feasibility; 29, 30–31, 33–4 about the key stages; 38, 75 for a rationale for a programme of study areas of activity.

CHAPTER 8

1   See, for example, Cole, A., 1989. My discussion throughout owes a debt to the work of Ann Cole, and detail may usefully be supplemented from the works she cites.

CHAPTER 9

1   (2004) A fuller discussion of misconceptions concerning rules, and their
    implications for understanding rule-related activity, is found in McFee,
    2004a esp. 47–52. The text as a whole also explores alternative pictures of
    rule-application.
2   The term 'inference' here signifies that there is a *conclusion* reached via a
    chain of *argument* from *premises* (Shaw, 1981: Ch. 1). For discussion of
    such an account of criticism, see Ground, 1989: 61–99; Wollheim, 1983;
    UD: 137–8.
3   The terms 'deduction', 'deductive' are here meant in a strict technical sense
    used in philosophy (by which much that Sherlock Holmes does is *not*
    deduction). It is typified by *syllogistic* reasoning (Shaw, 1981: 137–49)
    where there is a general, *major* premise ('all men are mortal'), a specific
    minor premise ('Socrates is a man') and a *conclusion* which — for valid
    arguments — be true if the premises are.
4   See, for example, De Man, 1979: Ch. 3; Norris, 1987, Ch. 7; Cavell, 1981b:
    Ch. 1. The point is contended in various ways by these different figures,
    and is most apparent through their practice.
5   This is an argument *against* the possibility of a private language (hence
    Aspin, 1981: 28 suggests it be called 'the public language argument'). It de-
    scribes a constraint on intelligibility or understandability on what must
    be the case in order that something be intelligible or be a fit subject for
    understanding. A key thought is that only when it is possible to maintain the
    distinction between *thinking one is right* and actually *being right* can one
    understand one's *own* words (Wittgenstein, 1953: §258): and this dis-
    tinction cannot be made within one's own private practice (Hacker, 1986:
    245–306).
6   (2004) For some discussion of themes from the Private Language
    Argument, see Supplementary Essay 3. Both the place of the argument in
    Wittgenstein's work and its importance are contentious. At the least, the
    'argument' must not simply be an affirmation of the thought that commu-
    nication (and hence *language*) requires more than one understander: even
    sceptics recognise that 'it takes two to tango' — they just dispute that this
    understanding can occur. A first (small) step lies in recognising that this
    cannot be an argument about *learning* psychological predicates, or about
    applying them to others (the problem of other minds), since it begins from
    the child who has mastery of the concepts (PI §257), enquiring in what
    mastery consists. For a more powerful reading, see Baker, 1998 esp. 346–
    354. For instance, Baker (1998: 325) urges that the Private Language
    Argument (in some version) has become 'one course in the prix fixe served
    ... to undergraduates studying philosophy', but (thus) read as 'signifying a

standard gambit in the chess game played out by modern philosophers ...
obscures Wittgenstein's intention to overturn the chess-board on which the
game is played' (Baker, 1998: 340).

CHAPTER 10

1 (2004) We can, of course, be clearer that the 'transformation' invoked here
is really transfiguration, as discussed (with quotation from Danto) in
Supplementary Essay 3.

CHAPTER 11

1 See also, for example, Burgin (1986: 204): 'the *end* of art theory *now* is
identical with the objectives of *theories of representation* in general: a
critical understanding of the modes and means of symbolic articulation of
our *criticial* forms of sociality and subjectivity'. Again Rorty (1991a: 116)
explicitly notes that Derrida 'does not distinguish between placid scientific
or legal text on the one hand and restless, self-deconstructing, literary texts
on the other'. The views of both Burgin and Derrida, therefore, will treat
art-objects and other popular cultural objects in the same terms.
2 See Shusterman (1992) for a philosopher who — because he denies the
artistic/aesthetic contrast — wishes to treat popular culture *as* art. To do so
is to remove the educational argument for the place of dance in schools.

CHAPTER 12

1 My thinking on this topic has been strongly influenced by discussions with
my colleague, Scott Fleming, and by his research on related topics. Some
of the examples are his — certainly more than the explicit citations
acknowledge. My thanks too for his careful comments on this chapter, even
when I have been unable to make changes he suggested.
2 This is a result from a very informal 'survey' based on company
programmes and telephone calls. At best, it is just suggestive of the true
position.
3 (2004) Indeed, some works by Shobana Jeyasingh might be understood in
exactly this way! Compare Rowell, 2000: 97; 107.

CHAPTER 13

1 (2004) The ideas of Stenhouse do not seem to have flourished in
educational theory since these passages were written in ways their author
clearly hoped. First, this leaves me simply older, rather than also wiser: to

me, these ideas still seem to offer a promising view of education. Second, the fine detail of Stenhouse's work was never fundamental — rather, its emphasis on *process* was taken to be useful in explicating the educational role of dance.

2 The original work was Tyler, 1949; it was modified in Tyler, 1973. For a discussion, to which the presentation owes much, see Lawton, 1989: 11–14.

3 Given the importance of the professionalism of teachers on this process account, it is hardly surprising that Elliott (1991) gives Chapter 7 to a thorough investigation of the place of teacher appraisal: the need for informed teachers is particularly emphasised once the process model is adopted.

4 As noted in the Appendix to Chapter 1, the National Curriculum has four Key Stages, representing particular age ranges. Those interested in more information here should consult the Key Stage statements in the document (DES, August 1991).

5 (2004) Recall here that — despite the criticisms offered by Sparshott (1995: 476), quoted in the Introduction to the Enlarged Edition — the focus was always on recognising the accountability of educational process: have we succeeded in teaching these pupils anything? Have they succeeded in learning? Such questions raise the possibility of commenting on education. And the choices as to how each is to be addressed may govern the claims of (in this case) *dance* to be educative.

CHAPTER 14

1 Perhaps the most important UK examinations, for our purposes, would be the General Certificate in Education, Advanced Level (A-level) typically taken by 18–year olds, and the General Certificate of Secondary Education (GCSE) typically taken by 16–year olds. For an outline of both, see Lawton, 1989: 71–78; on A-level dance, see Williams, 1986.

CHAPTER 15

1 The two senses of the word 'discipline' are, of course, that which relates to control and structure and that which relates to bodies of knowledge and methodology (academic disciplines). These come together once we see that (academic) disciplines provide — among other things — discipline. See Toulmin, 1972: 262–81; Cavell, 1981b: 269.

CHAPTER 16

1   On technical rationality, or instrumental rationality, see Carr & Kemmis, 1986: 131; Gibson, 1986: 6–8.
2   This idea is an important one in the thought of T.S. Kuhn. See Kuhn, 1970: 181–7; Kuhn, 1977: 320–25. However, its importance can be regularly missed or misunderstood (Chalmers, 1982: 82–99) because of failure to recognise the importance, for the view, of what Kuhn calls *normal science*. The practice of normal science 'has... assimilated a time tested and group-licensed way of seeing' (Kuhn, 1970: 89). It is this that Feyerabend (1988: 230) speaks of in his re-appraisal of Kuhn as 'a historical ... grounding of science'.
3   See, for example, Deforges & McNamara, 1979; McNamara & Deforges, 1978; Brown & McIntyre, 1988; Brown & McIntyre, 1986.
4   See Wittgenstein, 1969 §402; for a discussion see McFee, 1991.
5   See Lear, 1980: Ch. 3. The point is that, in practical reasoning, the aim is built-in: 'We deliberate not about ends but about means' [Aristotle *NE,* 112 B 18; Ross, 1925: p. 56].
6   On language and truth, contrast Baker & Hacker, 1984a: Ch. 10; on society, compare Lyotard, 1984: 71–82; Giddens, 1987: 242–52.

CHAPTER 17

1   Lyotard (1984: xxiii) defines the postmodern in terms of 'incredulity towards metanarratives'. Now a 'metanarrative' or 'metadiscourse' is concerned with 'legitimation with respect to its own status' (for discussion see Rorty, 1991a: 164–176). It is unclear how a dancework could fulfil such a metanarrative role, much less be incredulous in respect of one!
    For explicit discussion of how a post-modern dance might be conceived, see Jordan 1992, esp. 4–6.

SUPPLEMENTARY ESSAY 1

1   This looks slightly confusing, as readers are referred to the same text (Banes, 1987) for both views. But one view, introducing the modification, is in the Preface to the second edition (as we shall see below).
2   By 'criticism', I intend the whole variety of remarks made about artworks: as Wollheim (1980: 185) puts it, the English language has no single word, applicable across all the arts, which applies to 'the process of coming to understand a particular work of art'.
3   On a third issue, that of truth in fiction (at least for literature), see a 'No

Truth' theory as employed by Lamarque & Olsen, 1994 esp. 1–3.

4   Compare Luntley, 1995: 13; and see Jenks, 1986 especially some of his remarks (for example, re. 'Norman Foster's recently completed Hong Kong Shanghai Bank' p. 38) about recently completed buildings that cannot be read as postmodern: here we have postmodernism is treated as a (kind of) *style*.

5   J L Austin (1970: 203) noted that: 'there is no necessity whatsoever that the various models … should all fit together neatly as parts into one single, total model or scheme…'. So there is no reason to assume such a general theory: hence reason to be 'incredulous' about one offered us by some theorist. [NB this is the Austin of 1970 and not necessarily of Austin, 1962.]

6   Compare Lyotard, 1984: xxiii on 'incredulity towards metanarratives'. 'The idea of a 'grand narrative' or a 'metanarrative' vis-à-vis the arts is deeply implausible. For example, Ernst Gombrich (1960) asked the question: *why has representational art a history?* Or, as Wollheim (1973: 261) puts it: 'Why did Duccio and Rubens, Van Eyck and Monet, Uccello and Watteau, all of whom, it must be granted, were interested in depicting the visible world, depict it in such different, such bewilderingly different, ways? — as though all representational painting answered *one* project!'

7   As John Wisdom (1965: 102) comments, 'at the bar of reason, always the final appeal is to cases'. Wisdom elaborates the idea by contrasting what he calls 'the mother's method' of explanation with 'the father's method'. Asked what a greyhound is, the father replies with a kind of 'definition', that a greyhound is 'a dog of such-and-such a type'. [Wisdom comments 'Short, conclusive, the father's procedure. That's more what one might call a proof.' (Wisdom 1991: 48).] In contrast, the mother says (pointing): 'that's a greyhound, and you remember your uncle's dog, Entry Badge, well that was a greyhound. But now that [she says, pointing to a Borzoi] is not a greyhound, and even that [she says, pointing to a whippet] is not' (Wisdom 1965: 69).
Wisdom (1965: 69) also imagines that she might offer the rhyme:
   A foot like a cat, a tail like a rat,
   A back like a rake, a head like a snake
He concludes that the mother: 'replies with instances of what is and what is not a greyhound or by comparing greyhounds with what they are not, and these two procedures merge into one' (Wisdom, 1965: 70).
   Attempts to force knowledge and understanding into the straight-jacket of a set of criteria — the sort of thing 'the father's method' offered — seem doomed to failure. Instead, we need the reason from case to case, and to appeal to cases (compare Wisdom, 1991). Compare also McFee, 1978 Chapter 3.

8 For example, a politician from Mrs. Thatcher's government, discussing photographs of 'topless' women on Page Three of a British national newspaper, *The Sun*, 'made a widely reported observation to the effect that middle-class people could see spicier pictures of naked women on art gallery walls, and he really could not see that there was any difference between such things and the *Sun* Page Three girl' (from Fuller, 1988a: 211–212). Those who cannot see any significant difference between artworks and pin-ups are denying the idea of artistic value.

9 For 'narrative', see Carroll, 1993: 79–106; Carroll, 2001.

10 One of David Best's favourite examples: see, for instance, Best, 1992c: 174.

11 See, for example, Hirst, 1974: 30–53; 84–100.

12 For example, Hirst, 1974: 87–92; 152–64: Peters, 1966: 161–2.

13 Lyotard seems entranced by the very variety of language-games. But Wittgenstein's idea of a language-game (which Lyotard identifies as methodologically central: Lyotard, 1984: 9) cannot support Lyotard's use of it: language-games are not game-like in the sense of being *non-serious* (of being part of 'agonistics': Lyotard, 1984: 10). Contrast Baker & Hacker, 1980: 86–98.

   But why choose Lyotard as a theorist here: perhaps, say, Baudrillard's ideas ideas would be more fruitful? I have chosen Lyotard because, first, his is a *strong* position here, one worthy of contesting; second, his is a *widely-used* (and thus representative?) position; third, it is a position supported by (candidate) *arguments* and examples.

14 Contrast Derrida 1976: 158: 'The writer writes in a language and in a logic whose proper system, laws, and life his discourse by definition cannot dominate absolutely. He uses them only by letting himself ... be governed by the system. ... Without this recognition ... , critical production would risk developing in any direction at all and authorize itself to say almost anything'. Is the Derrida of this quotation in his 'playful' refusal to discuss with Searle? (See Norris, 1987: 177–186.)

15 This is a major insight of Wittgenstein: that we see persons first-and-foremost as *agents*, capable of *doing* certain things — and that the explanation of that doing should be see as typically 'after the fact'. Hence, it makes no sense to think of *reason* or knowledge as 'motivationally inert', at least in *all* contexts (especially those where the action is one of *judgement*). Compare McFee, 2001b: 109–110.

16 With Sibley (2001: 2), we may agree that 'normal intelligence and good eyesight and hearing' are required, without thinking that taste or sensitivity is to be cashed-out in other than these terms, combined with mastery of certain concepts-in-application.

17 Consider also his *Piano Piece* (1963): my thanks to Michael Finnissy who, a long time ago now, kindly went through these works with me, and shared his notes from a seminar with Feldman.

18 From DV8's manifesto, included in Mackrell, 1992: 127.

19 The first is from Mackrell, 1992: 124–125, describing *My Body Your Body* (1987); the second from 'DV8 — Physical Theatre in Rouen', *Dance Theatre Journal* Vol. 8 No 2 Summer, 1990 p. 4.

20 Contrast Lawson, 1981: 111: 'Throughout the 1940s and 1950s it could comfortably be assumed that not only was education 'a good thing' but that it was in safe hands'.

21 The role of the General Teaching Council makes the situation different in Scotland.

22 For any subjectivity here, if it is to be destructive of our position, must be 'necessarily subjective' (*UD*: 22–23; CDE: 5): and that is what is being denied.

SUPPLEMENTARY ESSAY 2

1 I am not claiming that the contrast between visual and performing arts *exhausts* the art field. So that, for example, I am not asserting that literature and film must fit into it in some place: it may be that they do, but it is no part of my purpose here to claim that (compare Shusterman, 1978).

2 In a sense, only the performance is really the dance, although its existence at times when it is not being performed, and the need to talk about 'the dance itself' apart from various performances, requires us to distinguish the dance from its various public existences in performance. My use of the word 'instantiated' (and its cognates) is designed to make explicit that only the performances give the dance physical 'being' as an art work. Hence this is the only time that one can engage with the art work. In particular, one is not confronted with a work of art when one confronts only a notated score or a film or a video, for none of these is the dance (see also Supplementary Essay 3).

3 A fuller account would consider the place of a patina, intended by the artist, for 'particular-object' art works.

4 Two pointer here: some dance might be of the 'particular object sort': for example, 'happenings'. Second, works of the multiple type need not be performing arts, even if/when one puts aside the case of literature. For etched prints and cast sculpture are multiples.

5 If we think of all the performances as tokens, we are precluded from treating them as an engineer might treat a model. For a fuller consideration,

see the discussion of *exemplars* in Baker and Hacker, 1980: 284–96: and my notion of 'a temporary paradigm' in McFee, 1978: 67–8.

6   N.B. this is to treat that first, rehearsal-room performance as a token.

7   See Austin (1976) for a discussion of the choreography of *Black Angels*.

8   But a dance is under-determined by the score to a greater degree than is music. See Carr, 1987: 356–7. Perhaps this is why dances are typically created by working on the bodies of dancers. For a score will not, typically, be *immediately* accessible to the dancers. Rather, the choreographer will have to teach the dance *from the score*.

9   A practical example: see the discussion of the retrieval of Doris Humphry's *New Dance* (1935) in Siegel, 1979: 80–81.

10 Video should be seen as both under-determining in the way described below (not specifying which are the crucial elements) and as over-determining, in tying future performances too closely to one particular performance. See the discussion in Supplementary Essay 3.

11 This idea originates in the work of Wollheim (1973: 257), who says 'Where such a notation is available, then there is a clear and determinate way of individuating tokens of a given type, and hence of identifying the work of art with the type'. Also of importance here is his discussion of 'internal producability' of type-works: Wollheim, 1973: 256–8.

12 That is one reason the thesis operates only 'in principle' and why the exposition of it is rough.

13 This point is central to Wollheim's discussion of multiple arts: see note 11 above

14 This may involve considering the relative importance of other features of dances — such as music and costume — which may vary from one work to another. Nor are these features incidental. It is no longer true that music is always a primary determinant of a dance work (See Armelagos and Sirridge, 1984). For example, Twyla Tharpe's *The Bix Pieces* has a variable music element. Similarly, many works of Alwin Nikolais require a particular costume. Here, first, a feature generally thought constant is variable and, second, a feature generally thought variable acts as a constant [see UD: 98].

15 That is, when we have the notated score. That we often lack such scores is one reason why the Thesis of Notationality cannot always offer practical help. In such cases, we might hope for a (future) score, or see such a score as an idealisation — catching the constraints of the type.

16 For me, of course, this will be a dance-critical matter — in line with my institutional account of art (above; and *UD*: 71–86).

17 For discussion of this difficult idea, see *UD*: 70; and Supplementary Essay 3.

18 See Meskin (1999), for some reservations about my entitlement to this combination of type/token and numerical identity.

19 Note that talk of 'numerically identical persons' amounts (as above) to there being only *one* person in the story: but the what is true of that person may differ at different times — *was* cheerful, short, hairy; *is* morose, tall, bald etc.

20 A problem raised by Sharpe (1979), and discussed below: not enough terms, with just 'type' and 'token', to cover the cases of abstract object, performers interpretation and particular performance. See McFee 1994b: 36–37.

SUPPLEMENTARY ESSAY 3

1 Thus Danto, 1997: 195: 'To be a work of art is to be (i) *about* something and (ii) to *embody its meaning*'.

2 In Danto (1981: 139), we are (familiarly) invited to consider 'confusable counterparts', 'where at least one of the counterparts is *about* something, or has a content, or a subject, or a meaning'.
Such-and-such is not 'about' anything, 'but *that* is because it is a thing, and things, as a class, lack aboutness just because they are things' (Danto 1981: 3). By contrast, 'artworks are ... typically about something' (p. 3), with '... "aboutness" being the crucial differentiating property' (p. 81) for artworks. This is something we learn in, roughly, learning 'how to go on' (PI §151; §179) in art. For, as Danto (1992: 46) puts it: 'The artworld is the discourse of reasons institutionalised, and to be a member of the artworld is, accordingly, to have learned what it means to participate in the discourse of reasons for one's culture.'

3 Kivy, 1975: 210 (rectified for the artistic/aesthetic contrast). See also McFee, 1997.

4 Most explicitly in McFee, 2003a: 122–125: see also McFee, 1999 esp. 169.

5 NB there is a commitment to value in the minimal sense that art-status gives one reason to ascribe value to the objects — but this may be defeated: see McFee, 1989b; and compare Cavell, 1969 on intention: 'I do not wish to claim that everything we find in a work of art is something we have to be prepared to say that the artist intended to put there. But I am claiming that our not being so prepared must be exceptional' (p. 253); 'Our concept of a work of art is such that what is not intended in it has to be thought of, or explained, in contrast to intention, at the same level as intention, as the qualification of a human action' (p. 253 n.). What goes for intention goes equally for some other artistic properties — including artistic value.

6 That Danto cannot take this line follows from his conception of role of any conditions he identifies. Finding that X is *sometimes* not relevant is taken to

show it *never* is!: for him, conditions must be (individually) necessary and (jointly) sufficient for art-status, on pain of breaking down the artwork/'real thing' barrier.

7   Although it would usually be odd to do so, the requirement for mobilisation might even be pressed (in some cases) for colour concepts: then (say) some blind people might be thought to *have* a concept they could not mobilise.

8   The issue of how to characterise 'the' meaning of artworks that are multiples (as dance is; see *UD*: 88–90) is postponed here.

9   Compare Beardsmore, 1971: 17–18. Note that we are not denying that Dickens' novels, say, might be sufficiently similar that *something* of the same 'aboutness' might be shared by two of them.

10 As in the case Jorge Luis Borges imagined ('Pierre Menard, author of *Don Quixote*', [Borges 1962: 42–51]), the difference in authorship (in 'history of production') between two works might well make them *distinguishable* for artistic purposes: for instance, the later work might be mannered in a way the earlier could not.

11 NB (i) see the *Mister Johnson* discussion in Beardsmore (1971: 9–15) for elaboration of the reasons to be offered here.
    (ii) cases of performing art (and some other multiples) are put aside, although clearly here difference between performances is tolerated by same-work continuity.

12 See Best, 1978: 121 on the different fates of Toller Cranston and John Curry.

13 One feature of the importance identified here (which is artistic importance): that such a third-person interest would not be required for aesthetic appreciation, which is amenable to performers' rendering ...

14 Both quotations are taken from the flyer for *The Challenge of Dance* conference, Uppsala, Sweden, 10th February, 2001.

15 See Mackrell, 1997: 32 for the quotation, although not (quite) this reading.

16 Of course, the claim must then be justified — or at least argued — by reference to the work's public features (whatever they are!).

17 We should of course recognise the 'intention implicit' in communicative acts: see Travis, 1989: 17–35.

18 However, a complication here (as with other cases) concerns whether we should take as intentional *all* the descriptions true of the artwork — or whether there could be unintended consequences here.

19 cf. Ryle (1970: 4): '...our copies of *Appearance and Reality* were dusty ...'; 'I cannot recall hearing one referring mention of the Absolute'.

20 Much needs to be added about the erotic *in* art. Bradley's idea here is that an erotic 'charge' might be part of the appeal of some art: but even then it would necessarily be a charge with a general appeal (with generalisable reasons, as we might say); and hence reference to the erotic is just one way

of explaining the 'charge' of *some* art — a way that recognises the place of the erotic in the life of humankind.

21 Consideration of the idea of decadence is extremely interesting here: as an idealisation, one may see the progressive 'feeding' of 'baser' instincts by a declining artworld/society. This might, say, be one case where, through demonstrating that such-and-such was a bad work of art, critics might have an untypical 'something' which was art despite its pornographic aspects — where those aspects were not sufficient to rule it out as art, but were clearly an aesthetic flaw: but the possibility of such examples should not be seen cumulatively.

22 Kant [1790] I §6: respectively, 1928: 51; 1987: 54; 2000: 96; see Guyer, 1979: 168fn.

23 The answer 'no' is surely inevitable — not least, of course, for anyone interested in the place of the arts in education.

24 For example, within the Republic: see Diffey, 1991. For my institutionalism, and democracy, and the need for other-acclamation, see *UD*: 71–4; 80–1: if the members of the relevant portion of the Republic can other-acclaim the work, then *they* are seeing something general (= non-personal?) in the work. Hence there is something to be seen, and therefore some basis for argument.

25 As I put it in 'Context, audience and understanding', read at a conference of Dutch Society for Analytic Aesthetics , Utrecht, February 2000: 'an artwork that requires of it audience, say, understanding the values of, say, *Victorian women* cannot thereby require that the audience be composed of Victorian women'.

26 A sophisticated reading might take what *I* have learned to be uniquely instantiated in what *I* do — but that begs the question.

27 One part of the problem relates to the term 'information'. There is a connection here to Wittgenstein's remarks on 'information' (PI §356: '... isn't it a misleading metaphor to say: "My eyes give me the information that there is a chair over there"?'): what exactly does this mean in the context of, for instance, some perceptual judgement? How can one's perceptions of, say, a table count as offering *information* (in the simplest or favoured cases)? There, I simply *see* whatever it is: the process is direct. Of course, if there is some *doubt* that what is before me *is* a table, I might begin by what seems uncontentious: 'Well, at the least, it looks to me, here, now, like a brown patch ...' But is that really *information*? For why is this less contentious (that is, *always* less contentious) than, say, my saying that I see a table — for I *might* come to dispute either, given my coming to accept other 'facts' about how the world is arranged. Perhaps, when I grant that the 'patch' was dried blood, I might modify my claim as to how it *looks* (here, now). So that might not provide a 'sub-strate'.

28 NB again the parallel with secondary qualities: you may not be able to see them, but they must be 'see-able'.

29 In contrast to sociological 'meaning', significance, association; see *UD*: 86; 114; 294–7.

30 This case is from Ground, 1989: 25–6.

31 Or suppose I confuse a work of decoration, such as some wallpaper, with a decorative artwork (with the Matisse *Red Interior*, say) which is clearly fine art. Here the object, the wallpaper, is both *designed* and designed *with beauty* (or something similar) in mind. Here too, as in the text, treating it as an artwork will involve mis-ascribing artistic concepts to it.

32 The example comes from Jorges Luis Borges, 1962: 236.

33 I take this from a paper by R. A. Sharpe, presented to the British Society of Aesthetics national conference in Oxford, September 2000.

34 I discuss this case in McFee, 2004c: 110-13; and see McFee, 2001b: 100–05.

35 Ian Ground (1989: 9; 30n) has argued against this idea, in conversation: its rejection is implicit in his view of art as operating *procedurally* or regulatively.

36 In a paper read to an Anglo-French Aesthetics Conference, Oxford, April 2000.

37 I am not saying (contrast McGinn, 1997: 20) that properties are not a bit like this — and I certainly am not suggesting that 'existence' might be used as a property which offers a counter-example to this view.

38 One difficult case (for any *general* thesis here: see UD: 130–131) is literature: and there are, in effect, two difficulties here — or two ways of identifying the difficulty. First, there is no perceptual verb for literature (see Diffey, 1991: 125–6): rather, we (typically) *read* literature. Second, that reading might be rooted in one's own seeing, or in touch (reading Braille); but one can also confront literature through another's reading the text — I am thinking here of poems and novels (dramas amount to another issue).

39 Notice (and see Putnam, 1999: 130) it is not as though *the whole scene* looks the same but that one aspect does — so, often, the illusion that there is a lake in the desert (a mirage) combines with there really being a desert!

40 Re. seeing dance on video, see arguments later.

41 For instance, an audience for painting which still had not assimilated, say, the advances of Cubism would be unlikely to be much use for contemporary art.

42 The force of 'precise' here is both important and difficult. The aim is to permit that, if I am in Eastbourne, one *might* not deny that, say, my pain is too; but that no final detail could be given. This point is easy to miss. Thus, for example, my antipathy to the *precise* temporal location of dreams (McFee, 1994c esp. 106) was intended to admit the claim that my dreams

took place *while* I was asleep without permitting further discussion of any 'precise location' (spatial, temporal). This strategy was misunderstood by Squires (1995 esp. 84–5).

43 Despite my seeing both as producers in some places (*UD*: 106) — and compare the discussion in Meskin, 1999 — I am nearer the truth elsewhere: for example, in contrasting the music case with 'for dance, ...performing (at least) movements of the body' (*UD*: 100). See also McFee, 1994b.

44 As Wittgenstein asks (with an implied 'no' answer): 'But you do speak of *understanding* music. You understand it, surely, *while* you are hearing it! Ought we to say that this is an experience which accompanies the hearing?' (Z §159).

45 Not for me, but for anyone who thinks that such an 'internal' perspective plays some crucial role in the dancer's *understanding* of the work. In a clear sense, I think of dancers first-and-foremost as *doing* (or making) dances — hence not as *understanding* them, if this were *contrasted* with performing them with understanding.

46 He actually says that *listening* is 'the core experience of all participants — composer, performer, audience and dancer' (Scruton, 1997: 456); but the context permits us to read it as *successful* listening; that is, as hearing.

47 See, for instance, Kivy, 1990: 95–101.

48 Gracyk (1997: 141) notes the view (from Thom, Godlovitch) that authenticity is 'a feature of performances, not merely of sounds': I take the point to be that sounds alone must be transfigured (that is, heard transfigured) to become the work — and it is the work that is performed.

49 How does one listen to musical works? — not *just* listening, but whatever follows from transfiguration. Consider Collingwood (1938: 140–41), who urged in respect of music: 'what we get out of the concert is ... something which remains for ever inaccessible to a person who cannot or will not make efforts of the right kind, however completely he hears the sounds that fill the room in which he is sitting'. We agree with Collingwood that *merely* hearing the sounds is insufficient for hearing the music.

50 As Michael Finnissy explained (in correspondence), with respect to a score of Webern's: 'The score is not "technically" difficult for any individual instrumental parts, although it demands (as with all of Webern's music) extreme refinement and sensitivity in performance. Making two notes "speak" in a way that is going to be meaningful to the listener is much more difficult than playing an entire melody. The problem of performing Webern well is the problem of *ensemble*, for sounding "together", of making your two tones blend with the two notes of someone else before and after you, and of sublimating individual virtuosity in an essentially unifying approach' (also quoted in McFee, 1978: 25 note).

51 With music by Peter Maxwell Davis.

52 Without wishing to preclude further arguments, I would be much happier
    with a view of music which — although it took recording to offer 'a
    superior mode of access to music' (Gracyk, 1997: 148) — still guaranteed
    a *performance tradition*, in which persons learned to play musical pieces,
    practiced them, and the like. My only worry would be whether this *could*
    be guaranteed once the ontological implications for music of the status of
    recording were acknowledged.

53 There *are* questions here about historicity: when is the case like 'plastic' in
    Akenside's 18th century poem, when like transformed answers? See
    McFee, 1992b esp. 313; McFee, 1995 esp. 281–2.

54 This means, of course, that he/she can perform it, not (necessarily) describe
    it, nor talk about it.

Bibliography

Abbs, P. (1991) 'From Babel to rhapsody: on the nature of creativity', *British Journal of Aesthetics*, Vol. 31, No. 4 pp. 291–300.

Abercrombie, N., Hill, S. and Turner, B.S. (1984) *The Penguin Dictionary of Sociology* (Harmondsworth: Middlesex: Penguin).

Adshead, J. (1981) *The Study of Dance* (London: Dance Books Ltd.).

Alvarez, A. (1971) *The Savage God* (London: Weidenfeld and Nicholson).

Anderson, P. (1976) 'The antimonies of Antonio Gramsci', *New Left Revue*, No. 100, pp.5–78.

Anscombe, G.E.M. (1957) Intention (Oxford: Blackwell).

Anscombe, G.E.M. (1981a) Metaphysics and the Philosophy of Mind (*Collected Philosophical Papers* Vol. II) (Oxford: Blackwell).

Anscombe, G.E.M. (1981b) Ethics, Religion and Politics (*Collected Philosophical Papers* Vol. III) (Oxford: Blackwell).

APU (1983) *Aesthetic Development: The Assessment of Performance Unit* (London: Department of Education and Science).

Aristotle (1965) 'On the art of poetry', in *Classical Literary Criticism*, trans. and ed. T.S. Dorsch (Harmondsworth: Penguin) pp.29–76.

Armelogos, A. and Sirridge, M. (1984) 'Personal style and performance prerogatives', in Maxine Sheets-Johnstone [ed.] *Illuminating Dance: Philosophical Illuminations* (Cranbury, NJ: Associated Presses) 85–100.

Aspin, D. (1981) 'Assessment and education in the arts', in M. Ross (ed.) *The Aesthetic Imperative* (Oxford and Elmsford, NY: Pergamon) pp. 25–52.

Austin, J.L. (1962) *How to Do Things with Words* (Oxford: Clarendon Press).

Austin, J.L. (1970) *Philosophical Papers* 2nd Edition (Oxford: Oxford University Press).

Austin, R. (1976) *Birth of a Ballet* (London: Vision Press).

Ayer, A.J. (1968) *The Origins of Pragmatism* (London: Macmillan).

BAALPE (1990) *Perceptions of Physical Education* (Dudley A.V. Unit, BAALPE).

Baker, G.P. (1977) 'Defeasibility and meaning', in P.M.S. Hacker and J. Raz (eds) *Law, Morality and Society* (Oxford: Clarendon Press) pp. 26–57.

Baker, G.P. (1986) 'Philosophy: Simulacrum and Form', in S.G. Shanker (ed.) *Philosophy in Britain Today* (London and Sidney: Croom Helm) pp. 1-57.

Baker, G.P. (1988) *Wittgenstein, Frege and the Vienna Circle* (Oxford: Blackwell).

Baker, G.P. (1991) 'Philosophical Investigations §122: neglected aspects', in R.L. Arrington and H.-J. Glock (eds) *Wittgenstein's Philosophical Investigations: Text and Context* (London: Routledge) pp.35–68.

Baker, G.P. and Hacker, P.M.S. (1980) *Wittgenstein: Understanding and Meaning* (Oxford: Blackwell).

Baker, G.P. and Hacker, P.M.S. (1984a) *Language, Sense and Nonsense* (Oxford: Blackwell).

Baker, G.P. and Hacker, P.M.S. (1984b) *Scepticism, Rules and Language* (Oxford: Blackwell).

Baker, G.P. and Hacker, P.M.S. (1984c) *Frege: Logical Excavations* (Oxford: Blackwell).

Baker, G.P. and Hacker, P.M.S. (1985) *Wittgenstein: Rules, Grammar and Necessity* (Oxford: Blackwell).

Banes, S. (1987) *Terpsichore in Sneakers: Post-Modern Dance* (with a new introduction) (Hanover, NH: Wesleyan University Press).

Beardsmore, R.W. (1971) *Art and Morality* (Basingstoke and London: Macmillan).

Beardsmore, R.W. (1973) 'Two trends in contemporary aesthetics', *British Journal of Aesthetics* Vol.13, No.4 (Autumn) pp. 346-66.

Bell, C. (1914) *Art* (London: Chatto & Windus).

Bennett, J. (1976) *Kant's Analytic* (Cambridge, England: Cambridge University Press).

Bennett, T., Mercer, C. and Woollacott, J. (eds.) (1986) *Popular Culture and Social Relations* (Milton Keynes: Open University Press).

Berger, J. (1969) *The Moment of Cubism and Other Essays* (London: Weidenfeld and Nicholson).

Berger, J. (1972) *Ways of Seeing* (Harmondsworth: Penguin).

Berger, J. (1978) 'In defence of art', *New Society* (28th September).

Best, D.N. (1974) *Expression in Movement and the Arts* (London: Lepus Books).

Best, D.N. (1978a) *Philosophy and Human Movement* (London: George Allen & Unwin).

Best, D.N. (1978b) 'Emotional education through the arts', *Journal of Aesthetic Education* Vol.12, pp. 71-84.

Best, D.N. (1979) "Free expression or the teaching of technique", *British Journal of Educational Studies*, Vol. XXXVII, No.3, pp. 210–220.

Best, D.N. (1983) 'A reply to my critics', *British Journal of Aesthetics* Vol.23, No.2 (Spring) pp. 148-63.

Best, D.N. (1984) 'The dangers of "aesthetic education"', *Oxford Review of Education* Vol.10, No.2, pp. 157-67.

Best, D.N. (1985a) *Feeling and Reason in the Arts* (London: George Allen & Unwin).

Best, D.N. (1985b) 'Primary and secondary qualities: waiting for an educational Godot', *Oxford Review of Education*, pp.73–84.

Best, D.N. (1986) 'Culture-consciousness: understanding the arts of other cultures', in J. Adshead (ed.) *Dance — a Multicultural Perspective* (Second Edition) (National Resource Centre for Dance) pp. 86-96.

Best, D.N. (1990a) *Arts in Schools: A Critical Time* Birmingham Institute of Art and Design [NSEAD Occasional Paper].

Best, D.N. (1990b) 'Learning from the arts', *Reflections* Vol.2, No.1, pp.11–28.

Best, D.N. (1991) 'Creativity: education in the spirit of enquiry', *British Journal of Educational Studies* Vol.39, No.3, pp.260–278.

Best, D.N. (1992a) 'Combined arts in education: the expedient generic myth', *Educational Philosophy and Theory*, Vol. 11, No. 1, pp. 27–46.

Best, D.N. (1992b) 'Feast as a dog's dinner', *The Higher*, Jan.31: p.18.

Biott, C. (1984) 'The centrality of enquiry and professional practice in a higher degree: craft/community knowledge and the identity of a field of study', Postgraduate Studies in Sport: seminar report (9th–13th July) (Sunderland, England: Sunderland Polytechnic) pp. 69–77.

Borges, J.L. (1962) *Fictions* [trans. A. Kerrigan] (New York: Grove Press).

Bradley, F.H. (1934) 'On the treatment of sexual detail in literature', in his *Collected Essays* Volume II (Oxford: Clarendon Press) pp. 618–27.

Brecher, R. and Hickey, T. (1990) 'In defence of bias', *Studies in Higher Education* Vol.15, No.3, pp.299–311.

Briginshaw, V., Brook, J., Sanderson, P. (1980) *Dance Artists in Education: Pilot Projects 1980* (London: Arts Council of Great Britain).

Brindle, R.S. (1975) *The New Music* (London: Oxford University Press).

Brinson, P. (1991) *Dance as Education: Towards a National Dance Culture* (Basingstoke: Falmer Press).

Brinson, P. and Crisp, C. (1980) *Ballet and Dance: a Guide to the Repertory* (London: David and Charles).

Brown, S. and McIntyre, D. (1986) 'How do teachers think about their craft?', in M. Ben Peretz, R. Brome. and R. Halkes (eds) *Advances of Research on Teacher Thinking* (Lisse: Swets & Zeitlinger BV) pp. 36–44.

Brown, S. and McIntyre, D. (1988) 'The professional craft knowledge of teachers', *Scottish Educational Review* (February) pp. 39–47.

Burgin, V. (1986) *The End of Art Theory* (London: Macmillan).

Burnside, F. (1990) 'Inside the magic box', *Dance Theatre Journal* Vol.7, No.4 (February) pp. 30–31.

Calabria, F.M. (1976) 'The dance marathon craze', *Journal of Popular Culture*, Vol, IX, No.1, pp.54–96.

Carr, D. (1978) 'Practical pursuits and the curriculum', *Journal of Philosophy of Education* Vol.12, pp.69–80.

Carr, D. (1984) 'Education, skill, and behavioural objectives', *Journal of Aesthetic Education* Vol.18, No.4 (Winter) pp. 67-76.

Carr, D. (1987) 'Thought and action in the art of dance', *British Journal of Aesthetics*, Vol.27, No.4 (Autumn) pp. 345-57.

Carr, W. and Kemmis, S. (1986) *Becoming Critical: Education, Knowledge and Action Research* (Basingstoke: Falmer Press).

Carroll, Lewis (1973) 'What the tortoise said to Achilles', in *The Complete Works* (London: The Nonesuch Press) pp. 1104-08.

Carroll, N. (1981) 'Post-modern dance and expression', in G. Fancher and G. Myers (eds) *Philosophical Essays on Dance* (New York: American Dance Festival) pp. 95-104.

Carroll, N. (1993) 'Essence, expression and history: Arthur Danto's philosophy of art', in M. Rollins (ed.) *Danto and his Critics* (Oxford: Blackwell) pp. 79–106.

Carroll, N. (1999) *Philosophy of Art: A Contemporary Introduction* (London: Routledge).

Carroll, N. (2001) 'Identifying art', in his *Beyond Aesthetics: Philosophical Essays* (Cambridge: Cambridge University Press) pp. 75–100.

Cavell, S. (1969) *Must We Mean What We Say?* (New York: Charles Scribner's Sons).

Cavell, S. (1979a) *The Claim of Reason* (Oxford, Oxford University Press).

Cavell, S. (1979b) *The World Viewed* (Enlarged Edition) (Cambridge, Mass: Harvard University Press).

Cavell, S. (1981a) *The Senses of Walden* (An Expanded Edition) (San Francisco: North Point Press).

Cavell, S. (1981b) *Pursuits of Happiness* (Cambridge, Mass: Harvard University Press).

Cavell, S. (1984) *Themes Out of School* (San Francisco: North Point Press).

Challis, C. (1999) 'Dancing bodies: can the art of dance be restored to dance studies?', in G. McFee (ed.) *Dance, Education and Philosophy* (Aachen: Meyer and Meyer) pp. 143–153.

Chalmers, A.F. (1982) *What Is This Thing Called Science? Second Edition* (Milton Keynes: Open University Press).

Chapman, J. (1984) 'XXX and the changing ballet aesthetic: 1828-32', *Dance Research* Vol. II, No.1 (Spring) pp. 35-47.

Chipp, H.B. (ed.) (1968) *Theories of Modern Art* (Los Angeles: University of California Press).

Cole, A. (1989) 'Dance artists in education', in *Young People Dancing: An International Perspective* Vol. I (London: Dance and the Child: International [DACI]) pp. 60–68.

Cole, M. (1989) 'Monocultural, multicultural and anti-racist education', in M. Cole (ed.) *The Social Contexts of Schooling* (Basingstoke: Falmer Press) pp.138–155.

Collingwood, R.G. (1938) *The Principles of Art* (Oxford: Clarendon Press).

Copeland, R. and Cohen, M. (eds.) (1983) *What Is Dance?* (London: Oxford University Press).

Croce, A. (1978) *Afterimages* (London: A&C Black).

Crowther, P. (1993) *Critical Aesthetics and Postmodernism* (Oxford: Clarendon Press).

Danto, A. (1981) *The Transfiguration of the Commonplace* (Cambridge, MA: Harvard University Press).

Danto, A. (1986a) *The Philosophical Disenfranchisement of Art* (New York: Columbia University Press).

Danto, A. (1986b) *Encounters and Reflections* (Los Angeles: University of California Press).

Danto, A. (1992) 'The artworld revisited' in his *Beyond the Brillo Box* (New York: Farrar, Strauss, Giroux) pp. 33–53.

Danto, A. (1993) 'Responses and replies', in M. Rollins (ed.) *Danto and his Critics* (Oxford: Blackwell) pp. 193–216.

Danto, A. (1994) *Embodied Meanings* (New York: Farrar, Strauss, Giroux).

Danto, A. (1997) *After the End of Art: Contemporary Art and the Pale of History* (Princeton, NJ: Princeton University Press).

Davies, S. (1990) 'Replies to arguments suggesting that critics' strong evaluations could not be soundly deduced', *Grazer Philosophische Studien* Vol. 38, pp. 157–176.

Davies, S. (1994) *Musical Meaning and Expression* (Ithaca, NY: Cornell University Press).

De Man, P. (1979) *Allegories of Reading* (New Haven and London: Yale University Press).

Dearden, R.F. (1968) *The Philosophy of Primary Education* (London: Routledge and Kegan Paul).

Deforges, C. and McNamara, D. (1979) 'Theory and practice: methodological procedures for the objectification of craft knowledge', *British Journal of Teacher Education*, Vol. 5, No. 2, pp. 145–152.

Derrida, J. (1976) *Of Grammatology* (Baltimore: Johns Hopkins University Press).

DES (1972) *Movement: Physical Education in the Primary Years* (Department of Education and Science).

DES (1989) *National Curriculum: From Policy to Practice* (Department of Education and Science).

DES (August, 1991) *Physical Education for Ages 5–16* (Department of Education and Science).

Diffey, T.J. (1969) 'The Republic of Art', *British Journal of Aesthetics*, Vol. 9, No. 2, pp. 145-56. [Also available as Chapter Two of Diffey, 1991, pp. 39–52].

Diffey, T.J. (1991) *The Republic of Art and Other Essays* (New York: Peter Lang).

Eagleton, T. (1976) *Marxism and Literary Criticism* (London: Methuen).

Eagleton, T. (1990) *The Ideology of the Aesthetic* (Oxford: Blackwell).

Eisner, E.W. (1972) *Educating Artistic Vision* (London: Macmillan).

Elliott, J. (1976) 'Developing hypotheses about classrooms for teachers' practical constructs: an account of the Ford teaching project', Interchange, Vol. 7, No. 2. Reprinted in S. Kemmis, et al. (eds.) *The Action Research Reader* (Victoria, Australia: Deakin University Press, 1982) pp. 293–311.

Elliott, J. (1991) *Action Research for Educational Change* (Milton Keynes: Open University Press).

Feyerabend, P.K. (1978) *Science in a Free Society* (London: Verso/NLB).

Feyerabend, P.K. (1988) *Against Method* (Revised Edition) (London: Verso).

Fleming, S. (1991) 'The role of sport in South Asian cultures in Britain and the Indian sub-continent' in J. Standeven, K. Hardman and D. Fisher (eds.) *Sport For All: Into the 90s* (Aachen, Germany: Meyer & Meyer Verlag) pp. 230–242.

Fleming, S. (1993) 'Multiculturalism and the physical education curriculum: the case of South Asian male youth, dance and South Asian dance', *Multicultural Teaching*, Vol. 11, No. 1 (Spring) pp. 35–8.

Flew, A. (1961) Hume's *Philosophy of Belief* (London: Routledge & Kegan Paul).

Foster, H. (ed.) (1985) *Postmodern Culture* (London: Pluto Press).

Forster, S. L. (1996) *Choreography and Narrative: Ballet's Staging of Story and Desire* (Bloomington: Indiana University Press)

Fuller, P. (1980) *Beyond the Crisis in Art* (London: Writers and Readers Publishing Cooperative).

Fuller, P. (1988a) *Seeing Through Berger* (London and Lexington, KY: The Claridge Press).

Fuller, P. (1988b) *Theoria: Art and the Absence of Grace* (London: Chatto & Windus).

Fuller, P. (1988c) *Art and Psychoanalysis* (Second Edition) (London: Hogarth Press).

Fuller, P. (1989) 'Editorial' *Modern Painters* Vol. 2, No. 4 (Winter) pp. 5–7.

Gallahue, D.L. (1982) *Understanding Motor Development in Children* (New York: Wiley & Sons).

Gibson, R. (1984) *Structuralism and Education* (London, Sydney: Hodder & Stoughton).

Gibson, R. (1986) *Critical Theory and Education* (London, Sydney: Hodder & Stoughton).

Giddens, A. (1987) *Social Theory and Modern Sociology* (Cambridge, England: Polity Press).

Gombrich, E. (1960) *Art and Illusion* (London: Phaidon).

Gracyk, T. (1997) 'Listening to music: performances and recordings', *Journal of Aesthetics and Art Criticism*, Vol. 55, No. 2, pp. 139–50.

Ground, I. (1989) Art or Bunk? (Bristol: Bristol Classical Press).

Gulbenkian (1980) *Dance Education and Training in Britain* (London: Calouste Gulbenkian Foundation).

Gulbenkian (1982) *The Arts in Society* (London: Calouste Gulbenkian Foundation).

Guyer, P. (1979) *Kant and the Claims of Taste* (Cambridge, MA: Harvard University Press).

Hacker, P.M.S. (1986) *Insight and Illusion* (Revised Edition) (London: Oxford University Press).

Hacker, P.M.S. (1987) *Appearance and Reality* (Oxford: Blackwell).

Hacker, P.M.S. (1990) *Wittgenstein: Meaning and Mind* (Oxford: Blackwell).

Hare, R.M. (1972) 'Principles', *Proceedings of the Aristotelian Society* 1972–3, Vol. 73, pp. 1–18.

Hargreaves, J. (1986) *Sport, Power and Culture* (Cambridge: Polity Press).

Hargreaves, J. (1992) 'Revisiting the hegemony thesis', in J. Sugden and C. Knox (eds) *Leisure in the 1990s: Rolling Back the Welfare State* (Eastbourne: Leisure Studies Association) pp. 263–280.

Hirst, P.H. (1974) *Knowledge and the Curriculum* (London: Routledge & Kegan Paul).

Hirst, P.H. (1989) 'The concepts of physical education and dance education: a reply', in G. Curl (ed.) *Collected Conference Papers in Dance* Vol. 4 (London: National Association of Teachers in Further and Higher Education) pp. 38-43.

HMI (1977) *Curriculum 11–16 (Report by Her Majesty's Inspectorate)* (London: Department of Education and Science).

HMI (1985) *Education from 5–16 (Curriculum Matters No.2)* (London: Her Majesty's Stationery Office).

HMI (1989) *Physical Education from 5–16 (Curriculum Matters No.16)* (London: Her Majesty's Stationery Office).

Homan, R. (1991) *The Ethics of Social Research* (London: Longman).

Hughes, D. (1990) 'Post-structuralist dance: some notes towards a working definition', *Dance Theatre Journal* Vol. 8, No. 2, pp. 28–31.

Jenks, C. (1986) *What is Post-Modernism?* (New York: St. Martin's Press).

Jordan, S. (1992) *Striding Out: Aspects of Contemporary and New Dance in Britain* (London: Dance Books).

Kaeppler, A. (1985) 'Structured movement systems in Tonga', in P. Spencer (ed.) *Society and the Dance* (Cambridge, England: Cambridge University Press) pp. 92-118.

Kant, I. [1790] *The Critique of Judgement* (1928) trans. J. C. Meredith (Oxford: Clarendon Press); (1987) trans W.S. Pluhar (Indianapolis: Hackett); (2000) trans. P. Guyer and E. Matthews, as Critique of the Power of Judgement (Cambridge: Cambridge University Press).

Katz, R. (1983) 'The egalitarian waltz', in R. Copeland and M. Cohen (eds) *What Is Dance?* (Oxford: Oxford University Press) pp. 521–32.

Kealiinohomoku, J.W. (1983) 'An anthropologist looks at ballet as a form of ethnic dance', in R. Copeland and M. Cohen (eds) *What Is Dance?* (London: Oxford University Press) pp. 533-49.

Kelly, A.V. (1990) *The National Curriculum: A Critical Review* (London: Paul Chapman Publishing).

Kenny, A. (1963) *Action, Emotion and the Will* (London: Routledge and Kegan Paul).

Kenny, A. (1973) *Wittgenstein* (London: Allen Lane).

Kirk, D. (1986) 'Health-related fitness as an innovation in the Physical Education Curriculum', in J. Evans (ed.) *Physical Education, Sport and Schooling: Studies in the Sociology of Physical Education* (Basingstoke: Falmer Press) pp. 167–182.

Kivy, P. (1975) 'What makes aesthetic terms aesthetic?', *Philosophy and Phenomenological Research*, Vol. 36, pp. 197–211.

Kivy, P. (1988) 'Live performances and dead composers', in J. Dancy, J.M.E. Moravcsik and C.C.W. Taylor (eds.) *Human Agency: Language, Duty and Value* (Stanford, Calif: Stanford University Press) pp. 237-57.

Kivy, P. (1989) *Sound Sentiment* (Philadelphia: Temple University Press).

Kivy, P. (1990) *Music Alone*: Philosophical *Reflections* on the Purely Musical Experience (Ithaca, NY: Cornell University Press).

Korsmeyer, C. (1977) 'On distinguishing "aesthetic" from "artistic"', *Journal of Aesthetic Education*, Vol. 11, No. 4, pp. 45–57.

Korsmeyer, C. (1999) 'Food and the taste of meaning', in P. Van Bonsdorff and A Haapala (eds) *Aesthetics in the Human Environment* (Lahti: International Institute for Applied Aesthetics) pp. 90–104.

Kuhn, T.S. (1970) *The Structure of Scientific Revolutions* (Second Edition) (Chicago: University of Chicago Press).

Kuhn, T.S. (1977) *The Essential Tension* (Chicago: University of Chicago Press).

Laban, R. (1948) *Modern Educational Dance* (London: MacDonald & Evans).

Lather, P. (1986) 'Research as praxis', *Harvard Educational Review*, Vol. 56, No. 3, pp. 257–277.

Lawton, D. (1975) *Class, Culture and the Curriculum* (London: Routledge & Kegan Paul).

Lawton, D. (1981) 'The curriculum and curriculum change', in B. Simon and W. Taylors (eds) *Education in the 80s* (London: Batsford Studies in Education) pp. 111–123.

Lawton, D. (1989) *Education, Culture and the National Curriculum* (London: Hodder & Stoughton).

Lear, J. (1980) *Aristotle and Logical Theory* (Cambridge: Cambridge University Press).

Levinson, J. (1996) 'Extending art historically', in his The *Pleasures of Aesthetics: Philosophical Essays* (Ithaca, NY: Cornell University Press).

Lewin, K. (1952) 'Group decision and social change'. Reprinted in S. Kemmis et al. (eds.) *The Action Research Reader* (Victoria, Australia: Deacon University Press [1982]) pp. 38–47.

Luntley, M. (1995) *Reason, Truth and Self* (London: Routledge).

Lyons, J. (1970) *Chomsky* (London: Fontana).

Lyotard, J-F. (1984) *The Postmodern Condition: A Report on Knowledge* (Manchester: Manchester University Press).

Maclure, S. (1988) *Education Re-formed: A Guide to the Education Reform Act 1988* (London: Hodder and Stoughton).

Maw, J. (1988) 'National Curriculum policy: coherence and progression?', in D. Lawton and C. Chitty (eds.) *The National Curriculum* (The Bedford Way Series) (London: Cogan Page).

McClellan, D. (1986) *Ideology* (Milton Keynes, Open University Press).

McDonagh, D. (1973) *Martha Graham: A Biography* (New York: Praeger Publishers Inc.).

McFee, G. (1976) 'What is the medium of gymnastics?', in *Focus on Gymnastics* (Eastbourne, UK: Association of Principals of Women's Colleges of Physical Education).

McFee, G. (1978) *Much of Jackson Pollock is Vivid Wallpaper* (Washington, DC: University Press of America).

McFee, G. (1980a) 'The fraudulent in art', *British Journal of Aesthetics* Vol. 20, No. 3 (Summer) pp. 215-28.

McFee, G. (1980b) 'The historicity of art', *Journal of Aesthetics and Art Criticism* Vol. XXXVIII, No. 3, pp. 307-24.

McFee, G. (1984) 'Wisdom on aesthetics: superstructure and substructure', in I. Dilman (ed.) *Philosophy and Life: Essays on John Wisdom* (The Hague: Martinus Nijhoff) pp. 83-122.

McFee, G. (1989a) 'The concept of dance education', in G. Curl (ed.) *Collected Conference Papers in Dance* Vol. 4 (London: National Association of Teachers in Further and Higher Education) pp. 15-37.

McFee, G. (1989b) 'The logic of appreciation in the Republic of Art', *British Journal of Aesthetics* Vol. 29, No. 3 (Summer) pp. 230-8.

McFee, G. (1990) 'Davies' Replies: a response', Grazer Philosophische Studien, Vol. 38, pp. 177–84.

McFee, G. (1991) 'Wittgenstein: understanding and "intuitive awareness"', in Wittgenstein: Towards a Reevaluation (Proceedings of the 14th International Wittgenstein Symposium, 1989) Part I (Vienna: Holder-Pichler-Temsky) pp. 37–46.

McFee, G. (1992a) Understanding Dance (London: Routledge).

McFee, G. (1992b) 'Triangulation in research: two confusions', Educational Research, Vol. 34, pp. 215–19.

McFee, G. (1992c) 'The historical character of art: a re-appraisal', British Journal of Aesthetics, Vol. 32, No. 4 (October) pp. 307–19.

McFee, G. (1994a) The Concept of Dance Education [original edition] (London Routledge) — CDE.

McFee, G. (1994b) 'Was that Swan Lake I saw you at last night?: dance-identity and understanding', Dance Research Vol. XII, No. 1, Summer, pp. 20–40.

McFee, G. (1994c) 'The surface grammar of dreaming', Proceedings of the Aristotelian Society, Vol. XCIV, pp. 95–115.

McFee, G. (1995) 'Back to the future: A reply to Sharpe', British Journal of Aesthetics Vol. 35, No. 3, pp. 278–83.

McFee, G. (1996) 'Postmodernism, dance and post-industrial society', in K. Gill (ed.) Information Society: New Media, Ethics and Postmodernism (Berlin: Springer Verlag) pp. 342–54.

McFee, G. (1997) 'Meaning and the art-status of music alone', British Journal of Aesthetics Vol. 37, No. 1, pp. 31–46.

McFee, G. (1998) 'Truth, arts education and the "postmodern condition"', in D. Carr (ed.) Education, Knowledge and Truth: Beyond the Postmodern Impasse (London: Routledge) pp. 80–95.

McFee, G. (1999) 'Technicality, philosophy and dance-study', in G. McFee (ed.) Dance, Education and Philosophy (Aachen: Meyer and Meyer) pp. 155–88.

McFee, G. (2000) Free Will (Teddington: Acumen).

McFee, G. (2001a) 'Wollheim on expression (and representation)', in R. Van Gerwen (ed.) Richard Wollheim on the Art of Painting (Cambridge: Cambridge University Press) pp. 151–68.

McFee, G. (2001b) 'Wittgenstein, performing art and action', in R. Allen & M. Turvey (eds.) Wittgenstein, Theory and the Arts (London: Routledge) pp. 92–116.

McFee, G. (2003a) 'Cognitivism and the experience of dance', in A. Sukla (ed.) Art and Experience (Westport, CT: Praeger) pp. 121–43.

McFee, G. (2003b) 'Art, audience and understanding: The case of dance', Nordisk Estetisk Tidskrift, Vol. 27/8 pp. 143–58.

McFee, G. (2004a) *Sport, Rules and Values* (London: Routledge).

McFee, G. (2004b) 'Normativity, justification and (MacIntyrean) practices': Some thoughts on methodology for the philosophy of sport', *Journal of Philosophy of Sport*, Vol. 31, No. 1, pp. 15–33.

McFee, G. (2004c) 'Wittgenstein and the arts: Understanding and performing', in P. Lewis (ed.) *Wittgenstein, Aesthetics and Philosophy* (Aldershot: Ashgate) pp. 109–36.

McGinn, C. (1997) *Ethics, Evil and Fiction* (London: Oxford University Press).

McNamara, D. and Deforges, C. (1978) 'The social sciences, teacher education and the objectification of craft knowledge', *British Journal of Teacher Education*, Vol.4, No.1, pp.17–36.

Mackie, J. (1977) *Ethics* (Harmondswort: Penguin).

Mackrell, J. (1992) *Out of Line: The Story of British New Dance* (London: Dance Books).

Meskin, A. (1999) 'Productions, performances and their evaluations', in G. McFee (ed.) *Dance, Education and Philosophy* (Aachen: Meyer and Meyer) pp. 45–61.

Mosston, M., and Ashworth, S. (1986) *Teaching Physical Education* (Third Edition) (London: Merrill publishing).

Murphy, R., and Torrance, H. (1988) *The Changing Face of Educational Assessment* (Milton Keynes, Open University Press).

Nagel, T. (1986) *The View from Nowhere* (Oxford: Oxford University Press).

NDTA (1990) *A Rationale for Dance in the School Curriculum* (London: National Dance Teacher's Association Working Group) February.

Norris, C. (1987) *Derrida* (London: Fontana).

Norris, C., and Benjamin, A. (1988) *What is Deconstruction?* (London: Academy Press).

Peters, R.S. (1966) *Ethics and Education* (London: George Allen and Unwin).

Pettit, P. (1980) *Judging Justice: An Introduction to Contemporary Political Philosophy* (London: Routledge & Kegan Paul).

Phillips, E.M., and Pugh, D.S. (1987) *How to Get a PhD* (Milton Keynes, Open University Press).

Preston-Dunlop, V. (1963) *A Handbook for Modern Educational Dance* (London: MacDonald and Evans).

Price, H. (1988) *Facts and the Function of Truth* (Oxford: Blackwell).

Putnam, H. (1983) *Realism and Reason* (*Philosophical Papers* (Vol.3) (Cambridge: Cambridge University Press).

Putnam, H. (1990) *Realism with a Human Face* (Cambridge, Mass: Harvard University Press).

Putnam, H. (1992) 'Irrealism and deconstruction', in his *Renewing Philosophy* (Cambridge, MA: Harvard University Press).

Putnam, H. (1999) *The Threefold Cord: Mind, Body and the World* (New York: Columbia University Press).

Quirey, B. (1976) *May I Have the Pleasure?* (London: BBC Publications).

Redfern, B. (1979) 'The child as creator, performer, spectator', in *Dance and the Child: Keynote Addresses and Philosophy Papers* (Canadian Association of Health, Physical Education and Recreation) pp. 3-24.

Redfern, B. (1983) *Dance, Art and Aesthetics* (London: Dance Books).

Redfern, B. (1986) *Questions in Aesthetic Education* (London: George Allen & Unwin).

Reid, T. [1815] (1969) *Essays on the Intellectual Powers of Man* (Cambridge, MA: MIT Press).

Rhees, R. (1969) *Without Answers* (London: Routledge & Kegan Paul).

Roith, O. (1990) *Research in the PCFC Sector* (Report of the Committee of Enquiry on Research in the Polytechnics and Colleges Sector, appointed by the Council) (London: Polytechnics and Colleges Funding Council).

Rorty, R. (1979) *Philosophy and the Mirror of Nature* (Princeton, NJ: Princeton University Press).

Rorty, R. (1989) *Contingency, Irony and Solidarity* (Cambridge: Cambridge University Press).

Rorty, R. (1991a) *Essays on Heidigger and Others* (*Philosophical Papers* Vol.2) (Cambridge: Cambridge University Press).

Rorty, R. (1991b) *Objectivity, Relativism and Truth* (*Philosophical Papers* Vol.1) (Cambridge: Cambridge University Press).

Ross, D. (1925) *The Nicomachean Ethics of Aristotle* (Oxford: Oxford University Press).

Rowell, B. (2000) *Dance Umbrella: The First Twenty-One Years* (London: Dance Book).

Russell, B. (1921) *The Analysis of Mind* (London: George Allen & Unwin).

Russell, J. (1958) *Modern Dance in Education* (London: MacDonald and Evans).

Ryle, G. (1949) *The Concept of Mind* (London: Hutchinson).

Ryle, G. (1970) 'Autobiographical', in O. P. Wood and G. Pitcher (eds) *Ryle: A Collection of Critical Essays* (London: Macmillan) pp. 1–15.

Salmon, R.O. (1977) 'The tango: its origins and meaning', *Journal of Popular Culture*, Vol. X, No. 4, pp. 859–866.

Schoenberg, A. (1975) *Style and Idea* (Berkeley, CA: California University Press)

Schön, D.A. (1983) *The Reflective Practitioner* (New York: Basic Books).

Schön, D.A. (1987) *Educating the Reflective Practitioner* (San Francisco: Jossey-Bass Publishers).

Scruton, R. (1997) *The Aesthetics of Music* (Oxford: Clarendon Press).

Searle, J. (1984) *Minds, Brains and Science* (London: BBC Publications).

Semple, M. (1990) 'Cultural diversity and dance', in G. Curl (ed.) *NATFHE Collected Conference Papers* (London: National Association of Teachers in Further and Higher Education) Vol. 5, pp. 38–40.

Seneca (1969) *Letters from a Stoic* (trans and ed. R. Campbell) (Harmondsworth: Penguin).

Sharpe, R.A. (1979) 'Type, token, interpretation and performance', *Mind* Vol. 86, pp. 437–40.

Shaw, P. (1981) *Logic and Its Limits* (London and Sydney: Pan).

Sherlock, J. (1989) 'Postmodern culture and dance study', in D. Botterill (ed.) *Leisure Participation and Experience: Models and Case Studies* (Eastbourne, England: Leisure Studies Association) pp.116–136.

Shusterman, R. (1978) 'The anomalous status of literature', *British Journal of Aesthetics*, Vol. 18, No. 4, pp. 317-329

Shusterman, R. (1981) 'Evaluative reasoning in criticism', *Ratio* Vol. 23, pp. 141-157.

Shusterman, R. (1992) *Pragmatist Aesthetics* (Oxford: Blackwell).

Siegel, M. (1972) *At the Vanishing Point* (New York: Saturday Post Review).

Siegel, M. (1977) *Watching the Dance Go By* (Boston MA: Houghton, Mifflin Co.).

Siegel, M. 1979) *The Shapes of Change* (Boston, MA: Houghton Mifflin Co.).

Simon, B. (1985) *Does Education Matter?* (London: Lawrence and Wishart).

Simon, B. (1988) *Bending the Rules: the Baker 'Reform' of Education* (London: Lawrence and Wishart).

Simons, H. (1988) 'Teacher professionalism and the new curriculum', in D. Lawton and C. Chitty (eds) *The National Curriculum (The Bedford Way Series)* (London: Cogan Page) pp. 78–90.

Sparshott, F. (1988) Off The Ground (Princeton, NJ: Princeton University Press).

Sparshott, F. (1995) *A Measured Pace: Towards a Philosophical Understanding of the Art of Dance* (Toronto: University of Toronto Press).

Spencer, P. (ed.) (1985) *Society and the Dance* (Cambridge, England: Cambridge University Press).

Squires, R. (1995) 'Dream time', *Proceedings of the Aristotelian Society*, Vol XCV, pp. 83–91.

Standish, P. (1995) 'Why we should not speak of an educational science', *Studies in Philosophy and Education* Vol. 14, pp. 267–81.

Stenhouse, L. (1975) *An Introduction to Curriculum Research and Development* (London: Heinemann Educational).

Stenhouse, L. (1983) *Authority, Education and Emancipation* (London: Heinemann Educational).

Stokes, A. (1935) *Tonight the Ballet* (London: Faber & Faber).

Stroud, B. (1977) *Hume* (London: Routledge and Kegan Paul).

TES (Feb.1, 1992) "Ballet stars boost lobby to save dance" (by Frances Rafferty) *The Times Educational Supplement*, p. 1.

TGAT (1987) *National Curriculum: Task Group on Assessment and Testing: A Report* (London: Her Majesty's Stationery Office).

TGAT (1988) *National Curriculum: Three Supplementary Reports — Task Group on Assessment and Testing (*London: Her Majesty's Stationery Office).

Thistlewood, D. (1981) *A Continuing Process: the New Creativity in British Art Education 1955–1965* (London: Institute of Contemporary Arts).

Thornton, S. (1971) *A Movement Perspective of Rudolph Laban* (London: MacDonald and Evans).

Toulmin, S.E. (1972) *Human Understanding* (Vol. 1) (Oxford: Clarendon Press).

Travis, C. (1984) 'Are belief ascriptions opaque?', *Proceedings of the Aristotelian Society* 1984-5, Vol. 85, pp. 73-100.

Travis, C. (1989) *The Uses of Sense* (Oxford: Clarendon Press).

Travis, C. (1997) 'Pragmatics', in B. Hale and C. Wright (eds) *A Companion to the Philosophy of Language* (Oxford: Blackwell) pp. 87–107.

Turner, M.J. (1971) *New Dance: Approaches to Nonliteral Choreography* (Pittsburgh: University of Pittsburgh Press).

Tyler, R. W. (1949) *Basic Principles of Curriculum and Instruction* (Chicago, Illinois: University of Chicago Press).

Tyler, R. W. (1973) 'The father of behavioural objectives criticizes them', *Phi Delta Kappan*, Vol. 55, p. 57.

Urmson, J.O. (1976) 'The performing arts', in H. D. Lewis (ed.) *Contemporary British Philosophy (Fourth Series)* (London: George Allen & Unwin) pp. 239–52.

Vasquez, A.S. (1973) *Art and Society, Essays in Marxist Aesthetics* (London: Merlin).

Walton, K. (1978) 'Categories of art' in J. Margolis (ed.) *Philosophy Looks at the Arts (Second Edition)* (Philadelphia, Pa.: Temple University Press) pp. 88–114.

Westhorpe, G. (1974) 'Physical education as a worthwhile activity', *Physical Education Association*, p. 4, p. 9.

White, J. (1988) 'An unconstitutional national curriculum', in D. Lawton and C. Chitty (eds) *The National Curriculum (The Bedford Way Series)* (London: Cogan Page) pp. 113–122.

Whittock, T. (1994) Book Review Understanding Dance, *Dance Research* Vol. XII, No. 1 Summer pp. 68–70.

Williams, J.L. (1986) "Public examinations in dance", in *Dance: the Study of Dance and the Place of Dance in Society (Proceedings of the VIII Commonwealth and International Conference on Sport, PE, Dance, Recreation and Health)* (London: E & FN Spon) pp.221–225.

Williams, R. (1961) *The Long Revolution* (London: Chatto & Windus).

Winch, P. (1973) *Ethics and Action* (London: Routledge and Kegan Paul).

Winch, P. (1987) *Trying to Make Sense* (Oxford: Blackwell).

Wisdom, J. (1953) *Philosophy and Psycho-Analysis* (Oxford: Blackwell).

Wisdom, J. (1965) *Paradox and Discovery* (Oxford: Blackwell).

Wisdom, J. (1991) *Proof and Explanation [The Virginia Lectures]* (New York: University Press of America).

Wittgenstein, L. (1953) *Philosophical Investigations* (trans. G.E.M. Anscombe) (Oxford: Blackwell).

Wittgenstein, L. (1969) *On Certainty* (trans. D. Paul and G.E.M. Anscombe) (Oxford: Blackwell).

Wittgenstein, L. (1974) *Philosophical Grammar* (trans. A. Kenny) (Oxford: Blackwell).

Wittgenstein, L (1993) *Philosophical Occasions 1912-1951* (ed. J Klugge & A Nordmann) (Indianapolis: Hackett Publishing).

Wolff, J. (1981) The Social Production of Art (London: Macmillan).

Wollheim, R. (1973) *On Art and the Mind* (Harmondsworth and London: Allen Lane).

Wollheim, R. (1980a) *Art and Its Objects* (Second Edition) (Cambridge, England: Cambridge University Press).

Wollheim, R. (1980b) 'Criticism as retrieval', in *Wollheim* 1980a, pp. 185-204.

Wollheim, R. (1983) 'Art, interpretation and perception', *Kant oder Hegel: Proceedings of the Stuttgart Conference 1982* (Stuttgart: Kleet-Cotta) pp. 549-59.

Wollheim, R. (1984) *The Thread of Life* (Cambridge: Cambridge University Press).

Wollheim, R. (1986) 'Imagination and pictorial understanding', *Proceedings of the Aristotelian Society* Supplementary Volume LX, pp. 45–60.

Wollheim, R. (1993) *The Mind and Its Depths* (Cambridge, MA: Harvard University Press).

Wright, C. (1992) *Truth and Objectivity* (Cambridge, MA: Harvard University Press).

Ziff, P. (1981) 'About the appreciation of dance', in G. Fancher and G. Myers (eds.) *Philosophical Essays on Dance* (New York: American Dance Festival) pp. 69–94.

Index

Ingram Content Group UK Ltd.
Milton Keynes UK
UKHW052259070623
423069UK00007B/231